Contact Languages

Pidgins and Creoles

Mark Sebba

First published 1997 by
MACMILLAN PRESS LTD
Houndmills, Basingstoke, Hampshire RG21 6XS
and London
Companies and representatives
throughout the world

ISBN 0-333-63023-8 hardcover
ISBN 0-333-63024-6 paperback

A catalogue record for this book is available
from the British Library.

This book is printed on paper suitable for recycling and made from fully managed and sustained forest sources.

10   9   8   7   6   5   4   3   2   1
06   05   04   03   02   01   00   99   98   97

Typeset in Great Britain by
Aarontype Limited,
Easton, Bristol

Printed and bound in Great Britain by
Antony Rowe Ltd
Chippenham, Wiltshire

Published in the United States of America 1997 by
ST. MARTIN'S PRESS, INC.,
Scholarly and Reference Division
175 Fifth Avenue, New York, N.Y. 10010

ISBN 0-312-17569-8 cloth
ISBN 0-312-17571-X paperback

Contents

Acknowledgements

Many people have played a part in the writing of this book. I am especially grateful to all those from whom, over the years, I have learnt about the field of pidgin and creole studies – in particular, to Tony Traill (who first taught me about this topic), to Ross Clark, to Bob Le Page (who introduced me to London Jamaican) and to Pieter Muysken (for stimulation and encouragement). For supplying information, texts and feedback of various kinds, I would like to thank Candida Barros, Michele Foster, Arthur de Graft-Rosenior, Val Hall, Paul Lareau, Susanne Mühleisen, L. H. Salt and Graham Turner. All creolists owe a debt to John Holm, for his encyclopedic volumes, which represent the mass of our knowledge about pidgins and creoles. Many thanks to Rosemary Anderson for help with the index. And as ever, my heartfelt thanks are due to my wife Sharon Dexter, for her support, but especially for her patience!

The author and publishers wish to thank the following for permission to use copyright material:

Chambers Harrap Publishers Ltd, for definitions from *Chambers Twentieth Century Dictionary* (1972);

Collins English Dictionaries, an imprint of HarperCollins Publishers, for definitions from *Collins Concise Dictionary* (1985);

Neal Oribio for 'Deaf Ear', © 1995 Neal Oribio.

Oxford University Press, for definitions from *The Concise Oxford Dictionary* (1982);

Wole Soyinka, for the extract from the lyrics 'Unlimited Liability Company' by Wole Soyinka from the record of the same name, Ewuro Productions;

J. W. Spear and Son PLC, Enfield, EN3 7TB, England, for permission to reproduce the Scrabble tiles as part of the cover design.

Every effort has been made to trace the copyright holders but if any have been inadvertently overlooked the publishers will be pleased to make the necessary arrangement at the first opportunity.

A Note on World Wide Web Resources

During the mid-1990s pidgin and creole resources have begun to become available via the World Wide Web. Some of these are excellent and others, of course, disappointing. For those with Web access, a good starting point is the *Creole Database Project*: http://www.ling.su.se:80/creole/ which has information and links to many pidgin and creole sites around the world.

Map of Pidgin and Creole locations

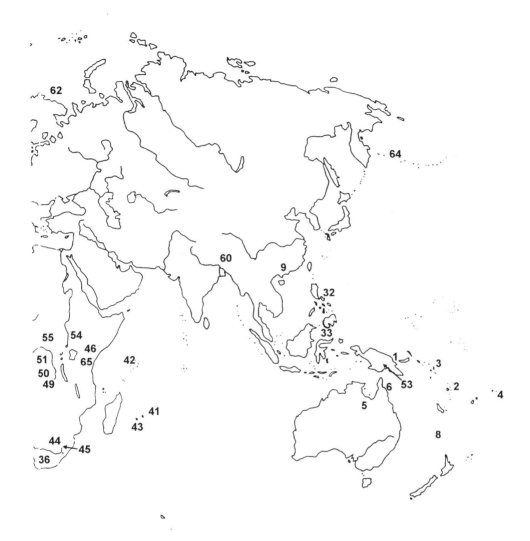

41	Mauritian Creole	47	Pidgin A-70	3	Solomon Islands Pijin
65	Mbugu	48	Pidgin Ewondo	23	Sranan
66	Media Lengua	49	Pidgin Swahili	39	St Lucia Creole
67	Michif	7	Pitcairnese (Pitkern)	19	St Vincent Creole
59	Mobilian Jargon	43	Réunionnais	1	Tok Pisin
60	Naga Pidgin	62	Russenorsk	6	Torres Strait Broken
61	Ndjuka-Trio Pidgin	4	Samoan Plantation Pidgin	17	Trinidad Creole
34	Negerhollands	55	Sango	63	Tupi (Língua Geral)
12	Nigerian Pidgin English	30	São Tomé Crioulo	11	West African Pidgin English
8	Norfolk	24	Saramaccan	33	Zamboangueño
31	Papiamentu	42	Seychellois		
32	Philippine Creole Spanish	46	Sheng		

English-Lexicon Pidgins and Creoles

1 Tok Pisin
2 Bislama
3 Solomon Islands Pijin
4 Samoan Plantation Pidgin
5 Australian Pidgin English
6 Torres Strait Broken
7 Pitcairnese (Pitkern)
8 Norfolk
9 Chinese Pidgin English
10 Hawaiian Creole English
11 West African Pidgin English
12 Nigerian Pidgin English
13 Cameroonian Pidgin English
14 Krio
15 Jamaican Creole
16 Guyanese Creole
17 Trinidad Creole
18 Grenada Creole
19 St Vincent Creole
20 Barbadian Creole
21 Belizean Creole
22 Central American Creole
23 Sranan
24 Saramaccan
25 Boni
26 Djuka
27 Gullah

Portuguese/Spanish-Lexicon Creoles

28 Guiné Crioulo
29 Cape Verde Crioulo
30 São Tomé Crioulo
31 Papiamentu
32 Philippine Creole Spanish
33 Zamboangueño

Dutch-Lexicon Creoles

34 Negerhollands
35 Berbice Creole Dutch
36 Afrikaans

French-Lexicon Creoles

37 Haitian Creole
38 Guadeloupe Creole
39 St Lucia Creole
40 Louisiana Creole
41 Mauritian Creole
42 Seychellois
43 Réunionnais

Bantu-Lexicon Pidgins and Creoles

44 Fanakalo
45 Fly Taal
46 Sheng
47 Pidgin A-70
48 Pidgin Ewondo
49 Pidgin Swahili
50 Kituba
51 Lingala

Other Pidgins, Creoles and Jargons

52 Eskimo Trade Jargon
53 Hiri Motu
54 Juba Arabic
55 Sango
56 Chinook Jargon
57 Delaware Jargon
58 Gastarbeiterdeutsch
59 Mobilian Jargon
60 Naga Pidgin
61 Ndjuka-Trio Pidgin
62 Russenorsk
63 Tupi (Língua Geral)

Mixed Languages

64 Copper Island Aleut
65 Mbugu
66 Media Lengua
67 Michif

---

* The numbers refer to those on the map on pp. x–xi.

1 Close Encounters between Languages

1 IS IT ENGLISH?

In *My South Sea Island* Eric Muspratt describes his life on an island in the South Pacific (San Cristobal in the Solomons group) where he was a plantation manager shortly after the First World War. At one point his servant, Peter, addresses his boss, who is seriously ill with fever, as follows:

> Master! Big feller fever he stop alonga you. Long time he stop. S'pose big fever he stop long time, bymbye man he die finish. Me think you close up die, master. You no savvy walk about no more – bymbye finish. S'pose you die, master, what name you want 'em? Me boss boy, me fix em what you want. (Muspratt, 1931, p. 125.)

If asked to put a name to this variety of language, you might well say that it is 'Pidgin' or 'Pidgin English', and in fact this is how Muspratt describes it in his book, with a disdain which is common in books written by Europeans:

> Thus one learns very quickly to use the native speech, and the boys [i.e. male islanders – MS] learn the names of the white man's accessories. 'Pidgin' or 'Bêche-de-mer' English, a simplified corrupted version of our language, is the lingua franca of the Pacific... Islands within sight of each other speak different dialects and some speak different languages, so that a crowd of mixed boys on a plantation talk together in 'Pidgin English'. (ibid., p. 81)

What exactly is pidgin? *The Chambers Dictionary* (1993) defines *pidgin* as:

> any combination and distortion of two languages as a means of communication...

and *pidgin English* as:

> any lingua franca consisting of English and another language.

So is what Peter speaks a language, or merely a 'corruption' or 'distortion' of English, or a 'jargon' of some sort?

1

The main subject of this book is the group of languages which linguists call *pidgins*, and a related group of languages known as *creoles*. Pidgins and creoles are two types of *contact language*, so called because they come about through contact between two or more previously existing languages. We shall see in the remainder of this book that although it is fair to describe Peter's speech in the extract above as 'pidgin English', this term does not have, for linguists, the negative connotations which are attributed to it by the *Chambers Dictionary* when it uses terms like 'distortion'. By way of doing this we shall first have to look at the whole notion of what a 'language' actually is, and the ideas of 'purity' and 'corruption' as they are applied to language.

2 WHAT IS A LANGUAGE?

What language do you speak?

Most people answer this question without hesitation (and many people, of course, can list more than one answer). But now comes a more difficult question: What makes what you speak a *language*, as opposed, say, to a dialect, jargon, argot, pidgin or gibberish? This question is not nearly so easy to answer. Dictionaries provide a number of definitions of 'language', for example:

> Vocabulary and way of using it prevalent in one or more countries
> (*Concise Oxford Dictionary*, 1982)

> A system for the expression of thoughts, feelings etc. by the use of spoken sounds or conventional symbols; . . . the language of a particular nation or people (*Collins Concise English Dictionary*, 1985)

> Human speech: a variety of speech or body of words and idioms, esp. that of a nation: mode of expression: diction . . .
> (*Chambers Dictionary*, 1993)

We can see from this sample of dictionary definitions that there is a close association between 'language' and 'nation', 'people' or 'country'. By contrast, if we look for a dictionary definition of 'dialect', we find that it is associated with lower social status or with geographical or social units smaller than a country or 'nation', or considered to be of less importance:

> Form of speech peculiar to a district or class; subordinate variety of a language with non-standard vocabulary, pronunciation, or idioms.
> (*Concise Oxford Dictionary*, 1982)

a. a form of a language spoken in a particular geographical area or by members of a particular social class or occupational group, distinguished by its vocabulary, grammar, and pronunciation. **b**. a form of a language that is considered inferior.

(Collins Concise English Dictionary, 1985)

A variety or form of a language peculiar to a district or class, esp. but not necessarily other than a literary or standard form; a peculiar manner of speaking.

(Chambers Dictionary, 1993)

The important point here is the association between 'language' and an identifiable political or social unit, usually a 'country' in modern-day terms (though note that English is particularly difficult to associate with any one 'nation' or country: most English speakers do not live in England. Spanish is even more problematic in this respect). Other terms like 'dialect' and 'jargon' are nearly always used to refer to the communication systems of groups which do not have the status of 'nations', and their connotations are nearly always negative, at least when compared with those of 'language'. Yet from a linguist's point of view, there is no systematic way to decide what is a 'language' and what is a 'dialect': both refer to exactly the same type of communicative system. Neither need necessarily be standardised and both may have high or low status, though dialects with high status (like Standard English) are not usually referred to as 'dialects' even though a minority of the population uses them.

We have to conclude that the *real* difference between 'languages' and 'dialects' is social; first, in terms of their social status; secondly, in that a language is associated with nationhood and, to some extent, with European ideas of 'civilisation'. (In articles by journalists, African languages, which are extremely diverse and differ as much from each other as English from Chinese, are often called 'African dialects'. This is almost certainly because the writers feel, subconsciously, that the African linguistic systems are not the equal of European 'languages'. The same journalists would almost certainly not dare to call, say, Dutch a dialect of German or Norwegian a dialect of Danish – though these statements would be slightly closer to the truth.)

The linguist Max Weinreich is credited with an often-repeated remark on this theme: *a language is a dialect with an army and a navy*. In other words, the difference lies not in the linguistic system, but in the social world where people organise themselves into political entities with boundaries and the mechanisms to defend them. A 'Language' is often just another national asset which the army and navy must be mobilised to protect.

3 'CORRUPTION' AND 'PURITY'

3.1 'Pure' Language, 'Pure' Race

The idea that the races of human beings can be, and should be, 'pure', has caused a great deal of turmoil and suffering in the twentieth century. Almost as obstinate and damaging an idea is the notion that languages can be, and should be, 'pure'. Purists reject foreign influences on 'their' language and use 'tradition' to justify their demands to preserve it in its 'pure' state. In contrast with the 'pure' language which they admire, and to which they attribute all sorts of positive properties (preciseness, musicality, logicality, lyricism, etc.), they deplore language as 'corrupt' when it deviates too much from the written standard, uses too many foreign words, or involves a mixture of languages.

Although purist attitudes are widely held in most English-speaking societies (and perhaps more so in some others, for example in France), it is important to see these attitudes for what they are: cultural phenomena which can, and do, change with time and which are not invariant from generation to generation or society to society.

How do you react to the following advertisement, which appeared in *Homes and Gardens* in November 1992?

This Coq au Vin lacks a certain je ne sais quoi. Wouldn't you like to know quoi?

If vous voulez cook Coq au Vin like françaises Coq au Vin, investez vous in a pack of Knorr Chicken Stock cubes, and follow cette recipe.

It is les Knorr stock cubes that make toute la difference to the flavour of any meal, be it the specialité de votre maison or a simple supper.

If your reaction is like that of most readers, and the sort of response the copywriters probably wanted, you will feel mild amusement, caused (1) by its slightly mocking stance towards pretentious people who use French cooking terms and French phrases like *je ne sais quoi*; but more importantly for us, (2) by the 'funny' mix of French and English ('Franglais'), which by now is quite well established in Britain as a written genre for humorous purposes (and is used elsewhere in advertising and marketing, e.g. 'Le Crunch' for French apples).

3.2 Serious Franglais

But why exactly is Franglais funny? And why is it appropriate only for humorous purposes? The following text, a letter written in 1403 to Henry IV, King of England, may surprise you.

Mon tressouveraigne et tres redoute Seignour,

Please a vostre tresgraciouse Seignourie entendre que a-jourduy apres **noone**...q'ils furent venuz deinz nostre countie pluis de .cccc. des les rebelz de Owyne, Glyn, Talgard, et pluseours autres rebelz des voz marches de galys, et ount prisez er robbez deinz vostre countie de Hereford pluseours gentz, et bestaille a graunt nombre, nient contre esteant la nostre trewe....

Car, mon tres redoute Seigneur, vous trouverez pour certein que si vous ne venez en vostre propre persone pour attendre apres voz rebelz en Galys, vous ne trouverez un gentil que veot attendre deinz vostre dit countee. **Warfore, for goddesake, thinketh on your beste frende, god, and thanke hym as he hath deserued to yowe! And leueth nought that ye ne come for no man that may counsaille yowe the contrarie; for, but the trouthe that I schal be to yowe yet, this day the Walshmen supposen and trusten, that ye schulle nought come there, and therefore, for goddesloue, make them fals men!**...

Tresexcellent, trespuissant, et tresredoute Seignour, autrement say a present nieez. Jeo prie a la benoit trinite que vous ottroie bone vie ove tresentier sauntee a treslonge durre, **and sende yowe sone to ows in help and prosperitee; for in god fey, I hope to almighty god that, yef ye come youre owne persone, ye schulle haue the victorie of alle youre enemyes.**

And for salvation of youre schire and marches al aboute, treste ye nought to no leutenaunt. Escript a Hereford, en tresgraunte haste, a trois de la clocke apres **noone**, le tierce jour de Septembre.

Vostre humble creatoure et continuelle oratour
Richard Kyngeston, deane de Wyndesore.

(*Royal and Historical Letters during the Reign of Henry IV*
vol. I, pp. 155–9)

This letter from Richard Kingston, 'Dean of Windsor', is about Welsh rebels' attacks on the King's territories. What is striking is that it begins in a form of French, switches to English in the middle of a paragraph, and then switches between English and French several times more. Fifteenth-century Franglais? But whatever else we may think of the Dean of Windsor's letter, we can be certain that it was not intended to be amusing. The matters discussed, in French and English, are deadly earnest. We can also be certain that today, no servant of the Crown would write an official letter in a mixture like this: Standard English would be expected in Britain, but even Standard French would be considered better (though odd) than a mixture of the two. Richard Kingston's letter would simply not be taken seriously today, any more than the advert for chicken stock cubes. (For more discussion of this text, see Knowles (1997).)

Nevertheless, the type of mixture seen in Kingston's letter is quite unremarkable in many situations of language contact where two or more languages are in regular use in a community. This was the case among the English nobility at the time the letter was written (though French was by then restricted almost entirely to official purposes and was not used as an everyday language by anyone in England; even nobles of French extraction had shifted to using English for everyday communication). In fact the kind of mixing of languages which Richard Kingston engaged in, called *code switching*, is a commonplace phenomenon in bilingual communities, especially in speech. The following example of conversational code switching between Alsatian (a dialect of German) and French in present-day Strasbourg (Gardner-Chloros, 1991, p. 121) recalls the closing passage of Richard Kingston's letter to Henry IV:

Der het's kauft vor zehn Johr, am achtzehnte *janvier; s'il le revend avant,* hett'r e *plus-value.*
(He bought it ten years ago, on the eighteenth *of January; if he sells it again before* [*ten years are up*] he'll have to pay *gains tax.*)

There are more examples of code switching in Chapter 7.

3.3 'Standard Coin'

In England in the six centuries since the letter to Henry IV was written, notions of standard language and language purity have gained such a hold that mixing languages, especially in writing, is felt to be appropriate only as a source of humour (or occasionally, of extreme sophistication!). According to McArthur (1993), 'Standard English' as a term was first used during the Industrial Revolution in Britain, when having 'standard' parts became important for mass-production. However, there is evidence that the idea of a 'standard' language – in this case Spanish – is much older than that. Later in the same century in which the Dean of Windsor wrote to Henry IV, Manuel de Nebrija addressed his Queen thus:

My illustrious Queen. Whenever I ponder over the tokens of the past that have been preserved in writing, I am forced to the very same conclusion.

Language has always been the consort of empire, and shall forever remain its mate. Together they come into being, together they grow and flower, and together they decline.

Your majesty, it has been my constant desire to see our nation become great, and to provide the men of my tongue with books worthy of their leisure. Presently, they waste their time on novels and fancy stories full of lies.

These words were written as the introduction to Nebrija's *Gramática Castellana* ('Castilian Grammar'), by which he sought to standardise the language of Castile (which has become modern Spanish), so making it fit, as he thought, for a language of Empire.

Queen Isabella, according to Illich (1981), was unable to understand why anyone would want a grammar book, and responded in these terms: 'What is the use of a grammar of a living spoken language? Every man has perfect dominion over his own tongue.' Nebrija's answer was as follows: 'Language is the mate of Empire. Let us turn the Castilian tongue into an artefact – a standard coin which will outlast time.'

In this we can see a link between the standardisation of languages and historical factors: standard languages had a functional role in nation and empire building during the era when large nation-states like Spain and France were being established in Europe and creating empires abroad through trade and colonisation; this trend was reinforced and consolidated by the advent of printed books (also around the time of Nebrija's 'gift' of the Castilian Grammar to his Queen) and, later, by industrialisation and the introduction of mass media.

We have to remember that before the notion of 'standard', 'national' languages existed, people in Europe did not have the same sense they have now of speaking either 'Language X' or 'a dialect of Language X'. People were simply aware of speaking the language of their own region. 'English', 'French' and 'Spanish' did not exist as concepts in the way they do now. Language varieties did not observe state or regional boundaries, and the notion of a 'nonstandard' language did not exist since there were no *living* standard languages. Latin – a language not used in everyday spoken communication – fulfilled the role of a medium for scholarship and long-distance communication.

Even today, dialect boundaries do not coincide with national boundaries. This is particularly so in certain parts of Europe, for example on the border between the Netherlands and Germany. The regional speech on either side of this border was, up to a few generations ago, as similar as any two varieties of one language which are separated geographically by only a few miles. Dutch and German are similar languages with a lot of shared linguistic history, so this should not be surprising. However, with the arrival of compulsory education and universal literacy, speakers on one side of the border became conscious of speaking a variety of 'German' while those on the other side felt they spoke a type of 'Dutch'. Influences from the written language norms have affected the spoken language as well, so the local varieties have also changed, each towards its own 'standard'. Although the boundaries for the spoken languages are still fuzzy, we are now closer than before to the situation as the public and politicians have long imagined it to be: Dutch people speak 'Dutch' and German people speak 'German'.

This idea of the link between language and nation being 'all in the mind' is taken up by one author, Benedict Anderson, in his book *Imagined Communities*. He stresses the importance of *print* in defining languages:

> Speakers of the huge variety of Frenches, Englishes, or Spanishes, who might find it difficult or even impossible to understand one another in conversation, gradually became aware of the hundreds of thousands, even millions, of people in their particular language-field, and at the same time that *only those* hundreds of thousands, or millions, so belonged. (Anderson, 1983, p. 47)

What Anderson calls 'print-languages' created large geographical regions with a common written standard which *included* large numbers of speakers while *excluding* all others. At the same time print-languages gave power to the dialects which were closest to the newly standardised form and disempowered others which were less similar. A status difference thus arose between prestigious dialects – the 'standard language' or 'print-language' and varieties nearest to it – and the rest. 'Standard' languages conferred economic and political power on their speakers. Any language variety which was not 'writable' or usable as a print-language was now second-class.

3.4 Focussing and Diffusion

But what of the situation beforehand? Apparently, the strict notion of 'correct' and 'pure' language did not exist, or at least not in the same way, among Europeans. Richard Kingston, 'deane de Wyndesore', was not – as far as we can tell, anyway – rebuked by the King for haphazardly mixing English and French, nor chastised over his spelling or points of grammar on which he differed from other nobles – who would certainly have spoken widely different varieties of English depending on which part of the country they came from. Some societies, it seems, can tolerate variation and indefiniteness of this sort, while others demand strict adherence to a norm, condemning deviations as 'corrupt', 'sloppy' or 'substandard'.

Le Page and Tabouret-Keller (1985) use the concepts of **focussing** and **diffusion** to account for these differences. A language which has highly focussed norms is one where the community of speakers puts rather strict limits on what is acceptable. They are likely to have clear notions of 'correct' grammar and 'standard' usage, and to refer to books such as dictionaries and grammars to back these up. Educational failure or low social status may be the prices paid by those who do not adhere to the norm. Most modern European countries, with their highly standardised national languages and literary norms upheld by authors, publishers, educators and academics, would fall into this category.

Other societies, meanwhile, have far more relaxed linguistic norms. Language may be valued more for its effectiveness in communicating messages than for whether its pronunciation or grammar meets some 'standard' set by society. Particular words and grammatical constructions are not stigmatised or ridiculed. If the language is written down at all, the rules of spelling are not strict. Such a society would be said to have *diffuse* linguistic norms in Le Page and Tabouret-Keller's terminology. Many pre-industrial societies, and marginal groups within industrial societies, fit this description.

3.5 Language Change and Family Matters

We have seen that in the perception of people in industrialised societies today, a 'language' is something which necessarily

- is 'pure',
- has clear boundaries separating it from all other languages,
- has clear, 'focused' norms of right/wrong, grammatical/ungram-matical.

We have also seen that these ideas are fairly recent and are social/cultural in origin. In this light, it is interesting to consider a model used widely by linguists to describe the relationships between languages – the **family tree model**. Although linguists nowadays do not speak of 'pure' or 'corrupt' languages (though others do), the family tree model in practice makes the assumption that languages are reasonably 'pure', or, to put it more neutrally, do not exert substantial influences on each other.

In the family tree model, a 'parent' language gives rise to two or more 'offspring', which are seen as having developed from it through more or less natural processes of sound, meaning and grammatical change. The 'offspring' languages are initially just different geographical or social varieties of the parent; but over time, as they become more geographically or culturally isolated from the parent, the results of the slow processes of change become so marked that they are no longer recognisable as variants of the parent. They will then be redefined – by linguists even if not by their own speakers – as separate languages from the parent.

The key assumption underlying this model of relatedness is that language contact, if it takes place at all, does not alter the 'true' or 'fundamental' character of a language. Though most linguists regard vocabulary as a relatively superficial aspect of a language, and one which is especially subject to influence from other languages, certain 'core' elements of vocabulary are widely believed to be resistant to change by outside influence. Thus words for some parts of the body like 'hand', and 'eye', common substances like 'blood' and 'water', and some abstract concepts like 'ten' might be considered so fundamental that no language would be likely to replace them with foreign terms. By contrast, words for new things or concepts coming in from a foreign culture, such as technological or religious terms, would be more likely to be taken from the language of the culture which first introduced them.

At the same time as assuming that language contact leaves languages to grow relatively undisturbed, the family tree model assumes that the pace of change is slow and gradual. Small changes take decades or centuries to become established; the 'evolution' of a language like Latin into modern Italian or Romanian is seen as a process taking centuries or millennia.

The 'family tree' model is one which is widely accepted, so much so that linguists and non-linguists alike will speak of French, say, being 'descended' from Latin, or Dutch and German being 'closely related'. However, the study of language contact provides a challenge to the family tree model, as we shall see later.

4 CLOSE ENCOUNTERS BETWEEN LANGUAGES: CONSEQUENCES OF SIX KINDS

We have seen above that even the concept of 'a language' is somewhat problematic. It is not as easy as all that to tie a string around a language and package it up neatly and separate it from all the rest. Language boundaries are fuzzy and often 'imagined'; furthermore, language contact may take place and confuse the boundaries further. However, there are different types of contact and potentially many different types of effect on the languages concerned. In this section we will take a look at some of the possible types of 'close encounters' between languages and their consequences.

4.1   Consequence 1: Vocabulary and Grammar 'Borrowing'

Taking another look at Richard Kingston's letter to Henry IV we can see that even those passages which are written in English contain words of French origin, for example *counsaille* (counsel), *supposen* (suppose), *enemy*. By the time this letter was written, French had had a presence in Britain for over 300 years (since the conquest of England by the Duke of Normandy in 1066), and during this time numerous French words had been 'borrowed' into English.

The term 'borrowing', although it is used very widely in linguistic textbooks, is rather misleading, since it suggests that the words or structures in question are taken in temporarily and will in due course be given back! What actually happens is more akin to 'adoption' or 'naturalisation': after a while, the 'borrowed' item is no longer felt to be strange or 'foreign' and is adapted to the sound and/or grammatical patterns of the new language. This is certainly the case with modern English, which contains many thousands of words of French origin which all English speakers use daily, nearly always unaware that these words were once 'foreign'.

For large-scale borrowing to take place, there must be at least a part of the language community which is bilingual in both languages. In the case of English, a situation of **diglossia** prevailed, with one language restricted to the upper class alone. In the period after 1066, only the nobles and the senior members of their households spoke French. The ordinary people of the country continued to speak English, in many different regional varieties. At the start of this period, in fact, most of the Norman overlords knew only Norman French. But quite quickly, in the course of a few generations, the French-speaking nobility first became bilingual in French and English, and then monolingual in English. (This process is called *language shift*.) Later, French became in effect a foreign language though it still had a role as an official language in England. It was during the relatively short period when a bilingual French/English community existed that most of the French influences on English were brought to bear, and a large quantity of French vocabulary became part of English.

Note the key 'ingredients' of this situation. One language (French) has much higher status than the other, because its speakers rule the country; but those speakers are also a tiny minority. Moreover, very few people are in a position to know both languages. Under these circumstances words, especially words for new concepts which previously did not exist in the 'host' language's culture, are able to pass from the high-status language to the lower-status one, with the small bilingual elite and their servants as their 'pipeline'. New words were able to enter English without displacing any of the existing ones, and the vocabulary of English grew substantially.

Although the French influence on English vocabulary was large, it had little effect on other systems of the language (for example, the grammar). The lexical system (vocabulary) of a language, although of great importance, is the most susceptible to external influences (see Thomason and Kaufman, 1988), and vocabulary changes are seen by most linguists as relatively superficial. Deeper-reaching effects – on the grammar and semantic systems – are only likely when a large proportion of the population has a knowledge of both languages and/or the contact continues over a very long period.

4.2   Consequence 2: Code Switching

Both *code switching* and the subject of the next section, *language convergence*, are characteristic of communities with a high degree of bilingualism, in other words, communities where some part of the population, possibly a large part, knows two or more languages *well*. Such communities are not rare, although those of us who live in western Europe and North America tend to overlook them in our assumptions that our societies are basically monolingual and have one single national language (obvious exceptions being Canada, Belgium and Switzerland). Probably a majority of the world's people live in bilingual or multilingual communities.

We have already seen two examples of **code switching**. The first, written example, came from Richard Kingston's letter to Henry IV. Although Kingston's conversational command of French may well have been poor, as French in England was becoming restricted to official purposes at the time when he was writing, we may look on him as *biliterate*, with the ability to read and write both French and English. Bilinguals who are fluent in two or more languages often switch between them if the social norms concerning language permit them to do so; this is much more likely in a society with *diffuse* rather than *focussed* linguistic norms.

The second example we saw above came from Strasbourg in Alsace, from a community where French and German have been in contact for centuries as ownership of the territory changed back and forth between Germans and French. In Strasbourg, virtually everyone speaks, reads and writes French, since all formal education is French-based. However, most people native to the area also speak Alsatian, a dialect of German, although they do not necessarily read or write German. Conversations like the one reported by Gardner-Chloros, where German and French intermingle even within the same sentence, are not unusual in Strasbourg; and in some contexts, they are the norm.

Code switching, although it may look haphazard and unsystematic, is actually systematic and often purposeful. In the mind of the code switcher, one language may be more appropriate than the other for expressing a particular idea; one language may be more intimate and personal than the other; one may show more authority, and the other, more solidarity. Code switchers construct a potent and finely modulated personal blend of languages each time they speak, and do so almost always without breaking any of the grammatical rules of *either* language! Since being 'noticed' as a linguistic phenomenon two or three decades ago, code switching has attracted a great deal of interest and there is now a huge literature on the subject (see, for example, Romaine, 1989; Heller, 1988). Like pidgin and creole languages, however, the phenomenon of code switching was ignored for a long time, even by linguists, because of the analytical difficulties it presented. For the general public, furthermore, it smacked of 'impurity' or even a 'barbarous' mingling of languages.

4.3   Consequence 3: Language Convergence

Code switching involves 'blending' two separate languages in conversation or writing. To switch, an individual must actually *know* both languages quite well. **Language convergence**, on the other hand, involves the languages within a community changing and adjusting their structures so that they all become more similar to each other. In a study reported by Gumperz and Wilson (1971), it was found that in Kupwar, a village in India, the languages Marathi, Urdu and Kannada had been in contact for 400 years. The Kupwar varieties of these three languages had grown so similar that there were virtually no differences in their grammatical structure. Although their vocabularies remained separate, a sentence in one of the three could be translated word for word simply by substituting the appropriate items of vocabulary. Anyone who has tried to do word-for-word translating from one language to another will know that this almost always leads swiftly to disaster, unless the languages are already very similar to each other – which standard Marathi, Urdu and Kannada are not. What has happened in Kupwar is that in the course of regular use by bilinguals and multilinguals in a community where all three languages have been used together for a long time, the languages' grammars have *converged* into a single system, although the vocabularies have remained intact.

Language convergence differs from *code switching* in that switching is something done by an individual speaker who knows both languages. Convergence takes place over time, in a community with a high degree of bilingualism, but the languages retain their separate vocabularies and individual members of the community may or may not be bilingual. The speakers themselves will not necessarily be aware that convergence has taken place (if they do not know about the more standard varieties of the 'converged' languages). Once the convergence is complete, the languages will be passed on to future generations of the community in that form, even if contact between the language groups stops (for example, if one of the language communities stops mixing with the others because of a new religious or political division).

4.4   Consequence 4: Pidginisation

Language contact phenomena of the first three types require that part or all of a community must have a reasonably high degree of bilingualism: in other words, at least some people must be fluent in the two (or more) languages involved. Where two communities with different languages settle side by side in relative harmony (even if the relationship is not without its problems, as in the case of the Norman French nobles who imposed their will on the English) there are usually ample opportunities for each group to learn the other's language, whether through formal education or simply through mingling with one another in daily life, especially as children. (Child-minders (servants and nannies) who use a low-status language have always had a special role in bringing about bilingualism in upper-class children who would otherwise learn only the high-status language. Some consequences of this will be apparent in later chapters.)

What happens, however, in cases where two groups of adults without a common language come into contact and neither group has the opportunity, or the will, to learn the other's language? In such cases, language learning will still take place, but imperfectly. A *pidgin* language is one potential outcome. 'Pidgin' is used here, not in the detrimental sense attributed to it by many dictionaries, but in a technical sense given to it by linguists. Pidgins result from the communicative strategies of adults who *already* have a native command of at least one language. Pidgins have therefore been called 'auxiliary' languages because they are needed by their speakers in addition to their own native languages, to bridge a communicative gap with speakers of some other language.

What I have said so far suggests that pidgins are made up 'on the spot' as a strategy to enable communication to take place. This is true in some cases, certainly. We know of several pidgins which have existed for short periods of contact between groups (for example, invading soldiers and local villagers) and have then disappeared. It is probably true to say that new pidgins are created, and die out, daily where tourists and travellers come into contact with local people with whom they share at most a few imperfectly pronounced words. The single words, simplified grammar and exaggerated gestures which accompany, say, tourists buying local crafts from a villager are the characteristics of a very basic type of pidgin. We shall be investigating such 'makeshift languages' in more detail in a later chapter.

Not all pidgins are so short lived or so basic, however. The pidgin spoken by the Solomon Islander Peter at the start of this chapter is a case in point. A pidgin form of English has existed in the South Pacific for about two centuries. During most of that time, it has remained *a language without native speakers of its own*, always learned by its speakers as an additional language. Yet, amazingly, it is still recognisably the *same* language as that first recorded in accounts of travellers and mariners in the eighteenth century – in other words, *it has had a recognisable set of conventions* over a long period. And while most of its vocabulary is recognisably English in origin, *it is very definitely a different language from English*. These points are three of the most important ones which traditionally define a pidgin (see Thomason and Kaufman, 1988, Chapter 7):

1. **Pidgins have no native speakers**, i.e. they are second languages for everyone who speaks them.

2. **They are governed by convention**, i.e. they have vocabulary and grammatical structures, however basic, which are accepted by their speakers. It is not the case that 'anything goes'.

3. **They are not mutually intelligible with their source languages.** Thus 'Pidgin English' is sufficiently different from English that a native speaker of English must learn it in order to be able to understand and speak it properly. (Of course, because many of its words are of English origin, learning the vocabulary may be a relatively easy task for an English speaker. Learning the grammar may present more challenges – a fact not always realised by Europeans trying to speak pidgin.)

A fourth point which may or may not be essential in defining a pidgin, and which will be discussed in more detail in Chapter 2, is the following:

4. **Pidgins have grammars which are simpler than the grammars of their source languages**. Simplicity of grammar is one of the characteristics of pidgins, and in fact is part of the meaning of the word in everyday use.

The next three chapters of this book are mainly devoted to a discussion of pidgins. Chapter 2 looks at the grammatical systems of pidgins and their characteristics. Chapter 3 discusses the question of how pidgins come into being. Chapter 4 deals mainly with how pidgins develop through time from rudimentary communication systems to fully fledged languages.

4.5   Consequence 5: Creolisation

While pidgins are languages without native speakers, they do not always remain so. Under conditions of social upheaval (such as slavery in the sixteenth to nineteenth centuries) or rapid social change (such as migration from rural areas to cities in the twentieth century) or where ethnically diverse groups mix closely together as in a colonial port or garrison, a settled community may come into being quite rapidly, in which the pidgin is the general language of communication. Once such a community has appeared, children are likely to follow soon afterwards, and will grow up surrounded by various languages – but in particular, by the pidgin. These children will acquire the pidgin – or something like it – as a native language (not necessarily their *only* language). The pidgin thereby begins to have native speakers. At this point we say that the pidgin has *creolised* and the resultant language is called a *creole*.

The above description is necessarily sketchy and over-simplified. Chapters 5, 6 and 7 are devoted to a discussion of creoles, their origins, and the problems and challenges they present to linguists. For the time being we can use the following definition: *creoles are pidgins which have become native languages for their speakers.* Because pidgins characteristically are simpler than their source languages, creoles too, typically have rather simple grammars.

4.6   Consequence 6: Language Mixing (also called *Language Intertwining*)

These are phenomena which have only recently attracted the attention of linguists. They involve two languages combining in such a way that (usually) the grammar of one language is 'grafted on' to the vocabulary of another – or vice versa. While there are some clear similarities with **pidginisation** and **creolisation**, in **language mixing** there is generally no loss of grammatical complexity – in other words, the grammar of one of the source languages is taken over intact, with no simplification of its rule system. At the same time, much or all of the vocabulary of the other language is incorporated into the resulting mixed language. This is clearly different from consequence 1 – *borrowing* – by virtue of its scale. Also, while borrowing is common, language mixing is rather rare. Because of the complexity of questions raised by language mixing, it will be discussed in more detail later, in Chapter 9.

5   PIDGINS AND CREOLES IN THE CONTEXT OF MULTILINGUALISM

Clearly, two people who both speak one language or dialect – or even different dialects of the same language – have no essential need for any other language in order to communicate with each other. It is only when a common first language is lacking that people necessarily have to find other strategies in order to communicate.

An alternative solution is to find a common second language. In many communities around the world which use their first language for all everyday purposes within the community, a second language is widely known and used for communicating with people from *outside* the community – for example, for trade or for dealing with the authorities. Such languages are known as **languages of wider communication** for their speakers. Where a language is widely used over a relatively large geographical area as a language of wider communication, it is known as a **lingua franca** – a common language but one which is native only to some of its speakers. The term 'lingua franca' itself is an extension of the use of the name of the original 'Lingua Franca,' a Medieval trading pidgin used in the Mediterranean region – an important maritime trading zone where traders' native languages included many very different languages such as Portuguese, Greek, Arabic and Turkish. 'Lingua franca' as a term for such a regional language does not imply that it is a pidgin. Swahili, a language widely spoken in East and some parts of Central Africa is a good example of an indigenous lingua franca – i.e. one that has its 'base' of native speakers within the area where it functions as a lingua franca.

In some countries English has the status of an *exogenous* lingua franca – in other words, it is widely used for inter-group communication even though there are few or no local native speakers. Due to the enormous economic influence of English-speaking countries, particularly the United States, English has become a lingua franca in many parts of the world and for many types of international communication.

These two examples of lingua francas – Swahili and English – are both languages which have native speakers of their own. In many regions of the world, however, lingua francas are in use which have their origins in language contact, and are not spoken natively by anyone: pidgins, in other words. Pidgins as lingua francas have the advantage of being simple in grammar and having relatively small vocabulary which is tailored to meet the functional needs of the pidgin's users. Thus they do not make too many demands on the learner. Pidgins may also have a social advantage, in that because they are no-one's native language, 'all speakers are equal' – there are no native speakers with a 'superior' knowledge of the language. Pidgins may therefore be seen as socially neutral, even though they may also have low status.

It is important not to lose sight of the fact that pidgins are solutions to a practical problem of communication among speakers who have no other common language. In other words, their main value at the *outset* is functional, though this may not be true forever. The most 'successful' pidgins – if we can apply this term to those which have survived longest, and are spoken over the widest areas – are those which also serve as regional lingua francas: for example, West African Pidgin English (spoken over a wide area of West Africa) and Melanesian Pidgin English (spoken in somewhat different forms in Papua New Guinea, the Solomon Islands and Vanuatu). We will now have a look in more detail at the latter.

6   CASE STUDY: TOK PISIN (NEW GUINEA PIDGIN ENGLISH)

6.1   Introduction

'Pidgin English' has been widely used in the Pacific region for about two centuries. Its origins are generally believed to lie in a nautical jargon used by seafarers in the Far East and South Pacific. This developed, under different circumstances of use and in different places, into several well-documented pidgins each similar, but with some differences. Today different varieties of this pidgin (called Melanesian Pidgin or Neo-Melanesian by some writers) are national languages, and partly standardised, in three countries. In Vanuatu (the former New Hebrides, a 'condominium' governed jointly by Britain and France) its connection with the trade in edible sea-slugs ('Bêche-de-mer' in French – cf. the quote from Muspratt at the beginning of this chapter) gave it the name Bislama. It is now one of the official languages of the Republic of Vanuatu. In the Solomon Islands, Pidgin (sometimes called Pijin or Neo-Solomonic) is not official, but is an important *lingua franca* as there are about 80 local languages.

The New Guinean variety of the pidgin seems to have its immediate origins in the pidgin used on German-owned plantations in Samoa (an island group in the South Pacific) at the end of the nineteenth century. (In spite of this there is relatively little trace of German in the pidgin – just a few words like *rausim* 'remove' from German *heraus* 'out' or 'get out!') Plantation labourers were recruited in New Guinea (also a German colony at the time) to work in Samoa, and the pidgin spread to New Guinea with their return. As there are estimated to be 750 indigenous languages in Papua New Guinea (Holm, 1989, p. 529), *Tok Pisin* – 'Talk Pidgin' or 'Pidgin Language' has become indispensable as a language for inter-group communication and for administration. Tok Pisin is now an official language in the independent Republic of Papua New Guinea of which New Guinea is the northern part.

6.2   Melanesian Pidgin Texts

The text below is an example of contemporary Tok Pisin. It is a short news item from the newspaper *Wantok*, published at Port Moresby, Papua New Guinea (see Figure 1.1). According to its masthead, *Wantok* has an audited circulation of 15,177. The name *Wantok* is significant: 'one talk' (one language) is the Melanesian Pidgin expression for a relative or clansman/clanswoman – a person who shares your language. In the case of the paper *Wantok*, the shared *second* language of all its readers is Tok Pisin.

This article appeared in the edition of *Wantok* dated *wik i stat long Fonde* ('week beginning Thursday'), 14 April, 1994. This extract is presented here in three versions. The first is the text as actually printed in the newspaper. This is a *mainly phonemic* spelling system which is used nowadays in Papua New Guinea to write Tok Pisin (a phonemic writing system is one where each character represents exactly one sound of the language). Underneath this is a representation of the English words from which the pidgin words derive, to help you to make that connection. A few words which are apparently not connected with any English word are given in translation in *italics*. Below this there is a translation into ordinary English.

Figure 1.1 *Wantok*, a newspaper in Tok Pisin from Papua New Guinea

Ol   meri   gat   bikpela   wari   yet
all   *women*   got   big-fellow   worry   yet
Women still have big worries

HELT   na   envairomen   em   ol   bikpela   samting
health   *and*   environment   him   all   big-fellow   something
Health and environment are two of the major things

ol   meri   long   kantri   tude   i   gat   bikpela   wari   long   en
all   *woman*   along   country   today   he   got   big-fellow   worry   along   him
which women in the country today have big concerns about.

Bikos   dispela   tupela   samting   i   save   kamap   strong
because   this-fellow   two-fellow   something   he   *know*   come-up   strong
Because these two things often have a strong effect

long   sindaun   na   laip   bilong   famili   na   komyuniti
along   sit-down   and   life   belong   family   *and*   community
on the situation and life of families and communities

insait   long   ol   ples   na   kantri.
inside   along   all   place   *and*   country
within villages and in the country.

Long   dispela   wik,   moa   long   40   meri   bilong
along   this-fellow   week,   more   along   40   *woman*   belong
This week, more than 40 women from

Milen   Be   provins   i   bung   long   wanpela   woksop
Milne   Bay   Province   he   *meet*   along   one-fellow   workshop

                                                        long   Alotau
                                                        along   Alotau
Milne Bay Province are meeting in a workshop at Alotau

bilong   toktok   long   hevi   bilong   helt   na   envairomen
belong   talk-talk   along   heavy   belong   health   and   environment
in order to talk about the difficulties of health and environment

long   ol   liklik   ailan   na   provins.
along   all   little   island   and   province
in the small islands and provinces.

Bung	**i**	**bin**	**stat**	**long**	**Mande**
Meeting	he	been	start	along	Monday

The meeting began on Monday

na	**bai**		**pinis**	**long**	**Fraide,**	**Epril 22.**
and	bye(-and-bye)		finish	along	Friday	April 22

and will finish on Friday, April 22.

Ol	**opisa**	**bilong**	**Melanesin**	**Envairomen**	**Faundesen**
All	officer	belong	Melanesian	Environment	Foundation

The officers of the Melanesian Environment Foundation

wantaim	**nesenel**	**na**	**provinsal**	**helt**	**opis**	**i**	**stap**	**tu**
one-time	national	*and*	provincial	health	office	he	stop	too

together with the national and provincial health office are there too

bilong	**givim**	**toktok**	**insait**	**long**	**dispela**	**woksop.**
belong	give-him	talk-talk	inside	along	this-fellow	workshop

in order to give talks in the workshop.

Finally, the original with its translation next to it:

Ol meri gat bikpela wari yet

Helt na envairomen em bikpela samting ol meri long kantri tude i gat bikpela wari long en.

Bikos dispela tupela samting i save kamap strong long sindaun na laip bilong famili na komyuniti insait long ol ples na kantri.

Long dispela wik, moa long 40 meri bilong Milen Be provins i bung long wanpela woksop long Alotau bilong toktok long hevi bilong helt na envairomen long ol liklik ailan na provins.

Bung i bin stat long Mande na bai pinis long Fraide, Epril 22. Ol opisa bilong Melanesin Envairomen Faundesen wantaim nesenel na provinsal helt opis i stap tu bilong givim toktok insait long dispela woksop.

Women still have big worries

Health and environment are two of the major things which women in the country today have big concerns about.

Because these two things often have a strong effect on the situation and life of families and communities within villages and in the country.

This week, more than 40 women from Milne Bay Province are meeting in a workshop at Alotau in order to talk about the difficulties of health and environment in the small islands and provinces. The meeting began on Monday and will finish on Friday, April 22.

The officers of the Melanesian Environment Foundation together with the national and provincial health office are there too in order to give talks in the workshop.

6.2.1 A note on orthography (spelling)

How the words of a pidgin or creole should be spelt is an issue which has aroused a lot of discussion at various times. Should the spelling of the lexifier language be used, with modifications? Or should there be a tailor-made, phonemic **orthography** which treats the pidgin or creole as unrelated to the lexifier? Each of these views has its proponents who use various arguments to support their case. The issues involved will be discussed in detail in Chapter 8. Meanwhile a variety of ways will be used to represent the written form of the languages mentioned in this book. Where there is an *accepted conventional orthography* for the language in question, it will be used. In other cases, I will use a *phonemic orthography* devised by linguists but not used by speakers of the language itself. For some texts, the *orthography of the source* (i.e. the writer or publisher of the text) is used. Which is being used will normally be made explicit if it is not clear from the context.

Here, for comparison, is the speech by the Melanesian Peter, which opened this chapter, transcribed in a spelling system consistent, as far as possible, with the one used by *Wantok*. The original version is printed immediately below each line.

Masta! Bik pela fiva i stap long yu.
Master! Big feller fever he stop alonga you.
Master! A great fever is upon you.

Longtaim i stap.
Long time he stop
It has been with you for a long time.

Supos bik fiva i stap longtaim,
S'pose big fever he stop long time,
If a great fever continues for a long time,

baimbai man i dai pinis.
bymbye [i.e. 'by-and-by'] man he die finish.
eventually a man will die.

Mi ting yu kolosap dai, masta.
Me think you close up die, master.
I think you are close to death, master.

Yu no save wokabaut nomo – baimbai pinis.
You no savvy walk about no more – bymbye finish.
You can't move any more – soon it will be finished.

Supos   yu   dai,   masta,   wanem   yu   wantim?
S'pose you die, master, what name you want 'em?
If you die, master, what do you want?

Mi   bosboi,   mi   fiksim   wat   yu   want.
Me boss boy, me fix em what you want
I'm the boss boy [i.e. chief servant], I'll arrange what you want.

[Note: *what you want* appears to be English rather than authentic Pidgin, cf. Tok Pisin *wanem yu laikim em.*]

Making allowances for regional differences and changes over the course of 70 years or so, if we compare the passage above with the newspaper article, we can see that they are in more or less the same language. If we study carefully the relationship between this pidgin and Standard English, it is also clear that Melanesian Pidgin is not just English haphazardly simplified. The word-for-word 'translation' of the pidgin in terms of the English source words simply does not make sense: the two languages are different in both vocabulary and grammar.

This illustrates a point about pidgins already made in 4.4 above, namely that *pidgins are not mutually intelligible with their source languages.* A knowledge of English is of limited help in understanding either of these texts (it is just about possible for English speakers to get the general idea of what they are about, but certainly they would not understand the finer points). Still less could a speaker of English who does not know Melanesian Pidgin 'translate' the English version of the texts back into Pidgin. Melanesian Pidgin has a grammar of its own, which is quite different from that of English.

If we compare the literal and free translations, it becomes clear that many of the Pidgin words, although they derive from English, have different meanings, for example:

ples (English *place*): usually means 'village' in Melanesian Pidgin.
hevi (English *heavy*): here means 'difficulty' rather than 'heavy'.
wokabaut (English *walk about*): means 'move' or 'move about' in Melanesian Pidgin.
stap (English *stop*): in Melanesian Pidgin means 'stay' (its dialectal meaning in many parts of England, e.g. 'Are you stopping overnight?') and hence also 'continue' or simply 'be in a particular place'.

More striking are the *grammatical* functions taken on by words like *baimbai* (*bai* in the newspaper text, from the old-fashioned English *by-and-by*, meaning something like 'soon') and *belong*, which are adverb and verb respectively in English, but are used quite differently in Melanesian Pidgin. (There is an exercise on this below.)

To conclude this section, we can see that a pidgin is much more than a random simplification of a European language, 'a simplified corrupted version of our language' as Muspratt calls it. Melanesian Pidgin, although much of its vocabulary is derived from English, clearly *uses* that vocabulary in a distinctive and non-English way. If most of its vocabulary is English, how much of the grammar of Melanesian Pidgin is derived from indigenous languages of Melanesia? This is one of the questions which will be examined in more detail in later chapters.

6.3   Exercise

You can find data to answer these questions in the two Melanesian Pidgin texts above.

1. Compare the spelling of the original versions of the two passages (the original version of the speech of 'Peter' is at the beginning of this chapter). Which method of writing the pidgin do you think is more appropriate, and why?

2. Compare the meaning of *sindaun* and *wokabaut* in the texts with their English source expressions 'sit down' and 'walk about'. In what way has the meaning changed and how do you think this has come about?

3. Write down all the prepositions you can find in the pidgin texts. (Hint: rely on the *free translation* to decide what is a preposition, not on the English source words.) How many are there altogether? What English words translate each one?

4. Find one example of negation. How does Melanesian Pidgin show negation?

5. Find an example of (a) a sentence with past meaning and (b) a sentence with future meaning. How does Melanesian Pidgin indicate past and future tense?

6. Make a list of the words which are translated as plurals in the *free* translation. How does pidgin indicate the plural of a noun?

7. Make a list of the words which have the suffix *-pela*. What is the grammatical function of *-pela* in the texts? (Hint: ignore the literal translation 'fellow'.)

8. Translate: **Ol meri bilong komyuniti i bung long dispela ples bilong toktok long bikpela wari**.

9. Translate into Melanesian Pidgin: **This officer will stay in the village of the big man**.

7 'LEXIFIER', 'SUPERSTRATE', 'SUBSTRATE' AND 'RESTRUCTURED' LANGUAGES

The notion of a pidgin as a 'mixture' of two languages underlies many of the ways of talking about the origins of pidgin grammars. The fact that many pidgins and creoles are apparently nonstandard variants of European languages – and in particular, English, French, Portuguese, Dutch and Spanish, the languages of colonial empire – has led to a formula for naming pidgins and creoles by the place where they are spoken and the name of the European language from which they appear to derive, thus: Nigerian Pidgin English, Philippine Creole Spanish, Mauritian Creole French, etc.

A common view (and one that has some truth in it, but not the whole truth) is that a pidgin or creole is a language which takes its vocabulary from one language and its grammar from another. The merits of this idea will be discussed in later chapters; for the meantime, we will just note that it is often the case that the great majority of the lexicon of a pidgin or creole derives from just one language, with a small (usually less than 20 per cent) contribution from other languages. This fits in well with the idea that *one* language – in colonial situations, usually the European colonisers' – was the original target of language learners.

Where a single language is identified as the source of the majority of the lexicon of a pidgin or creole, it is known as the **lexifier**. As mentioned above, the lexifier often equates with the European colonisers' language where there is one. However, the lexifier need not be a European language: for example, the Papuan language Motu is lexifier of the pidgin Hiri Motu and the African (Bantu) language Kikongo is the lexifier of the pidgin Kituba.

That the grammar of pidgins and creoles is derived from the 'other' partner(s) in the language contact is both harder to demonstrate and more controversial. In this book, this will be discussed at much greater length in later chapters. It relates to another of the metaphors which linguists use when describing the origins of pidgins and creoles: the notion of **substrate**. The 'substrate' or 'layer below' in this case refers to the grammars of the indigenous languages with which the lexifier came into contact. In the case of Tok Pisin the *lexifier* is English, while the *substrate* would be a collection of more or less closely related indigenous languages of the South Pacific, some of them sharing some vocabulary and grammatical features.

The concept of a 'top layer' – also called a **superstrate** – of European vocabulary resting on a 'bottom layer' (substrate) of indigenous grammar bears more than a passing resemblance to the colonialists' model of a (European) social elite resting (literally!) on a socially inferior indigenous underclass. Unfortunately, this is an accurate picture of social relations in many of the situations where pidgins and creoles came into being – slavery and plantation labour being two of the most frequent. For this reason if not for any other, we should be cautious in using the term 'substrate', which suggests that indigenous speakers somehow played a secondary or inferior role in the formation of these languages. In fact, there is ample evidence that the grammatical structures and semantic systems of the indigenous languages have had a significant impact on the form of pidgins and creoles, as we shall see in Chapters 3 and 6. Where clear superstrate and substrate languages are not identifiable, the term **adstrate** is sometimes used to indicate a more-or-less equal contribution from several languages. Finally, all of the languages involved in the creation of a pidgin or creole may be termed **input languages**.

Since **creolisation** can take place to a greater or lesser extent, and since **decreolisation** – where the creole becomes more like its lexifier as a result of social pressures – is also possible, the more general term **restructuring** is sometimes applied to languages which appear to have gone through processes of pidginisation and/or creolisation. So the expressions 'restructured English', 'restructured French', 'restructured Arabic' etc. may be used to refer to pidginised or creolised language varieties which are lexically related to English, French and Arabic respectively. Use of the term 'restructuring' implies that the structures of the language (grammar, morphology, phonology etc.) have undergone substantial changes as a result of language contact but does not specify whether the result is a pidgin, a creole, or the result of partial creolisation or decreolisation.

8   PIDGIN AND CREOLE TYPES

8.1   Introduction

Let us now have a look at some of the different pidgin and creole languages from around the world. In this section we will classify pidgins according to the circumstances in which they first came into being (or in some cases, how they came to be spoken over a wide area). This classification is based on the *social* context of the language's origins rather than on linguistic factors such as the languages involved in the contact. While many pidgins do not fit neatly into one category, it is still useful to divide them into seven broad types:

1. Military and police pidgins
2. Seafaring and trade pidgins and creoles
3. Plantation pidgins and creoles
4. Mine and construction pidgins
5. Immigrants' pidgins
6. Tourist pidgins
7. Urban contact vernaculars

8.2   Military and Police Pidgins and Creoles

The earliest known European pidgin, *Sabir* or *Lingua Franca*, seems to have originated during the Crusades, when soldiers from many different places – with Southern Europe predominating – came together. Probably throughout history there have been ethnically and linguistically mixed armies, and these naturally provide the sort of environment where a pidgin not only may come into being, but also will have immediate functional value. Several recent pidgins are known to have a military origin.

Juba Arabic, a pidginised form of Arabic which was developed among Sudanese soldiers in the Egyptian army which occupied Southern Sudan in the middle of the nineteenth century, spread from the army bases to the multilingual region around Juba, the major city of the Southern Sudan. It is still spoken there today and is apparently becoming a creole as some people now speak it as a native language.

Hiri Motu, formerly called *Police Motu*, a pidginised form of the Papuan language Motu, is associated with the police force established by the British colonial administration in Papua (now part of Papua New Guinea) at the end of the nineteenth century. However, there was already a tradition of trade-voyage (*hiri*) languages among the Motu, so modern Hiri Motu may be a continuation of this tradition. Hiri Motu, like *Tok Pisin*, is widely used in Papua New Guinea, but is more regional, confined to its traditional 'home' of Papua (the southern part of the country).

The fact that many pidgins seem to have had their origins among the ranks of armies or police forces is simply testimony to their usefulness for communication in situations where speakers from diverse linguistic backgrounds are 'thrown together' and have to find a common means of communication. Several of the other types of pidgin described here – for example, plantation pidgins and mine/construction pidgins – share with military pidgins the feature of being products of an environment where workers, mainly or all male, live away from home and mingle with speakers of other languages for a long period.

8.3   Seafaring and Trade Pidgins and Creoles

Scholars like Reinecke (1937, p. 434, quoted by Mühlhäusler, 1986) have been convinced of the importance of the role of seafarers in creating pidgins:

One of the most favourable situations for the formation of such dialects is found aboard merchant vessels which ply the seven seas and ship large numbers of foreign sailors – and indeed the seaman is a figure of the greatest importance in the creation of the more permanent makeshift tongues.

In spite of this, though scholars trying to explain the origins of pidgins and creoles have often had recourse to a notion of a 'nautical jargon' or seafarer's pidgin (see below, p. 76), there are very few cases of pidgins which clearly have a nautical *origin* (for example, on ships with linguistically diverse crews). On the other hand, there are a number of pidgins which have undoubtedly been spread by a combination of seafaring and trading (the two activities often being inseparable). The earliest form of *South Seas Pidgin*, which has evolved into modern *Tok Pisin, Bislama, Solomon Islands Pijin* and a number of creoles, appears to have been a 'nautical jargon' (see Clark, 1979). One of the descendants of this proto-pidgin, *Bislama*, owes its name to the edible sea-slug, bêche-de-mer, which was the object of trade by English seafarers among the inhabitants of the South Pacific (the sea-slugs were destined for the Chinese market, as an ingredient of soup (Hall, 1966, p. 10).)

The various pidgins and creoles of West Africa similarly seem to have their origins in both seafaring and trade. According to some scholars (see below), a Portuguese-lexicon pidgin – possibly *Sabir*, already mentioned in 8.2 – was brought to West Africa by mariners on Portuguese ships. There it became the lingua franca of the slave trade, and the forerunner of the *Portuguese-lexicon creoles* spoken today in Guiné, Cape Verde, São Tomé, Angolar and Annobón. It may also have been the precursor of the English pidgin which is today widely spoken in West Africa (*West African Pidgin English*, or WAPE) and which in some parts of Nigeria is now a creole with native speakers of its own. Again, the seafaring origins of this pidgin are largely conjecture, while the trading uses (in the slave trade) are reasonably well documented. Still in West Africa, the creole language *Krio* is spoken in Sierra Leone by the descendants of freed slaves, for whom the Freetown colony was founded by the British. It is very similar to West African Pidgin English. In the Philippines, what was originally a Portuguese-lexicon creole seems to have evolved into a Spanish-lexicon one (see Holm, 1989, pp. 316–17) in several coastal cities. *Philippine Creole Spanish* now exists in several varieties, with perhaps a quarter of a million speakers (Holm, 1989, p. 317). The most widely spoken of these is *Zamboangueño*.

In the case of *Russenorsk*, a Russian–Norwegian pidgin which developed among seafarers in far northern waters, the distinction between a pidgin used by seafarers and one developed for trade is similarly blurred. Some scholars hold that Russenorsk was the product of a nautical pidgin used by mariners in the Arctic Ocean – which would partly explain the surprising range of languages represented in its lexicon (see Holm, 1989, p. 621). In more recent times, however, Russenorsk seems to have been used in the course of trade between fishermen. (See Chapter 2 for a detailed case study.)

A number of pidgins clearly owe their origins to trade, without the involvement of prior nautical pidgins. *Chinook Jargon*, a well-documented trading pidgin of the American Northwest, was the language of the fur

trade, used by speakers of several different Amerindian languages, English
and French. Its lexicon came mainly from Chinook, a language whose
speakers mainly inhabited what are now the US states of Washington and
Oregon. It may have pre-dated the arrival of Europeans in the area around
1800. As the centre of the fur trade moved further north, Chinook Jargon
became confined to British Columbia, north of the Canadian border.
Chinook Jargon religious literature was published there until the 1920s.
There were still a few speakers in 1975 (Holm, 1989, p. 597). Two other trade
pidgins based on Amerindian languages are also known to have existed and
been spoken over large areas of North America: *Mobilian Jargon* in the
Southeast around the Mississippi River, and *Delaware Jargon* in what is
today the Northeastern United States.

Other trade pidgins have also existed in the Arctic regions; for example,
Eskimo Trade Jargon was used for contact between European whalers and
Inuit (Eskimo) people in the Arctic reaches of North America.

The Chinook and Eskimo pidgins are good examples of contact languages
which are spoken over a very large geographical area, by traders who speak
several different native languages. There are also some examples of trade
pidgins which serve the needs of relatively less diverse groups, for example
where only two or three languages are involved. The interior of Surinam,
South America, is home to *Ndjuka-Trio Pidgin*, based on Ndjuka (itself a
creole, and a relative of Sranan, discussed in Chapter 5) and Trio, an
Amerindian language. This pidgin is used for trade between the Ndjuka
(the descendants of slaves who escaped into the interior of Surinam
and established their villages beyond European control) and the Trio and
Wayana Indians (Holm, 1989, p. 604). In a similar category, but more
widely spread, we might include *Chinese Pidgin English*, described in
Chapter 2.

8.4 Plantation Pidgins and Creoles

Plantation farming was a frequently employed method of exploiting
resources – environmental and human – under colonial regimes established
by Europeans in tropical countries. In contrast to traditional methods of
agriculture, which usually involved subsistence farming of small plots,
plantation farming was only possible where large quantities of cheap labour
were available to work large farms. This was possible where the labour was
provided by slaves or indentured labourers working for very low wages.

Since plantation labour was typically provided not just by local people
but by migrant labourers from a wide area, multilingual plantations have
provided a fertile ground for the growth of new pidgins and the development of existing ones. Indentured labourers, unlike slaves, would usually
return to their home villages at the end of their contracts, spreading the

pidgin over a wide area. Plantations based on slave labour, on the other hand, have tended to give rise to creoles, as generations of slaves were born and died in one place.

The use of indentured plantation labour has been responsible for the origin or spread of pidgins in Hawaii, Samoa, New Guinea and Queensland within the last century or so. The modern descendants of these include *Tok Pisin*. The plantation system has also given rise to creole languages in many parts of the *Caribbean* (English-lexicon creoles in Jamaica, Guyana, Trinidad, Grenada, St Vincent, and the Caribbean Coast of Central America, Costa Rica and Nicaragua) as well as elsewhere; French-lexicon creoles in Haiti, Guadeloupe, St Lucia and Louisiana; Dutch-lexicon creoles in the Virgin Islands ('Negerhollands') and Berbice (Guyana); and the Spanish-lexicon creole *Papiamentu* in Aruba, Bonaire and Curaçao, Hawaii (English-lexicon creole), Mauritius (French-lexicon creole), and the islands off the coast of West Africa (Portuguese-lexicon creoles). In the case of all of these except Hawaii, an earlier pidgin stage is not documented, and may not have existed (see Chapter 6).

While plantation and slave labour systems have been productive breeding grounds for pidgins and creoles, contact languages do not inevitably result from forced-labour situations. Indeed, it is interesting to speculate why no Spanish-lexicon creole ever developed, so far as we know, in Cuba (see Perl and Grosse, 1994), while no Portuguese-lexicon creole is documented for Brazil. Both countries employed slave labour extensively in plantation farming and are in regions where creoles, originating from the plantation slavery time, are widely spoken.

8.5 Mine and Construction Pidgins

Although *Fanakalo* (See Chapter 2) appears to have originated as a trade pidgin for contact between the Zulus and European settlers in Kwazulu Natal (South Africa), its development and spread were undoubtedly dependent on its role in the mines of the Witwatersrand, as returning mine workers were responsible for its spreading over much of Southern Africa.

Further north, in Cameroon, Pidgin A-70 (also called *Pidgin Ewondo*, *Ewondo Populaire*, *Bulu-Yaoundé* and *Truck-drivers' Bulu*) is a pidginised form of the Bantu languages Ewondo (Yaunde) and Bulu, closely related members of the language group called A-70 in the standard classification of Bantu languages (Guthrie, 1967–72). According to John Holm (1989, p. 561) Pidgin A-70 came into being as a result of the construction of a railway line to Yaoundé (now capital of the Republic of Cameroon) in the 1920s. From its origins among labourers drawn from a mix of linguistic backgrounds, it spread to become 'a lingua franca wherever different ethnic groups came into contact and needed a means of communicating: in towns, in markets, and along the railroads and highways' (ibid.). However, it is not used elsewhere (e.g. in the home, or for religious purposes).

8.6 Immigrants' Pidgins

In some countries, identifiable contact-language varieties spoken by new immigrants have come into being: for example *Cocoliche*, spoken by Italian migrants in Argentina. Though discussed in the literature on contact languages (Whinnom, 1971), *Cocoliche* is usually regarded not as a pidgin but as an unstable blend of two closely related languages (Italian and Spanish). Because these languages are already very similar, there is no need for grammatical simplification, and *Cocoliche* has no stable grammar of its own. Thus there seem to be inadequate grounds for calling *Cocoliche* a pidgin. However, immigration may lead to pidgin-like outcomes in cases where the immigrant group has limited contact with the language of the 'host' community, for example among the so-called 'guest workers' of Germany. *Gastarbeiterdeutsch* (Guest-worker German) is described in a detailed case study in Chapter 3.

8.7 Tourist Pidgins

While in practice *any* encounter between buyers and sellers who have no common language might result in a makeshift language for bargaining just for that occasion, to speak of a 'tourist pidgin' proper, we would want there to be some indication of *continuity*, of a 'tradition' of tourists and locals communicating in a language which shows the kinds of simplification typical of pidgins. It is probably safe to assume that there are quite a number of such pidgins, used in places where foreign tourists have been regular visitors for some time. However, since encounters like these are typically short-lived from the participants' point of view, linguistic descriptions are almost completely lacking.

Recently, there have been reports of a possible English-lexicon pidgin used by street traders in tourist areas in Bangkok, Thailand (Gwyn Williams, personal communication). Hinnenkamp (1982) describes a process of pidginisation in progress in a Turkish village where a number of foreign tourists visit regularly and tend to come back season after season.

Apart from this, we have very little information about tourist pidgins. There is ample scope here for research by linguists on holiday.

8.8 Urban Contact Vernaculars

'Urban contact vernacular' here refers to a type of language which seems to evolve in a particular type of urban setting. Where large-scale migration from the countryside to urban areas creates poor communities which are linguistically and sometimes ethnically diverse, the youth of those communities may create or develop a vernacular language which has many of the characteristics of pidgin. Such a language is *Sheng* ('Swahili-English') of Nairobi, Kenya, which so far has not been properly described by linguists. A reasonable description would probably be 'simplified Kiswahili (a lingua franca in Kenya, but spoken natively by a small minority) with a large amount of English vocabulary, including much that is slang or new coinages'. Extracts from an article by Kwendo Opanga entitled 'Humour by the Ringside' in the Nairobi *Daily Nation* (8 December, 1989) give a flavour of what it is like (and, incidentally, of the journalist's attitude!):

> The sport they love may be the most brutal, but they are the most hilarious sports fans in Kenya. They are the Sheng-speaking group, mainly from Nairobi's Eastlands, who are driven into a wild frenzy by what they call *boki, mkono, muhand, ndondi*, and *masumbwi* [words for 'boxing' in Kiswahili and Sheng]....
>
> In boxing, punches to the tummy and the sides are said to cut out a boxer's ability to breathe well, so the fans talk of *kata pumzi* (cut short one's breath) through a barrage of body punches (*job mob ya tumbo*) and then a haymaker or killer punch (*nyundo* – Kiswahili for hammer) to knock out the boxer. The killer feast is also called *kiboko*, which, in Kiswahili, literally means a whip.

'Jokiness' at the level of vocabulary seems to be pervasive in Sheng. For example, in Sheng, Whites are referred to as *yuro*, 'Euro', i.e. 'Europeans'. By analogy, Africans are called *miro* – a play on 'you' versus 'me' which nicely encapsulates the attitudes of Sheng speakers. This continual playing on words not only enhances the racy and rebellious 'feel' of Sheng, but makes it very hard for outsiders to understand – one of the main functions of slang varieties in any language.

A few thousand miles further south, in South Africa, *Fly Taal* or *Tsotsi Taal* is a pidginised urban variety of Afrikaans used exclusively by Africans. (See Chapter 5 for a description of Afrikaans. Most Afrikaans speakers are white, and Standard Afrikaans in South Africa is much more closely identified with white than with black speakers.) According to Holm (1989, p. 350) Fly Taal's 'innovative character, not to say multilingual virtuosity, has given Fly Taal the aura of urban cool and the advantages of a language that can be totally opaque to outsiders'. Exactly the same could be said of Sheng (above). According to Janson (1984) citing a study reported by Schuring (1978), Johannesburg (and perhaps more generally the province of

Gauteng) is the main location of its speakers, and 'the users are typically young, male, and with an education above average for the group'. According to a speaker of the language, Morena Monareng (personal communication), Fly Taal is mainly used by men, and is regarded as 'street language' unsuitable for use in a family home.

Although its structure is essentially a reduced form of Afrikaans, Fly Taal has borrowed heavily for its vocabulary from Bantu languages such as Tswana and Zulu, and from English. The lexical composition of Fly Taal varies from area to area in which it is spoken: thus the word for 'money' varies from region to region even within Soweto, the black city adjacent to Johannesburg: Monareng (personal communication) mentions *tshelt* (Afrikaans *geld* [xelt]), *isholo* (?from Zulu), *ingwexa* (?from Xhosa), *tsika* (unknown origin). Janson (1984) reports *lozi, zak, smega, tshin, tsaris* (all of undetermined origin) as well. For 'to beat' we find the Afrikaans word *slaan*, but also the more colourful *coward* (?from English), and *panel-beat* or just *panel*. Such vocabulary terms are also short lived as they are quickly replaced by new coinages.

Like Sheng, Fly Taal has much in common with slang varieties of language in general. Its use of 'mainstream' words with semantic changes – for example, English *feature* to mean 'arrrive', as in *hy sal môre feature*, 'he will arrive tomorrow' (Janson, 1984, p. 174), is typical of slang in general, and so is the variability and quick turnover of its vocabulary.

The above list of pidgins and creoles is by no means exhaustive; those named are examples only. In many cases a pidgin may reasonably be put in any of two or more categories; for example, Fanakalo seems to have originated in the course of inter-ethnic contact and trade but has continued in existence mainly as a mining pidgin. Creoles are also under-represented here, and in this list nearly all have arisen through slave trading or conditions of plantation labour – though in Chapter 5 we shall introduce some which have not.

9 LANGUAGE CONTACT: WHAT CAN IT TELL US?

All this has taken us a long way from the pidgin of the Solomon Islander Peter. However, it has shown us some of the reasons for the low status of pidgin languages – their perceived 'corruption' or 'impurity' – and also explains an important fact about the history of the study of pidgins and creoles: until recently, very few people – even including linguists whose life's work was the study of language – found them worthy of serious study.

Two nineteenth-century linguists, Schuchardt and Hesseling, are famous exceptions to this; they can be said to be founders of the study of pidgins and creoles. Hugo Schuchardt (1842-1927) was an opponent of the prevailing belief in the 'family tree' model of language relationships: he found his counter-evidence in pidgin and creole languages. In a lifetime of descriptive work, he produced detailed accounts of many pidgin and creole languages then spoken in the world's colonial outposts – especially those languages with Portuguese-derived vocabulary. Of these, some are still spoken today, while others have disappeared. Dirk Hesseling (1859–1941) made creole languages with Dutch-derived vocabulary his main interest. Both these men were regarded as minor scholars until recently by the linguistic establishment; but apart from them, there was little interest in 'mixed' or 'makeshift' languages, as they were sometimes called, until the second half of the twentieth century. A third 'founder', John E. Reinecke, began reporting his research from Hawaii – home of both a pidgin and a creolised form of English – from the 1930s.

One of the earliest reasons why pidgins and creoles excited the interest of linguists like Schuchardt was because of the way they provided a challenge to the 'family tree' model of language relatedness. Linguists, especially those of the nineteenth century, were very interested in discovering the relationships between languages, both modern and ancient. We saw above that the 'family tree' model needs us to assume that language contact does not make very fundamental changes to existing languages. A second assumption commonly made is that language change is slow and gradual. A third assumption is that if any fundamental changes *do* take place, we will be able to detect them. These assumptions had become orthodoxy in the nineteenth century.

However, none of them is necessarily true. Language contact may have profound effects on some languages, as we have seen. But also, *completely new* languages can arise out of contact between two languages which are not related under the 'family tree' model. Pidgin languages are one example of this. Furthermore, language change is not always slow. Creole languages, which are another main topic of this book, compress the 'centuries of slow evolution' into just one or two decades, as they originate from pidgins and go through rapid changes to become fully-fledged languages complete with native speakers.

Contact languages like these pose a real problem for the 'family tree' model. Where is there a place in the conventional tree for languages originating from two very different parts of the world which somehow combine to form a 'mixed language'? And how do we *know* which languages have a mixed origin, when we have no written records going back more than a few hundred years for most languages? Unless we have historical records about the origins of such 'mixed' languages, we will have no way of knowing that mixing occurred in earlier times. There is a possibility that many of the existing languages may have mixed origins, without us being any the wiser.

Pidgins and creoles also have something to tell us about the nature of human language generally. 'Ordinary' languages differ a great deal in their structure and often have elaborate systems of gender, case, tense and aspect. They frequently have many different word classes and complicated morphology. None of these things prevents children from learning such languages; all normal children acquire their native language within five or six years of birth, whatever their language. Pidgins and creoles, however, can tell us something about how *basic* languages can be, when stripped of all these complex systems. They can help us to separate the *essentials* of language – those aspects which humans require for an effective communication system, and which are part of our genetic specifications – from those which are characteristic of certain languages, but which are not a necessary part of every language.

Pidgins and creoles, along with other varieties of language which were thought to be substandard, did not really come into their own as a field of study until relatively recently. When the potential interest of these languages became clear, there was a mushrooming of interest which continues today and has led to a large amount of research and many books and articles on the subject.

To the general public, however – even those who are themselves speakers of pidgin or creole languages – these are mostly still 'substandard' or 'broken' forms of another, standard language such as English or French. Behind this attitude lies the belief that there is only one correct norm for a language, and that that norm does not allow for mixing of languages or language varieties.

10 EXERCISE: LANGUAGES AND VALUES

All of the following terms have been used in tourist guide books to describe New Guinea Pidgin. Have an argument with a friend, real or imaginary, in which you argue for or against using them to describe this language:

'baby talk'
'broken'
'demeaning'
'far from ideal'
'extremely clumsy'
'roundabout and wordy'
'absurd'

KEY POINTS: Pidgins, Creoles and Mixed Languages

Pidgins

- have no native speakers;
- are the result of contact between two or more languages;
- are not mutually intelligible with their source languages;
- have a grammar of their own;
- have simpler grammars than their source languages;
- usually draw most of their vocabulary from one language (the *lexifier*).

Creoles

- are the result of contact involving two or more languages;
- develop out of a pidgin;
- have native speakers of their own;
- are usually grammatically simple.

Mixed Languages

- are the result of contact between two languages;
- have native speakers of their own;
- are grammatically as complex as their source languages.

2   The Character of Pidgins

1   WHAT MAKES A PIDGIN?

Up until now I have discussed pidgins as though they formed an identifiable group with characteristics in common, but I have not shown why this should be so. This chapter will look at some of the features which typify pidgins, leading to remarkable similarities among pidgins widely separated in time and space.

In the rest of this chapter we will look at these pidgin features in more detail. We will start with an overview of pidgin grammars in Section 2 using Melanesian Pidgin (the pidgin introduced in Chapter 1) as the main source of examples. The remaining sections will look at each aspect of the grammar and lexicon in turn; syntax in Section 3, morphology in Section 4, phonology in Section 5, semantics in Section 6 and the lexicon in Section 7. The chapter ends with three case studies of pidgins at different stages of development and with different lexifiers.

2   PIDGIN GRAMMARS

2.1   Some Features of Melanesian Pidgin

Note: In this chapter *Melanesian Pidgin* is used as a general term to cover the English-lexicon pidgins spoken in Papua New Guinea, the Solomon Islands and elsewhere in the South Pacific (see Chapter 1, Section 8.3). These all share similar, but slightly different, grammar and vocabulary. Sometimes reference will be made to *Tok Pisin* ('Talk Pidgin'), the New Guinea variety of this pidgin, which is now one of the national languages of Papua New Guinea.

Chapter 1 stated that the grammars of pidgins were characteristically less complex than the grammars of their source languages. Relative grammatical simplicity is thus one of the distinguishing marks of a pidgin. Taking Melanesian Pidgin as an example, this section lists some of the ways in which pidgins display such 'simplicity'. (Where possible, examples come from the texts in Chapter 1.)

2.1.1   Nouns and pronouns lack inflections
In Standard English, nouns have distinct morphological markers (inflections) to indicate plurals (e.g. women, ship*s*), possession (someone'*s*) and, sometimes, object function (*her, them* as opposed to *she, they*). By contrast, in Melanesian Pidgin, we find:

(i)   No plural marking – the plural is indicated by a number, by context, or by the separate word *ol* (English *all*); the noun does not change form.

(ii)   An *analytic* possessive form (*laip bilong famili*) which indicates possession by means of a separate word ('life of family') rather than by a morphological change in the noun.

(iii)   Object forms are not marked, even for pronouns; *em* stands for both 'he' and 'him', as well as 'she' and 'her' (gender is not marked either); likewise *ol* is 'they' and 'them' as well as indicating the plural of nouns.

2.1.2   Verbs also have reduced inflection

Standard English usually marks past tense by adding -*ed* or -*t* to the stem of the verb. Sometimes there is a change in the stem vowel (*strike*, *struck*) or the whole stem changes (*go*, *went*). The continuous aspect marker -*ing* is another inflection which is added to the end of the stem. However, in Melanesian Pidgin:

(i)   All tense markers are external to the verb, i.e. they are separate words: *bin* for past, *bai* (from *by and by*) for future.

(ii)   Tense is not marked at all when it is clear from the context, e.g. when time adverbials like 'yesterday' occur in the same sentence.

(iii)   All verbs have just one form – hence there are no irregular verbs.

(iv)   Continuous aspect may be marked by a separate verb, e.g. *stap*, 'stay'.

2.1.3   There is a reduction in the use of the copula

In English, the **copula** or linking verb 'to be' is used to join a noun with its noun complement (*Mona is a place*), adjective complement (*Mona is hot*), and its location (*Mona is in Jamaica*). In Melanesian Pidgin:

(i)   There is no verb *to be* in the present tense, thus *em ples bilong mi*, 'it's my place/village'.

(ii)   There is no verb *to be* with adjectives, e.g. *haus i-bik* 'the house is big' (in fact adjectives which follow the noun (**predicative adjectives**) behave like verbs in Melanesian Pidgin, taking the same tense markers *bin* and *bai*).

2.1.4   There is no definite or indefinite article (the *or* a)

In fact *ol* (which also means 'they') is sometimes used like a definite article in the plural (and thus helps to make up for the lack of plural morphology), as in *ol meri*, 'the women'. Apart from this, articles are absent from Melanesian Pidgin.

2.1.5 The negator 'no' is always external to the verb
Unlike the English *not* which follows the verb and may be joined to it, the Melanesian Pidgin negation morpheme always precedes the verb and all other tense/modality markers:

yu	**no**	**save**		**wokabaut**
you	no	know (how to)		move

you can't (= *can* + NEGATOR) *move*

2.2 Some General Features of Pidgin Grammars

The Melanesian Pidgin features discussed in 2.1 are in fact fairly typical of pidgin grammars. Although not every pidgin has all these features, most pidgins have nearly all of them; and a language which has only a few of them would quite likely not be a pidgin, though it might result from language contact of some sort.

Here is a list of features which are typically associated with pidgins; some of them are also associated with creoles, and will be discussed in more detail later. We can classify these features under five headings: syntactic, morphological, phonological, semantic and lexical.

Syntactic features:

(a) no definite or indefinite article;
(b) no copula *to be* (at least in present tense);
(c) tense, aspect, modality and negation marked externally to the verb – often by a content word like an adverb;
(d) no complex sentences (e.g. sentences involving relative clauses); if there is sentence embedding, it may not be morphologically marked;
(e) no passive forms.

Morphological features:

(f) very few or no inflections, e.g. no morphologically marked number (singular/plural), case (subject/object), tense, gender or grammatical agreement;
(g) analytic constructions used to mark possessive, e.g. X of Y rather than Y's X.

Phonological features:

(h) avoidance of 'difficult' sounds (i.e. those which are 'highly marked' in phonological terms);
(i) simple syllable structure – consonant, vowel (CV);
(j) tone is not used to distinguish words.

Semantic features:

(k)   preference for semantic transparency (see Section 6).

Lexical features:

(l)   small vocabulary;
(m) very small inventory of prepositions or postpositions;
(n)   preference for short words, i.e. a small number of syllables per word
       (this could also be regarded as a *phonological* feature);
(o)   small number of compounds (i.e. derivational morphology is not well
       developed).

It should be said at this point that most of the grammatical features listed
above can also be found in languages which are not regarded as pidgins or
creoles. For example, Russian lacks articles and the verb *to be* in the present
tense; Chinese almost totally lacks inflections, while French has the
possessive structure *X de Y* ('X of Y') but nothing corresponding to *Y's X*
in English. Likewise, simple CV syllable structure is widespread, and some
languages, such as those of the Polynesian family, have few or no
phonologically marked sounds. However, most languages have at most a
few of the features from this list, and those that have several are usually
complex in other respects; for example, although Chinese lacks inflections it
makes very extensive use of tones in its phonology; although Russian lacks a
copula and articles, it has a rich system of noun cases and inflections for
nouns, verbs and adjectives.
    The rest of this chapter will look in more detail at the grammatical,
phonological and lexical systems of pidgins.

3   SYNTAX

3.1   Word Order

Of the six possible relative orderings of subject, verb and object, we find that
most of the world's known languages have opted for one of SVO (subject–
verb–object), SOV or VSO. However, most of the well-studied pidgins and
creoles have SVO word order. This has led to the claim sometimes being
made that this is the only possible word order in pidgins and creoles (at least
in those which have stable norms of word order), suggesting that somehow
it is simpler or more 'natural' than other word orders. Bakker (1994a,
pp. 33–4) points out that in fact, while 'virtually all creole languages have
strict SVO order', a major difference between pidgins and creoles is that a

number of different word orders are found in pidgins: some such as Trio-Ndjuka Pidgin and Hiri Motu (Chapter 1) are strictly SOV, Mobilian Jargon has OSV and others have OVS. Some pidgins, like Russenorsk, alternate SOV and SVO.

We cannot therefore claim that all pidgins have SVO word order, and even the fact that nearly all creoles have this order may be due to the fact that most of them have SVO languages as lexifiers.

3.2 Word-order in Questions

What is certain is that pidgin word order does not have the complexity of word ordering that is found in many other languages. For example, Woolford (1978), writing about Tok Pisin, notes that it lacks all the constructions which are usually regarded as involving movement of words within a sentence, including subject–auxiliary movement and passivisation.

With this in mind, we can look at the ordering of words in questions and statements. Many languages have different word orders for questions and statements (sometimes this is only one of several stylistic possibilities), for example in English:

Sarah is an engineer → *Is Sarah an engineer?* (Subject–verb inversion)
Sarah designs machinery → *What does Sarah design?* (Movement of object noun phrase to first position in sentence, plus inversion of the subject and auxiliary verb)

Similar processes of question formation are found in many languages, including several European languages which are lexifiers of pidgins and creoles, for example French:

Elle est professeur ('She is a professor') → *Est-elle professeur?*
Vous allez au marché ('You are going to the market') → *Où allez-vous?*

However, within pidgins and creoles, syntactic processes which rearrange the words within sentences seem generally to be rare. Typically, yes/no questions (those without a 'question word' like *who?*, *what?* or *where?*) tend to have identical word order with the corresponding statements, but may be distinguished by intonational patterns. Where 'wh-questions' are concerned, however, some pidgins do require the question word to be the first element in the sentence, e.g.

Fanakalo
Yini lo-msebenzi   wena   azi?
what the-work   you   know
'What sort of work can you do?'

Russenorsk
Kak   pris?
how   price
'What is the price?'

Other pidgins have the question word in the same position as the corresponding word or phrase would occupy in a statement:

Tok Pisin
Yu   lukim   wanem?
you   see   what
'What do you see?'

This is an example of an aspect of pidgin grammar which may be closely linked with the grammars of the substrate and superstrate languages. The fact that in both Norwegian and Russian, question words occupy first position in the sentence may, for example, be responsible for the fact that Russenorsk question words behave in the same way. We can also compare Tok Pisin with the historically related Australian Pidgin English (this example was collected by Robert A. Hall (Hall, 1966, p. 152) from a native speaker of English who had served as a judge in the Northern Territory):

wotnem shi bin tok? 'what did she say'?

3.3   Negation Marking

The negator is always a separate word and invariant in form. In the majority of known pidgins and creoles, negation markers occur before the verb; however, there are some exceptions to this (the negator in Hiri Motu comes *after* the verb). This may be because of a universal preference among languages with SVO word order for preverbal modification.

3.4   Tense, Aspect and Modality Marking

In the most rudimentary pidgins, context alone indicates **tense, modality** and **aspect** (TMA). Sometimes adverbials like *before, tomorrow* and *perhaps* provide the necessary clues. Pidgins show a preference for TMA marking external to the verb itself, and sometimes even externally to the verb phrase. There are exceptions (sometimes affixes are used to indicate tense, like the Fanakalo past tense affix *-ile*), but as a general rule, pidgin TMA markers are separate lexical items which are invariant (i.e. have only one form). The morphemes which pidgins use to mark these categories are often not the ones which the lexifier would use, though they usually originate from the lexifier. In

Melanesian Pidgin, for example, past tense is marked using *bin* although English *been* is never used alone in this way. (Compare *mi bin lukim haus* with its English translations 'I looked at the house' and 'I have been looking at the house'.)

Frequently, we find that the pidgin TMA markers are actually *content* words in the lexifier language, i.e they do not have a grammatical function in the lexifier, where they are typically verbs, or adverbs. We can see how this works in Fanakalo (see below for a sketch of Fanakalo grammar). Fanakalo *mhlaumbe* (from Zulu *mhlawumbe*) 'perhaps' is used to express modality, e.g. *mhlaumbe mina zo hamba* (literally, perhaps I FUTURE go) 'I may go', 'I might go', 'perhaps I shall go'.

Similarly, in Tok Pisin, the future marker *bai* derives from the earlier form *baimbai* 'by-and-by', i.e. 'soon': *Bung...bai pinis long Fraide*, 'The meeting...will finish on Friday' (*Wantok*, Port Moresby, 14 April 1994).

Some more examples of modality and tense/aspect markers derived from content words in pidgins and creoles are given below.

West African Pidgin English

don 'COMPLETIVE' from English 'done' (in the sense of 'finished'): *a don kom* 'I have arrived'.

go 'FUTURE' from English 'go': *a go kom* 'I will come'.

fit 'be able, can' from English 'fit (to do X)', e.g. *a fit si am* 'I can see him'.

Tok Pisin

pinis 'COMPLETIVE' from English 'finish': *mipela i ting olsem i mas dai pinis*, 'we think he must have died (finish)'.

4 MORPHOLOGY

4.1 Inflectional and Derivational Morphology in Pidgins

Morphologists usually make a distinction between **inflectional morphology** – processes of word formation which mark grammatical relations – and **derivational morphology**, which affects word-class membership and meaning. The English ending *-ing*, which attaches to verbs to signal a continuous tense, is an example of inflectional morphology, while the suffix *-er*, which makes the noun *writer* from the verb *write*, is an example of derivational morphology.

It is inflectional morphology which typically fares worst in a pidgin. Many pidgins have none at all: all grammatical functions will then be indicated either by separate words or by word order. This often implies the loss of grammatical categories like gender or tense which are indicated by means of inflectional morphology in the input languages. Nagamese, a pidgin spoken in Nagaland (India) and lexically based on two related languages, Assamese and Bengali, is typical.

> Unlike Assamese, it has no verbal inflections marking person. While Assamese has six cases, Nagamese has only the locative and the dative.... Morphologically, Nagamese shows only a two-way opposition in tense: simple past and non-past. (Bhattacharjya, 1994, p. 37)

Some pidgins, like Nagamese, have a few grammatical **inflections**. These are always regular, and usually represent a reduction of the inflectional system of the lexifier. The Fanakalo plural prefixes (see detailed case study later in this chapter) provide an example: Fanakalo has only two, *ma-* and *zi-* (the latter mostly used with animals) while Zulu nouns have a system of about ten different singular and plural prefixes.

4.2 Morphology Types

Morphological classifications of languages usually divide them into five broad types, *synthetic* (*inflecting* or *fusional*), *analytic* (*isolating*), *agglutinating*, *incorporating* and *infixing*, depending on how the grammar 'packages' meanings into words. For a fuller discussion, see Katamba (1993, pp. 56ff). For this discussion we will consider only three of these, namely *synthetic*, *agglutinating* and *analytic*.

In languages with **synthetic** morphology words typically contain several morphemes. However, the morphemes tend to have irregular forms and meaning is not always predictable from form. For example, the English words *caught* and *women* could each be said to contain two morphemes, incorporating the past tense and the plural respectively. However, these two morphemes cannot be identified as separate parts of the two words, and are different in form from the past tense morpheme found in *carried* and the plural morpheme of *horses. Caught* and *women* can be said to show synthetic morphology while *carried* and *horses* demonstrate morphology of the **agglutinating** type, which is more regular; this shows that English, like most languages, contains a mixture of morphology types.

In *agglutinating* or *agglutinative* morphology, words are built up of several morphemes, but the meaning of each is 'transparent', i.e. there is a one-to-one correspondence between form and meaning. *Strictly agglutinating* languages are very regular; words tend to contain large numbers of morphemes.

In **analytic (isolating)** morphology, each meaning is separately packaged as a word on its own, on the principle 'one word = one morpheme'. Bound morphemes are very rare.

An idea of the different morphology types can be given by comparing one phrase – 'in our houses' – in several languages displaying different degrees of synthetic, agglutinating and isolating morphology.

English (mixed morphology, mainly *isolating* type):

in	**our**		**houses**
in	1stPERSON + PLURAL + POSSESSIVE		house + PLURAL

(Total: 3 words, 6 morphemes)

Latin (*synthetic/inflecting* type)

in	**domibus**	**nostris**
in	house + ABLATIVE + PLURAL	1stPERSON + PLURAL + ABLATIVE + PLURAL

(Total: 3 words, 8 morphemes)

Turkish (*agglutinating* type)

ev + ler + im + iz + de
house + PLURAL + 1stPERSON + PLURAL + in
(Total: 1 word, 5 morphemes)

(Mandarin) Chinese (*analytic/isolating* type)

wo	**men**	**de**	**fangzi**	**li**
I	PLURAL	POSSESSIVE	HOUSE	IN

(Total: 5 words, 5 morphemes)

For comparison, one **Tok Pisin** equivalent would be:

long	**haus**	**bilong**	**mipela**
in	house	POSSESSIVE	1stPERSON + PLURAL

(**Total**: 4 words, 5 morphemes)

4.3 Pidgins Prefer Isolating Morphology

From the example above we can see that pidgins have a tendency toward the *isolating* (analytic) type of morphology. Where this is not strictly adhered to, there is a tendency to *agglutinating* morphology, which combines morphemes within a word but in a regular way which makes the meaning transparent.

Since it is unusual for any word to contain more than two or three morphemes in pidgins, the agglutinating morphology is also very simple. Synthetic morphology, which produces unpredictable forms like *caught* and *women*, is very rare in pidgins. The concept of 'semantic transparency', which seems to be important in pidgin grammars, will be discussed in more detail in Section 6.

The preference for isolating and agglutinating morphology can probably be explained in terms of the need for pidgins to be easily learnable: for example, learners of the pidgin will not be confronted with more than one form for any verb, while the tense and aspect are indicated by separate, and invariant, markers.

For an illustration of the preference for isolating and agglutinating morphology and semantic transparency, let us consider the pronoun system of Tok Pisin. The pronouns of Tok Pisin are as follows:

	singular	**dual**	**plural**
1st	mi	mitupela yumi (tupela)	mipela yumipela
2nd	yu	yutupela	yupela
3rd	em	tupela	ol

Note that the forms *mitupela* and *mipela* represent exclusive 'we' – where the hearer is not included in the 'we', as in 'We're going to a film, what about you?' The forms based on *yumi* – rather transparently – indicate inclusive 'we', i.e. 'you and me'. This distinction is found in most of the languages of the Pacific region and this is probably why it is found in Tok Pisin. The *dual* is a form used when exactly *two* people are referred to; here too, 'two' is explicit in the form (= *tu*).

The pronoun system is a good example of the fact that in pidgin languages – like in others – everything is not always neat and tidy. The third person pronouns have different forms in singular, dual and plural. However, in the first and second persons, the plural is formed by adding *pela* (from English *fellow*) to the singular, while the dual is formed by adding *tu* ('two') + **pela** to the singular.

Concerning pronoun systems, Mühlhäusler (1986, p. 158) remarks 'the pronoun systems of stabilized pidgins in all likelihood illustrate the minimal requirements for pronoun systems in human language'. He gives the interesting example of the pronoun system of Samoan Plantation Pidgin, a historical precursor of Tok Pisin, where the plural pronouns are regularly formed from the singular ones by the addition of the word *ol* (from English *all*) (Mühlhäusler, 1986, p. 159). This system is thus even more regular and predictable than that of Tok Pisin.

Pronoun System of Samoan Plantation Pidgin

	singular	**plural**
1st	mi	mi ol
2nd	yu	yu ol
3rd	em, him, hi	emol, himol

4.4 Morphological Development

Because pidgins are characteristically very poor in morphology in their early stages, this is one of the areas in which they tend to develop over time. Inflectional morphology, which has a grammatical role, is very slow to develop, but derivational morphology, which enables the lexicon to expand, develops more rapidly. We shall examine this in more detail in Chapter 4, which deals with the development of pidgins over time.

5 PHONOLOGY

5.1 The Sound System of Pidgins

The phonology of pidgins tends to be unstable and to some extent is dependent on the individual speaker: everyone brings his or her own 'accent' to the pidgin. Speakers tend to interpret the sounds of the lexifier language in terms of the phonological system of their native language. This is not to say that pidgins lack a sound system of their own. Typically pidgins avoid phonologically *marked* sounds (for example, those which are acquired late by children learning a first language) – pidgins thus tend not to have front rounded vowels or doubly articulated stops. Vowel systems are likely to be simplified to a symmetrical system of five vowels, thus:

```
i              u
   e       o
      a
```

As a general rule, we may say that pidgins prefer sounds which are common to the main languages involved in the contact, and tend to exclude sounds which would be difficult for a significant number of speakers. However, some pidgins do make use of relatively rare sounds. Fanakalo has click consonants which elsewhere are found only in a few languages (including the lexifier, Zulu), though these are not used by all speakers; hence, we cannot say that phonological simplification will always take place in a pidgin.

5.2 Syllable Structure

Perhaps for reasons outlined in 5.1, pidgins have a preference for CV syllable structure. Consonant clusters tend to be broken up by the insertion of vowels (epenthesis), e.g. Fanakalo *sikis*, 'six', Tok Pisin *sitiret*, 'straight'. In other cases, clusters are simplified by losing one of the consonants. There is also a preference for short words (approximately two syllables). This is discussed in more detail in Chapter 4.

The phonological tendencies described above may lead to pidgin words which bear little resemblance to the form of their source words, expecially when several changes take place together. For example, Tok Pisin *banis*, 'fence, enclosure, bandage', is derived both from English *fence* and *bandage* through phonological processes like those shown below (the intermediate stages are not all attested and some may have taken place simultaneously or in a different order from that below):

/fens/   → /fenis/ (vowel insertion to break up cluster)
             → /penis/ (change of fricative to stop: commonly applies to
                 initial /f/)
             → /benis/ (voicing of initial /f/ – applies only sporadically)
             → /**banis**/ (lowering of front vowel – applies sporadically)

/bændɪdʒ/   → /bandidʒ/ (reinterpretation of /æ/ as /a/ and /ɪ/ as /i/ within
                 a five-vowel system)
             → /bandis/ (simplification of affricate, accompanied by de-
                 voicing to /s/)
             → /**banis**/ (simplification of cluster through loss of /d/)

These sound changes also have consequences for the lexicon of Tok Pisin – see Section 7.3.

5.3 Tones

Those pidgins that are known to have lexifiers which are tone languages are not tone languages themselves. This is true of Fanakalo (Zulu, the lexifier, is a tone language) and Pidgin Sango (whose lexifier, Sango, is tonal) as well as other languages whose lexifiers are not tonal but which have tonal substrate languages, e.g. Chinese Pidgin Russian. Bakker (1994a, p. 35) points out that nearly all the speakers of Pidgin Sango speak tone languages natively, and Sango itself (the non-pidgin variety) is tonal. Pidgins therefore seem to have a strong preference for *not* being tone languages. Language contact (between Bantu and Arabic speakers) is often cited as a reason for the loss of tone in Kiswahili, the only non-pidgin Bantu language which is not tonal. Tone therefore seems to be an early casualty of language contact between tonal and non-tonal languages.

6 SEMANTICS

6.1 Semantic Transparency

As in all human languages, the relationship between the sign (word) and the signified (meaning) in a pidgin is arbitrary; however, there are degrees of arbitrariness in any language, especially where meanings can potentially be broken down into smaller components. In general, pidgins will tend to be at the less arbitrary end of the scale.

In English, for example, we have a number of words for animals (including ourselves) where the forms denoting male and female have different roots: *man – woman, dog – bitch, bull – cow, stallion – mare*. We have other animal names where the male and female are usually distinguished by adding the adjectives 'male' and 'female': *male mouse, female mouse; male parrot, female parrot*. In a third set of animal names, the name of the female is derived from the name of the male, usually by adding *-ess: lion – lioness*.

We can describe as 'semantically transparent' those words where the meaning can be relatively easily determined from the component morphemes. In terms of semantic transparency, the second of these strategies produces the most transparent terms, because by knowing the independent meanings of 'male', 'female' and the animal in question, we can determine the meaning of the expression directly. The strategy of adding *-ess* is somewhat less transparent, as it requires knowledge of one additional morpheme; but as it is a productive strategy which applies to a large number of forms (mostly words for humans, in fact: *actor, Count*, etc.) it could be said to cause relatively little extra work for a learner of the language. Seuren and Wekker, developing a more general theory of how 'semantic transparency' could apply to pidgins, say that 'semantic transparency, in an overall sense, limits learning and computing efforts to a minimum' (1986, p. 68).

The least transparent of the three strategies is to have separate words for the male and female of the species. It is interesting that most languages seem to use this strategy only with a relatively small set of nouns, which denote animals that are culturally or economically important to them – the most familiar animals, in other words.

In Tok Pisin, as in other pidgins we shall look at, there is a strong tendency to semantic transparency. Thus in the case of names for the male and female of species, we should expect, and in fact we find, that gender is always marked by the use of a separate word: *man* for the male, *meri* for the female in Tok Pisin. The human species is thus the only one where male and female have separate terms!

Mühlhäusler (1986, p. 169) calls the principle which underlies this kind of semantic transparency the 'one form = one meaning' principle. Another example he gives is the prevalence of compound words formed by suffixing a word meaning 'man' or 'woman' to derive a new meaning:

kaisman   'left man' = 'left-handed person'
kamman   'come man' = 'new arrival'
masman   'march man' = 'marcher'

According to Mühlhäusler (p. 171), similar examples can be found in most pidgins. Virtually identical sets can be found in creole languages as well, for example the creole Sranan Tongo (see Chapter 5 for more on this language):

wrokoman   'work + man' = 'worker'
wakaman   'walk + man' = 'drifter'
wrokosani 'work + thing' = 'tool'
(see Sebba, 1981, p. 107)

6.2   Question Words in Pidgins and Creoles

While probably most languages (including the European lexifiers of pidgins) have single monomorphemic words like *what?* (English), *quoi?* (French), *wat?* (Dutch) as question words, pidgins and creoles have a tendency to agglutinative compound expressions. Many question words in historically unrelated pidgins have similar forms consisting of two morphemes: a nounlike morpheme which is the ordinary word for man, thing, time etc. and another which derives from a wh-question word in the lexifier language. Following Muysken and Veenstra (1994, p. 125) we could represent this abstractly as QUESTION PARTICLE + QUESTIONED SEMANTIC UNIT.

These are some examples of the word for *what?* in various pidgins:

Kenya Pidgin Swahili	titu gani	'thing which'
Fanakalo	yini + ndaba	'what-thing'
New Guinea Pidgin	wa(t) + nem	'what-name'
Nigerian Pidgin English	we + tin	'what-thing'

(+ here indicates a morpheme boundary within a word, while a space indicates a word boundary)

Compare also these forms from creole languages:

Sranan Tongo (archaic)	o sani	'how thing'
Pitcairnese	wothing	'what thing'
Papiamentu	kiku	'what thing' (Spanish: ¿qué cosa?)

Muysken and Veenstra (1994) show that many, though not all creole languages have these 'transparent' forms. However, this does not mean that those which lack them now never had them, since over time, 'transparent' forms may develop into 'opaque' forms (e.g. single-morpheme forms). This has happened, for example, in Sranan, where the *o* (from English *how*) has been dropped, and the normal word for *what?* is just *san? San* has now become lexically distinct from the word for 'thing', which is *sani* (derived from English *something*). Given this developmental perspective, Muysken and Veenstra suggest that semantic transparency may represent 'a basic strategy of creolisation'.

6.3 Exercise

List the systematic phonological changes needed to derive Sranan *o sani* from the English *how something*. (See the Tok Pisin example in 5.2 above.) What semantic changes are involved and why might these have occurred?

7 THE LEXICON

7.1 Maximising the Minimal

The principle of maximum semantic transparency goes hand in hand with what Mühlhäusler (1986, p. 171) calls 'maximum use of a minimum lexicon'. The *basic* vocabulary of most pidgins is indeed minimal, severely reduced by comparison with their lexifier languages (the languages which provide the sources of the vocabulary). It is always difficult to get an accurate word count for any language, but estimates for pidgins range from less than 100 words for the most rudimentary jargons to a few thousand words for older and better established pidgins such as Tok Pisin. Since pidgins need to place as small as possible a burden on their learners, it is understandable that the actual list of words which have to be learnt should be as small as the functions of the language will allow. At the same time, there will be a need to make the best *use* of the available word-resources. The remainder of this section will give illustrations of how pidgins do this in practice.

7.2   Prepositions in Melanesian Pidgin

In the exercises in section 6.3 of Chapter 1, you were asked to find all the prepositions in the Melanesian Pidgin texts. There were in fact only three 'true' prepositions: *long*, *bilong* and *wantaim* (*insait* is always compounded with *long*, and *kolosap* is adverbial in function). This is typical of pidgins, which often manage with only a handful of prepositions.

Of the three 'true' prepositions, *wantaim* (from English 'one time', probably because if two people go somewhere or do something with each other, they do so at *one time*) is quite uncommon compared with the other two, *long* and *bilong*. Leaving *wantaim* aside on the grounds that it is relatively uncommon, we can say that *long* and *bilong* between them divide up the 'semantic space' of Melanesian Pidgin prepositions, in the following way:

Long: a relationship between a noun and a location in space or time, i.e. a place or a period, or a comparison, e.g.

*ol meri **long** kantri*	'women in the country'
*bung i bin stat **long** Mande*	'The meeting began on Monday'
*toktok **long** hevi bilong helt*	'talk about the difficulties of health'
*moa **long** 40 meri*	'more than 40 women'

Bilong: a relationship between two nouns, e.g. possessor and possessed, a personal or family relationship, or a relationship of appropriateness, e.g.

*laip **bilong** famili*	'family life'
*Ol opisa **bilong** Melanesin Envairomen Faundesen . . .*	'The officers *of* the M.E.F. . . .'
*. . . i stap tu **bilong** givim toktok*	'. . . are there too *in order to* give talks'

As Edward De Bono has put it,

> One of the most powerful words I have come across in any language is the word 'bilong' which is to be found in Pidgin in Papua New Guinea. The word has nothing to do with property or possession but simply indicates a perceptual field – its very lack of specificity is its strength. (De Bono, 1981, quoted by Mühlhäusler, 1983)

Other space and time relationships can be expressed by means of prepositions combined with words which actually belong to other word classes, e.g.

insait   **long**   **woksop**
inside   LOC   workshop
'*in*(*side*) *the workshop*'

where *insait* behaves grammatically like a noun and is always compounded with *long*. Note that here *long* is glossed as LOC, i.e. a generalised locative marker, with possible translations *in*, *on*, *at* etc.

7.3   Extension of Meanings

Pidgins generally have very few synonyms. Unlike older languages, which often have several terms for more-or-less the same thing (in English, often derived from Latin, Saxon and French), in the compact vocabulary of the pidgin, there is no room for two words with the same meaning. From the viewpoint of the speaker of an older language, pidgins often seem to lack specificity: thus the Tok Pisin word *ston* could be used to translate not only English 'stone' but also 'boulder' (*bikpela ston*, 'big stone'), 'pebble' (*liklik ston*, 'little stone'), and other near-synonyms like 'rock'. Similarly, the word *lek* can mean 'leg', 'foot', 'hind leg', 'footprint'.

A more striking example is Tok Pisin *nil*, which can mean roughly 'any pointy thing' and encompasses the semantic range of English *nail, needle, thorn, syringe, bodkin* etc. Specific types of *nil* can be described by the addition of adjectives, e.g. *nil diwai*, 'nail wood = peg'.

The origins of *nil*, with such a broad meaning, seem in part to be due to a coincidental similarity between the English words *needle* and *nail*. Though on phonological grounds the source of *nil* seems to be *needle* (because of the vowel sound), it is also similar in sound to *nail* (by virtue of the same consonants in the same order). Many researchers in the field of pidgin, and creole studies (for example, Mühlhäusler) have become convinced that 'reinforcement' of one vocabulary item by another – for example, in Russenorsk where /po/ happens to be a common preposition in both Russian and Norwegian – is a significant factor in determining which lexical items from the source language become part of a pidgin's lexicon and which do not.

A somewhat similar example from Tok Pisin is the word *banis*, which means 'bandage', 'ribbon', 'fence' or 'enclosure'. If we knew nothing of the origins of this word, we could easily think of it as an example of polysemy – two related meanings represented by a single word. It is not hard to think of a fence as being a kind of 'ribbon' around a piece of land, or a bandage being used to 'enclose' a wound. Indeed, speakers of Tok Pisin may think of it in just this way, just as speakers of English may feel there is a connection between an 'ear' of corn and the 'ear' we hear with, though historically, these words are completely unrelated. In the history of Tok Pisin, it seems likely that *banis* derives on the one hand from *fence* and on the other hand, from *bandage* via phonological simplification (see Section 5.2). Of course, similarity of meaning may have reinforced this process. The result is a single word with a broader meaning than either of its supposed English sources.

7.4 Multifunctionality of Lexical Items

'**Multifunctionality**' refers to the same word functioning as two or more different syntactic categories (parts of speech), for example, the word *kaikai*, which can mean either 'food' (noun) or 'to eat' (verb). Multifunctionality of this kind is common in many languages (English has many examples such as *(to) look*, *(a) look*) but is especially common in pidgins and creoles. The advantage of this for learners of the pidgin is that they only need learn one vocabulary item rather than two or three.

8 LANGUAGE LEARNING AND THE 'DESIGN FEATURES' OF PIDGINS

We have identified a number of features typical of pidgins. We can summarise them briefly in terms of four *principles*:

1. Lack of surface grammatical complexity – this shows itself both through the small number of grammatical categories (small number of tenses, no plural, no gender etc.) and through the absence of movement rules and embedded sentences.
2. Lack of morphological complexity – as shown by a lack of inflection, and a tendency to have one morpheme per word.
3. Semantic transparency – as shown both in the morphological preference for isolating and agglutinative morphology, and in the preference for semantically transparent compounds in the lexicon.
4. Vocabulary reduction – meaning both a small overall wordstock and a small number of grammatical function words, e.g. pronouns and prepositions.

At this stage we may ask: *why* do pidgins have these characteristics exactly? Chapter 3 is devoted to answering this question in terms of how pidgins come into being. For the time being, it is useful to think of the four points above as 'design features' of a pidgin, and ask: why should a pidgin be designed in precisely this way?

A first answer can come from thinking about *who* the users of the pidgin are. Since a pidgin is, by definition, not a first language, its speakers are *second language learners* of it. We need to make a clear distinction between **language acquisition** – the process whereby a child acquires a language natively – and **language learning**, the process of gaining competence, to a greater or lesser degree, in a second or subsequent language. These processes are alike in some ways, but different in others – particularly in terms of outcome.

The outcome of *language acquisition* is normally complete competence in the native language. The child will not even be conscious, in most cases, of having to 'learn' the language, and formal instruction in the language (e.g. at school) does not usually begin until *after* the child has acquired the language almost fully. The child will normally have perfect competence in the phonology of the language (i.e. will not have any 'foreign accent') and will not have any sense of whether the language is grammatically 'difficult' or 'easy', 'complex' or 'simple'.

Language learning, by contrast, is an activity which typically takes place *after* the learner has acquired a *first* language. Its outcome is much less certain. Learners may progress to the point where they have a native-like command of the new language (sometimes even perfecting their pronunciation to the point where they have no 'foreign accent') or may learn only a few words or phrases, poorly pronounced. Most learners attain a level of competence in a second language which is somewhere between these two extremes. The outcome will depend on a large number of factors, including exposure to the target language (the language being learnt), the method of learning, the learner's motivation, and the extent to which the target language is different from their own language. Second language learners will almost certainly be conscious of some of these differences (whether or not they receive formal 'lessons' in the language) and will be aware of certain 'difficult' aspects of pronunciation or grammar. They will be conscious of the fact that the target language, like their native language, has a large vocabulary but that they know only some of it. They will be conscious of the fact that there are words in the new language which they do not understand, and concepts in their own language which they cannot translate because they do not know the target language word.

If we return now to the four principles which I have called the 'design features' of pidgins, we can see how each of these is oriented towards making a pidgin easier for a language learner who wants to gain competence in the pidgin, probably under less than ideal learning conditions:

- *Lack of surface grammatical complexity* means that the learner does not learn complicated grammatical constructions.
- *Lack of morphological complexity* means that the learner has only a few, regular, forms to learn and can make direct connections between forms and functions.
- *Semantic transparency* allows the learner to make direct connections between forms and meanings.
- *Vocabulary reduction* means the learner has a smaller number of words to learn.

From this it is clear that pidgins are 'well-designed' from the point of view of language *learners*. Whether they are well-designed for language *acquirers*, i.e. children learning a first language, is a separate issue, which will be taken up in Chapter 6.

To end this chapter, we will look at three detailed case studies of very different pidgins.

9   CASE STUDY 1: FANAKALO

9.1   Introduction

Fanakalo (also spelt Fanagalo) is a pidgin which draws its lexicon mainly from the Zulu language (a language of the Bantu family) and is spoken in parts of southern and south central Africa. It is particularly associated with the main mining regions of the area, especially the Witwatersrand region centred on Johannesburg, where the South African gold mines are located.

Fanakalo appears to have its origins in the mid-nineteenth century in contacts between European settlers and the indigenous inhabitants of KwaZulu/Natal, the region on the east coast of South Africa where the Zulus predominate (Mesthrie, 1989). The arrival of indentured labourers from the Indian subcontinent in the second half of the nineteenth century created a very multilingual community, in which the pidgin was able to stabilise. (One theory of the origin of Fanakalo – that it arose from contact between Zulus and Indians – has now been discounted on the basis of historical evidence which shows that Fanakalo existed before the arrival of the Indian immigrants (Mesthrie, 1989).) From its original base in KwaZulu/Natal the pidgin spread, following the patterns of migration to the mining areas, to establish itself in the mining regions of the Witwatersrand, Zimbabwe and Zambia. It is still widely used in the South African mines. The name Fanakalo probably comes from the phrase *enza fana ga lo*, 'do it like this' (Bold, 1974; Holm, 1989).

The special circumstances of gold mining in South Africa have contributed to the preservation of Fanakalo, which despite its usefulness for inter-group communication is reviled by many Africans because of its association with colonialism and the *Apartheid* system (strict racial separation with entrenched economic and political domination by the Europeans over Africans). The South African mining industry is heavily dependent on migrant labour. For many years, men were recruited to the mines of the Witwatersrand from all over southern Africa – over a radius of up to a thousand miles or even more. This brought together a large pool of workers who had no language in common. For the most part they spoke related languages of the Bantu family, which are fairly similar in grammar but have substantial lexical and phonological differences. The mine workers on the whole lacked formal education and therefore did not speak the language of the Europeans; the Europeans (who without exception held the managerial and supervisory positions in the mines) would know at most one, and frequently none, of the African languages. Fanakalo provided a solution to the problem of communication in the mines, in a situation where lives might depend on the ability to understand and be understood.

The South African Chamber of Mines itself was therefore instrumental in promoting Fanakalo and training all miners in its use – a rare example of mass language instruction in a pidgin! This has done nothing to lessen the associations of Fanakalo with racism and white supremacy, but has ensured that Fanakalo is reasonably well documented and standardised, with several manuals and small dictionaries available.

9.2 Fanakalo Text (Bold, 1974)

Sakubona!
(Greeting)
Good day

Bani lo gama gawena?
what the name of-you
What is your name?

Yini lo mhlobo gawena?
what the tribe of-you
To what tribe do you belong?

Wena azi kuluma lo Singisi?
you know speak the English
Can you speak English?

Cha, mina kuluma Fanagalo kupela.
no I speak Fanagalo only
No, I can only speak Fanakalo.

Yini lo msebenzi wena azi?
what the work you now
What sort of work can you do?

Mina yazi lo msebenzi ga lo ndlu.
I know the work of the house
I know housework.

Mina hayifuna lo lova.
I not-want the loafer
I don't want a loafer.

Wena   una   lo   skafu,   na?
you   want   the   food,   QUESTION
Do you want food?

Ipiskati   wena   zo   qala   lo   msebenzi?
what-time   you   FUTURE   begin   the   work
When will you start work?

Yinindaba   wena   hayikona   figile   izolo?
what-thing   you   not   come-PAST   yesterday
Why did you not come yesterday?

Upi   lo   muntu   ena   sebenzile   lapa   lo   gadin?
where   the   man   he   work-PAST   in   the   garden
Where is the boy [sic] who worked in the garden?

Sula   lo   baf   kuqala;   washa   lo   eplon   gawena   baimbai.
clean   the   bath   first   wash   the   apron   of-you   by-and-by
Clean the bath first and wash your apron later.

Basopa   zimvwana   yena   hayi duka;...
take-care   lambs   he   not stray
Take care the lambs don't stray;...

noko   wena   lahlegile   yena   mina   zo   shaya   wena.
if   you   lose   he   I   FUTURE   beat   you
if you lose any I will beat you.

9.2.1   Characteristics of Fanakalo
Compared with its main source language, Zulu, Fanakalo is grammatically
greatly simplified. Perhaps the best demonstration of this claim is the fact
that the 'grammar' section of Bold's *Fanagalo Phrase Book Grammar and
Dictionary* (1974) is only five pages long! Bold also mentions that

> by means of 'crash courses' in 'language laboratories' on the gold mines,
> White miners and other skilled personnel have been taught Fanagalo in
> sessions totalling only 15 hours.   (p. 6)

9.3   Grammatical Systems of Fanakalo

9.3.1   Pronouns
The pronouns of Fanakalo as given by Bold are as follows:

	singular	plural
1	mina	tina
2	wena	wenazonke (zonke = 'all') *or*: nina
3	yena	yenazonke

The separate pronouns *mina, wena, tina, nina* exist in Zulu but are used mainly for emphasis. In an 'unemphatic' Zulu sentence, the pronoun is indicated by a verbal prefix, for example: *ngiyakubona* 'I see you' is made up of four elements: *ngi-* '1st person singular', *-ya-* 'tense marker', *-ku-* '2nd person singular', and the verb root *-bona*, 'see'. In Fanakalo this would simply be *mina bona wena*. Note the plural pronouns *wenazonke*, 'you-all', and *yenazonke*, 'he-all', and compare the Samoan Plantation Pidgin (Section 4.3 above): *mi ol, yu ol, emol/himol*.

9.3.2 Tenses

The otherwise unmarked form of the verb, e.g. *bona*, 'see', functions as the present tense, and probably for other tenses and aspects of the verb. The future is formed with a separate word *zo* placed before the verb, e.g. *mina zo bona wena*, 'I shall see you'. This particle *zo* is derived from the Zulu future marker *-zo-*, but in Zulu *-zo-* is a bound morpheme affixed to the verb, e.g. *ngizokubona*, 'I shall see you'.

The past tense is formed with the suffix *-ile* added to the verb, e.g. *mina bonile wena*, 'I saw you'. Here Fanakalo is in agreement with Zulu grammar, as in Zulu the past is also indicated by the suffix *-ile*.

Generally, Fanakalo shows a greatly simplified system of tenses compared with Zulu. Zulu has a rather large set of verbal prefixes and suffixes which can be combined to convey a range of complex tenses and modalities, e.g.

ngidladla ibhola	'I am playing football'
ngisadladla ibhola	'I am still playing football'
bengingadladla ibhola	'I could (in the immediate past) play football'
	(Nyembezi, 1957)

Such nuances can be conveyed in Fanakalo, if at all, by a combination of separate words.

9.3.3 Possession

Possession is indicated by *ga* before the possessor, e.g. *lo msebenzi ga lo ndlu* 'the work of the house = housework', *eplon gawena* 'apron of you = your apron'.

In Zulu, nouns are divided into a number of classes, each with its own prefix. The class of a noun is determined by grammar rather than semantics, i.e. it is not predictable on the basis of meaning, although most humans belong together in one class and most animals in another. The prefix of each noun has an important role in Zulu grammar, as it appears in modified form as a prefix to other nouns or adjectives to show their relationship. This is how possession is shown in Zulu, e.g.

aba + ntwana **ba** + madoda	'children of the men'
izi + nkomo **za** + bantu	'cows of the people'

The Fanakalo possessive marker *ga-* does not correspond to any actual form in Zulu, although in function it resembles the Zulu possessive prefixes.

9.3.4   Plurals

Bold (1974, p. 10) gives a general rule that plurals are formed by adding the prefix *ma-*, e.g. *foshol* 'shovel' – *mafoshol*, 'shovels', but he adds that some nouns, including many animal names, form their plural by adding *z-* or *zi-*.

Zulu plurals are formed by prefixes different from the singular prefixes of the same noun; which of the plural prefixes is used depends on the particular class the noun belongs to, and is not reliably predictable from the meaning of the noun, or even from its singular form. Thus we have *umuntu – abantu* 'person – people', *indoda – amadoda*, 'man – men', *izwe – amazwe*, 'country – countries', *inhlanzi – izinhlanzi*, 'fish – fishes'. In practice some of the Zulu plurals seem to have carried over into Fanakalo, e.g. *zimbuzi*, 'goats' (Zulu *izimbuzi*), *zinkomo*, 'cows' (Zulu *izinkomo*), while other plurals are formed using the 'general rule' of adding *ma-*. This *ma-* prefix corresponds to the Zulu prefix *ama-*, which is a common, but by no means universal, plural prefix.

9.3.5   Morphological typology of Fanakalo

While Zulu displays a strongly *agglutinating* type of morphology, with a single word sometimes corresponding to a four- or five-word sentence in English, Fanakalo is predominantly *isolating* in its morphology. Thus the four- or five- word sentence of English is likely to be a four-, five- or six-word sentence of Fanakalo as well. To return to our earlier example:

Fanakalo	lapa	zindlu		ga	tina
	in	PL-house		POSS	we
Zulu	e + zi + ndl + ini			ze + thu	
	LOC-PL-house-LOC			POSS-we	

English	**in our houses**

Furthermore, where Zulu has analytic morphology in nouns and adjectives (which can never occur without prefixes) Fanakalo may simply discard these prefixes or analyse them as part of the stem:

Zulu	*i + zinyo*, 'tooth', *i + sela*, 'thief'
Fanakalo	*zinyo, sela*

Zulu	*-bomvu,* 'red', with forms: o-bomvu, e-bomvu, eli-bomvu, esi-bomvu, ezi-bomvu, olu-bomvu etc. in agreement with the noun qualified, thus: *umuthi obomvu*, 'red tree'.
Fanakalo	*bomvu,* 'red' invariant, e.g. *bomvu mti*, 'red tree'.

9.4 The Lexicon of Fanakalo

The lexicon of Fanakalo is predominantly Zulu. Cole (1964) estimated the Zulu contribution to be about 70%, with 24% from English and 6% from Afrikaans, the other main language of Europeans in South Africa. Where words have been adopted into Fanakalo from English or Afrikaans, they may have undergone some phonological changes to bring them into line with the sound systems of Bantu languages – for example *foroko*, 'fork', *steshi*, 'station', *dayimani*, 'diamond', from English; *festele*, 'window', from Afrikaans *venster* [fenstər], and *bulughwe*, 'bridge', from Afrikaans *brug* [brœx].

Where words in Fanakalo have English origins, they are not necessarily from Standard English. Thus 'food' is *skafu* from nonstandard English *scoff* – which also turns up in Russenorsk with the meaning 'eat'. Bold gives the Fanakalo for 'aeroplane' as *flaimashin* ('flying machine') although 'fly' is *ndiza* and 'machine' is *mtshini*. It is quite common to find in pidgins and creoles that their vocabulary includes nonstandard, dialectal, slang or obsolete words from their source languages.

The vocabulary of Fanakalo, as expected, is substantially reduced compared with that of its source languages. Bold's *Fanagalo Phrase Book Grammar and Dictionary* lists about 2000 Fanakalo words. Again as expected, we find many examples of one word having a broad range of meanings. For example, the Fanakalo word *litshe*, like the Tok Pisin *ston*, is glossed as *rock, stone, pebble, boulder*, while *hlinza* is glossed in Bold's dictionary as '*cheat, defraud, skin, flay, slaughter*' and, worryingly, 'surgical operation'.

9.5 Phonological Simplification

The phonology of Zulu is very unlike the phonology of English. To start with, in Zulu most syllables consist either of a vowel alone or of a consonant followed by a vowel and (possibly) a nasal consonant. Two consonants may come together without an intervening vowel if the first consonant is a nasal one produced at the same point of articulation as the second; there are only a few other clusters, e.g. *tl*, *tw*, *kw*. Thus words like *amanzi*, 'water', *abantwana*, 'children', and *ukudabula*, 'to tear', show the typical syllable structure of Zulu.

Secondly, there are a number of sounds in Zulu which are very unusual to English ears and in fact are found in only a few other languages. The click sounds written *c*, *x*, *q* in Zulu are produced by creating a vacuum between the tongue and the roof of the mouth and then releasing the tongue so that the air can rush in. The *c* click (alveolar click) resembles the disapproving 'tut-tut' sound made in the English-speaking world, and the *x* click (lateral click) is the sound used by English speakers to urge on horses. These sounds are not used as regular speech sounds in English, but they are ordinary consonants in Zulu.

Thirdly, there are likewise several sounds of English which are not found in Zulu. These include the consonant clusters such as *str-* and *-ld*, which are forbidden by the rules of Zulu syllable structure. There are also the sounds [θ] and [ð] as in *think* and *that*, which do not occur in Zulu.

Fourthly, Zulu, unlike English, is a *tone language*, i.e. in Zulu, tone is *phonemic*. This means that the intonation pattern or 'tune' of a word is part of its structure and can distinguish one word from another: hence the possibility of minimal pairs like *ithanga* ('thigh') and *ithanga* ('pumpkin') which differ only in tone ('thigh' has the tone pattern High-Low-High and 'pumpkin' has High-Low-Low).

In English, intonation patterns are used to distinguish questions from statements and can be used to convey feelings such as anger or boredom, but they do not function to distinguish words. To the untrained English ear, two Zulu words which differ only in their tones may well sound identical.

The phonology of Fanakalo is the result of the compromise that might be predicted, given that Zulu and English speakers were trying to make themselves understood using mainly Zulu vocabulary.

1.   Fanakalo words usually display Zulu-like syllable structure. English and other non-Zulu words often have an epenthetic (extra) vowel inserted to make a final syllable open: *sirinji*, 'syringe', *lampu*, 'lamp', *wilibero*, 'wheelbarrow'. On the other hand, a number of clusters are possible which are not allowed in Zulu, for example in *stim*, 'steam', *streyit*, 'straight', *smesh*, 'smash'. Not all non-Zulu words are adapted to end in a vowel: so we have *ges*, 'electricity', *bendej*, 'bandage', and *ketsh*, 'cage (a lift used to transport miners)'.

2.   The Zulu clicks are present in Fanakalo but are not always pronounced as clicks by speakers of languages which do not have clicks. Bold (1974, p. 7) advises: 'if you find you can't manage the clicks, even after coaching, you can at a pinch use the letter k instead'.

3.   Fanakalo does not use tone to distinguish words. As mentioned above, tone is important in Zulu phonology, but phonemic tone is absent in English.

9.6   Exercise

Go through the list of 'general features of pidgin grammars' in Section 2.2 of this chapter. Try to find a Fanakalo example of, or counter-example to, each of the features listed. Make a note of any difficulties you have in deciding whether your example is appropriate.

10 CASE STUDY 2: RUSSENORSK

10.1 Introduction

Unlike Fanakalo, which is an example of a **stable pidgin** (to be discussed in Chapter 4), Russenorsk represents a more basic stage of development, a *jargon*. We shall see in Chapter 4 that a **jargon** is the most basic stage of a pidgin. It is in the nature of jargons that they are often short-lived – they either die out completely or mutate into a more durable stable pidgin. They are usually perceived as purely functional and of low status by their speakers, who seldom take the trouble to analyse them or write them down. We therefore have to make do with limited accounts of a fairly small number of jargons, although we can be sure that many more have existed and disappeared without leaving any trace. One relatively well documented jargon is *Russenorsk* ('Russo-Norwegian'). Russenorsk was spoken along the Arctic coast of northern Norway from the eighteenth until the early twentieth century (Broch and Jahr, 1981). It also has at least two other names, *moja po tvoja* ('mine in yours') and *kaksprek* 'how-speak' or '*kak*-speak' (Fox, 1983, p. 101). It was used by Russian sailors and Norwegian fishermen, mainly for the purposes of bartering during the short summer season. Since the contact between the two groups was not only restricted, but seasonal, in a sense Russenorsk had to be 're-created' each year by a slightly different set of people. An unusual feature of Russenorsk (pointed out by Holm, 1989, p. 621) is that the two groups in contact were social equals rather than 'colonisers' and 'colonised' as in many other situations where contact languages have come about. This may account, says Holm, for the fact that the vocabulary of Russenorsk is drawn almost equally from the two source languages: 39% from Russian and 47% from Norwegian (Fox, 1973, p. 62).

10.2 Russenorsk Text

The sentences of Russenorsk in Figure 2.1 are a selection of examples given by Ingvild Broch and Ernst Håkon Jahr (1981), who draw their data from a number of sources, especially O. Broch (1927).

Note on the transcription: here,

å = Norwegian å, approximately [ɔ]
j = [j]
x = [x]
è = [tʃ]
ž = [ʒ]
š = [ʃ]

RUSSENORSK	NORWEGIAN	RUSSIAN	ENGLISH
kak ʃprek? how speak	**hva sier du?** what say you	**čto govoriš?** what say-2SG	*What do you say?*
kak ju snakka? how you speak	**hva sier du?** what say you	**čto govoriš?** what say-2SG	*What do you say?*
kak ʃprek po norsk? how speak in Norwegian	**hva heter det på norsk?** what is-called it in Norwegian	**kak nazyvaetsja po-norvežski?** how calls-1SGtself in-Norwegian	*What is this called in Norwegian?*
tvoja ʃprek russki? you speak Russian	**du taler russisk?** you speak Russian	**ty govoriš po-russki?** you speak-2SG in-Russian	*Do you speak Russian?*
tvoja kupom planka? you buy plank	**(vil) du kjøpe planker?** (want) you buy planks	**ty kupiš li doski?** you buy-2SG Q-MKR planks	*Do you want to buy planks?*
kak pris? how price	**hva er prisen?** what is price-the	**kakaja cena?** what price	*What is the price?*
kak stojit? how costs	**hva er prisen?** what is price-the	**skol'ko stojit?** how-much costs	*How much does it cost?*
moja kupom fiska. I buy fish	**jeg kjøper fisk.** I buy fish	**ja pokupaju rybu.** I will-buy-1SG fish	*I buy fish.*
fiska po den sija. fish in the side	**fisken til denne siden.** fish-the at that side	**rybu na etu storonu.** fish on that side	*Fish is on that side.*
principal po lan. boss in land	**skipperen er i land.** captain-the on land	**xozjain na beregu.** captain on shore	*The captain is ashore.*

Russenorsk	Norwegian	Russian	English
tvoja ligom. / you lie	du lyver. / you lie	ty vrjoš / you lie-2SG	You are lying.
moja ikke ligom. / I not lie	jeg lyver ikke. / I lie not	ja ne vrju. / I not lie-1SG	I'm not lying.
moja po vater kastom. / I in water throw	jeg vil kaste deg på sjøen. / I want throw you in sea	ja v vodu brošu. / I in water throw-1SG	I'll throw you in the water.
grut stoka na gaf. / big storm in sea	sterk storm på havet. / strong storm in harbour	sil'nyj štorm v morje. / strong storm in sea	There's a strong storm at sea.
tvoja kralom tros! / you steal rope(s)	du har stjålet en trosse! / you have stolen a rope	ty ukral tros! / you steal-PAST rope	You've stolen the rope!
moja pos[lagom po tvoja! / I hit in you	jeg vil slås med deg! / I want beat with you	ja budu drat'sja s toboj / I will-1SG fight with you	I will hit (fight) you!
jung grebi moja po lan! / boy row me in land	gut, ro meg til land! / boy row me to land	mal'čik pervezi menja na bereg! / boy row me to shore	Boy, row me ashore!
norsk man kom po rus man. / norweg man come in Russian man	nordmannen kom til russeren. / Norwegian come to Russian	norvežec prišel k russkomu. / Norwegian come-PAST to Russian	Norwegian, come to the Russian.
vil ju po moja stova po / want you at my room on	vil du spise hos meg imorgen? / want you eat by me tomorrow	ty xočeš kušat' zavtra / you want-2SG eat-INF tomorrow	Do you want to eat at my place tomorrow?
morradag skaffom? / tomorrow eat		u menja? / at me	

Figure 2.1 Russenorsk Text

10.3   Exercise

Compare the Norwegian, Russian and Russenorsk sentences given in Section 10.2.
What do you notice about the following?

1. Word order – does Russenorsk follow the word order of Russian, Norwegian or neither? Look at both statements and questions.

2. Prepositions – how many prepositions are used in Russenorsk, and how does this compare with the two source languages?

3. Tenses – how does Russenorsk show tense?

10.4   Notes

Of the two source languages, Russian is the more highly inflected, with distinct verbal endings for first, second and third person singular and plural (marked 1SG, 2SG etc.). Nouns and pronouns also have inflected forms, e.g. /ja/ 'I' but /menja/ 'me', /o mnje/ 'about me'.

The pronouns *moja* and *tvoja* ('I' and 'you') in Russenorsk are actually *adjective* pronoun forms in Russian, inflected to agree with a feminine noun, e.g. /moja ryba/ 'my fish'.

The frequency of the preposition *po* is remarkable. Hall (1966, p. 61) notes that 'the formation of Russenorsk seems to have depended on the chance similarity of the preposition /po/ "on, in" in both Norwegian and Russian', though he gives no evidence to suggest that without this similarity, Russenorsk could not have come into being.

The origin of the verb ending *-om* in Russenorsk is mysterious. It may be related to a similar verb ending *-im* in the pidgins of the Pacific Ocean (see Chapter 4, Sections 4, 5 and 6), or the ending *-um* often reported in the pidgin English of Native Americans (Indians) (see Miller, 1980).

11   CASE STUDY 3: CHINESE PIDGIN ENGLISH

11.1   Introduction

Chinese Pidgin English (CPE) is one of the oldest varieties of English-lexicon pidgin. The English established a 'factory' (trading station) at Canton (Guangzhou) in 1664, and 'immediately a variety of Pidgin English grew up there' (Hall, 1966, p. 8). According to Hall, the English regarded the language of the Chinese as unlearnable, while the Chinese were unwilling to learn the language of the foreigners (whom they held in contempt) but were prepared to learn a reduced variety of it. Pidginised English thus served the interests of both sides, who 'wanted to hold [each other] at arm's length' (ibid.). Holm (1989, p. 512) notes that the Chinese were forbidden to teach their language to foreigners, 'since it was deemed convenient for them to be able to communicate in Chinese to one another during trade without the foreigners understanding'.

CPE may have its roots in an earlier Portuguese pidgin which was used around the Portuguese colony of Macao from 1555 onwards, a possibility suggested by the fact that 'some of the earliest fragments of CPE [...] seem to be more Portuguese than English' (Holm, 1989, p. 514).

CPE was used mainly in Canton until about 1843, when Britain won a war with China and forced the Chinese to open several ports to foreign trade. CPE thus spread along the Chinese coast during the nineteenth century. Its heyday or 'classical period' (Hall, 1966) lasted until about 1900; from that date on its use declined, as CPE came to acquire the stigma which often attaches to pidgins, and Chinese who were able to do so began to learn to speak Standard English. Whinnom (1971) states that in Hong Kong, the last of the British colonies on mainland China, CPE became a lingua franca for use among Chinese with different linguistic backgrounds. ('Chinese' refers to a language with a single, ancient writing system but several mutually unintelligible spoken languages. Hong Kong, as a 'melting pot' which has attracted Chinese from different parts, is predominantly Cantonese-speaking but also has speakers of other types of Chinese.) CPE has now fallen out of use even in Hong Kong. It can thus be said to have undergone a complete 'life cycle' – from creation to disappearance – in around 300 years.

The range of functions of CPE was severely restricted. Bauer (1974, p. 86) estimates that a lexicon of 750 words was sufficient for most speakers. Holm (1989, p. 515) states that 'the overwhelming majority of pidgin words were derived from English but most were modified to fit Chinese phonotactic rules', i.e. to fit the normal rules of Chinese syllable structure.

Grammatically, some constructions can be traced to a Chinese origin, for example the use of *-pisi* ('piecee') after numerals and demonstratives, which echoes the use of numeral classifiers in Chinese. In Chinese, numerals and demonstratives do not directly precede the word they modify; instead a *classifier* must intervene. Which classifier is used is dependent on the semantics of the noun it modifies: thus there is one classifier for leaves, paper, and windowpanes (flat things), another for pencils, pipes and sticks, etc. CPE does not reflect the elaborate semantics of this system, but retains an echo of its grammatical function in using *-pisi* to mark numerals and demonstratives.

11.2   Chinese Pidgin English text

The CPE text below is from Bauer (1974, p. 154) and originally appeared in
Household Words, vol. 15, p. 452, in 1857.

Foreigner. – Chin-chin fookkee?

F. – How do you do, John
Chinaman [or friend]?

Chinaman. – Belly well, belly well.
Chin-chin: whafo my no hab see
taipan sot langim?

C. – Quite well, thank you, sir.
How is it that I have not had the
honour of seeing you for so long?

F. – My wanchee wun pay soo
belly soon. Spose fookkee too
muchee pigeon: no can maykee.

F. – I want a pair of shoes soon.
But I fear you are too busy to
make them for me now.

C. – Cando cando: whafo no can:
no cazion feeloo: my sabbee belly
well: can fixee alla popa.

C. – Most certainly I can. Why
not? Don't be afraid of that. I am
sure I can make them all right.

F. – Wanchee maykee numba wun
ledda: feeloo no hab eulop ledda?

F. – I want a pair made of the best
leather; but perhaps you are out
of European leather?

C. – No cazion feeloo. Can skure
hab numba wun popa ledda.

C. – Don't be afraid of that. I can
guarantee the leather to be the
very best.

F. –   Patchee wun piece sulek
insigh all popa; wanchee finis
chopchop; can do?

F. – Well, line them with silk
nicely. I want them at once, if
you can.

C. – Can see, can sabee; skure you
day afoo mollo: taipan can sen
wun piece cooly come my sop
look see.

C. – I'll see. I promise you them the
day after tomorrow. Please, sir,
to send a servant to my shop for
them.

F. (seeing a woman in the back part
of the shop) – High ya, fookee:
my see insigh wun piecee wifoo.
Dat you wifoo? My no sabee
fookkee hab catchee wifoo.
Tooloo?

F. – Well, friend, who is that
woman inside there? Is that your
wife? I did not know that you
had got married. Is it so or not?

C. So fashion tooloo. Beefo tim
wun moon, countee alla popa
day, my catch dat piece wifoo.

C. – Yes, sir, quite true. Last
month, on the most auspicious
day I could select, I married her.

11. 3 Exercise

1. Make a list of CPE words with their English source words. What phonological changes do you notice between English and CPE? Are these changes regular? Can you suggest any reason for them?

2. Identify as many CPE words as you can in the above text which have meanings different from the meaning of the English source word. How can you account for the change in each case?

3. How does CPE express
    (a) Tense?
    (b) Negation?

Are there any similarities with Tok Pisin, Fanakalo or Russenorsk?

KEY POINTS: Pidgins

Pidgins

- have no native speakers;
- are the result of contact between two or more languages;
- are not mutually intelligible with their source languages;
- usually draw most of their vocabulary from one language (the *lexifier*);
- have grammars which are *simplified* and *reduced* compared with the grammars of their input languages;
- tend to have simple phonological systems;
- tend to have analytic (*isolating*) or agglutinating morphology;
- tend to have *semantically transparent* relationships between words and meaning;
- have small vocabularies where words cover a wide semantic range.

3 Pidgin Origins

1 INTRODUCTION

In Chapter 1 we saw that pidgins were one possible outcome of language contact, while in Chapter 2 we saw that pidgins typically have simple grammars in comparison with the native languages of their speakers, and have a reduced vocabulary. We saw that these features make pidgins more accessible to language learners, but we did not have any explanation of how these features actually came to characterise a particular pidgin language. In this chapter we will look for an explanation of the typical characteristics of pidgins in terms of their origins. We know that pidgins come into being under somewhat unusual circumstances, which necessarily involve language contact. Are simplification of the grammar, and vocabulary reduction, always a result of a particular *kind* of language contact? What exactly are the conditions which give rise to languages with the kind of structure we have seen?

We saw in Chapter 2, Section 8, that simplification and reduction provide practical solutions to the problems of learning a new language in a context where that language needs to be learnt as quickly and with as little effort as possible. The small vocabulary – restricted to a specific range of functions, depending on the speakers' requirements – will not tax the learner's brain unnecessarily. The grammar, stripped of redundant categories, will likewise minimise the possibility of mistakes or misunderstanding.

At this level, simplification and reduction are easy to explain. But by what mechanism do they come about? It is very clear that no-one in a language-contact situation sets out consciously to 'invent' a maximally simple language. There have been several attempts to invent artificial languages for international communication, of which Esperanto is probably the most famous and successful – but none of these have much resemblance to pidgins, and all have actually been more complex than any of the known pidgins. Pidginisation is the result not of conscious strategies but of unconscious processes. The rest of this chapter will explore some of the hypotheses about them.

2 SIMILARITIES BETWEEN CONTACT LANGUAGES

2.1 Grammatical Similarities

At this stage we should note that the similarities which are widely shared among pidgins and creoles are not just at a general level, but extend to specific patterns. If we consider the verb systems of various pidgins and creoles from around the world we find some remarkable similarities, for example, in the ordering of negation, tense and aspect markers. Consider one sentence from a sample of contact languages. Each of the sentences below is a translation of the English 'I did not see him' or 'I have not seen him'.

Tok Pisin	mi no bin lukim em
Chinese Pidgin English	mai no hav si
Sranan Tongo	mi no ben si en
Haitian Creole	m pa te wè li
Papiamentu	mi n' a mir' e

In each case, the contact language has similar word order:

1. Subject pronoun (derived, as it happens, from the *object* pronoun in the lexifier language)
2. Negator
3. Past tense marker
4. Main verb (*see*)
5. Object pronoun (omitted in Chinese Pidgin English)

We can note first that although the first three languages of the sample have English as their lexifier, English has a different word order from all three for this sentence. In English, the past tense marker is incorporated in an auxiliary verb (*do* or *have*) which precedes the marker of negation *not*. The fact that all three are historically 'related' to English therefore does not explain why they have similar word order – and we still need an account of why it should be *different* from English. Next, note that Haitian Creole has French as its lexifier, but that the French translation of this sentence is *je ne l'ai pas vu*, literally *I not him have not seen*, where the negation is expressed by the items *ne* and *pas*, which are not adjacent to each other. In Haitian Creole, *pa* expresses the negative, but it is located before the verb rather than after, as in French. Spanish, the main lexifier of Papiamentu, has similar word order to French, without the double negation: *I not him have seen*. We now have to explain how the contact languages in the sample come to resemble each other grammatically, while all being significantly *different* from their lexifier languages.

2.2 Similarities in Lexical Composition

Another fact which clearly needs some explanation is that most contact languages derive the majority of their vocabulary from just one language, the lexifier. One could easily imagine different outcomes, where the various groups involved in the contact contributed vocabulary in proportion to their numbers, or the vocabulary was divided equally among the different source languages. Russenorsk is an example of something close to the latter arrangement – so it is *possible*, but unusual. In most cases the majority of the vocabulary comes from *one* language, which is often spoken by a numerically *small* group, for example Europeans, who were heavily outnumbered by indigenous inhabitants or slaves in the majority of contexts where pidgins and creoles have come into being.

3 THEORIES ABOUT THE ORIGIN OF PIDGINS AND CREOLES: AN OVERVIEW

We are now ready to examine some of the most important theories about how pidgins and creoles come into being. Here we will mainly be concerned about the origins of *pidgins*, since in many cases these exist for some time prior to creoles, which develop from them. Some of the theories which have been proposed, however, offer accounts for the origins of both. We will consider in future chapters (especially Chapter 6) exactly what the relation is between pidgins and creoles.

In 3.1 we will discuss *monogenetic* theories and *relexification*, which aim to provide an account of a common origin for many of the world's pidgins and creoles. In 3.2 we will discuss the possibility of *polygenesis* and independent parallel development of pidgins. In later sections we will concentrate on specific 'mechanisms' which have been claimed to be relevant to pidgin and creole genesis: *second language learning* (Section 4), *simplified input* or *foreigner talk* (Section 5), *substrate* influence (Section 6) and linguistic *universals* (Section 7).

3.1 Monogenesis and Relexification

In view of the challenge which creoles offer to the family tree model of linguistic change (see Chapter 1) it is ironic that one of the most-discussed theories of pidgin and creole genesis accounts for similarities among pidgins and creoles by means of genetic relationships and descent from a common ancestor. The essence of the **monogenesis** (single-origin) theory is that the present-day pidgins and creoles of the world are linked either directly or indirectly with an earlier Mediterranean pidgin, possibly Sabir or a later version of it (see Chapter 2). According to the monogenesis hypothesis, this proto-pidgin, drawing its lexicon mainly from Portuguese (itself a descendant of Latin), was carried around the world in the course of European colonisation, giving rise to pidgins (and later, creoles) in many places.

An essential component of this theory is the notion of **relexification**. We have seen that pidgins and creoles tend to draw most of their vocabulary from just one source language ('the lexifier'). The monogenesis theory proposes that as the proto-pidgin came into use among different groups of European colonisers – Spanish, Dutch, French and English – it underwent a near-total replacement of its vocabulary with items from the new coloniser's language, while undergoing little or no grammatical change. This 'near-total' substitution of vocabulary is given the name *relexification*. The 'near' in 'near-total' is significant because in many of the world's pidgins and creoles we find a few words representing the earlier 'strata' of vocabulary: in particular, a few items of Portuguese origin are remarkably persistent and widely spread. Thus *savvy*, 'know' (Portuguese *saber*, Tok Pisin *save*, Chinese Pidgin English *savvy*, West African Pidgin English *sabi*, Sranan Tongo *sabi*, Papiamentu *sabi*, Jamaican Creole *sabi*), and *piccaninny*, 'small' or 'child' (Portuguese *pequenho* /pekenyu/, West African Pidgin English *pikin*, Sranan Tongo *pikin*, Jamaican Creole *pikni*), are found in pidgins and creoles widely separated geographically and with different lexifiers.

While the monogenesis theory to some extent explains the origin of this shared Portuguese 'core', its main strength is that it accounts for the similarities in pidgin and creole grammars in terms of a common origin. The grammar of Sabir reappears, basically unaltered, in its descendants. Thompson (1961), one of the early proponents of monogenesis, drew attention to the similarities in the way creoles with different lexifiers nevertheless had very similar tense, mood and aspect marking. Each creole essentially has three preverbal markers: one for 'durative', indicating a continuing action; one for 'perfective', indicating a completed action; one for 'contingent or future' indicating an action to take place. Certain combinations of these markers are allowed, while others never occur. Thus we get:

Sranan Tongo (English-lexicon)	mi	ben	e	go
Papiamentu (Spanish/Port.-lexicon)	mi	taba	ta	bai
Haitian (French-lexicon)	m	te	ap	ale
	I	PERF	DUR	*go*

The similarity of patterning across lexically 'unrelated' creoles is remarkable. In each creole the perfective marker comes first, then the durative, and the meaning is approximately: 'I was going'. These similarities remain the subject of various theoretical attempts at explanation; obviously, a common origin in a proto-pidgin is one possible explanation, but a common linguistic 'blueprint' or universal tendency to simplify in a particular way is another.

If – but only if – relexification can be shown to be a real possibility rather than a purely theoretical notion, then the monogenesis theory has some merit, for the spread of European-lexicon pidgins and creoles has followed the major trade routes and it is not inconceivable that the main seafaring nations could have 'taken over' an existing pidgin, one from another, as first the Portuguese and later the English, French and Dutch dominated the Atlantic slave trade and the sea routes to the East. Since the Portuguese were first to find a sea route from Europe to the East, and the first to trade slaves along the West African coast, the possibility of a Portuguese-lexicon proto-pidgin seems quite likely (though we have no record of it). The historical links between some of the creoles, furthermore, are quite well documented: for example, Keith Whinnom (one of the earliest names associated with the monogenesis theory) showed in his 1957 book that the Spanish-lexicon creoles still spoken today in the Philippines had their origins in a Portuguese-lexicon creole once spoken on the Indonesian island of Ternate, and which was transported to the Philippines in the seventeenth century. The connections between the various West African slave trading forts (which at different times were in the control of different European powers) and the Caribbean plantation colonies to which the slaves were sent (and which also changed hands from time to time) are likewise matters of historical record.

Is relexification a real possibility? There is evidence that it is. One source of evidence is languages like *Media Lengua* (Muysken, 1981; 1994), not a pidgin but a 'mixed language' resulting from *language mixing* (see Bakker and Mous, 1994), which was mentioned briefly in Chapter 1 and will be discussed in more detail in Chapter 9. Media Lengua, spoken in Ecuador, is a 'mixture' of Quechua, an indigenous language which has agglutinative morphology, and Spanish, the other main language of Ecuador. Media Lengua has about a thousand native speakers in Central Ecuador. In Media Lengua (literally 'Half Language'), Quechua word stems are replaced with Spanish equivalents, maintaining the rest of the Quechua structure. Thus most of the grammatical morphemes and the syntactic structure of Media Lengua are Quechua, but nearly all the 'content words' are Spanish. Media Lengua could well be described as Quechua grammar with Spanish vocabulary. Muysken offers Media Lengua as an example of relexification – although Media Lengua cannot be described as a pidgin because of its syntactic complexity.

Mühlhäusler has studied the progress of lexical change in the pidgins of Papua New Guinea. He emphasises (1986, pp. 108–13) the importance of making it clear at what stage in the development of a pidgin relexification occurs. Until a pidgin has developed a stable lexicon, which is not the case in the earliest stages (see Chapter 4), relexification is an irrelevant concept. However, Mühlhäusler believes that relexification can take place at different stages after stabilisation has occurred, and in two different ways: either gradually (with alternative words drawn from different languages available simultaneously) or abruptly, where a new word replaces an existing one. According to Mühlhäusler (1986, p. 108) 'gradual relexification is associated with a prolonged period of bilingualism and the simultaneous presence of more than one prestige lexifier language'. Such conditions might have been found, perhaps, in slave trading forts as one European power took over from another, with a period of overlap. Mühlhäusler concludes that relexification of both types has played a role in the history of a number of pidgins and creoles, but that 'there is no indication that *all* these languages are related in this way' (p. 113).

Proponents of monogenesis are not always explicit about *which* of the world's pidgins and creoles the theory is meant to take into account. Clearly, a number of contact languages are good candidates for descent from a Portuguese proto-pidgin, namely those on either side of the Atlantic with either a Portuguese lexical base or a connection with the slave trade, and those in the Far East and Oceania where Portuguese seafarers were the first European traders and colonisers. Equally, there are pidgins and creoles for which a Portuguese connection, however indirect, is virtually unimaginable: for example, the pidgins of Africa which draw their lexicon from various Bantu languages (e.g. Fanakalo), Juba Arabic, Naga Pidgin spoken in the Indian subcontinent, and so on. Mühlhäusler also points out that proponents of monogenesis usually ignore the possibility that some of the existing pidgins and creoles with European lexifiers could be relexified forms of earlier contact languages with *indigenous* lexicons, i.e. if relexification really can take place, then the European lexicons we find at the moment in many pidgins and creoles around the world may not be the 'original' ones.

To conclude, the notion of relexification seems to be relevant to pidgin genesis, but it needs to be viewed in the context of a pidgin developing over time, under particular historical circumstances (though we are not sure at present exactly what these would have to be). A wholesale appeal to relexification to explain similarities among contact languages leaves too many other things unexplained: in particular, we might ask why the proto-pidgin had the grammatical features which it must have had (i.e. the grammatical features we find in its 'descendants', mentioned in 2.1), since these are *not* found in Portuguese or similar languages such as Spanish and Italian. Furthermore, although the monogenesis theory is meaningless without relexification, if relexification really occurs it does not follow that the monogenesis theory is right. Even if there was no proto-pidgin, relexification may still take place locally under the right conditions – as Mühlhäusler has shown. Nevertheless, the monogenesis theory has drawn attention to the historical connections between many of the world's existing pidgins and creoles, and further research may shed light on the exact conditions which promote large-scale relexification.

A theory of pidgin and creole origins which has some features in common with the 'classical' monogenetic theory is the so-called *nautical jargon* theory. This theory exists in different versions, which relate pidgins and creoles around the world either to a seafarers' jargon based on English or to one based on French. Earlier scholars such as Reinecke (1937) and Hall (1966) are convinced of the importance of nautical language in the formation of pidgins, and there is no reason to doubt this, as even if the earliest European-lexifier pidgins did not originate at sea, they were certainly spread by sea voyagers.

Comparative work by Ross Clark (1979) points to the importance of a tradition of seafaring English which could account for many of the lexical similarities in pidgins and creoles of the Pacific region, some of which are shared with pidgins and creoles further afield (the Caribbean and Atlantic). While this kind of historical reconstruction is valuable for helping us understand the historical relationships between various contact languages better, and may reveal the sources of some lexical items, it is not useful as a theory of pidgin origins in general. There are too many pidgins and creoles *outside* the regions where such a jargon might have been spoken, which nevertheless share grammatical similarities with the Atlantic and Pacific creoles.

3.2 Polygenesis and Independent Parallel Development

On the opposite side from the monogenesis theory stand several theories which may jointly be termed **polygenetic** theories, in other words theories which propose *multiple* independent origins for different pidgins and creoles.

The notion of *independent parallel development*, associated with the work of Robert A. Hall, suggests that the similarities between pidgins and creoles world-wide can be ascribed to similar processes at work producing similar results from different starting-points. There is no need to postulate the existence of a proto-pidgin which gave rise to all existing pidgins and creoles. Likewise, it is not a problem for the proponents of independent parallel development that pidgins and creoles exist which show the grammatical similarities mentioned in 2.1, but which have *no* plausible historical connection with a Portuguese pidgin.

One problem for polygenetic theories until fairly recently has been that it was difficult to find clear cases of *genuinely* independent development. The complex network of European trade routes and the pervasiveness of Portuguese involvement on every continent have made it possible for proponents of monogenesis to find a connection of some sort between almost any two European-lexifier pidgins and creoles, especially if the probability of a nautical jargon is taken into account. Even similarities between Pitcairnese (Chapter 5) and Jamaican Creole (Chapter 7) could be explained by the fact that one of the 'founding fathers' of Pitcairnese was a man from St Kitts in the Caribbean!

In the last few decades detailed descriptions have become available of pidgin and creole languages without European connections – in particular, a number of African pidgins (e.g. *Sango* of the Central African Republic, *Lingala* of Zaire, *Juba Arabic*), Asian pidgins (e.g. *Nagamese* of India) and Oceanic pidgins (e.g. *Pidgin Fijian*) which were previously not well documented. All of these studies have found much the same kinds of basic structural similarities as noted previously. This suggests that any theory of pidgin genesis which is to be general enough to cover *all* cases of pidginisation must be a polygenetic one. There is still room for dispute, however, over the exact mechanism whereby the 'different starting points' lead to 'similar outcomes'.

These are briefly reviewed in the rest of this section.

3.3 Universalist Theories

Universalist theories (Section 7 below) put emphasis on the existence of *universal strategies* for simplifying language which are part of the innate tacit knowledge of all humans – including, of course, those actively involved in 'creating' a pidgin.

One specific universalist theory which we will look at in detail below, the *'foreigner talk' theory*, suggests that the learners' input – i.e. the model offered to those learning the pidgin by speakers of the lexifier – was a simplified **foreigner talk** register of the lexifier language. This will be discussed in more detail in Section 5 below. Since foreigner talk involves simplification of the speaker's own language, and speakers are apparently able to do this without being taught what to do (i.e. they have some *innate* understanding of how to simplify), this can also be seen as a type of universalist theory (Section 7).

3.4 The 'Common Core' Hypothesis

This accounts for similarities among contact languages through *similarities in the 'combinations' of grammars* (e.g. of European languages + indigenous languages) which gave rise to the pidgins concerned. Thus the combination of a European lexifier with African languages in the Caribbean might produce a similar result to the combination of another European language with indigenous Austronesian languages in the South Pacific, given that there are considerable structural similarities between most European languages on the one hand, and accidental similarities between African and Austronesian languages on the other.

The 'common core' hypothesis holds that the pidgin which results from contact between languages A and B will have in its grammar just that part of the grammar of A which is also found in B, i.e. the overlap between the grammars of A and B. (This theory was put forward by Robert A. Hall (1961).) For example, Fanakalo (Chapter 2) is somewhat unusual among pidgins in having a past tense suffix *-ile*, which is identical to the Zulu one. Inflection, as we have seen, is not highly developed in pidgins; and the majority of tense markers, including the future marker *zo* in Fanakalo, are preverbal. However, we could explain the Fanakalo suffix by the fact that the English past tense is also formed by suffixation (usually of *-ed*) and so the grammars of Zulu and English overlap at this point. However, this explanation does not work in the case of the Fanakalo definite article *lo*, as Zulu does not have articles.

To take another African example, it was mentioned in Chapter 2 that Pidgin Sango is a product of contact between several languages, all of which have phonemic tone. However, Pidgin Sango is not a tone language itself.

Of course, the 'common core' of the grammar of two languages is just the part where any *universal*s of human language are likely to be found, and the more languages involved in the contact, the smaller and more 'universal' the common core is likely to be. This theory is therefore sometimes hard to distinguish from a more general 'universalist' theory (see Section 7 below).

3.5 Substrate Theories

The *substrate* languages (see Chapter 1, Section 6) are usually all those involved in initial or continuing contact, apart from the lexifier. *Substrate theories* focus on the role of substrate languages (usually the indigenous languages of the region where the pidgin is spoken) in providing the grammatical structure of a pidgin. The involvement of similar substrate languages in contacts which gave rise to pidgins or creoles with different lexifiers can be used to explain the similarities found in the languages in question, if it can be shown that similar features are also found in all or most of the substrate languages. For example, we know that in different parts of the Caribbean a mix of related West African languages were in contact with different European languages during the slavery period. The fact that many West African languages share certain features of grammar could be used to account for the appearance of these features in English-lexicon, French-lexicon and Spanish-lexicon creoles (for example, Jamaican Creole, Haitian Creole and Papiamentu respectively).

In the remainder of this chapter we will look in some detail at different theories about the origin of pidgins. We will begin by looking at pidgins as cases of second language learning, as many of the theories start from the basic assumption that pidgins involve language learning of some kind, whether complete or incomplete, of a 'normal' model or a reduced model.

4 PIDGINS AS SECOND LANGUAGE LEARNING

4.1 Successful or Not?

Pidgins are sometimes seen by linguists as examples of *unsuccessful* or incomplete second language learning. Hesseling, one of the 'founders' of creole studies, was probably first to put this idea forward. To take this view, however, is very much to assume that second language learning is only successful if the end result is the achievement of a native-like command of the *target* language (the language supposedly being learned). A more pragmatic view would be that pidgins represent *successful* second language learning from the point of view of their users – who learn just enough to communicate what they need to communicate and no more. Thus effort is not wasted on the unrealistic goals of learning the finer details of grammar and pronunciation: the focus is on successful communication within a limited range of interactions. The learner's communicative goal is thus adequately achieved, even though the supposed target language is not learned well from its own speakers' point of view.

Some researchers in this field have therefore chosen to treat pidginisation as a type of imperfect second language learning, with the lexifier as target language. What this means is that in a given contact situation, some (usually a powerful or prestigious minority) speak the lexifier natively while the rest (usually a powerless majority) try to learn it, but under less than ideal conditions. Their unsuccessful efforts result in the pidgin: a grammatically impoverished version of the lexifier with a very restricted vocabulary.

This theory, stated straightforwardly, has its attractions. It can explain the disproportionate amount of vocabulary from one source. If we can also show that learners tend to simplify their language in certain ways, it could explain the types of grammatical structure we find in pidgins. On the other hand, we need explanations of why the learners never improve beyond this very inadequate stage, and how it is that everyone reaches the *same* stage and gets stuck there. Second language learning in normal circumstances is characterised by considerable *differences* in the progress of learners. In this section, we will look at some data which bears on these issues.

In Europe and North America, 'knowing foreign languages' (which nearly always is taken to mean knowing a European language or Arabic, Chinese or Japanese) is usually seen as a personal educational accomplishment. Individuals may choose to learn a foreign language for career purposes, to enhance their enjoyment of holidays, for pleasure or simply out of curiosity. Relatively few people are put in the position of having to learn a new language simply in order to survive; and those who are in that position are often helped by attending language classes or having personal tuition.

There are also, however, many instances of people forced to learn a new language out of necessity, without the benefit of teachers or books. In

Europe and North America, most of the people in this category are
economic migrants or refugees from poor countries. Their efforts to learn
the language of the new country are often hampered, not only by a lack of
tuition, but by limited access to native speakers of the language. For
example, migrant workers may have some contact with native speakers in
their workplace but socialise almost entirely with people from their own
language group; while women from some cultures live rather secluded lives,
rarely leaving their homes, and almost never meeting people who speak the
language of the new country natively. Some recent studies of untutored
learners' language have given us insights into how learners go about
communicating in a new language which they have not been formally
taught. These communication systems share a number of features with
pidgins: they are always learnt by adults as additional or second languages,
and their grammars and vocabularies show signs of simplification and
reduction in comparison with those of the target languages.

4.2   Case Study: *Gastarbeiterdeutsch*

In Germany, the term *Gastarbeiterdeutsch* (guest-worker German) is applied
to the simplified German of so-called 'guest workers' – migrant workers
mainly from the Mediterranean countries of Europe and North Africa. There
is disagreement among scholars as to whether *Gastarbeiterdeutsch* should
really be termed a pidgin. The doubts arise partly from the questionable
stability of *Gastarbeiterdeutsch*. Is it really a language with its own norms and
conventions, however rudimentary, or a 'continuum of interlanguages'
(Hinnenkamp, 1984, p. 153) – a collection of personal 'versions' of German
showing different degrees of success at second language learning? If it is the
latter, this can be explained by the fact that 'the foreign worker community
has not been totally cut off from the superstrate [i.e. German-speaking]
population, and thus exposure to the target language still prevails'
(Blackshire-Belay, 1993, p. 437; see this article also for an overview of
the debate). Whatever the answer, *Gastarbeiterdeutsch* shows many of the
features of pidgins, for example, grammatical simplification and vocabulary
reduction. Many of these cannot be explained simply by reference to
'interference' from the speaker's native language.

Here, for example, is what Klein, Perdue and others found concerning the
variety of German spoken by 'Vito', a Sicilian who at the time of the study
was aged about 31 and had lived in Germany for about eighteen months
(Klein and Perdue, 1993a, pp. 7–11). He was married to an Italian, worked
in the kitchen of an Italian restaurant, and had little contact with Germans.
Nevertheless, he was 'talkative, self-confident, lively and very interested in
questions of language'. Klein and Perdue's summary of Vito's linguistic
repertoire (based on a sample of 31 utterances) shows the following, which
might be of interest to those studying pidginisation:

Morphology: 'no inflectional morphology, hence no case marking, no agreement, no tense'.

Prepositions: 'There is only one frequent preposition, *in* (30 occurrences), which, just as the six or seven other ones he occasionally uses is strongly overgeneralised to denote all sorts of spatial relations.'

Quantifiers: 'They are very rare: *viel* 'many, much' (5 occurrences), *all* 'all' (3 occurrences), *zwei* 'two' (1 occurrence).'

Pronouns: The only third person pronoun used is *sie* (Standard German 'she') (28 occurrences) – mostly used to refer to a male. The only second person pronoun is *du* (3 occurrences), appropriate only with intimates and children (see also the text below).

Vocabulary: The authors warn that estimates of Vito's vocabulary may be misleading, because 'his active use is clearly determined by the nature of the task' (he was asked to re-tell the story of a shortened version of *Modern Times*, the film featuring Charlie Chaplin). For many words it was also difficult to decide on a part of speech category. Nevertheless, their findings are indicative. Vito has 60 different nouns, 40 different verbs 'some of them with a rather overgeneralised meaning', about a dozen adjectives, and a dozen or so adverbs.

In the above summary we can see a number of the features which characterise pidgins: lack of inflection, a small number of prepositions, a very limited vocabulary with (over-)generalisation of meaning to compensate and a preponderance of nouns over other parts of speech. Furthermore, from Klein and Perdue's description of the grammar of Vito's utterances, it is clear that there is considerable reduction and simplification of the grammar as well, in comparison with Standard German. On the other hand, as Blackshire-Belay points out, 'there is more inflectional morphology [in the speakers in her own study] than would normally be expected in a *true* pidgin' (emphasis in original). Below, we look at a short extract from an interview with a 'guest worker' which shows some of the kinds of grammatical simplification which characterise *Gastarbeiterdeutsch*.

Gastarbeiterdeutsch **text** (based on Klein and Dittmar, 1979, p. 110)

Interviewer (in Standard German): Sie waren krank, hat es da Probleme gegeben mit der Firma, wenn Sie krank gewesen sind? *You were sick, did that cause you any problems with the firm, when you were sick?*

Miguel (Spanish migrant worker):
Wann ich krank, Ingenieur mir sagen, 'meine Büro kommen, Arbeit?
When I sick, engineer to me say, 'my office to come, work?

Ich sag 'ah, ich krank, ich nicht kommen Arbeit.'
I say 'ah, I sick, I not to come work.'

– 'Warum? Wieviel Wochen du krank?'
– 'Why? How many weeks you sick?'

Ich sag 'ah, ich weiss nichts, ich nicht Doctor.'
I say, 'ah, I know nothing, I not doctor.'

Und dann Ingenieur sagen 'nächste Monat nicht kommen Arbeit,
And then engineer say, 'next month not to come work

du fort Spanisch auch'
you away Spanish [Spain] too'

– 'Warum? Das Monat bezahle, warum ich fort?'
– 'Why? The [whole] month pay, why I away?'

Note: Klein and Dittmar use phonetic notation for Miguel's speech. I have re-transcribed it into Standard German orthography for ease of reading by readers who may know German. The English gloss is a literal translation but does not show up some of the unusual features of Miguel's language, for example the use of *du* (familiar form of you, normally used with close friends and family, or children) where only the formal *Sie* would be appropriate in Standard German, and the use of the infinitive forms *kommen* 'to come' and *sagen* 'to say' when a present-tense form (*komme*, *sage*) is required.

Studies like those on *Gastarbeiterdeutsch* and others have indicated that untutored second language learners, at least in their early stages, produce language which shares quite a lot of similarities with pidgins. Some learners, furthermore, 'stabilise' or 'fossilise' at this stage, and do not progress any further in the direction of the target language which they are trying to learn. Schumann, whose study is described and critiqued by Cook (1993, p. 75), goes so far as to say 'that pidginization may characterize all early second language acquisition and that under conditions of social and psychological distance it persists' (Schumann, 1978, p. 110). This means that while all second language learners produce 'pidgin-like' utterances at first, *restricted access* to the target language (through social factors) and/or *rejection* of the target language (as a result of a negative attitude towards its speakers) may lead learners to 'fossilise' at that stage.

Just these psychological and social factors might be expected in the type of situation where pidgins typically come into being. Where Europeans or other colonising groups have come into contact with indigenous peoples, the latter have been expected to learn to communicate with the colonisers – who would not stoop to learn their language properly – but have been forced to do so without formal teaching and often with very limited access to native speakers of the language. Social distance was inherent in such a situation. Moreover, each side often had a negative attitude towards the other: there was thus little desire to learn to speak the other group's language 'properly'. An active desire for social and linguistic distance, for example, seems to have been one of the conditions which gave rise to Chinese Pidgin English (see Chapter 2).

5 PIDGINISATION AS SECOND LANGUAGE MODELLING

Another way to view pidginisation is as a process of second language *modelling*. Here, we take the viewpoint of the learner of the pidgin who is trying to identify and learn a particular *target* language – the lexifier. The theory of pidginisation most frequently advocated in this connection is that of *foreigner talk* or simplified input, where learners (consciously or unconsciously) learn a simplified version of the target language.

5.1 Pidginisation as Interaction

Whatever else it may be, pidginisation must surely be an interactive process, involving communicative efforts on the part of several parties, and on many occasions. To treat it purely as a process of second language *learning*, then, seems to be to treat the speakers of the target language as involved only passively in the process, and this is surely a mistake. Pointing out how 'pidginisers' at the outset of contact seem to select words which are similar in form in two or more of the languages involved, such as Russian *po* and Norwegian *på,* which give Russenorsk its all-purpose preposition *po,* James A. Fox (1983, p. 101) goes on:

> These sorts of matching, and the early accounts in general, seem to indicate that the interlocutors in initial contact situations are consciously involved in arduous negotiation and 'implicit teaching'.... In fact, it is

often clear from dialogues that the speakers are consciously (not just implicitly) teaching, as in this line from a dialogue recorded by a Russian (Broch, 1930, p. 134): *Burmann zakrepiko trosa lita gran nemnosko* 'Fisherman make fast hawser little bit a little', to which is added:

> The Norwegian does not understand the word *zakrepitj* 'make fast' but the Russian, while uttering the sentence, gives him the end of the hawser and shows him what to do.

If we accept that all parties to the process of pidginisation are likely to be 'teachers' as well as learners, a new question now arises: what exactly is the target language which is being modelled for the learners? In other words, what is it that they are being offered as a goal? Up to this point we have assumed that the target was more or less *Standard* English, *Standard* German, and so on; but there is evidence to suggest that in contexts where pidginisation takes place, the target language itself (or target languages themselves) may be represented by a simplified and reduced variety. We examine this possibility in 5.2.

5.2 Foreigner Talk

If I go to a French language class with a view to becoming a fluent speaker and writer of French, I assume as a matter of course that my teacher will take care to speak to me in what he or she regards as 'best French', correcting any errors which I might make in my responses. On the other hand, if I approach a passer-by in a French street and haltingly, in ungrammatical French, ask them for directions, they may decide that the most helpful thing they can do for me is to reply not in 'best French' but in a simplified version which reduces to a minimum the potential for mis-understanding.

According to Charles Ferguson (1971, p. 143):

> ... many, perhaps all speech communities have registers of a special kind for use with people who are regarded for one reason or another as unable to readily understand the normal speech of the community (e.g. babies, foreigners, deaf people). These forms of speech are generally felt by their users to be simplified versions of the language, hence easier to understand and they are often regarded as an imitation of the way the person addressed uses the language himself.... [S]uch registers are, of course, culturally transmitted like any other part of the language and may be quite systematic and resistant to change.

Such a 'simplified register' of a language which is used for communication with 'foreigners' (i.e. non-speakers of the language) is called *foreigner talk*.

'Foreigner talk' (FT) is thus a term for a special style in which native speakers talk to foreigners, not the other way round.

Foreigner talk shares a number of features with pidgins. It is grammatically simplified, has a limited vocabulary and is used in a restricted range of interactions or encounters – normally only those where communication is essential, and no alternative language or interpreter is available. In a comparsion of German FT (used by Germans speaking to 'guest workers') and Turkish FT (used by Turks speaking to foreigners), Hinnenkamp (1984, p. 157) found the following ten 'most typical instances of simplification':

1. Loss of pre- and postpositions
2. Loss of nominal inflection and agreement
3. Deletion of the copula
4. Generalisation of the infinitive
5. Change in word order
6. Loss of overt question marking
7. External placement of propositional qualifiers
8. Juxtaposition in place of subordination [i.e. using conjoined phrases in place of one phrase embedded in another]
9. Lexical and grammatical multifunctionality
10. Periphrasis [circumlocution]

All of these are typical of pidgins as well.

If we look at some examples of German foreigner talk, we can see some similarities with the German of the *Gastarbeiter*.

German Foreigner Talk (Hinnenkamp, 1982)

(The following utterances represent the speech of Germans to foreign 'guest workers', recorded by Hinnenkamp. These examples are selected more or less randomly to show typical features of German FT. The numbers are Hinnenkamp's.)

(62) **Alle in Betrieb wählen, können so wählen, mit äh, Zettel schreiben, wer soll uns vertreten?**
All in company vote, can vote so, with er, write note, who will represent us?

(71) **Türkisch Mann, du?**
Turkish man, you?
(Standard German: Sind Sie Türke? *Are you a Turk?*)

(116) **Wenn Uni sagt: hier Deine Flugticket, dann alles klar.**
       If Uni says: here your flight ticket, then everything
       ready.

(138) **Wievel Leute, wieviel Kollegen bei Beyer, wieviel?**
       How many people, how many colleagues at Beyer, how
       many?

In a situation of language contact where there is pressure to communicate, perhaps aggravated by social distance between speakers from different groups, we may conjecture that foreigner talk may be used to a significant extent by some or all parties. It may even provide the main, or perhaps the only *model* for speakers trying to learn each other's languages, or a particular target language. If this is so, the kind of simplification we find among second language learners in such situations (for example, the 'guest workers' in 3.1) may be due as much to a simplified model (i.e. simplified *input* in language-acquisition terms) as to simplification by the learner in the course of learning the target language.

5.3   Case Study: English Foreigner Talk

The following are transcripts of actual encounters between native speakers of English and others with a minimal knowledge of English. The researcher, Edith Harding, accompanied Health Visitors on their rounds visiting the mothers of young babies and recorded the conversations between the Health Visitor (H.V.) and the mothers, who were mostly Urdu or Bengali speakers.

Key: capital letters: very loud ('very high amplitude')
         lower case: normal loudness
         / rising pitch
         \ falling pitch
         . (dot) pause

(1)
H.V.   ME SEND . TEACHER
M.   all right
H.V.   TEACH ENGLISH
M.   yea
H.V.   (*to the researcher*) y'see if they will accept. i
       think. y'know it is important –
       (*to the mother*) COME . HERE . TEACH YOU . ENGLISH
M.   all right

(2)
H.V.   HUSBAND . WORK /
M.   yes
H.V.   FACTORY/
M.   factory yes
H.V.   ALL DAY/
M.   yes all day so
H.V.   SO YOU . ON YOUR OWN\
M.   yes

(3)
H.V.   HOW . MANY . OUNCES/
M.   (*pause of 1.5 seconds*)
H.V.   BOTTLE/ . FULL/
M.   all right
H.V.   IK IK OUNCE/ (*counting on fingers*)
          (*IK = H.V.'s version of Urdu for* one)
M.   (*1 second pause*) full bottle
H.V.   FULL BOTTLE\
M.   bottle
H.V.   TCHOP . TCHOP OUNCE\
          (*TCHOP = H.V.'s version of Urdu for* four)
M.   yes
H.V.   yea

(*Source*: Harding, 1984, pp. 142–7)

5.4   Exercise

Study the Health Visitor's utterances in the above data collected by Edith Harding. What do you observe about the following:

- Length of utterances, as measured in words. What is the longest utterance of the Health Visitor? What is the average utterance length?
- Loudness and intonation. Which words are loudest, what intonation patterns are marked as important?
- Which word classes are present, and which are absent? Which class of words is commonest?
- What kind of vocabulary is present?

5.5   Notes

From these extracts, several characteristics of the Health Visitor's foreigner talk can be identified:

- Very short utterances; the conversational turns of both the Health Visitor and the mother tend to be only two or three words long.

- Key words are spoken loudly and with exaggerated intonation.
- Sentences consist mainly of pronouns, nouns and verbs: there are very few other parts of speech – no prepositions, for example.
- Vocabulary is very limited and there are few references to things outside the immediate context.

Foreigner talk provides one possible source of the simplified and reduced grammar which characterises pidgins. But this begs the question: how do we know how to 'do' foreigner talk? Since it seems that speakers of many, perhaps all, languages know intuitively how to produce foreigner talk when confronted with a 'foreigner', we now have to explain this intuitive ability to simplify our language.

5.6   Foreigner Talk in Pidgin Genesis

The 'foreigner talk' theory of pidgin genesis has its origins in an earlier theory, often called the 'baby talk' theory. Schuchardt, one of the first linguists to take an interest in pidgins and creoles, regarded the simplification found in contact languages as resulting from a simplification of the model presented by Europeans to indigenous peoples: 'The White was Teacher to the Black' (1979, p. 74). The notion that Europeans simplified their language in talking to their colonial subjects was publicised by Bloomfield, an eminent linguist (but not a pidgin or creole specialist), in his book *Language* (1933, p. 472):

> Speakers of a lower language may make so little progress in learning the dominant speech, that the masters, in communicating with them resort to 'baby-talk'. This 'baby-talk' is the master's imitation of the subjects' incorrect speech.... The subject, in turn, deprived of the correct model, can do no better now than to acquire the simplified 'baby-talk' version of the upper language.

Ferguson (1971) took up the idea of 'baby-talk' (in this case meaning simplified speech directed *at* babies, not the speech *of* babies) and compared it with foreigner talk (analogously, talk directed at foreigners) and pidginisation. Noting some of the features which we have already seen characterising FT and pidgins, he suggests (1971, p. 147):

> the foreigner talk of a speech community may serve as an incipient pidgin. This view asserts that the initial source of the grammatical structure of a pidgin is the more or less systematic simplification of the lexical source language which occurs in the foreigner talk register of its speakers, rather than the grammatical structure of the language(s) of the other users of the pidgin.

One issue which arises for proponents of the 'foreigner talk' theory is the question of whether the speakers whom Ferguson calls 'the other users of the pidgin' are aware that the model they are being offered is a simplified version of the lexifier, or believe that they are hearing, and learning, the 'normal' conversational variety of their target language.

Certainly, a 'foreigner' may be unaware that what he or she is hearing is foreigner talk, mistaking it for the 'ordinary' language. If, after studying French for six months with a teacher, I visit France and ask haltingly for directions, there is a good chance that if the reply is in FT, I will recognise it as such. If, however, I had no conception of what French was like in the first place, I would have no way of knowing that what I was hearing was foreigner talk French and might innocently assume that what I had heard was the way French people speak to each other.

Encounters with completely new languages must have been relatively common events during the era of colonialism. In particular, there must have been many cases where Europeans met indigenous people, with neither side having any idea what the other's language was really like. In their efforts to communicate, each side may have used their own 'foreigner talk' register to the other. Hence each side would go away from the encounter with a false view of what the other's language was like; but at the same time, they would have a practical grasp of some important vocabulary and some idea about word order and sentence structure which would serve them well in the next communicative encounter.

It seems that the belief that each side is speaking the other's language, when in fact both are speaking some kind of foreigner talk or jargon, may play a role in the early development and transmission of pidgins. Silverstein (1972) calls this a 'double illusion' which ultimately is what makes communication possible. From a commentator on the early expansion of Europeans into the interior of Australia, for example, we learn that an early pidgin was spread by

> the stockmen and sawyers [who supposed it] to be the language of the natives, whilst they suppose[d] it to be ours, and which [was] the ordinary medium of communication between the squatters and the tame black-fellow.　　　　　(Hodgkinson, 1845; quoted by Sandefur, 1979, p. 3)

The same kind of observation (reported by Silverstein, 1972, p. 14, and quoted by Romaine) was made by Father Paul de Jeune, a French Jesuit living in Quebec, in 1633:

> I have noticed in the study of their language that there is a particular jargon between the French and the Indians, which is neither French nor Indian, and nevertheless when the French use it, they think they are speaking Indian, and the Indians in taking it up think they are speaking good French.

The arrogance and ignorance of many European colonisers would only be reinforced by the impression that the 'natives'' language was very simple and limited. Here, for example, is an account by Eric Muspratt (1931) of one of the local Polynesian languages spoken in the Solomon Islands:

> 'The language was limited to a couple of hundred, mostly simple, words, although some were complicated enough, such as *manumanagausuhu* which means swamp duck and is a variation of *manu* or bird. . . . There is no grammar, so that speech is so simple that should anyone make a mistake it would be laughed at for weeks and weeks afterwards. Thus the verbs have no conjugations and there is no person, number, gender, case, also pronouns or adverbs are absent. A gloriously simple language relating to a simple world of primarily natural things. . . .

One observer who was apparently *not* fooled was the Rev. Calloway, living among the Zulus. According to Mesthrie (1989, p. 231), Calloway experienced difficulty in getting his informants to speak 'real' Zulu to him (Calloway, 1868, p. i):

> In common conversation the native naturally condescends to the ignorance of the foreigner, whom, judging from what he hears from the colonists, he thinks unable to speak the language of Zulu: he is also pleased to parade his own little knowledge of broken English and Dutch; and thus there is a danger of picking up a miserable gibberish, composed of anglicised Kafir and kafirised English and Dutch words, thrown together without any rule but the caprice and ignorance of the speaker.

From what has been said above, it seems that foreigner talk is potentially present in contexts where pidginisation takes place. However, this does not mean that pidginisation results directly from FT. Mühlhäusler, from a study of the role of English FT in the formation of Tok Pisin, concludes that 'the importance of foreigner talk is restricted to the very early stages of pidgin formation, but of little relevance for later development' (1986, p. 105). According to one researcher, Hinnenkamp, FT is too inconsistent and occurs too unpredictably (only a quarter of Hinnenkamp's German sample *ever* used simplified FT, and those who did used it inconsistently) to provide a model for second language learning. He concludes that (1984, p. 161)

> inconsistency and high variability of FT use does not allow for model simplification to play a decisive role as an input source for the target language learner. . . . Simplifications do of course occur. [But] although the ability of a native speaker to simplfy her or his native language is an indisputable fact, model simplification as such is not a *sufficient* condition for the inception of pidginization.

On the other hand, Hinnenkamp's observations in a Turkish village (see above) suggest that through an interactive process, with Turkish speakers using a conventionalised Turkish foreigner talk (*Tarzanca* or 'Tarzan Talk') on the one hand, and German speakers using simplified or 'broken' Turkish on the other, a true 'tourist pidgin' may be emerging (Hinnenkamp, 1982; 1984).

A crucial factor here may be the *conventionalisation* of the FT register, recalling Ferguson's suggestion (from 5.2 above) that the FT register may be 'culturally transmitted like any other part of the language and may be quite systematic and resistant to change'. If there is a 'tradition' of using FT with foreigners, so that FT itself has accepted conventions – which seems to be the case with the Turkish *Tarzanca* – then it may be the case that it is used consistently enough for foreign learners to treat it as a model. The issue of just what the learners think they are learning can be treated separately. As we have seen, there are situations where considerations of social distance make learners unwilling to learn the 'proper' version of the target language anyway.

Taking into account both the historical evidence that foreigner talk has been present in contexts where pidginisation has taken place, and Hinnenkamp's observation that conventionalised FT has its place in an interactive process of pidgin creation, we can conclude that FT is likely to be involved in pidgin genesis, at least in some contexts. However, as Hinnenkamp points out, this is not a *sufficient* condition for a pidgin to come into being; and at the moment, there is not enough evidence to suggest that it is a *necessary* condition either.

6 SUBSTRATE: THE ROLE OF SPEAKERS' NATIVE LANGUAGES

6.1 Transfer in Second Language Learning

Research into second language acquisition (SLA) suggests that the role played by 'interference' or 'transfer' from the learner's first language may account for only a small proportion of the 'errors' (here, meaning deviations from the target language grammar) made by learners. Current SLA theory emphasises the importance of the learner's own 'interlanguage', a system which is different from both the learner's native language and the target language. This would suggest that first-language transfer might be relatively unimportant in the pidginisation process.

This seems to be the conclusion of Klein and Perdue, summarising the findings of their large collaborative project, which studied learners of different linguistic backgrounds learning several different Western European languages:

...apart obviously from the word-stock, development to a 'basic variety' proved to be remarkably impermeable to the specifics of SL [source language – the speaker's native language] and TL [target language].... Further development takes the learner varieties towards the specificities of the TLs, but overall, the structure of the process shows strong similarities cross-linguistically; what differs more is the *rate* and ultimate *success* of the process.   (Klein and Perdue, 1993b, p. 257)

And again:

The general conclusion is that: *SL influence affects the rate and success of the process, but tends not to affect the sequence/order.*

(ibid., p. 262; italics in original)

In spite of this, there is plenty of evidence that speakers' native languages *do* have an effect on the emerging pidgin. In respect of the lexicon, this is obviously true – most of the vocabulary of any pidgin is drawn from the native languages of the speakers involved in the initial contact (though these are not necessarily the same groups who use the pidgin later on). Although typically one language, the lexifier, contributes a high proportion of the vocabulary, other languages are always represented in the word-stock.

6.2   Lexical Patterns: Calques

However, substrate influence may amount to more than simply the presence of certain words of substrate origin: it may take the form of word *patterns* which occur in the substrate languages, and are translated literally into the pidgin or creole – relexified, in other words. Such relexified patterns are termed *calques*. Nigerian Pidgin English provides several examples of **calques** (described by Elugbe and Omamor, 1991, p. 159, as 'translations of West African concepts'), for example:

domot   'door mouth', i.e. 'doorway'
switmaut   'sweet mouth', i.e. 'flattery, greed'
strong hed   'strong head', i.e. 'stubbornness'

Also (from Barbag-Stoll, 1983, p. 77):

gudbele   'good belly', i.e. 'kindhearted'
longatrot   'long throat', i.e. 'greed'
openai   'open eye', i.e. 'aggressive'

Some of these calques are also found in Caribbean creoles, which, through slavery, have a connection with languages of West Africa. For example, Sranan Tongo (see Chapter 5 and Sebba, 1981, note 3) has:

bigi-ay 'big-eye', i.e. 'greedy'
bun-ati 'good-heart', i.e. 'generosity'
bun-ede 'good-head', i.e. 'luck'

6.3 Grammatical Influences

Where the grammar is concerned, pidgins typically show features which coincide with one or more of the languages involved in the initial contact. Fanakalo, for example, resembles either English or Zulu in various respects where the grammar of the two differs:

Resemblances to English:

Articles: the Fanakalo word *lo* (of Zulu origin) is used as a definite article (though not always in the same way as in English), although Zulu does not have any definite or indefinite article. Examples: *lo skafu*, 'the food'; *lo msebenzi*, 'the work'.

Morphological type: as noted in Chapter 2, Fanakalo has much more isolating morphology than Zulu. In this respect it is much more similar to English.

Word order: quantifiers (including numerals) and adjectives, which in Zulu always follow the noun they modify, *precede* the modified noun in Fanakalo:

mathathu skati   'three times' (Zulu *izikhathi izithathu*)
lo nyuwan muti   'the new medicine' (Zulu *umuthi omusha*)
zonke pikanin mti 'all the small trees' (Zulu *imithi emincane yonke*)

Resemblances to Zulu:

Plurals: plurals are formed using a prefix in Fanakalo, as they are in Zulu (though Zulu has a much more complex set of prefixes).

Possessives: possessives are formed by adding the prefix *ga-* to the possessed. This applies also to the personal pronouns, hence *lo hashi gamina*, 'my horse', *motokali gayena*, 'his car'. Zulu similarly uses prefixes for this purpose, though it has far more of them.

6.4   Exercise

In the exercise in Chapter 2, Section 9.6, you were asked to find a Fanakalo
example of, or counter-example to, each of the features listed as 'general
features of pidgin grammars' in Section 2.2. In the light of the discussion in
6.3 above, go through your list again, and decide which of these features of
Fanakalo could be the result of influence from English, which could result
from Zulu influence, and which appear to result from neither.

6.5   Substrate and Lexifier

Although if we look at the lexicon of Fanakalo it is overwhelmingly Zulu, if
we look at the grammar – including aspects like word order and
morphological type – there are far more resemblances to English than to
Zulu (see Mesthrie, 1989, p. 213). This brings us again to an observation
often made in the course of pidgin and creole studies: namely, that contact
languages frequently draw their vocabulary mainly from one source (the
lexifier language) and their grammar from another language, or several
related languages (the substrate). In the case of Fanakalo, Zulu must be
regarded as the lexifier, and English (and/or Afrikaans, the other European
language of the frontier contact) as the substrate (Mesthrie, 1989, p. 231). In
this case, as in many others, it is difficult to say to what extent the
similarities between the pidgin grammar and the substrate grammar derive
from the grammar of the substrate itself, and to what extent they are present
in the pidgin as a result of simplification of the lexifier on the basis of
'universal' principles of simplification which could be applied to any
language. For example, though Fanakalo has a strong preference for
isolating morphology – making it look like English – this could just be
because *all* pidgins have a preference for isolating morphology, because that
is the simplest kind and most accessible to learners trying to learn a language
in less-than-ideal conditions.

We are on stronger ground if we can find features or constructions in a
pidgin (or a creole) which are also found in one of the source languages but
which are not likely to be in the pidgin on grounds of simplicity. The
Fanakalo preference for placing adjectives and enumerators before the noun
they modify, for example, is unlikely to be the result of a process of
simplification of Zulu, as Zulu has the opposite order; nor is it simpler
per se, because in languages around the world which typologically are
similar to Fanakalo, there is no particular preference for one order or the
other. The conclusion seems to be that Fanakalo in this respect has followed
the word order of English (and Afrikaans).

We can reach a similar conclusion – that substrate influences are
responsible – if we consider the pronoun system of Tok Pisin. We saw in
Chapter 2 that there were separate forms, *mipela* and *yumipela*, representing

exclusive 'we' (where the addressee is not included) and inclusive 'we' (including the addressee) respectively. We noted then that this distinction is found in most of the languages of the Pacific region and this is probably why it is found in Tok Pisin. The justification for this explanation is that while the distinction *is* found in most of the substrate languages of Tok Pisin, it is *not* found in English (the lexifier) and there is no reason to suppose that its presence represents a simplification of the grammar in any way.

The extent of substrate influence is very much a live question in scholarly discussion of pidgins, but even more so for creoles. We shall therefore be discussing it in more detail in Chapter 6. In the next section we move on to another live issue, the question of the role of *universals* in the genesis of pidgins and creoles.

7 THE ROLE OF UNIVERSALS IN PIDGIN GENESIS

We have noted a number of times already that pidgins (and as we shall see later, creoles) tend to share a number of specific characteristics with respect to their syntax, morphology, phonology and semantics. We have also seen in this section that quite similar outcomes can result from 'natural' second language learning (without heavy intervention from tutors), and from speakers' 'intuitive' attempts to make their speech intelligible to foreigners. Thus Hinnenkamp (1984, p. 160) notes that:

> languages that are structurally quite different may be simplified in very similar ways, yielding nearly identical surface structures. . . . Every language has its way of arriving at this kind of surface structure.

What all this points to is the possibility of the existence of *universal* principles which are at work in the pidginisation process. By definition, these would be part of the innate tacit knowledge of all humans (or at least, all those who have successfully acquired a first language). This is how it is put by Todd (1990, p. 40):

> The similarities in all pidgins from the past as well as the present, and from all continents, may well be accounted for if we can show that human beings are biologically programmed to acquire *Language* rather than any particular language, and that the programming includes an innate ability to dredge our linguistic behaviour of superficial redundancies where there is a premium on transmitting facts, on communicating, as it were, without frills. It is not being suggested that we are consciously aware of *how* we adjust our language behaviour. But the fact that we do adjust and the fact

that people of different linguistic backgrounds adjust their language behaviour in similar ways, suggests that the behaviour is rule-governed and may be the result of linguistic universals.

Hypothetically, universal principles might take different forms, which would affect the process of pidginisation in different ways:

- They could take the form of constraints on what it is possible for an adult to learn, or at least provide a scale of learnability on which some types of structure or vocabulary would be too difficult to learn under given circumstances. Pidgins would thus be limited to containing structures which lay below this threshold. The absence of complex sentences (e.g. relative clauses) or words of more than two syllables in rudimentary pidgins, for example, could be accounted for by saying that these structures are, or are thought to be, too difficult to learn (see Chapters 2 and 4 for examples).

- They could take the form of constraints on the permissible relationships between form and meaning. Principles like *semantic transparency* (Chapter 2) would determine the limits of what is possible in a pidgin.

- They could take the form of strategies for simplifying language in interaction with other speakers in order to achieve maximum communicative efficiency – resulting in 'reduced registers' such as foreigner talk, on the one hand, and simplified 'learners' interlanguage' like *Gastarbeiterdeutsch* on the other.

The notion of 'universals' of human grammar is central to much current linguistic thought, which views the possible types and structures of language as fairly tightly constrained by a set of universal principles, with individual languages differing structurally only in terms of their specification of certain parameters from a universally-available set. The human child is born with innate knowledge of the principles and possible parameters ('Universal Grammar') but will choose the parameter *settings* on the basis of input from speakers of the language s/he is acquiring. Non-pidgin languages mostly have complexity at some level of their grammar, but pidgins might choose the simplest, or minimal, specification of each of these parameters, making pidgins the 'default case' of human grammar. One argument against this is that pidgins are 'created' by adults, who may not have access to 'Universal Grammar' (see Cook, 1993, p. 214), and who do not necessarily use the same learning strategies as children acquiring a first language. In spite of this, adults may have an intuitive idea of what is 'simple'. In Chapter 6, we will discuss the implications of similar arguments with respect to *creoles*.

It is important to be clear about what counts as 'universal' in this context. While pidgins and creoles show remarkable similarities to each other in spite of having different input languages and being widely separated in time and space, it is very difficult to find a single feature which occurs in *all* pidgins without exception. This should not invalidate a 'universals' approach to pidgin origins, however, since we are not always comparing like with like. As we shall see in the next chapter, pidgins go through stages of development, and universals may be much more relevant at some stages than at others: specifically, in the early stages universal communicative strategies may predominate, while later on, the pidgin will begin to develop its own resources in the same way as other languages, and there may be more influence from other languages which are in contact with the pidgin. This applies equally to creoles.

8 CONCLUSION

In spite of all the academic interest focussed on the topic, the way pidgins come into being remains uncertain, for a simple reason: we have no first-hand observer accounts of the phenomenon from trained linguists. The nearest thing we have is excellent contemporary observations on the development of Tok Pisin, a kind of 'linguistic laboratory', from linguists like Peter Mühlhäusler, Suzanne Romaine, Gillian Sankoff and others, together with Mühlhäusler's painstaking historical work based on written records. But unfortunately, it is too late to observe the moment of emergence of this pidgin. It is already well established, and in the process of becoming a creole (also under careful observation from a battery of linguists!). The title of Hinnenkamp's paper 'Eye-witnessing pidginization?' suggests that perhaps in German industrial settings, or in the interactions between tourists and Turkish villagers, we might be able to do just that: yet no-one, unfortunately, has actually succeeded in taking a 'snapshot' of a pidgin being formed.

Even if some linguists were privileged to be eye-witnesses to the formation of a pidgin, there would still be room for debate about the correct explanation for what they were observing. Almost certainly, all the hypotheses outlined in this chapter have something to contribute to that explanation (even the monogenetic theory, though it has nothing to say about pidgins unconnected with the European trade routes, has the concept of relexification to offer). While substrate influences are undoubtedly relevant in some cases, universals seem to be at work in others. Even if conventionalised foreigner talk is not involved in all cases of pidgin formation, it seems to involve principles of simplification which probably play a role in any interactive situation where the parties have to make themselves understood to each other in the absence of a common language.

In this chapter we have focussed on the likely components of a situation where a pidgin first comes into being. However, it is very important to remember that pidginisation is actually a process which takes place over time, and is followed by the structural and functional development of the pidgin over a longer period. We have to take an interest not just in the moment of formation of a pidgin, but in its whole history. This developmental perspective on pidgins will be the focus of the next chapter.

KEY POINTS: Pidgin Origins

Theories about pidgin origins

Monogenesis: all pidgins have a common origin. *Relexification* accounts for the lexical differences.

Polygenesis: pidgins and creoles arose independently. Similarities can be explained by:
- Universalist approach: universal tendencies of simplification/innate properties of language.
- Substrate approach: similarities due to influences of structurally similar substrate languages.

Language learning in Pidginisation

- Pidginisation as second language *learning*: simplification is the result of imperfect or incomplete learning of target language.
- Pidginisation as second language *modelling*: simplification is the result of learners being given a simplified/reduced model, i.e. *foreigner talk*.

4 From Pidgin to Creole: Stages of Development

1 THE PIDGIN DILEMMA: SIMPLICITY VERSUS EXPRESSIVENESS

For any language which is a native language for someone, there is an enormous range of potential functions which that language can fulfil. From a private and involuntary curse uttered on hitting one's thumb instead of a nail with a hammer, to a carefully crafted poem or song, to a lively argument about sport or politics, there is hardly any limit to what people can do with a language which they speak natively.

At the same time, much can be done with little or no language. Where the context makes the intention clear, a minimum of words or even no words at all will suffice to convey a message. This is especially true of activities like trade or barter, where the items involved may be spread out for both parties to see, and reference to abstract concepts is unnecessary. Where groups who have no common language come together for short-term encounters like this, a 'minimal language' may develop and be used by both parties to facilitate interaction. There are two somewhat conflicting requirements of such a communication system. On the one hand, *it must be adequate to the function* it is needed to perform, even though it may be unsuitable for other kinds of interaction which require more linguistic complexity. At the same time, *it must not make excessive demands on the language learning capabilities* of those who have to learn to speak it.

Research into language acquisition – both of the first and subsequent languages – shows clearly that the ability to learn a language natively is lost progressively from the age of about six onwards. By the arrival of adolescence, the child's inborn and instinctive capability to learn a language natively has seriously diminished. This is not to say that human beings cannot learn languages after the onset of adolescence: many of us do, with great success. However, after the crucial cut-off point – the so-called 'critical stage' – has been reached, it seems that it is very difficult for a learner to achieve 'native-like' command of a language. Learners of a second language rarely attain the same level of knowledge in the second language (L2) as in the first language (L1), and often become 'fossilised' at some stage and fail to progress any further. This does not happen with normal children learning a first language. It seems likely that in order to learn a second language, we employ a different set of strategies from those we use to learn a first language. It is this set of strategies which most pidgin speakers will use in learning a pidgin, and which in some sense pidgins must be 'designed' to

99

accommodate. Put another way, this means that the structure of pidgins must match *adult* language-learning strategies while the structure of non-pidgin languages meets the requirements of *child* language-learning strategies.

It may be useful at this stage to have a reminder of the key differences between (first) *language acquisition* and (second) *language learning* which were discussed in Chapter 2 (Section 8), in the form of a table (see Table 4.1).

To return to the 'somewhat conflicting requirements' of the 'minimal communication systems' mentioned above, we can now rephrase these as being, on the one hand, the need for as much *expressiveness* as possible to meet the demands of the situation, and on the other, the need for maximum *simplicity* to enable adults to learn to communicate as quickly and effortlessly as possible. 'Old' languages – meaning those which are not pidgins or creoles – usually sacrifice simplicity for expressiveness. They normally have large – expressive – vocabularies and often have complex grammars as well, allowing one meaning to be expressed in several alternative styles, from informal to poetic. Pidgins, by contrast, typically have simple grammars and small vocabularies.

At this stage we need to look again at the definition of 'pidgin'. To say that pidgins are languages without native speakers is not a sufficient definition in itself (and is also not quite true, as some pidgins do have native speakers). Not all languages which lack native speakers are pidgins – for example, there are made-up or 'artificial' languages such as Esperanto, which lack most of the identifying characteristics of pidgins. On the other hand, the term 'pidgin' covers a range of communicative systems which differ greatly in the range of functions they can serve. At one end of the range, we have *jargons* such as Russenorsk (Chapter 2), which can be used to discuss only the most limited topics. At the other, we have Tok Pisin, described in Chapter 1, which now serves as the medium of parliamentary debates and newspapers, as well as in everyday conversation between people who do not share a first language.

Table 4.1

language acquisition	language learning
first language (L1)	second or subsequent language (L2)
child learner	(usually) older learner
unconscious process	conscious process
no systematic teaching	may involve systematic teaching
progresses to completion	may stop before completion
learner unaware of target	learner conscious of target/model
learner unaware of complexity	learner aware of 'difficult' aspects
outcome: competence in L1	outcome: varies, often partial competence

What this means is that pidgins, like other communication systems, are dynamic, responding to the needs of the situation, or rather, to the needs of the speakers in that situation. As the complexity of social interaction increases, so the demands on the pidgin increase, and it will evolve into a linguistic system of greater complexity, with a greater range of functions. Sometimes the reverse will happen: a pidgin, brought into being to meet a particular set of communicative needs, may die out when there is no further need for it. The last two centuries have provided examples of both outcomes. Tok Pisin has evolved from a rudimentary maritime jargon, widely used across the South Pacific among sailors and traders, to become the national language of Papua New Guinea; Russenorsk, which similarly arose to meet the communicative needs of sailors and fishermen in the Arctic waters, died out after a few centuries without ever developing beyond the most basic stage. Chinese Pidgin English (Chapter 2) was widely used for some centuries but has also died out.

What has been said above indicates that there is a *developmental continuum* for pidgins; in other words, a pidgin can be seen as evolving through a number of stages in a regular order. Circumstances may cause the development to be stopped at a particular stage – as in the case of Russenorsk. However, some pidgins continue developing until they reach a stage where there is little difference in terms of functional range between the pidgin and a first language.

It was mentioned in Chapter 1 that a *creole* comes into being when children are born into a pidgin-speaking environment and acquire the pidgin as a first language. What we know about the history and origins of existing creoles suggests that this may happen at any stage in the development of a pidgin. In other words, having a fully-developed language ready for children to acquire natively is not a prerequisite for children being born! However, the form which the creole takes may depend on the stage which the pidgin has reached before undergoing creolisation, i.e. the process of becoming a creole. In Chapters 5 and 6 we shall look at a selection of different creoles and theories about how they came into being.

2 THE DEVELOPMENTAL CONTINUUM

2.1 A Model of Pidgin Development

We have seen that the term 'pidgin' actually covers a range of communication systems, some of which can fulfil the barest communicative needs, while others are the equal of much older languages. Pidgins, once they have come into being, do not remain static, but change in terms of both their structure and their functional capabilities, evolving to meet the needs

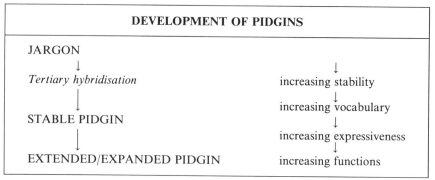

Figure 4.1

of their users. We need to distinguish, therefore, between the stages of pidgin *formation* and pidgin *development*.

For Mühlhäusler (1986, p. 54), this is an important distinction:

> The formative period of pidgins and creoles embraces their development up to the point where a socially accepted grammar emerges, that is, a grammar which is transmitted without significant restructuring, to a subsequent group of speakers. As a rule, formation occurs within a single generation of speakers. By development, I mean the subsequent history of the language over a number of generations.

The diagram in Figure 4.1 gives a schematic representation of the developmental continuum for pidgins and creoles. Under appropriate circumstances, a pidgin will evolve from the stage of a *jargon* into a *stable pidgin* usually via a process of **tertiary hybridisation**. Over time, a stable pidgin may become an **extended** (or **expanded**) pidgin. At any of these stages, *creolisation* of the pidgin may occur if the language acquires native speakers. (This is discussed in Chapter 5.)

In the rest of this section we will discuss the development of pidgins in terms of this model, looking briefly at each of the stages in turn.

2.2   The Jargon Stage

A jargon is linguistically the least structured stage of pidgin development; at the same time, it has the most limited range of functions and is used in the most restricted of social situations. Russenorsk is sometimes given as an example of a jargon; this is consistent with its restricted functions, its unstable vocabulary (with the word for a particular concept sometimes being drawn from Russian, sometimes from Norwegian) and somewhat inconsistent grammar. However, Romaine (1988, p. 124) argues that Russenorsk was a stable pidgin 'albeit . . . short-lived'.

Jargons are characterised by great instability in both grammar and vocabulary. Mühlhäusler (1986, p. 147) says:

> Jargons are unstable both linguistically and socially. Moreover, they are not transmitted in any consistent way from generation to generation, but invented in an ad-hoc fashion.

As is apparent from the dispute over the nature of Russenorsk, linguists do not agree completely on what constitues a jargon. The most important characteristic of a jargon, however, is definitely the lack of stable *norms* among its speakers concerning what is, and what is not, a word or phrase of the jargon. Thus a meaning may be conveyed very differently on different occasions, with varying proportions of the source languages used. Communication is the only important goal, and it does not really matter how this is achieved.

Jargons are typically the result of contact and communication between just *two* groups, each with their own language. To advance beyond this stage, it seems to be necessary for more groups and languages to become involved. We will consider this in the next section.

2.3 'Tertiary Hybridisation'

Keith Whinnom (1971) draws analogies between the development of languages and of living species by adopting the biological term *hybridisation*. *Primary* hybridisation in biology refers to the 'smooth' development of several different species from one ancestral species, comparable with the development of languages in the 'family tree model'. *Secondary* hybridisation, often just called hybridisation, in biological terms, means the interbreeding of distinct species to form a new one.

It might be thought that pidgins could be taken as linguistic examples of secondary hybridisation; after all, many of them appear to result from the 'interbreeding' of a European language with an indigenous one. However, this may be too simple. Mixed communication systems do, indeed, arise from contact between two languages; but according to Whinnom, in such cases one side is invariably trying to learn the other's language. The resulting 'mixture' will lack stability because as long as the target language is available as a model, the speakers of the other language will continue to learn it in its normal form: in fact what we will have will be a continuum of learners' interlanguages. Rather than a stable language with its own norms, we will find a range of different 'versions' of the target language, depending on the proficiency of the individual speakers. *Cocoliche*, spoken by Italian immigrants in Argentina, seems to have this character, and in Chapter 3 we discussed the characteristics of *Gastarbeiterdeutsch*, which suggest, again, that it represents attempts to learn German with varying degrees of success.

The key stage in the formation of a pidgin proper, according to Whinnom and others who have followed his lead, is *tertiary* hybridisation. This occurs when the pidgin comes to be used for communication between speakers who are *not* speakers of the original target language. What we now have is a language which is not native to any of its speakers, being used as a *lingua franca* by people who have no other language in common. It would also be necessary at this stage for the pidgin to have a degree of stability – in other words, for norms of vocabulary and grammar to have become relatively fixed – since the groups using the pidgin to communicate would no longer have access to the target language.

To summarise so far, the stages leading to the formation of a stable pidgin would be as follows:

Stage 1: Two groups, A and B, communicate by means of each other's languages. A tries to learn B's language, B tries to learn A's language. However, A and B may both be simplifying their language for the benefit of the other group, so that A may be modelling a *foreigner talk* version for B, and vice versa (see Chapter 3).

Stage 2: The norm for communication becomes a version of one of the languages, say language A. This is likely to be the language whose speakers dominate the interactions by virtue of greater power, for example the language of a coloniser. Group B continues to learn the language of Group A but does not have full access to it (and may only hear the foreigner talk register of it) so people in Group B never learn A's language fully, but learn a reduced version of it which is adequate for their interactions with Group A. This reduced (i.e. pidginised) version of Language A becomes the norm for inter-group communication between A and B.

Stage 3: Group B start to use their reduced version of Language A to communicate with members of Group C. B and C are now communicating by means of a pidgin form of A. Speakers of A are not involved and may no longer be present at all, so there will be no model for the 'native speaker' version of Language A and no pressure to learn it 'correctly'. A fairly stable form of 'Pidgin A' is the result.

Whinnom (1971, p. 105) illustrates the difference between secondary and tertiary hybridisation by suggesting that a 'French-based' pidgin (a pidgin where the original target language was French) could not arise 'in stable form' from attempts to communicate by an English and a French schoolboy. However, such a pidgin French might well develop between an English and a German schoolboy, if they had no other language in common. In the absence of a speaker of the target language (French), their main interest would be communication, not 'correctness', and they would be limited by their accented pronunciation and imperfect knowledge of grammar and vocabulary. Their version of 'French' – reduced in vocabulary, simplified in grammar, and lacking sounds which they found difficult to pronounce – might well be unintelligible to a French person.

The idea that pidgins only become 'proper' pidgins with stable norms of grammar, pronunciation and vocabulary when they are taken up by 'third parties' seems to be supported by the fact that the most successful pidgins of today – that is, those with the longest histories and spoken most widely – are also lingua francas used by speakers of large numbers of mutually unintelligible languages. By contrast, Russenorsk, whose speakers were nearly all either Russians or Norwegians, disappeared quickly when contact between the two groups of speakers ended. Cases like Russenorsk and Chinese Pidgin English show that it is certainly possible, though, for a pidgin to result from contact between only two languages (see Thomason and Kaufman, 1988, pp. 197–9, and Fox, 1983, pp. 105–6, for a critique of tertiary hybridisation based on Russenorsk).

2.4 The Stable Pidgin Stage

From an unstable jargon a *stable pidgin* with its own norms of grammar, pronunciation and lexicon may emerge. Linguists are not agreed on the nature of the process by which this happens: for some, like Whinnom, 'tertiary hybridisation', where the jargon begins to be used between groups who do not speak the original lexifier, is crucial if a more stable communication system is to develop. For others, it is just the emergence of established norms that counts. To the extent that Russenorsk and Butler English (see Section 8.1), for example, have their own norms distinct from their source languages, they could be described as 'pidgins' rather than jargons (cf. Romaine, 1988, p. 124, as noted above). Crucially, for a pidgin to stabilise it must develop its *own* norms of grammar, lexicon and pronunciation; *the speakers' target is now the pidgin, not the lexifier language.*

Mühlhäusler (1986, p. 176) regards the following as the 'truly salient, if not universal' features of the stabilisation stage:

1. the reduction of variability found in preceding jargon stages;
2. the establishment of relatively firm lexical and grammatical conventions;
3. the development of grammatical structures independent from possible source languages.

We have already seen many of the characteristics of stable pidgins, in our case studies of Tok Pisin, Fanakalo and Chinese Pidgin English (though the first two of these have actually gone beyond the stable pidgin stage and have become *expanded* pidgins).

2.5   The Extension or Expansion Stage

'Stable pidgins' do not emerge overnight, but in the course of a generation or so. However, once stable norms have begun to emerge, the process of development does not necessarily stop. What happens at this point largely depends on the uses to which the pidgin's speakers decide to put it, in other words, the *functions* which it is used to perform, and the *domains* (areas of life) in which it is used.

If the pidgin continues to be used in a narrow range of functions – for example, solely for the purpose of trading between people from different towns – it is unlikely to develop significantly once it has stabilised. In this case, it will be left with a reduced and limited vocabulary, and a grammar whose simplicity severely limits stylistic expression. Such a pidgin cannot move forward unless its users extend its functions into new domains. If this does not happen, it may nevertheless remain stable over a long period of time, perhaps centuries. Equally, however, its usefulness – which depends on the pidgin being needed for a very restricted purpose – may decline (for example, through changes in trading patterns) and it may die out.

An alternative scenario is possible: the pidgin may develop into an extended or expanded pidgin. This idea was first articulated by Todd (1990, p. 5):

> An extended pidgin is one which, although it may not become a mother tongue, proves vitally important in a multilingual area, and which, because of its usefulness, is extended and used beyond the original limited function which caused it to come into being.

Once a pidgin has entered the expansion stage, it is potentially on course to become a language, with the full referential range and expressive capabilities of any other language. As Mühlhäusler (1986, p. 204) puts it, 'the study of expanding pidgins suggests that the differences between first and second languages may be very tenuous'; in other words, fully expanded pidgins may function very much like first languages for many of their speakers, though whether they actually become first languages (through creolisation) will depend on historical circumstances.

At the same time, the expansion of the pidgin into new domains of use may result in the creation of new *genres* of communication in the pidgin. Whereas, at an earlier stage, it may have been used purely for spoken conversation between traders, it may now come into use, for example, in religious activities. This would result in the pidgin being used for a number of new types of spoken or written communication – scriptural translations, church newsletters, hymns and sermons, each with its own particular style.

Stylistic variation is an important characteristic of the expanded pidgin stage which sets it apart from the earlier stages of development. In recently-stabilised pidgins, norms provide a reference point for speakers, but variation within a fairly wide range is acceptable. This variation is likely to result from different native languages and other factors (including personal factors such as age or gender) but is not likely to have any stylistic meaning. Once the pidgin is on the road to expansion, however, already existing variations may be *reinterpreted* as belonging to a stylistic dimension (for example, as 'formal' vs 'informal' etc.)

2.6 Beyond Expansion: From Pidgin to Creole

By the time a pidgin has reached the expanded pidgin stage, it is only a short step away from becoming a creole, by becoming a native language for some or all of its speakers. 'Some or all of' here points to one of the complexities of this kind of contact situation. As a pidgin develops, it may become the *main* language of a stable community of speakers, none of whom speak it natively. This would typically happen where migration from rural areas to an urban centre brings together people from different language backgrounds. The pidgin – call it X – as the only common medium of communication, becomes the usual medium of everyday interaction in many domains – even within the family if the household contains people without a common first language.

At this stage X is still a pidgin for everyone. Quite soon, however, children may come along, and for them X will be a *first* language. Even if they learn another language as well as the pidgin from their carers, they will have only the pidgin in common with most of the other children in their community. These children are now first-generation *creole* speakers of X. At the same time, they are surrounded by adults who speak X, but not as a first language. In this rather complex situation, X is *both* a pidgin and a creole, but for different groups of speakers.

Tok Pisin is in exactly this situation. Following a long period of stability and expansion, during which time it acquired prestige as a language of social mobility, Tok Pisin started to become the main home language among families whose adults came from different linguistic backgrounds, especially in the urban areas. From the 1960s onwards, significant numbers of children began to acquire Tok Pisin as a native language (often in a multilingual setting where they acquired other languages natively as well). Mühlhäusler (1982, p. 441) estimated the number of native speakers at 90,000 while Wurm (1977) put the total number of speakers at one million.

Since Tok Pisin has so recently become a creole, it has been possible for linguists to observe some of the changes taking place. Linguists have been particularly interested in the question of whether the creolised, i.e. native, form of Tok Pisin is different in any observable way from its pidgin form. This will be discussed in Chapter 6.

The scenario above describes the process whereby a pidgin becomes *nativised* within a community, i.e. becomes a native language for that community. In so doing, it achieves the status of a language learnt natively by children (rather than as a second language by adults) and becomes a creole. However, many linguists would argue that **nativisation** of a pidgin is not the only route to creolehood. Rather, creolisation may occur at *any* of the stages, from jargon to expanded pidgin. This would be unlikely except under unusual or extreme social circumstances, as it would involve children learning, not their parents' language or languages, but an unexpanded pidgin. However, according to some researchers, the 'extreme social circumstances' of slavery produced just such an outcome. Some examples of this will be discussed in more detail in the next two chapters.

As a pidgin moves through the different development stages, so development takes place in each of its sub-systems: phonology, morphology, syntax and lexicon. The pace of development is not always the same in each sub-system, and of course each pidgin will develop somewhat differently, as a result of different local conditions. Nevertheless, the developmental picture is broadly the same for all pidgins – though of course some never get beyond the earlier stages. In the rest of this chapter, we shall look at the structural aspects of pidgin development, taking in turn each of the sub-systems of the language.

3   PHONOLOGICAL DEVELOPMENT

In the pre-stabilisation stage of a pidgin, there is a great deal of scope for native speakers of different languages to bring aspects of their own phonology into the language. Jargons are characterised by the lack of definite norms, with the result that different strategies may be used by different speakers, with successful communication being the ultimate justification. Substrate influence from the native languages of speakers is likely to be most significant in the jargon stage. This suggests that each speaker will pronounce words of the jargon in the way that comes most 'naturally', in other words according to the phonology of his or her language. However, this is not necessarily so, because speakers may make conscious efforts on the one hand to simplify their own pronunciation – along the lines of foreigner talk – or to approximate the pronunciation of speakers from another group. The extent to which this happens will vary from speaker to speaker. We can recall Bold's advice to English-speaking learners of Fanakalo, mentioned in Chapter 2, that they should try earnestly to learn to pronounce the click consonants, but if all attempts fail, 'you can at a pinch use the letter k instead' (1974, p. 7). This suggests the possibility, in any similar contact situation, of a wide range of 'styles', from minimal to almost complete adaptation.

Once stabilisation of the pidgin has begun, the effect of substrate languages diminishes, as the pidgin acquires its own phonological norms. According to Mühlhäusler, words consisting of a maximum of two syllables are the norm for stable pidgins, as are open syllables (those which end in a vowel). Chinese Pidgin English, with forms like *piecee* and *wifoo* from monosyllables *piece* and *wife*, and *cazion* from *occasion*, shows both tendencies – which, as it happens, are also present in Chinese.

In the *stable pidgin* stage, pronunciation and phonology are the least stable elements of the grammar, according to Mühlhäusler. We have seen that pidgins tend to reduce the number of sound contrasts (i.e. the number of phonemes required) in comparison with the source languages, tending to eliminate those contrasts that are rare or would present difficulties for the speakers of one or more of the languages in contact. The absence of tone in Fanakalo compared with Zulu is a good example of this.

As the pidgin moves into the *expansion* stage, Mühlhäusler (1986, p. 177) notes three main phonological tendencies: an *increase in phonological distinctions*; the *emergence of phonological rules*; and *the use of former 'free variants'* (i.e. variants without stylistic meaning) *for stylistic purposes.*

The first two of these affect the structure of the phonological system of the pidgin and can be seen as two sides of the same coin. On the one hand, new consonant distinctions may be introduced – for example, distinctions between [s] and [t], [f] and [p], and [l] and [r], which were not present in an earlier stage of the language. Likewise, Mühlhäusler shows that a number of pidgins have expanded their vowel systems from a system of only five contrasting vowels to a system with seven contrasts – an increase in the number of distinctions which a speaker must be able to make. Thus according to Mühlhäusler (1986, p. 178), West African Pidgin English (see case study below, Section 9), Torres Strait Broken (a pidgin/creole spoken by Aboriginal Australians) and Tok Pisin all seem to have started out with a five-vowel system as in (A) but, after some time, developed a seven-vowel system, (B):

(A)

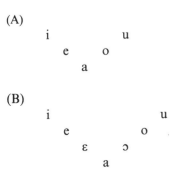

(B)

Speakers of these pidgins thus now had to be able to recognise, and make, distinctions between /e/ and /ɛ/, and /o/ and /ɔ/.

At the same time as new contrasts emerge, phonological rules may develop which reduce some forms. Consonant clusters may arise through the development of rules which allow the deletion of intervening vowels; thus Tok Pisin *sitiret*, 'straight', has recently returned to a pronunciation closer to its lexifier: *stret* (Mühlhäusler, 1986, p. 180). An increase in *speech tempo* which comes with the development and expansion of the pidgin also involves the reduction, in flowing speech, of 'full' forms, especially those with a grammatical function. Thus the Melanesian Pidgin suffix *-pela* [pɛla] (from English *fellow* and often so written in early accounts) may be reduced to [pəla] or [pla] in speech.

4   MORPHOLOGICAL DEVELOPMENT

We saw in Chapter 2 how pidgins favour isolating and analytic morphology and avoid synthetic morphology.

In stable pidgins derivational morphology typically exists, but is very limited. An example would be the affixation of the word for *man* or *woman* to another word, to produce a derived meaning. The use of this strategy in Tok Pisin was noted in Chapter 2, but it is commonly found in other pidgins. In fact, derivational morphology in stable pidgins is usually limited to forming compounds of two existing words. This helps to increase the size of the lexicon but maintains maximum semantic transparency, as the meaning of the word can be deduced from the meaning of its parts.

The expansion of a pidgin is perhaps most obvious at the morphological level. This affects both the grammar and the lexicon as well. Lexical expansion (discussed below) largely takes place through derivational morphology – underdeveloped at the stable pidgin stage, but increasingly significant as the pidgin expands.

Inflectional morphology also tends to become more important in a pidgin as it expands, although as far as we can tell, it never becomes as complex as in the lexifier or substrate languages. Tok Pisin, for example, has several inflectional morphemes:

- The suffix *-im*, which marks a transitive verb, as in *mi katim kopra*, 'I cut copra', in contrast with *mi kat*, 'I cut'. This has its origin in the English object pronoun *him*.

- The prefix *i-*, which is attached to verbs with third person subjects, e.g. *ol masta i-kik*, 'the white men were kicking'. This seems to have originated from English *he*.

- The suffix *-pela*, which attaches to adjectives used attributively (i.e. before the noun they modify), e.g. *bikpela haus*, 'big house', in contrast with *haus i-bik*, 'the house is big'. Historical records show that the origin of this suffix is the English word *fellow*. Inflectional endings on attributive adjectives are a feature of many languages, though not of modern English. German makes a distinction similar to Tok Pisin: *ein grosses* Haus, 'a big house' vs *das Haus ist gross*, 'the house is big'. However, the Tok Pisin suffix is invariant (i.e. has just one form) while German *gross* may require the ending *-er*, *-es*, *-e*, or *-en*.

5 SYNTACTIC DEVELOPMENT

5.1 The Functional Load

The grammatical work which in many languages is done by inflectional morphology – signalling grammatical relations between words within a phrase, and between phrases in a sentence – in pidgins must be done, if it is done at all, by syntax – in effect, by word order. This suggests that the syntactic system of the grammar of pidgins may carry a heavier *functional load* – in other words, have to do more work – than in other languages. In practice, this may not be the case. Pragmatic information – the context of the utterance – and extralinguistic information – gesture and gaze – may make up for what is lacking in both syntax and morphology.

5.2 Word Order

We saw in Chapter 2 that pidgins have a variety of word orders, though SVO is the most frequent. Word order in pidgins seems to depend mostly on the word order of the substrate language(s), where these are identifiable. The word order in the jargon stage may be unstable if the contributory languages have different word orders. In the case of Russenorsk, which resulted from contact between an SVO language (Norwegian) and a language with SVO and SOV as possible variants (Russian), sentence word order seems to have been unstable, either SVO or SOV. We might guess, though, that since SVO is a possibility for Russian speakers, and the only possibility for Norwegian speakers, the pidgin word order would finally have stabilised to SVO if Russenorsk had lasted long enough.

5.3 Grammaticalisation of Content Words

We saw in chapter two that grammatical categories such as tense, aspect and modality in pidgins are often marked by what in the lexifier are content words – for example, adverbs and verbs. In the early stages of a pidgin, it is likely that these markers still have the status of content words; for example, Fanakalo *mhlaumbe* in *mhlaumbe mina zo hamba*, 'I may go, I might go, perhaps I shall go', is probably an adverb, although its function here is to indicate modality.

As the communicative complexity of a pidgin increases, content words (i.e. those which bear independent meaning) may be re-analysed to take on a grammatical function. This process is called **grammaticalisation**. Naturally, it is more likely to affect those aspects of the pidgin grammar which are most impoverished at the outset, so the marking of tense/modality/aspect (TMA) is an area where grammaticalisation often occurs.

We mentioned in Chapter 2 the Tok Pisin future marker *bai*, derived from English 'by-and-by' (also found as an adverb in Fanakalo). We have enough historical documentation to be able to chart the different stages of this word in Tok Pisin. According to Sankoff and Laberge (1974), in its earliest stages, *baimbai* functioned as a sentence adverbial meaning 'afterwards' or 'later'. It later became a preverbal particle, and subsequently a verb prefix indicating future. At the same time, it has undergone phonological change: from *baimbai* to *bəmbai* to *bai* to *bə*. This kind of grammatical re-analysis going hand in hand with phonologial reduction is typical of grammaticalisation as a process. As an item alters in status from content word to grammatical morpheme, it loses much of its phonetic 'baggage' as well.

Given that a pidgin starts out with minimal grammar, its grammatical development along the developmental continuum will largely consist of developing new and more elaborate grammatical categories, complete with the appropriate marking. The means whereby this takes place is largely through the grammaticalisation of existing content words. TMA marking is not the only area affected. The development of the Tok Pisin subject marker *i-* and the object marker *-im* from the pronouns *he* and *him* is another example (Section 4 above).

Similar developments take place in creoles, where the origins of such TMA markers are sometimes apparent in unusual word ordering. In Papiamentu *lo* 'FUTURE' probably derives from Portuguese *logo*, 'soon, immediately': *lo mi bai*, 'I shall go'. Unlike all other TMA markers in Papiamentu, *lo* is external to the verb phrase, coming before the subject –where we might expect to find an adverb like 'soon'. The same applied to Tok Pisin *bai* in its earlier stages of development.

We saw in Chapter 2 that in the creole language Sranan (described in Chapter 5), the earlier form meaning 'what?' was *o sani?*, where the *o* derives from English *how* and *sani* (meaning 'thing') from English *something*. In modern Sranan *o* has been dropped, and the normal word for 'what' is just *san? San?* is now lexically distinct – through phonological reduction – from the word *sani* 'thing'. *Sani*, from its original status as a content word meaning 'thing', has thus kept its original content-word meaning on the one hand, and undergone grammaticalisation to become a question word on the other.

5.4 Complex Syntax: Relative Clauses and Complementation

Relative clauses are interesting to look at in connection with pidgin development because they involve a 'step up' in the complexity of sentence structure. The process of **relativisation** involves embedding one sentence inside another and at the same time signalling that there is a shared noun phrase common to both. In the English sentence

Where is the child [who wants food] ?

the word *who*, subject of the relative clause, stands for *the child*. (The relative clause is marked by square brackets.) In English and many other languages, special relative pronouns (*who*, *which*) are available for this function, though in some circumstances other strategies are used. Pidgins at an early stage of development are likely to have a much simpler strategy, illustrated by the Fanakalo translation of the above:

Fanakalo: Upi   lo   pikanin [yena funa   skafu]?
              where the   child   s/he   want   food

No relative pronoun is available but the ordinary third person pronoun *yena* is used to supply the subject of the relative clause. On the surface, there is no structural difference between this and a compound sentence: 'Where is the child, s/he wants food.'

A similar example shows that the same strategy is used when the relativised phrase is the object of the verb in the relative clause:

Fanakalo: Lo   ambulens [wena bizile   yena] yena fikile.
              the ambulance you   call-PAST it   it   come-PAST
              'The ambulance you called has arrived.'

                                        (Heine, 1973, p. 144)

As usual, our historical documentation is better for Tok Pisin than for most other pidgins. In this case, we can actually see the development of strategies for making relative clauses where only the most rudimentary ones existed in early stages. In early examples (Wawn, 1893) we find that relative clauses were not marked by overt means at all:

South Seas Pidgin: **You savez two white men [stop Maputi] he got house.**
                        'You know two white men who live at Maputi who have houses.'

Transcriptions by Hall (1943) of the speech of New Guineans who were born around the beginning of the twentieth century show the same:

Tok Pisin: **Spos yu   lukim man [i-kisim poisen] yu   i-ken   tok**.
if   you see   man SM-get magic   you SM-can   talk.
'If you had seen the man who made black magic, then you might talk'.
SM = Subject Marker

More recently, from the 1950s onwards, an important change has taken place in the way relative clauses are marked in Tok Pisin. Sankoff and Brown (1976), documenting this change, show that Tok Pisin relative clauses are now optionally marked by the demonstrative *ya* ('here'), which may occur twice: once after the head noun and once at the end of the relative clause. Both the first and second *ya* are optional, but the second one is unlikely to occur without the first. For example:

Tok Pisin: **meri   *ya*   [i-stap   long hul   *ya*]   em i-hangre.**
woman   REL   SM-stay   in   hole   REL   she SM-hungry
'The woman who stayed in the hole was hungry.' (Wurm et al., 1979)
SM = Subject Marker

Sankoff and Brown show how *ya*, originally used as a *discourse focus marker*, developed over time into the relative-clause-marking *ya* – hence the title of their paper: *'On the origins of syntax in discourse'*. This is, of course, yet another example of the grammaticalisation of a content word, as *ya* has lost its original meaning 'here' (in this context) and is now a grammatical particle.

A second way of increasing sentence complexity is to embed one sentence within another as the complement of the matrix (larger) sentence. In English, this is usually accomplished by means of a *complementiser* (especially *that*), for example:

he believes that [this will really help the provinces]

where *that* serves to introduce the embedded sentence. In English the complementiser is optional in sentences like this. From an earlier stage where there were no complementisers, Tok Pisin has developed three, by grammatical re-analysis (i.e. altering the grammatical function) of three existing words: the preposition *long*, 'in', 'at', etc.; the adverb *olsem*, 'thus'; and the conjunction *na*, 'and' (Woolford, 1979). The Tok Pisin translation of the example above, which occurs in the Port Moresby newspaper *Wantok*, 14 April 1994, is thus

(em)	i	bilip	olsem	[dispela	bai	helpim
he	SM	believe	that	this	FUT	help-TM

			tru	ol	provins]
			true(ly)	the-PL	province

SM = subject marker
TM = transitive marker
tru = 'truly, really, very much'

There are almost certainly many other examples of 'complementiser creation' to be found in other pidgins and creoles.

5.5 Overview

At the same time as a pidgin expands its expressive and referential range, its syntax becomes more complex. In particular, we find that sentence embedding becomes more common, and that new syntactic means for marking embedded clauses may develop. These syntactic structures appear to be necessary if the pidgin is to have sufficient expressiveness.

Syntactic complexity is something which is not easily measured. Insofar as it can be measured, the syntactic complexity of pidgins probably never reaches that of the most complex non-pidgins. Compare, for example, the Fanakalo sentence from 5.3 with its Zulu equivalent, where the subject and object are marked on the verb in the relative clause by means of prefixes ('concords') and the whole verb is marked as 'relativised' by means of a suffix:

Fanakalo:	Upi	lo	pikanin	[yena	funa	skaful]?
	where	the	child	s/he	want	food

Zulu:	Uphi	umntwana	[o + ku + funa + yo	ukudla]?
	where	child	SUBJ + OBJ + want + REL	food

SUBJ = subject concord (agrees with *child*)
OBJ = object concord (agrees with *food*)

Nevertheless, over time pidgin syntax may develop complex structures. Markers for syntactic categories can be introduced where none existed before, often through grammaticalisation of existing words. Everyday discourse may provide the occasion for such new developments, as Sankoff and Brown have shown. What this means is that when a pidgin reaches the stage where speakers find a need to mark a particular grammatical category which does not already have a grammatical marker, they will create a marker. This may be equally true in all languages, but is especially significant for pidgins, which start with much less surface grammatical marking than other languages.

6   LEXICAL DEVELOPMENT

A key characteristic of stable pidgins which distinguishes them from jargons is the existence of fairly clear-cut norms concerning what is and what is not a word of the pidgin. The vocabulary of Russenorsk shows many cases where a meaning can be expressed in more than one way – for example, *ʃprek* and *snakka*, both meaning 'speak'. In a stable pidgin, efficiency is maximised by having just one word for a particular referent, i.e. by reducing the number of synonyms. This implies an (unconscious) acceptance by the speakers of the pidgin that it is a language in its own right, and not simply an attempt to speak the ordinary form of one of the languages involved in the contact.

Conflicting demands are made of the pidgin lexicon. On the one hand, it must be reasonably small and easy to learn. On the other, it has to be large enough to meet the requirements of its speakers. These requirements, in a community where a pidgin is stabilising, are likely to increase and the pidgin will have to develop accordingly. However, the grammar of a stable pidgin, as we have seen, largely lacks derivational morphology.

The stable pidgin therefore has to rely on some simple strategies for expanding its lexicon. We will now look at some of the possible ways of doing this.

6.1   Circumlocution

While circumlocution or paraphrase does not actually increase the number of lexical items, it provides a means of increasing the referential range of the language. Circumlocutions are more typical of the jargon stage than of a stable pidgin, but in practice they can also function as definitions for new words and so have a use even in the later stages of pidgin development, and in non-pidgin languages.

Unfortunately, 'amusing' circumlocutions have become part of the folklore of amateur linguistics, and are often used to put pidgins down. Mühlhäusler (1986, p. 26) provides us with a brief history of reports, from 1902 to 1969, of the name for 'piano' in Pacific Pidgin English. These are all variations on the theme 'big-fellow box, suppose you fight (hit) him, he cry' (modern Tok Pisin: *bikpela bokis, supos yu paitim, em i-krai*). However, we can be fairly sure that no speaker of this pidgin ever intended that this should be interpreted as the *word* for piano. It is just a *description* of the piano in terms of its appearance and function. Similarly, Muspratt (1931) says 'a boy [i.e. adult male Solomon Islander] once described a cross-cut saw as a "pull-him-he-come, push-him-he-go, brother-belong-axe" '.

Circumlocutions are a strategy available in any language for giving a description of something which does not (yet) have a name in that language. It is not surprising, therefore, to find that pidgins use them, and probably use them more than most languages. A recent example of a circumlocution being used to define a word which is new to the language (i.e. to explain it to speakers who may not recognise it) is the following, from the 1991 Enga Province Business Directory (*Nambawan buk bilong toksave long ol bisnis long Enga*) from Papua New Guinea. In the editor's preface, under his signature we find printed: E*dita (Man husat i raitim dispela buk)* – 'Editor (man who wrote this book)'.

In the stable pidgin stage, according to Mühlhäusler (1986, p. 171), it is common to have 'phrase-like formulas for the description of new concepts'. He gives examples from Hiri Motu (a pidgin spoken in Papua New Guinea which is lexically based on the indigenous Papuan language Motu): *kuku ania gauna*, 'smoke eat thing' = 'pipe'; *traka abiaisi gauna*, 'truck raise thing' = 'jack', etc.

6.2 Borrowing

A pidgin which has reached the stable pidgin stage by way of tertiary hybridisation has become a language with its own norms. Its vocabulary has to be seen as its own, rather than as 'borrowed' from the lexifier language. Two facts underline this argument. First, we know of cases where the lexifier language has disappeared from the scene at the point where tertiary hybridisation took place, or even earlier. This happened in New Guinea, when a German colonial administration took over, leaving pidgin speakers without English models for about 30 years. It also happened in Surinam (see Chapter 5), where Dutch plantation owners replaced English ones.

Secondly, many words in the pidgin do not have the meaning of their source words in the lexifier language. Mühlhäusler (1986, p. 168) notes that a weakening of meaning in the transition from lexifier to pidgin is quite common, so that lexifier words which may sound extreme or crude have mild or 'normal' meanings in the pidgin. Well-known examples include *bagarap*, 'spoilt', from English *bugger(ed) up*; and *as*, 'origin, cause, base, buttocks', from English *arse*, in Tok Pisin. It seems to be true generally of pidgins that their vocabulary includes words drawn from a 'low' or vulgar register in the lexifier language, but that these have quite neutral meanings in the pidgin. More examples from Tok Pisin would be *shit*, 'excrement, remains, residue' (*shit bilong faia* = 'ashes'), and *kok*, 'penis', both based on words which are not part of the polite register in English. Nagamese provides a similar example: *dud* (Nagamese 'breast') is a word for milk in most dialects of Bengali, but is slang for 'breast' in one Bengali dialect. According to Bhattacharjya (1994, p. 43), 'it is evidently this usage that the Nagas heard . . . and retained'.

In addition, there are many cases where lexifier-language words have been altered in meaning to fit a differently structured semantic field, in keeping with an indigenous culture or concept of the world. Thus Tok Pisin *lek* means not only 'leg' in the English sense, but also 'foot', for which there is no separate word. Hall (1966, p. 92) and Mühlhäusler (1986, p. 169) give the examples of Tok Pisin *brata* (English 'brother'), meaning 'sibling of the same sex', and *susa* ('sister'), meaning 'sibling of the opposite sex', which correspond to categories in indigenous kinship systems but not in the English one. Note that these terms would have the 'right' reference from the point of view of an English speaker if they were used by a *male* pidgin speaker: a man's *brata* will be his brother, though a woman's *brata* will be her sister. This may result from the fact that the pidgin developed among male plantation workers. Hall notes that some Europeans misunderstood the pidgin usage and even believed that indigenous women could not tell the difference between the sexes!

During and after the stable pidgin stage, 'true' borrowing of words – the adoption into the pidgin of words which are not already part of its established word-stock – is likely to take place. The source of these may be either the lexifier, if it is still in contact with the pidgin, or other languages (indigenous or coloniser). 'New' borrowings (i.e. those which take place after stabilisation) will have to fit in with the phonological norms of the pidgin rather than the source language, so they may undergo considerable changes in form. While words borrowed from some other language than the lexifier should be easy to identify (though the actual language they come from may be very hard to determine, and is often disputed), it may be difficult to know where to draw the line between 'originally pidgin' words and 'borrowed' words from the lexifier language.

Mühlhäusler (1986, p. 174) points out that in fact pidgins are quite constrained in what words they may borrow. Pidgins have 'a marked preference for bisyllabic or at least short words', and they tend to impose strict limits on consonant clustering. (In fact probably most languages have a preference for words no more than two or three syllables long in common use. Pidgins are only different in that three syllables seems to be close to an absolute limit, while non-pidgins have no problem with much longer words – they just tend not to be used so much.)

In keeping with these constraints, words can only be borrowed if they fit, or can be made to fit, the preferred syllable-structure and word-structure patterns of the pidgin. We saw above that the Chinese Pidgin English lexicon tended to contain monosyllabic and bisyllabic words and that syllables tended to contain one consonant followed by one vowel. Under these circumstances the pidgin would be unlikely to borrow English words of four or five syllables. As the pidgin develops and expands beyond the stable pidgin stage, however, these constraints may become more flexible, and longer and phonologically more complex words may be borrowed into the pidgin.

Here, for example, are some words used by Tok Pisin speakers in the documentary *Raskols* (about robber gangs in Papua New Guinea), which was broadcast by Channel 4 television in June 1995: *impossible, fertilisers, insecticide*, *provincial*, *security*, *project*, *subtract*. Most of these break the two-syllable rule while others have 'difficult' final consonant clusters (/kt/). Borrowing from English, which is pervasive in Papua New Guinea and has high prestige, is transforming the vocabulary of Tok Pisin (so much so that a distinctive 'anglicised' variety is emerging, which is unintelligible to the mainly rural speakers of the 'standard' variety).

6.3 Metaphorical Extension

Probably every language enlarges the referential power of its lexicon by taking existing words for common or familiar objects and extending their ranges of reference to things or concepts which are in some way similar. English provides examples such as *hand* (of a clock), *bonnet* (of a car), *window* (an empty space in one's diary). In each case, the new meaning involves an extension of the original meaning beyond the original 'concrete' meaning. Sometimes the metaphor underlies our way of conceptualising an object, so that we speak not only of the *hands* of a clock but also of its *face* (though not of its *legs*, *waist*, or *ears*!)

Pidgins also use this strategy to extend the referential range of their lexicons. Somewhat like English clocks, Tok Pisin houses are conceptualised using the same terms as the human body. Thus a house (*haus*) has a face (*pes bilong haus*) – the front; eyes (*ai bilong haus*) – gables; and a skeleton (*bun bilong haus*) – a frame.

Sometimes a metaphor like this may be an innovation from within the pidgin as it stabilises and expands, while sometimes it may represent a *calque* on an indigenous lexical pattern found in the substrate languages. A calque is a 'literal translation' of a lexical item or pattern, which produces a word or phrase that in form resembles the lexifier language but semantically reproduces the structure of the substrate.

Tok Pisin *brata*, mentioned in 6.2 above, is almost certainly a calque on indigenous kinship terms: it has English form, but refers to an indigenous New Guinean category of meaning, 'sibling of the same sex'. In practice, unless one knows a lot about the substrate languages and the culture behind them, it is often difficult to know whether a pidgin word or phrase represents a new **metaphorical extension** of an existing word, or a calque on an indigenous term with the same range of meanings.

6.4 Multifunctionality of Lexical Items

We already noted this as a feature of the pidgin lexicon in Chapter 2. Probably most languages have a degree of multifunctionality, so that some lexical items can function as members of different grammatical categories. This is certainly common in English, e.g. *curtain* (noun), *to curtain* (verb). Historically, we can be reasonably sure that the noun came first, and the verb developed from it, though sometimes it is the other way around. Many writers have noted that pidgins have a tendency to multifunctionality in their lexicons, but as Mühlhäusler points out, it is actually much *less* used than it could be by pidgins at an early stage of development. 'When considering multifunctionality in Tok Pisin, for instance, one is struck not only by the absence of numerous mathematically possible forms, but also by the fact that restrictions on productivity appear to have been inherited from substratum resources' (1986, p. 173).

In spite of this, multifunctionality can be quite productive in pidgins which have reached the appropriate stage. The derivation of verbs from nouns (*lokim*, 'to lock', from *lok*, 'lock, padlock'), adjectives (*bikim*, 'to enlarge', from *bik*, 'big') and other verbs is widespread in Tok Pisin (see the exercise in 6.6 below).

6.5   Derivational Morphology

As mentioned in 6.2, pidgins at the *stable pidgin* stage tend to have very limited derivational morphology. We usually find a few word compounds but little else. Mühlhäusler has shown that significant derivational morphology, like the multifunctionality mentioned in 6.4 above, only develops when the pidgin has moved on to the expansion stage of its development.

Developments in derivational morphology go hand in hand with an increase in the permitted size level of lexical items (Mühlhäusler, 1986, p. 197). In the earlier stages of development, words are strictly limited in length and complexity; hence phrases consisting of several words will be required to express a concept. In the stable pidgin phase these are gradually replaced by polysyllabic single words formed by *compounding*. Mühlhäusler gives examples such as *wara bilong skin* ('water of skin' = 'sweat'), now being replaced by *skinwara*, and *man bilong save* ('man of know(ledge)' = 'wise person', now replaced by *saveman*.

Reduplication and affixation are two morphological processes which may be used to enlarge the lexicon. Reduplication is sometimes said to be a very widespread feature in pidgins and creoles but in fact the evidence on this is conflicting. In Tok Pisin it seems to be rather limited in its scope, but is sometimes used to derive new words from existing ones, e.g. *saksakim*, 'fill many bags', from sak, 'bag'.

New grammatical categories such as causatives may develop and be signalled by morphological means. Mühlhäusler (1986, p. 185) gives an historical account of the emergence of causatives in Tok Pisin, formed by adding the 'transitive suffix' *-im*. From the earlier Samoan Plantation Pidgin English, he gives the example of *yu mekim sam wara i boil*, indicating that *boil* in the pidgin could not be used transitively in the sense of 'cause to boil' at that time (cf. English *boil some water*). By 1927 New Guinea Pidgin permitted *boilim* to be used causatively, as in *yu boilim sampela* (i.e. 'some' + 'fellow') *wara*. At the same time, the first causative use of many other verbs was recorded, indicating that this was not a one-off change but the introduction of a new grammatical category, 'causative', with morphological marking. Mühlhäusler also shows that there is a natural progression for the development of these forms: the causative first develops in intransitive **stative** verbs like *slip*, 'sleep' (*slipim*, 'to make lie down'), later in adjectives (*bikim*, 'to enlarge'), next in non-stative verbs (*noisim*, 'to make noise'). As recently as 1973 the first causative derived from a transitive verb was found: *dokta i dringim sikman*, 'the doctor makes the patient drink' (Mühlhäusler, 1986, p. 186).

6.6 Exercise: Lexical Expansion in Tok Pisin

Discuss the Tok Pisin words listed below. For each word or expression, which of the lexicon-building processes mentioned in Section 6 are involved?

1. *skelim* 'to weigh', from *skel* 'scales'
2. *bulitim* 'to glue', from *bulit* 'glue' (from a brand name?)
3. *hevi* 'difficulty'
4. *kamapim* 'to make come up', from *kamap* 'come up'
5. *luklukim* 'appearance', from *lukim* 'look'
6. *bunlo* 'constitution', from *bun* 'bone' and *lo* 'law'
7. *rop bilong blut i karim blut i go long hat* 'rope of blood which carries blood to the heart' = 'artery'
8. *giabokis* 'gear box'
9. *kalabus* 'prison; cage; vice (tool), brake'
10. *nil diwai* 'nail tree' = '(wooden) peg'
11. Parts of a bicycle:
    (a) *baisikel* 'bicycle'
    (b) *wilwil* (wheel-wheel) 'bicycle'
    (c) *bun baisikel* (bone bicycle) 'frame'
    (d) *so* (saw) 'gearwheel'
    (e) *sindaun* (sit-down) 'saddle'
    (f) *sia* (chair) = 'saddle'

(Data from P. Mühlhäusler, *The Development of Word Formation in Tok Pisin*, and elsewhere.)

7 STYLISTIC DEVELOPMENT

The development of new and more complex forms at every level of grammar and vocabulary at one and the same time *results from* increased expressive needs on the part of speakers and *permits* speakers to indulge in a wider range of referential meanings and styles. From the jargon to the pidgin stage this may not be so obvious; but as the stable pidgin expands and takes on a wide range of culturally appropriate functions, the increase in stylistic range is as notable as the development of the grammar.

It is very important to remember that expanded pidgins are invariably used in multilingual communities, where knowledge of *at least* two languages is the norm. In such communities, different languages typically are used for different functions, possibly with some overlap. The expansion of the pidgin enables it to take on functions new to the community (for example, connected with the modern way of life) and possibly to replace some existing functions of languages which were used in the community before the arrival of the pidgin. At the same time, appropriate *styles* of the pidgin will develop to meet the needs of particular functions.

Wurm and Mühlhäusler (1982) document the emergence of at least ten different stylistic registers in Tok Pisin. These include *tok piksa* ('picture talk', using similes 'more or less readily understood by a general audience'), *tok pilai* ('play talk', where a metaphor is 'used repeatedly in light-hearted conversation'), *tok bokis* ('box talk', in which special conventionalised lexical items are used whose meanings are not predictable from the 'mainstream' vocabulary), *tok hait* ('hide talk', a kind of *tok bokis* for the purpose of excluding outsiders), *tok mainus* ('backslang', where words are reversed phonologically to avoid taboos or exclude outsiders, e.g. *kepkep* for *pekpek*, 'defecate'), foreigner talk, narrative style, Church Pidgin, Official Pidgin and Heavily Anglicised Pidgin.

While, in West Africa, the stylistic development of Pidgin English is not so well documented, we have evidence of its stylistic diversity from the range of its functions. Elugbe and Omamor (1991, p. 123) note that Nigerian Pidgin 'has basically been a spoken language in Nigeria and it would appear that it has managed to sustain a virile and vital oral literature. It has been used as a vehicle for songs, folktales, proverbs, work-chants and the like. There is also some use in written literature.' (See Section 9.4.)

An interesting example of the expansion of West African Pidgin English for culturally appropriate functions comes from Cameroon. According to Marie-Lorraine Pradelles de Latour (1984), the following exchange might take place in Douala, the largest city in Cameroon:

Father: *Jean-Marc, yu kam chop?* ('Are you coming to eat with me?')
Son, aged 8: *Hau papa, yu chop ol di tin, yu no lif mi som tin?* ('What, papa, have you eaten everything, didn't you leave me something?')
Father laughs.

What is interesting here is the light-hearted nature of this exchange. The father laughs at his son's remark, but according to Pradelles de Latour

(1984, p. 266), 'it would be absolutely unthinkable for this young boy to say such a phrase in Bangwa [their first language] or for the father to accept such a comment in his language'.

Somewhat like Tok Pisin, Cameroonian Pidgin is a language of secrets, according to Pradelles de Latour; but according to her description, the 'hidden message' will often be conveyed in front of the third party who is not supposed to know it, and who will understand it perfectly well. It seems that the function of the pidgin, rather than to hide the meaning, is to signal the private nature of the message: something like a 'stage whisper' in English, which indicates playfully that something is meant to be a secret. Cameroonian Pidgin also has a 'backslang' form, called Makro Pidgin, which is used by underworld elements to exclude outsiders.

These examples show that once a pidgin has become part of an indigenous culture, it may diversify in all sorts of ways, developing different stylistic registers in accordance with the needs of its users. As languages of wider communication which at the same time have associations with modern (often urban) life, pidgins can be seen both as extensions of an *existing* culture and as the vehicles of a *new* culture.

8   CONCLUSION

Perhaps the most important conclusion that can be drawn from studying the development of pidgins – apart from the simple fact that they *do* develop – is that they develop in their own way, through maximising their own resources. Mühlhäusler's work on the lexicon of Tok Pisin has shown that the development of syntactic and morphological processes takes place in an ordered fashion, with new rules added only when the appropriate stage is reached. Meanwhile, evidence from several pidgins indicates that syntactic categories are likely to be added by means of grammaticalising content words, not by borrowing categories or structures directly from the lexifier or substrate languages. In other words, once a pidgin has reached the crucial stable pidgin stage, it 'has its own mind' in terms of how it develops. While continued contact with the lexifier is bound to have an effect, the pidgin is none the less master of its own resources. This fact is of great importance in considering not just the development of pidgins, but also that of *creoles*, to which we turn in the next chapter.

To end this chapter, we look at two case studies from opposite ends of the developmental continuum: *Butler English* of India is a contemporary language variety which is probably best treated as a jargon rather than a stable pidgin; *Nigerian Pidgin* is a variety of West African Pidgin English which is an expanded pidgin and has native speakers of its own in some areas.

9 CASE STUDY: SIMPLICITY AND VARIATION IN BUTLER ENGLISH

Butler English (so called after the head of the household servants in wealthy Indian families), is described by Hosali (1987, 1992) as one of a 'network of varieties' (1992, p. 59) of English on the Indian subcontinent, which date back in their origins to the earliest English (later British) contacts with India. It is spoken mainly by Indians with little formal education, but who come into contact with speakers of Standard English through their work (typically as house servants, hotel staff, street vendors or guides). Thus it has the classic features of a 'secondary hybrid': Standard English is ostensibly the target language for all speakers of Butler English, who succeed in varying degrees in reaching the target. The result is a communication system with a great deal of variability – of 'fluctuating and unsystematic character' (Hosali, 1992, p. 71) – which is grammatically simplified and reduced in vocabulary in comparison with Standard English.

The following example of Butler English appeared in *The Times* (London) in 1882 (cited in Schuchardt, 1891, and quoted by Hosali, 1992):

> Discovery has been made of a butler stealing large quantities of his master's milk and purchasing the silence of the subordinate servants by giving them a share of the loot; and this is how the ayah (nurse) explains the transaction: *Butler's yevery day taking one ollock for ownself, and giving servants all half half ollock; when I am telling that shame for him, he is telling, Master's strictly order all servants for the little milk give it – what can I say, mam, I poor ayah woman?*

A modern example collected by Hosali (1992, p. 64) – a recipe for pickle:

> All right, I can tell. Cut nicely brinjal. Little piece. Ginger, garlic, hm chilly – red chilly, mustard and eh *jira* – all want it, grind it in the vinegar. No water. After put the boil – then put it all the masala, little little slowly fry it – nice smells coming – then you can put the brinjal. Not less oil. Then after is cooking in the hoil make it cold – put it in the bottle.

Here, with some modern examples (drawn from Hosali, 1987, pp. 55–63), are some of the types of grammatical simplification found in Butler English.

(a) *Absence of plural suffixes.* Butler English uses numerals to indicate number, but has no plural inflections.

> ... then two spoon coffee ...
> ... Only Indian drink there ...

(b) *Absence of possessive suffixes.* In Butler English, possession is shown by placing the possessor before the possessed without any possessive marker corresponding to *'s* in Standard English.

> ... I living next to my memsahib sister house ...

(c) *Reduction of tense marking.* The form of the English verb ending in *-ing* (the present participle in English grammatical terminology) is heavily used in Butler English, in contexts where it would not be used in Standard English. According to Hosali 'it is used not just for the present and the future but for many of the other tenses in English as well.... Distinctions relating to time and continuity of action are understood either from the context or are indicated by adverbials' (1987, p. 58).

> Those days I not *working* ...
> ('In those days I was not working/doing)
> I *starting* work twenty years ago
> ('I started my work twenty years ago')
> ... Only *taking* gin and lime cordial
> ('They only take gin and lime cordial')

(d) *Lack of a copula (verb* to be*).* According to Hosali, 'All the butlers interviewed ... tended to use copulaless clauses in English regardless of the other language(s) they spoke. This feature then seems to have its source in a simplification technique – a universal pattern of linguistic behaviour appropriate to contact situations' (1987, p. 62).

> That the garden.
> 'That is the garden.'
>
> Those foreign drinks no here.
> 'Those foreign drinks are not here.'
>
> Only Indian drink here.
> 'Only Indian drinks are here.'

At the same time as Butler English fairly consistently shows the four types of grammatical simplification above, it shows a great deal of variation in the use of pronouns. While Hosali says that 'with pronouns there has been a simplification of the English system', in fact individual speakers seem to behave idiosyncratically:

My working Spencer's officer	'*I* was working for...'
Me not drinking Madam	'*I* do not drink...'
I age eh about fifty-one	'*My* age eh is about...'

To sum up, Butler English is a language with some of its own grammatical and stylistic norms, which are different from Standard English. At the same time, individual speakers may be influenced to a greater or lesser extent by Standard English, depending on how much they come into contact with it. The result is an *unstable* grammatical system and a high degree of *variation*.

10   CASE STUDY: EXPANSION IN WEST AFRICAN PIDGIN ENGLISH

10.1   West African Pidgin English

West African Pidgin English (WAPE) is a cover term for several related pidgins spoken over a wide area of West Africa including Ghana, Nigeria and Cameroon. The varieties of pidgin spoken cover a range from rudimentary to expanded, but at least in the three countries mentioned, there are substantial numbers of speakers who are using the pidgin in an expanded form. Although because of the similarities between regional varieties it is reasonable to talk of 'West African Pidgin English', there are enough specifically regional features to make it possible to talk of Nigerian Pidgin English, Cameroonian Pidgin English (called *Kamtok*, see Todd, 1990) and other varieties.

WAPE has a long, but only partially understood, history in West Africa. European ships traded along the West African coast from the late fifteenth century, making it likely that a Portuguese-lexicon pidgin was spoken there, although we have no direct evidence of this. From the beginning of the seventeenth century, the English became the main European traders along this coast, establishing coastal slave trading posts (forts), or seizing existing ones from the Dutch, in what are now Ghana, Togo, Benin and Nigeria. Although there is only partial historical evidence about what actually happened, an English-lexicon pidgin (perhaps replacing the earlier Portuguese-lexicon one) seems to have come into use around these forts, being used for communication not only between English traders and Africans, but also among Africans who had no other common language. Some English traders had families with African women living close to the forts; the

English-lexicon pidgin or creole spoken among these families may have been significant in maintaining and spreading the pidgin. Some indigenous groups like the Kru, who live in what is now Liberia and were often employed on English ships, may have been important in transporting the pidgin further afield along the West African coast.

10.2 Nigerian Pidgin English

In Nigeria, the pidgin was very much a creation of the slave trade. In the 1780s, Antera Duke, a trader from Calabar and a native speaker of the Efik language, kept a diary in a version of Pidgin (with some admixture of English, which he had probably been taught to write). The diary, published in 1968 (Forde, 1968), is a fascinating historical and linguistic document.

Having been the preserve of British traders and trading companies for some centuries, Nigeria became a British colony in the nineteenth century and eventually became independent in 1960, with English as the official language.

Elugbe and Omamor (1991, p. 12) point out that Nigerian Pidgin today has its largest proportion of speakers in the former slaving ports of Calabar, Port Harcourt and Warri. In Lagos (until recently the capital of Nigeria), pidgin is 'decidedly a recent development'. This relationship between 'old' and 'new' Pidgin locations is made clear by Mafeni (1971, p. 98):

> Nigerian Pidgin is essentially a product of the process of urbanization. While its origins lie historically...on the coast, its development and spread is the result of contacts between Africans. The rapidly growing towns of Nigeria have increasingly become the melting pots of the many tribes and races which constitute Nigeria and Pidgin seems to be today a very widely spoken lingua franca, many town and city dwellers being at least bilingual in Pidgin and an indigenous language.

10.3 Cameroonian Pidgin English

According to Ian Hancock (1969), Cameroonian Pidgin grew out of the eighteenth-century Calabar variety of Pidgin English. British missionaries and traders were probably significant in spreading the pidgin in coastal Cameroon in the mid-nineteenth century. Cameroon was annexed by Germany in 1884 but by then the English-lexicon pidgin was so well established that the Germans had little option but to use it to communicate with their subjects. The introduction of a plantation labour system by the Germans and the adoption of the pidgin by German missionaries for their work led to its spread to the interior of Cameroon. After the defeat of the Germans in Cameroon by Allied forces during the First World War, Cameroon was divided up as mandated territories between the English (in the west, bordering Nigeria) and the French (in the east). Pidgin in Cameroon continues to be widely used, although since independence, in 1960, the official languages have been French and English. (Information from Todd, 1984, and Holm, 1989.)

An interesting development in the expanding Cameroonian Pidgin of Douala is its *gendered* nature. According to Pradelles de Latour (1984), the secret 'bandits' backslang', Makro Pidgin, is exclusive to men. But in the everyday language of the markets, French 'appears as the language of specialized trade and of young men, Pidgin being that of basic food and women' (p. 266). The probable reason is that only those with education have access to French, and women are less likely to be educated.

10.4 The Post-Pidgin Continuum

Although the English-lexicon pidgins of Nigeria and Cameroon are very similar and share much of their history, the differences between them reveal how social and political factors may affect the development of a pidgin in the expansion stage.

In Cameroon, the pidgin was able to develop independently of Nigerian Pidgin to some extent because of Cameroon being administratively separate from Nigeria. What may be more significant is that the language of colonial administration in Cameroon was first German, later (in the larger part of the country) French: Standard English thus played virtually no role in colonial Cameroon (except in the British part). The pidgin thus developed in isolation not only from its related pidgin in Nigeria, but from its lexifier, English.

Meanwhile in Nigeria, the pidgin has throughout its history been involved in continuing language contact with English. The first contacts clearly involved native speakers of English. Subsequently, while few Nigerians would have had contact with native English speakers, Standard English has had a high profile in Nigeria. It has been the main language of administration and education in most parts of the country (in some areas, there are major regional languages) both during the colonial period and since then. With the expansion of education since independence, and the advent of radio and television, increasing numbers of Nigerians have some exposure to a local variety of Standard – or near-Standard – English.

While Nigerian Pidgin is widely used as an oral medium (cf. the quotation from Elugbe and Omamor in Section 7), as yet there is no consistent *literary* use of Nigerian Pidgin for complete works. Though many writers have portrayed their poor or rural characters as speaking Nigerian Pidgin, the main body of the text is usually in a local Nigerian form of Standard English; 'the more common routine in literary works has been to occasionally feature bits and pieces, snippets in NP used in a number of different ways...' (Elugbe and Omamor, 1991, p. 127).

10.5 Nigerian Pidgin English Text

The text below is from a work which straddles the boundary between an oral and a literate form. Written by Wole Soyinka, one of the best-known Nigerian writers and author of plays and novels in Standard English, it is a recorded dialogue spoken against a musical background. The record is sold in a sleeve which incorporates a written version of the text. The text is a satire in which the 'common shareholder' (ordinary Nigerian) accuses the Chairman of the Company (representing the Nigerian government and corrupt elite). Although the text is not really 'pure' Nigerian Pidgin (there are some parts which seem to be Standard English) and is probably best regarded as a mixture of Pidgin and Standard, it still shows many of the commonest structures which characterise the pidgin. Written 'pidgin' typically includes a proportion of near-Standard English, according to Elugbe and Omamor. This may be because it is typically the work of those who are already literate in Standard English; though in the case of *Unlimited Liability Company* it might also be a realistic portrayal of a character who has some education and whose pidgin has moved closer to Standard English.

Extract from *Unlimited Liability Company*
(Music and Lyrics by Wole Soyinka)

Chairman, wetin you dey find for home?
We tink say you still dey overseas
Ah, I forget, it's getting near the time
For a meeting of all the shareholders.

wetin: what (what-thing)
you dey find: you are finding
we tink say: we thought that
for home: at home
dey overseas: are overseas

Chairman, you sabi waka o
We look for you from Tokyo to New York
In Bulgaria, they say you just commot
Your executive jet pass us for Argentina

sabi: know
waka: walk, i.e. travel about, wander
o: an exclamation
commot: leave, 'come out'; *you just commot*, 'you just left'
for Argentina: *in* Argentina

Chairman, dis meeting go hot o
Your directors done chop all we money
While you dey shake hands with Kings and Presidents
Your business partners done shake the treasury loose

go hot: will get hot
chop: eat
done chop: have eaten up
dey shake hands: 'are shaking hands'

Each time they sneeze, millions of Naira go scatter
When they snore, the bank itself go shake
Mobilisation fee is the order of the day
The contractor collect, take we money and run away

Naira: Nigerian unit of currency

My eye see wonder the other day for Yola
When your Directors meet for society wedding
Private jet and helicopter na de fashion
Mercedes na dash to their favourite singers

for Yola: at Yola
na de fashion: are the fashion
na dash: is a bribe

Forty aeroplanes, all private, fly in the guests
Each director and wife spray at least twenty thousand
When money finish at midnight they open the bank
For brand-new Naira to continue the lovely spray

You say you fit be Chairman
You lobby to be chairman
You say you go try for me o
You swear you go try for me o
Make meself I tanda small
Make I get small sugar for my tea

make: let (me)
tanda: stand (up)

Chairman, no to say I vex
I be just a common shareholder
I never say I want butter for my bread
I fit to drink my tea without sugar

I vex: I am angry

How many million you spend to clear the bush
Where you say you wan grow food for chop
Soil erosion na in alone dey grow
Common farmer do better on in own

chop: eat
na in alone dey grow: (it) is that alone that grows
in: he/she/it/his/her/its

How many many I go talk o
How many many I go shout o
what of that Two point Eight billion
Wey you take play Hide and Seek o?
Make you take yourself commot
Unless you give me my share of Two point Eight

wey: which
make you take yourself commot: get rid of yourself

10.6   Exercise: Nigerian Pidgin English

1. Go through the text above and mark each stretch of text according to
    whether you think it is Standard English or Nigerian Pidgin English
    (assume that any usage which is not Standard English is Nigerian
    Pidgin English). Do you notice any systematic way in which each is
    used differently in the song?

2. What are the different functions of *for* in the pidgin parts of the text?
    Is there any resemblance here to anything in Tok Pisin?

3. Find all the pidgin expressions in the text which indicate tense or
    aspect. List each tense/aspect marker and its apparent function. Also
    make a note of verbs where tense and aspect are *not* marked. Do you
    notice any similarities with Tok Pisin?

4. Find all the pidgin expressions in the text which in English are
    translated by the copula (some form of the verb *to be*). Try to work
    out under what syntactic conditions each is used.

10.7   Grammatical Notes

10.7.1   Prepositions in West African Pidgin English
Like many other pidgins, WAPE has few prepositions. The preposition *for* is
an all-purpose locative preposition, translatable as *in*, *at*, *on*, *to* etc. It also
has some of the uses of Standard English *for*.

10.7.2   The tense and aspect system of West African Pidgin English
Markers before the main verb are used to show tense and aspect:

progressive aspect:	you *dey* find
completive aspect:	your directors *done* chop
future tense:	dis meeting *go* hot

There is also an anterior (past) marker *bin*, which can combine with the
aspect markers, thus: *bin chop*, *bin dey chop*, *bin done chop*: 'ate', 'was
eating', 'had eaten' (this is a rough translation; the actual translation will
depend on the context).
    This pattern of preverbal tense and aspect markers and their permitted
combinations is almost identical to that found in many other English-
lexicon pidgins and creoles – a fact to be discussed in more detail later.

10.7.3   The copula in West African Pidgin English
WAPE has (at least) three distinct possible ways of translating the English
copula 'to be':

(a)   as zero, with an adjective: *I vex, dis meeting go hot*
(b)   as *dey*, with a location: *you still dey overseas*
(c)   as *na*, when linking two noun phrases: *Mercedes na dash*, 'Mercedes
      (cars) are a bribe'

This pattern of the 'threefold copula' is found in many other creoles, some
of which we will look at later. In the kind of Pidgin represented by the text,
which is heavily influenced by Nigerian (Standard) English, the English
form *be* also appears in some contexts, especially where a less Anglicised
variety of the pidgin would have *na*; for example, *I be just a common
shareholder*.

KEY POINTS: From Pidgin to Creole

Stages of development:

- Jargon;
- 'Tertiary hybridisation';
- Stable pidgin;
- Extended/expanded pidgin;
- Creolisation may occur during the expansion stage or earlier.

Patterns of development

- Phonological: word length and structural complexity increases.
- Morphological: derivational morphology becomes significant; some inflectional morphology.
- Syntactic: grammaticalisation of content words, 'movement rules', relative clauses and complementisers may develop.
- Lexical: lexicon extends through metaphorical extension, multi-functionality of lexical items and development of derivational morphology.
- More stylistic choices evolve as language serves a wider range of functions.

5 Creolisation

1 INTRODUCTION

1.1 Problems with Defining 'Creole'

Earlier in this book I gave a definition 'for the time being' of creoles as *'pidgins which have become native languages for their speakers'* (Chapter 1, Section 4.5). The purpose of this chapter is to fill out this definition of a creole, showing that it is in some ways problematic. Through case studies of a range of creoles with different histories, we will be able to see that creoles actually form a fairly diverse group.

A key issue in creole studies recently, and one that we shall come back to in this and the next two chapters, has been the *stage* at which the transformation from pidgin to creole takes place. We saw in the last chapter that pidgins, given the right circumstances, go through a series of stages in which they develop from rudimentary jargons to 'expanded pidgins'. Clearly, once a pidgin has reached the expansion stage, there is a good chance of it becoming the lingua franca of a settled community, for some if not all of its speakers. In such a settled community, children will be born and will acquire the creole as a first language (perhaps along with other languages). Tok Pisin, which has become a creole through nativisation of a pidgin after decades without native speakers of its own, is a good example for which we have a mass of historical evidence.

In this case, it also makes sense to speak of 'pidgin Tok Pisin' (Tok Pisin spoken *as a pidgin*, i.e. by those for whom it is a second language) and 'creole Tok Pisin' (Tok Pisin spoken *as a creole* by those who learnt it natively as small children). Thus it is possible for a language to be both a pidgin and a creole at the same time, though for different groups of speakers.

At the time Tok Pisin began to creolise (in the 1960s), it had been a stable pidgin for perhaps a century, and an expanded pidgin for several decades. By this time, there was little difference in terms of referential and stylistic possibilities between Tok Pisin and the indigenous languages of the communities where Tok Pisin was used: hence the transformation of Tok Pisin from pidgin to creole could be seen as simply another – inevitable – stage in the development of the language.

However, just as we know that children are likely to be born into a settled community where a stable or expanded pidgin is spoken, we can also be sure that children will not *wait* to be born *until* a rudimentary pidgin has become a stable one. Thus there is a possibility, at least in theory, that children may be born under circumstances where the only lingua franca used by adults is a pidgin in an *early* stage of development – no more than a jargon.

Where a creole comes into being in a situation of language contact before a stable pidgin has had time to emerge, we can speak of **abrupt creolisation** (a term coined by Thomason and Kaufman). *Abrupt creolisation* necessarily takes place within a short space of time, probably at most one generation. The resulting creole will have the features of a contact language but historically would not have gone through any of the stages discussed in Chapter 4, except perhaps the first (jargon) stage.

Thomason and Kaufman write (1988, p. 150):

> In this process the emerging contact language at once becomes the primary language of the community and is learned as a first language (though not necessarily as their only first language) by any children born into the new multilingual community. The contact language therefore expands rapidly into a creole rather than stabilizing as a functionally and linguistically restricted pidgin, though its formative period, before it crystallizes as a language, corresponds to what is generally called a prepidgin stage.

Clearly, for a community to create a new language for itself within the space of one generation will not happen without a good reason. But the upheaval of slavery, which we know has given rise to many of the known creole languages, may be just such a good reason.

1.2 Normal and Abnormal Transmission of Language

Because of the possibility of abrupt creolisation, we cannot assume that all creoles are the result of the steady process of development which Tok Pisin has undergone. To refine our definition some more, we can make use of the concept of **normal transmission** (as used by Thomason and Kaufman, 1988). Normal transmission is the method by which languages are 'normally' passed from generation to generation, children learning the language from adults, older children and peers. Language change under normal transmission is slow and gradual, and significant differences between language varieties only emerge in the course of several, or many, generations. This is in fact the type of change, and the type of language transmission, which the 'family tree' model of language history (see Chapter 1) assumes to be universal. Having accepted the idea of 'normal transmission' and that it applies to the majority of existing languages, we can look at the cases where 'normal transmission' does not take place. These are just those languages where some social change – possibly a very traumatic one such as slavery – has led to a community acquiring a new language in less than one generation. This certainly would apply to all the languages which result from 'abrupt creolisation'.

1.3   A Definition of 'Creole'

We can now give a definition of a creole as *a language with native speakers which results from language contact without normal transmission*. We can note that there are two ways a creole can come into being according to this definition:

1. Through *abrupt creolisation*, where a creole arises without a preceding stable pidgin, through a sharp break in the transmission of language in some community;

2. Through **nativisation** of a pidgin (in practice this means a stable or expanded pidgin). 'Nativisation' here refers to the process whereby a community will take on a new language as its native language. Although in this case, the transmission of the pidgin to children (who become the first generation of creole speakers) is more or less 'normal', there is nevertheless a break in normal transmission at the stage where the *pidgin* comes into being.

Some case studies of creolisation

In the next section we will look at a few historically well-documented cases of creolisation. We will see that there can be different 'ingredients' in situations which end in creolisation, with respect to such features as the number of languages involved, the relative numbers of their speakers, and whether or not a pidgin establishes itself prior to the appearance of the creole. We shall first look at Pitcairnese, a creole which we know must have established itself with little or no prior pidgin stage; next we look at Mauritian Creole, a case of abrupt creolisation; then at Sranan, which some believe to have creolised abruptly, but for which there is also a **'gradualist'** argument. Next we will look at Krio, an African creole with strong Caribbean connections, and finally at Afrikaans, which is sometimes called a **'creoloid'** because it has some creole features but not enough to be a 'clear' creole.

2   CASE STUDY 1: PITKERN AND NORFOLK – LINGUISTIC CONSEQUENCES OF THE MUTINY ON THE *BOUNTY*

Lexifier: **English**
Languages in contact: **English and Tubaian (Tahitian)**
Relative numbers in initial contact: **approximately equal**
Outcome: **creolisation without a clear pidgin stage**

2.1 Background

In 1789, after setting the harsh Captain Bligh and his loyal crewmen loose in an open boat somewhere in the South Pacific, the nine male mutineers on the *Bounty* sailed to the Polynesian island of Tubai (near Tahiti) where they swelled their ranks with nineteen islanders, some of whom did not come of their own free will. Seeking a place to hide from the British navy, the mutineers and their companions reached Pitcairn (an uninhabited island about 5 sq km (2 sq miles) in area) in 1790.

Thanks to detailed records, we know the origins of the whole community that settled there: the mutineers included four English men, two Scottish, one American, one from St Kitts in the Caribbean and one from Guernsey; the Polynesians from Tubai were six men ('servants') and twelve women ('consorts'). At the time of the departure from Tubai, one of the women had a child with her; by 1800, all but one of the men (John Adams) had died, but ten Polynesian women and twenty-three children remained. The language varieties spoken by some of the mutineers have left some clear marks in Pitcairnese: for example, the negative imperative dʌnə, from Scots, and mɔgə 'thin', from the speech of Edward Young, the mutineer from St Kitts (Ross and Moverley, 1964, p. 244; also quoted by Holm, 1989). As might be expected, much of the lexicon referring to local plants and products is of Polynesian origin. Tahitian (or Tubaian) seems to have had a substantial influence on the phonology.

We can be sure that Pitcairnese came into being very soon after the arrival of the mutineers and their company, and the new language was learnt by the children born on Pitcairn as their first language. According to Thomason and Kaufman (1988, p. 148), 'Pitcairnese certainly developed immediately as a creole, without a definite pidgin stage.'

In 1856, due to depletion of natural resources on the island, the entire population of Pitcairn – 194 people – was moved to Norfolk Island, almost 4000 miles further west. Between 1859 and 1864, however, 43 of them returned to Pitcairn, where their descendants still live. The languages of Pitcairn and Norfolk can thus be considered to be dialects of the original Pitcairnese, with Norfolkese considerably more influenced by Standard English than Pitcairnese. Ross and Moverley (1964) is a study of the languages of Pitcairn and Norfolk. More recently (1991) Anders Kallgård, having spent three months on Pitcairn, produced a word-list with the title *Fut Yoli Noo Bin Laane Aklen?* ('Why didn't you all teach us?'), which includes etymologies for many Pitcairnese words. (Note: *Fut* = 'why?', *aklen* = 'us'.)

Although Pitcairn, with no airport and only infrequent visits from ships, is among the remotest places in the world, it is now possible to 'visit' Pitcairn via its World Wide Web site, to find out something about each individual on the island, and even to order local crafts. According to an electronic mail posting in June 1996, 'Pitcairn Island Council has declared the "Pitcairnese Language" to be an official language of the Island. The language will be henceforth called PITKERN, which is the way it is referred to in the language itself' (P. J. Lareau, e-mail dated 3 June 1996). This is confirmed by a letter from the Commissioner for Pitcairn (L. H. Salt, personal communication), who believes that the decision was brought about by concern that Pitkern might die out. This concern is also expressed by Kallgård (1991, p. 1) who considers that 'Pitcairnese may well be a "dying language". A flourishing Pitcairnese will be possible only if the status of the language is raised, and the printing of this word-list is an attempt to contribute to that.'

In 1996 it was noted that none of the children on the island were speaking Pitkern spontaneously, though all understand it when it is spoken to them. However, 'Pitcairn's Education Officer is actively encouraging the use of Pitkern at school and there has been a heightening of awareness among adult Pitcairners of the need to encourage the use of Pitkern by children' (L. H. Salt, personal communication).

The Pitcairn World Wide Web site contains information about the Pitcairnese language including a word-list, but no texts. The following texts are from Norfolk Island and would be easily intelligible to Pitcairn Islanders.

2.2   Texts from Norfolk Island

The orthography is that of the sources, and appears to be more or less phonemic.

Mais Tintoela (Maree's Sohng)
(words and music by Donald Christian-Reynolds)

Hieh mais tintoela,
Watawieh mais darlen?
Mais taim lornga yuu gat noe en
Daa san se miek yus hea shain
Mais haat se skip a biit
Awaw law se miek aklan wan

Chorus
Ai law yuu mais darlen
Tek mii lornga yuu
Dem ai f'yoen miek mais haat kepsais

Yus haan iin main daa tenda
Miek ai fiil guud
Yuu d'wan iin mais haat mais darlen
Ai law yuu

Kam work orn 'sehn
Uni aklan ya nau
Laan baut daa taim wi fas kiis
Awas haat se kaina pili
We semes wan faas boet
Awas law naewa gwena dan

watawieh: what-a-way, i.e. 'how'
aklan: we/us
pili: stuck together (Polynesian origin, Kallgård, 1991)
done: finish (English *done*)

[Hey my sweetheart
How are you my darling?
My time with you has no end
The sun makes your hair shine
My heart has skipped a beat
Our love has made us one

Chorus
I love you my darling
Take me with you
Your eyes make my heart capsize
Your hand in mine is so tender
It makes me feel good
You're the one in my heart
I love you

Come walk on the sand
We're on our own now
Talk about the time we first kissed
Our hearts joined together
We're like a 'fast-boat'
Our love will never end.]

Instructions for use of the Norfolk Telecom Phonecard
(from the Norfolk Island World Wide Web site, http://www.ozemail.
com.au/~jbp/pds/, June 1996)

Norfolk Telecom Foenkaad

Dieh kaad es uni f'dem kaad foen orn Norfuk – kaa yuuset enisaid aels. Dem punch hoel shoe baut hau mach mani laef in. Dieh kaad uni el yuuset f' ring weih from Norfuk.

Norfolk Telecom Phonecard

This card is for Card Phones on Norfolk Island only. Punched holes show approximate credit remaining. For international calls only.

2.3 Exercise

1. Go through the texts above and pick out all the personal pronouns. What forms do you notice?

2. Now find all the verbs in the two texts. By looking at the translations, see if you can work out how tense and aspect are marked in Pitkern/ Norfolk.

2.4 Grammatical Notes

2.4.1 Pronouns

The Pitkern/Norfolk pronoun system has separate forms for subject/object and possessive, thus *ai* 'I', *mais* 'my'; *aklan* 'we/us', *awas* 'our'; *yuu*, 'you', *yus* 'your'. The plural of you is *yoli* or *yorlyi*, which can be traced either to an archaic English form like *all ye* or *you-all-ye*, or to Tahitian *'orua* (Kallgård, 1991). The English forms *wi* 'we' and *mii* 'me' are also each found once in the first text: this may be a sign of English influence. While the English origins of the forms (apart from *aklan*, which is obscure) are obvious, the possessive forms are not those of English.

2.4.2 Verbs

Pitkern/Norfolk verbs have not retained English inflections. Verbs may be unmarked for tense and aspect (*ai law yuu*) but some are marked by preverbal markers *gwena* (future, e.g. *awas law naewa gwena dan*), *sa* or *se* (completive, e.g. *mais haat se skip a biit*) and *bin* (past, e.g. *fut yoli noo bin laane aklen?* ('why didn't you teach us?'). There is no copula with adjectives: *whataway hem* (literally 'how he').

2.4.3 Possessives

The possessive construction has the form X *fa* Y (e.g. *dem ai f' yoen*). *Fa* is also used to introduce purpose clauses (where Standard English would use an infinitive marked by *to*), as in *yuuset f' ring*, 'use it to ring'.

3 CASE STUDY 2: MAURITIAN CREOLE

Lexifier: **French**
Languages in contact: **French, West African languages, Bantu languages, Malagasy (Austronesian family) and Indian languages**
Relative numbers: **approximately equal numbers from each group**
Outcome: **creolisation without a clear pidgin stage**

3.1 Introduction

Mauritius is a small island in the southern Indian Ocean. Its closest neighbouring land masses are Madagascar – a much larger island – and the African mainland. It was uninhabited when discovered by the Portuguese at the start of the sixteenth century, but was settled by the Dutch in the seventeenth; after abandonment by the Dutch it was claimed by the French East India Company in 1715. French settlers arrived from the neighbouring French island of Réunion and from Europe, and began to import slaves from Madagascar, West Africa, East Africa and India. The number of slaves grew rapidly after 1727 and the proportion of Europeans in the population dropped accordingly, to 11 per cent by 1777 (Papen, 1978, p. 13). By this time there were already references to a local creole language. Britain captured and kept Mauritius during the Napoleonic wars, and English became the language of government and education; nevertheless French remained the language of a small elite, with Creole the language of the majority. After the emancipation of the slaves in 1835, indentured labourers were brought from India in large numbers; their descendants now speak Creole as well as some Indian languages such as Bhojpuri. (Information from Holm, 1989, pp. 396–8.)

There has been a lively debate among scholars about the exact origins of Mauritian Creole (MC). One theory, put forward by Robert Chaudenson (1974) is that Mauritian was an offshoot of the creole of Réunion, which provided some of the first European settlers on Mauritius during the French period. Two other scholars, Baker and Corne, have argued that the Réunionnais contribution to Mauritian was not substantial, and that MC came into being on Mauritius itself, without going through a full pidgin stage, in the period 1727 to 1738. During this period, 465 children were born to slave mothers, according to the parish registers. Baker writes (Baker and Corne, 1982, p. 248): 'I am satisfied that it was these children, or at least a proportion of them, who were responsible for transforming pidgin into something better suited to their needs, and thus for determining some of the more basic characteristics of MC.' Baker notes that in 1773, a newspaper advertisement concerning a lost slave, aged 13, mentions that 'he does not understand the creole language', indicating clearly that by that stage, only 22 years after the first wave of slave imports, an identifiable local language had developed.

This is not just a matter of getting the history of MC correct. If Baker and Corne are right, then Mauritius presents a clear example of abrupt creolisation (cf. the quote from Thomason and Kaufman in Section 1). Furthermore, the predominance of slaves (speakers of African languages and Malagasy) over Europeans (speakers of French) in the population at the time of creolisation can explain how on the one hand, MC is so different from Standard French, while on the other, it resembles the French-lexicon creoles of the Caribbean, where the 'mix' of speakers of European and African languages was comparable. By contrast, Réunionnais is much closer to Standard French than is Mauritian – and in Réunion, the ratio of Europeans to Africans was much higher. Le Page, in his preface to the book by Baker and Corne (1982), suggests a Caribbean parallel: the creole of Barbados, which is much closer to Standard English than, say, Jamaican Creole, also arose in a situation where the numbers of Europeans and Africans were more evenly matched.

3.2 Mauritian Creole Text

Extract from *Li* by Dev Virahsawmy (1982), translated as *The Prisoner of Conscience* by Ramesh Ramdoyal (the original title can mean 'he, 'she' or 'it'). The translation is published together with the original in the same book, but is given here immediately after the MC original. Note that Mike also uses some Standard French for effect (*voilà, c'est fait* and *Oh, la douce créature!*) and there is at least one borrowing from English (*training*). This is as would be expected in the present-day multilingual situation in Mauritius.

Note on orthography: the spelling is that of the source. In this system, the circumflex over a vowel (â, ê etc.) indicates nasalisation. Hence *bô* is pronounced similarly to Standard French *bon*.

MIKE

Bô, *voilà, c'est fait. (Li poz sizo la lor latab, met so laglas dâ pos.)* Serzâ, fin midi. Mo bizê alé. Mo pa kapav rat mo rândevu... *Oh, la douce créature!*

There, [French] that's perfect. (*He places the scissors on the table, puts the mirror inside his pocket*). Sergeant, it's twelve o'clock. I must be off. Can't keep my date waiting... [French] Oh, the sweet little thing!

RAWANA

To pa kapav alé, to râplasâ pa âkor arivé. Ki to presé! En vié renar kuma twa kon biê ki plis to fer ên fam atan twa, plis li kôtâ twa.

You can't go yet. Your replacement hasn't arrived yet. What's the rush anyway! An old fox like you ought to know that the more you keep them [lit. a woman] waiting the more they love you for it.

MIKE

Saken sa teknik... Kifer li âretar? Kisanla sa?

I know what I'm doing. Why's he late? Who is this bloke anyway?

RAWANA

Ki sa?

What?

MIKE

Kisanla pu râplas mwa.

Who is this bloke who's replacing me?

RAWANA

En sa ban zên jukal ki fek sorti Training.

Oh that! He's fresh from training school, still wet behind the ears.

MIKE

Li pa pu ser nu kwê?

He won't be in our way, will he?

RAWANA

Ser nu kwê! To kapav kwar. En kut kraking, mo fer li vin ên bô tutu. Dé tut fasô, to bizê returné dezer. Pa bliyé tu plâ fin dresé pu dezer-redmi. Avâ trwazer, tu bizê fini dâ lord.

In our way! You must be joking! By the time I finish with him he'll be eating out of my hands. In any case you've got to be back at two o'clock. Don't forget, everything is fixed for two and a half. Before three it must be over and done with.

3.2.1 Notes on the phonology of Mauritian Creole

MC phonology is characterised by the unrounding of the French front round vowels: /zen/ 'young', from French *jeune* /ʒœn/; /dite/ 'tea', from French *du thé* /dy te/ 'some tea'. The French palatal fricatives /ʒ/ and /ʃ/ are replaced by /z/ and /s/: /laz/ 'age', from French *l'age* /laʒ/ 'the age'; /sez/ 'chair', from French *chaise* /ʃez/. (Examples from Baker, 1972, p. 43.)

3.2.2 Notes on the lexicon

The great majority of MC words are of French origin, though Baker (1972) notes that more than 150 words are derived from English, more than 50 from Indian languages and several from Malagasy and Chinese.

One striking feature of the MC vocabulary when compared with that of French is the number of words which derive from a French word plus the article (*l'*, *le*, *la*, *de*, *du*, etc.). The French definite article is used in more contexts than the English one and is phonologically more closely bound (proclitic) to the noun it modifies. Compounding of the article with the preposition *de*, 'of', is also very common. Thus in spoken French, we are more likely to hear *le pied* /lə pje/ 'the foot' than simply *pied*; *du blé* /dy ble/ 'of the wheat' (also 'some wheat') than *blé* on its own. This fact probably accounts for the MC forms of these words: *lipye*, 'foot', *dible*, 'wheat', and many others, for example *liver*, 'winter' (French *l'hiver*), *dilo*, 'water' (French *de l'eau*), *lezwa*, 'goose' (singular) (French *les oies* (plural)) (Baker, 1972, p.p.77–8). It is interesting to note that MC does not itself have a definite article (though there is an indefinite singular article, *en*) so that, for example, *lipye* in a given context can mean 'foot' or 'the foot'. The part of the MC word which corresponds to the French article is definitely not a prefix; for MC speakers, it is simply part of the word.

The incorporation of articles as part of the form of the word is a feature of many French-lexicon creoles in different parts of the world. Bollée (1980) notes that different French-lexicon creoles have different sets of nouns with this feature, suggesting that they have developed independently of each other, at least to some extent.

3.3 A Comparison of the Grammar of MC and French

3.3.1 Pronominal system

Standard French has separate forms for subject, object and possessive pronouns. In addition there are separate masculine and feminine forms in the third person. MC has just one form for all three.

	Mauritian Creole		Standard French		
	singular	plural	singular		plural
1	mo	nu	je	(subject)	nous
			moi	(object)	
2	to	zot	tu	(subject)	vous
			toi	(object)	
3	li	zot	il	(masc. subj.)	ils
			elle	(fem. subj.)	elles
			le	(masc. obj.)	les
			la	(fem. obj.)	les

3.3.2   Verb tense and aspect

According to Baker (1972), MC has one tense marker, **ti** (Past) and four aspect markers (**pe**, Progressive; **fin**, Perfective; **a**, Indefinite Future; and **pu**, Definite Future). The past tense marker, **ti** can combine with each of the aspect markers, or they may occur singly, or not at all, for example:

mo mahze	'I eat'	French: *je mange*
mo pe mahze	'I am eating'	French: *je mange*
mo fin mahze	'I have eaten'	French: *j'ai mangé*
mo ti mahze	'I ate'	French (spoken): *j'ai mangé*
mo ti pu mahze	'I was going to eat'	French: *j'allais manger*

(Note: *h* signifies nasalisation in Baker's orthography; **mahze** = **mâze** in Virahsawmy's system.)

Not only are the MC verbal forms unlike the French ones in structure, there is no correspondence between them. MC makes distinctions (for example, between 'I eat' and 'I am eating') which are not made in the French system.

3.3.3   Negation

There is a single, invariant preverbal negator **pa**.

> MC: **mo mohte pa pe travay**, 'my watch isn't working'
> French: *ma montre ne travaille pas.* (Negation is performed by a combination of preverbal *ne* and postverbal *pas*.)

3.3.4   Determiners

In MC plurals are marked by the particle **ban** placed before the noun, e.g. **ban solda**, '(the) soldiers', **ban latab**, '(the) tables'. Plural marking is only used for emphasis or where contextually necessary. By contrast, in French, plurality is generally marked in speech by plural forms of modifiers or verbs which agree in number with the noun, e.g. *le garçon sait* /lə garsɔ̃ se/ ('the boy knows'), *les garçons savent* /le garsɔ̃ sav/ ('the boys know'). Here the spoken form of 'boy' is invariant but the article and verb inflect to show plural.

MC does not have a definite article (though it has a preverbal *in*definite article *en*) but it has a 'proximity marker' *-la*, which may be suffixed to a noun. This 'denotes proximity of time or place, that the nominal has been referred to a moment earlier or is close at hand' (Baker, 1972, p. 81): e.g. *latab-la*, 'the, this table'. French has prenominal articles (*la table*, 'the table') and demonstratives (*cette table*, 'this table') but nothing equivalent in sense to the MC *-la*.

4 CASE STUDY 3: SRANAN TONGO

Other names: **Sranan, Taki-Taki** (this term is found in older works on
  Creole languages, but is never used in Surinam; as it means 'chit-chat' it
  is somewhat insulting)
Lexifier: **English**
Languages in contact: **English, various languages of West Africa**
Relative numbers: **not stable, but Africans have outnumbered Europeans
  from the earliest stages**
Outcome: **either abrupt creolisation following a very brief pidgin stage, or
  'gradual creolisation'** (see discussion below)

4.1 Introduction

Sranan Tongo ('Surinam Tongue') is the native language of about one-third
of the half-million inhabitants of Surinam, on the north coast of South
America, and is a *lingua franca* for all of them. Mother-tongue speakers of
Sranan are mostly the descendants of African slaves; other major ethnic
groups in Surinam are East Indians, Javanese and Amerindians. In the
interior, other, related creoles, Djuka and Saramaccan, are spoken.

The historical facts of the early years of the colonial era in Surinam are
not disputed, but important questions remain concerning the formation of
Sranan. To sum up the history briefly: in 1651 English planters first settled
in Surinam. Around 1665 we know there were 1500 English planters and
3000 Arican slaves, mostly on small plantations (Holm, 1989, p. 434).
Virtually all these slaves would have been African-born. In 1667 the Dutch
captured Surinam, and kept it by the same treaty which gave present-day
New York to the English. The Dutch began to import new slaves, and the
English began to leave, though slowly; it was only in about 1675 that
the new slaves outnumbered the old ones. By about 1690 no English planters
were left in Surinam. The number of Dutch planters grew steadily, as did the
number of slaves in the colony.

The plantation system, with slavery, continued in the Dutch colonies until
1863. Throughout the slavery period, new slaves were brought to Surinam
from Africa to replace those who died in the harsh conditions there
(Surinam was thought to be one of the worst places for slaves to be sent to,
and the survival rate for slaves there was lower than elsewhere) or who
escaped into the interior. Slave escapes or *marronage* were a recurrent fact in
the Caribbean. Slaves who tried to escape and failed were, of course, very
severely punished; but those who reached the safety of the interior jungles of
Surinam (or elsewhere, the safety of the mountains) often set up villages
where they were able almost to re-establish an African way of life.
In Surinam the descendants of the maroons (escaped slaves) still live in

villages on the rivers of the interior, and speak creole languages such as Djuka, Boni and Saramaka Tongo (Saramaccan), which are not mutually intelligble with Sranan Tongo. (There are some grammatical differences from Sranan Tongo and major lexical differences, including a higher proportion of Portuguese and African vocabulary.)

Surinam continued under Dutch rule until 1975, when it became an independent state. A large number of Surinamese people (by birth or descent) now live in the Netherlands.

From what has been said it is clear that Sranan Tongo speakers have not had much opportunity to hear English spoken for over 300 years. On the other hand, Dutch (the official language, even now) and various African languages have been present in Surinam for most of that period. Not surprisingly, Sranan does not closely resemble English.

Two simple facts – (a) that the 'core' lexicon (the most basic vocabulary) of Sranan is mainly English, and (b) that all the English planters had left Surinam by 1690 – point to the conclusion that Sranan, or at least its *lexicon*, developed rapidly in less than 40 years to a stage where its main characteristics had been determined. The first known text in Sranan dates from 1718, and shows a language quite similar to today's. Sranan thus seems to be a good candidate for 'abrupt creolisation'. The conventional view until recently was that Sranan – either as a pidgin or as a creole – must have formed no later than 1680, probably earlier, and that it was transmitted to the new (Dutch) slaves by the old (English) slaves during the transition period, 1667–90.

While there can be hardly any doubt that an English-lexicon pidgin was in use in Surinam during the era of the English planters, exactly what happened next is unclear. If the pidgin was 'abruptly creolised' by children learning it as a first language during the 'English' era, those children may have been the instruments whereby it continued as a native language in Surinam, being learnt as a second language (perhaps in a pidgin form) by the newly-arrived slaves brought by the Dutch. However, there is no concrete evidence for this. On the contrary, the number of children born in Surinam was always rather low in comparison with the number of new slaves. Birth rates among slaves were low (probably due to overwork, unhealthy conditions and a positive desire not to bring children into the world of slavery) while new slaves were constantly having to be imported owing to the short lifespan of slaves in Surinam.

On the basis of these demographic factors, as well as structural changes in the language itself, Arends and Bruyn (1994, p. 114) argue for a *gradualist* account of Sranan's origin. According to Arends and Bruyn, 'it seems unlikely that nativization by children took place during the first one or two generations of slaves, simply because the children required to perform such a process were not present in sufficient numbers'. It seems possible that even after four generations, only 10 per cent of the slave population was locally born. They suggest that 'it was probably not until the balance between locally-born and African-born blacks had shifted further in favor of the former that the nativization of Sranan really started'. They add, however, that there is no agreement about how many children are required for this process to be carried out.

The idea that Sranan creolised gradually over several generations, developing structurally and lexically as it did so, may help to explain the high proportion of *substrate* features which can be identified in the language. African grammar seems to have had a particularly strong influence on Sranan: indeed many aspects of African culture are reflected in the language. This topic will be taken up later in this chapter.

Lexically, Sranan can be likened to a tree-trunk: at the very core are a few Portuguese-derived words such as *kaba*, 'finish' (Portuguese *acabar*), and *pikin*, 'small' (Portuguese *pequenho*). Around this slender core we have a more solid stem made up of English words. These include most of the words for the most basic everyday activities and things, people, animals, parts of the body and some numbers: *taki*,'talk', *oso*, 'house', *uma*, 'woman', *dagu*, 'dog', *finga*, 'finger', *tu*, 'two'. Next comes another thick stratum of Dutch words, some of them only slightly less basic than the English ones: *denki*, 'think' (Dutch *denken*), *spikri*, 'nail' (Dutch *spijker*), *srudati*, 'soldier' (Dutch *soldaat*), *feyfi*, 'five'. All these were already an integral part of the language in the nineteenth century and probably earlier. Lexical borrowing from Dutch has probably continued at a steady rate since then. More recently, with increasing influence from English internationally, new words have been borrowed from English. (For a more detailed account of the origins of the Sranan lexicon, and what the authors call 'lexicon archaeology', see Geert Koefoed and Jacqueline Tarenskeen, 1996.)

In addition, dotted about in the lexicon, are words taken from the other languages with which Sranan has been in contact, including Amerindian languages and Javanese. A number of words derive from contact with the Portuguese Jews who were among the early settlers in Surinam. Interestingly, these words refer to Jewish religious practices but have been nativised to refer to Surinamese ones. *Kaseri* (from *kosher*, in the Sephardic Jewish pronunciation) refers to ritual cleanliness while *trefu*, (from *trayf*, meaning non-Kosher food in Jewish practice) is used to describe 'secret taboo' foods, particular to each individual, which will bring the eater out in a rash.

As creoles go, Sranan and some of the other creoles of Surinam are exceptionally well documented. Missionaries were active in Surinam from early on, and from the middle of the nineteenth century we have a dictionary by the Moravian missionary Wullschlägel (1856) and a grammar probably by the same author. The fact that the missionaries used Sranan as a written medium in education in the nineteenth century (until stopped by the Dutch colonial regime) means that we have a fair number of written texts spanning the last two centuries, as well as a few earlier ones. This has enabled scholars like Jacques Arends and others to do historical studies of the developing Sranan language. Others have concentrated on detailed phonological studies of the Surinam creoles (for example, Norval Smith, 1987), or on the syntax of Saramaccan (Francis Byrne, 1987).

4.2 Traditional Sranan Text: 'Why Dog Goes About Naked'

An oral narrative recorded by Melville J. Herskovits and Frances S. Herskovits (1936). They transcribed this folktale about Anansi the Spider using the International Phonetic Alphabet. I have standardised the spelling in accordance with proposals made by Pieter Seuren in 1980.

Wan dansi ben de. Dagu no ben abi
one dance PAST BE Dog NEG PAST have

                                   krosi fu go dansi.
                                   clothes for go dance

Dan a leni wan bruku na Anansi.
then he lend one trousers LOC Anansi

Ma di den go dansi, a bruku ben pikin fu Dagu.
But when they go dance the trousers PAST small for Dog

Te Dagu e dansi, a e bradi en futu.
when Dog ASP dance he ASP broad his foot (leg)

A fosi tron Anansi kari en kon na wan sey, a taki,
the first time Anansi call him come LOC one side he say

'Mati, luku bun, yu broko mi bruku.'
friend look well you break my trousers

A libi en.
he left him

Di den e dansi baka, Dagu bradi en futu baka.
when they ASP dance again Dog broad his leg again

Anansi kari en baka, a taki,
Anansi call him back he say

'Mati, luku bun, yu broko mi bruku.'
friend look well you break my trousers

Ma di fu dri tron di Dagu bradi en
but REL for three time when Dog broad his

                                   futu baka, nomo
                                   leg again at-once

Anansi	kisi	a	bruku,	hari	puru	na	Dagu	skin.
Anansi	get	the	trousers	haul	pull	LOC	Dog	skin (body)

Dati	meki	te	tide	Dagu	e	waka	na	soso	skin.
that	make	till	today	Dog	ASP	walk	LOC	only	skin

Note: ***bruku***, 'trousers', from Dutch *broeken*.
ASP = aspect marker
REL = relative clause marker

Translation (by Mark Sebba)

There was going to be a dance. Dog had no clothes to go to the dance in, so he borrowed a pair of trousers from Anansi. But when they went to dance, the trousers were too small for Dog. When Dog danced, he kicked out his legs. The first time, Anansi called him to one side, he said, 'Look here, my friend, you're tearing my trousers!' He left him. When they danced again, Dog kicked out his legs again. Anansi called him again, he said, 'Look here, my friend, you're tearing my trousers!' But the third time Dog kicked out his legs, Anansi immediately took his trousers and pulled them off Dog's body.

   That's why, to this day, Dog walks around naked.

4.3   Modern Sranan Text: *Uma fu Sranan* (Women of Surinam)

From the *Redi Dron* (Red Drum) *Songbook*, *c.*1980

Wi	na	den	uma	fu	Sranan
we	BE	the-PL	woman	of	Surinam

We are the women of Surinam

Wi	na	den	mama	fu	a	kondre
we	BE	the-PL	mama	of	the	country

We are the mothers of the country

Na	wi	e	wasi	den	pikin
BE	we	ASP	wash	the-PL	child

It's we who wash the children

Den	mangri	anu	nanga	fesi
them	thin	hand	with	face

Their thin hands and faces

Dan	wi	e	luku	in'	den	bigi	ay	fu	wi	pikin
then	we	ASP	look	in	the-PL	big	eye	of	we	child

Then we look into the big eyes of our children

Pikin   nanga   angri
child   with   hunger
Hungry children

En   wi   e   pramisi:
and   we   ASP   promise
And we promise

'dyonsro   mama   sa   tyar'   a   nyan'
just-now   mama   FUT   carry   the   food
'Soon Mama will bring the food'

Go   prey   now,   go   prey   now
Go   play   now   go   play   now
Go play now, go play now

dyonsro   mama   sa   tyar'   a   nyan
just-now   mama   FUT   carry   the   food
Soon Mama will bring the food.

Wi na den uma fu Sranan
we are the women of Surinam

wi na den Sranan wroko uma
we are the Surinam work(ing) women

na wi e wroko na bigi mevrouw
is we work for big madams

luku pikin sondro angri
look children without hunger

dan wi e prakseri un eygi pikin na oso
then we think our own children in house (at home)

pikin nanga angri
children with hunger

en wi e prakseri san un ben taygi wi pikin
and we think what we have told our children

So a ben de so langa ten
so it has been so long time

so a ben de someni yari
so it has been so-many years

na so den yari ben pasa
is so the years have pass

dati no wani taki dati a sa tan so
that not want talk that it shall stay so (i.e. that doesn't mean it will always
be so)

bika wi sabi taki a dey sa kon dati wi sa fri
because we know that the day will come that we shall (be) free

Sranan tron fri kondre
Surinam turn free country

uma sa feti ina strey fu kon fri
women shall fight in the battle to (be)come free

Note words not of English origin:
pikin, 'small'; *sabi*, 'know' (?Portuguese)
mevrouw, 'Madam'; *prakseri*, 'think'; *eygi*, 'own'; *strey*, 'fight' (Dutch)

4.4   Exercises

1. (a)   In the texts above, find the Sranan words for the following:

     look, leave, break, wash, hand, face, work, want, talk, turn, fight

     What systematic differences are there between the English and
     Sranan words?

    (b)   What would you expect the Sranan words for the following to be?

     live, knife, burn, love, sing

    (c)   What do you think the following Sranan words mean?

     neti, waka, prani, sribi, krey

2. On the basis of the above, what can you say about what clusters of
    consonants are allowed in Sranan? And are there any rules about
    syllable structure?

3. The following are words in Akan, a West African language which
    formed part of the Sranan substrate. (Tones are not indicated,
    although Akan has phonemic tone.)

kasa	'speak'
kyerε	'show'
goro	'play'
abɔfora	'child'

> | *dadesan* | 'pot' |
> |---|---|
> | *pɔŋkɔ* | 'horse' |
> | *hene* | 'king' |

Do you notice any similarities with Sranan in terms of their syllable structure or phonological characteristics?

4. Go through the Sranan texts above and note all the possible Sranan forms which are equivalent to the English copula (i.e. translated by any form of *be*).

    (a)   What forms does the Sranan copula have?

    (b)   When is each of these forms used? (Under what syntactic conditions?)

    (c)   Now compare the Sranan copula system with that of Nigerian Pidgin English, described at the end of the previous chapter. What do you notice?

4.5 Grammatical Notes

4.5.1 *The pronoun system of Sranan*

	singular	**plural**
1	mi	wi
2	yu	unu
3	a (subject)	den
	en (object/possessive)	

Standard English has separate forms for subject, object and possessive pronouns, and a three-way gender distinction in the third person singular (*he/she/it*). Sranan has just one form for each pronoun, with the exception of the third person singular, which has one form for the subject and another for the object/possessive. The Sranan form is sometimes derived from the English subject form and sometimes from the object form.

We can compare the Standard English and Sranan systems in terms of their numbers of *dimensions*. The English pronoun system can be thought of as having four dimensions: *person* (first, second, third), *number* (singular/ plural), *case* (subject/object/possessive) and *gender* (masculine/feminine/ neuter). Sranan could be said to have at most three of these: person, number and case. Of these, case is marginal since it only applies to the third person singular. Gender does not apply at all.

Sranan is thus 'simpler' than English by at least one dimension. But notice another difference: Sranan also has distinct singular and plural second person forms ('you-singular' *yu* and 'you-plural' *unu*, of African origin).

This makes the Sranan system more symmetrical than the English one, and could be taken as evidence that Sranan is 'simpler' (but more 'expressive') than English in this respect.

4.5.2   Plurals
In Standard British English, plural marking is the norm e.g. book–books, woman–women.

In Sranan, either the plural is not marked at all or it is marked through the definite article, which has a separate singular form *a* and plural form *den* (note that these are also the forms of the third person pronouns). Examples: *a pikin*, 'the child'; *den pikin*, 'the children', *pikin*, 'child/children'.

4.5.3   Tense and aspect
Sranan has aspect markers **e** (progressive) and **o** (future), which can combine with the tense marker **ben** (anterior) to give combinations like

mi e waka	'I am walking'
mi ben waka	'I walked'
mi ben e waka	'I was walking'
mi ben o waka	'I was about to walk'

The unmarked form *mi waka* can have present habitual or anterior meaning: 'I walk (habitually)' or 'I walked (on a particular occasion)'. The form **kba** (from *kaba*, 'finish') can also be used to mark completion of an action: *mi waka kba*, 'I had walked'.

The tense and aspect markers are similar in form and function to those of West African Pidgin English (see Chapter 4). Also compare Mauritian Creole (above).

4.5.4   The copula
Standard English uses the copula *to be* for a variety of purposes. In particular, it is used (in all tenses) with locative complements (I *am* at home), with equatives (I *am* a writer) and with adjectival complements (I *am* tired). In Sranan, we find that each of these cases would require a different form of the copula, or none:

Locative complement: **de**
Rudy de na oso, 'Rudy is at home'

Equative: **a**
Rudy a stukaman, 'Rudy is (a) student'

Adjectival complement: **(absent)**
a siki, 'he is sick'

The full story is slightly more complex than this, since **de** may also occur with certain adjectival phrases, e.g. *a liba de so bradi*, 'the river is so broad' (compare *a liba bradi* 'the river is broad') (see Sebba, 1986) and noun phrases used attributively. In any case, it can be seen that the copula system of Sranan uses none of the English lexical forms and has no one-to-one relationship with the English system.

4.5.5   Possession
Sranan possessives can be formed in either of two ways:
  (a)   X **fu** Y: *a pikin fu Mary* ('the child of Mary')
  (b)   YX: *Mary pikin* ('Mary's child')

Note: *fu* is also a verbal marker corresponding to English *to*, e.g. *mi wani fu taki nanga en* ('I want to talk with him'). Note the similarity with Pitcairnese: *yuuset f' ring*, 'use it to ring'.

5   CASE STUDY 4: KRIO – ACROSS THE ATLANTIC AND BACK AGAIN

Lexifier: **English**
Languages in contact: **English-lexicon creole and pidgin, various languages of West Africa especially Yoruba**
Relative numbers: **Europeans had minimal involvement**
Outcome: **creole followed by possible repidginisation and recreolisation**

5.1   Introduction

Krio (Holm, 1989, pp. 412–21) is the native language of about half a million inhabitants of the West African republic of Sierra Leone. Europeans had been trading in the area which is now Freetown, capital of Sierra Leone, since the fifteenth century, and it is likely that an English-lexicon pidgin was spoken in the area, as in other parts of West Africa where English traders and slavers had an interest. At the end of the eighteenth century, in 1772, slavery was abolished in England. Sierra Leone became the focus of projects by abolitionists to repatriate former slaves and other Africans to Africa. The Freetown colony was initially established in 1787 by a mixture of freed slaves of African descent from England and North America (the latter having won their freedom by escaping to fight for the Crown against the rebellious colonies which became the United States). More former American slaves turned soldier came in 1792. In 1800, these were joined by 550 Jamaican maroons (escaped slaves). For most of the next six decades Freetown was a base for British navy anti-slavery patrols, which intercepted slaving ships of other countries, liberated the slaves, and brought them to Freetown, where they were settled (few were able to return to their original homes). In the linguistic history of Krio we can identify the following likely sources:

1. A possible pidgin or creole form of English spoken around Freetown before the settlement of the ex-slaves.
2. A possible pidgin or creole form of English spoken by the North American slaves who were 'founder citizens' of the colony. (See Chapter 9 for a discussion of the language of African-Americans.)
3. The English-lexicon creole of the Jamaican maroons who came in 1800. The maroon creole is usually regarded as more distant from English (i.e. more 'creole') than other varieties of Jamaican creole.
4. A wide range of African languages brought by freed slaves during the nineteenth century. From lexical evidence it is clear that Yoruba, a language spoken mainly in Nigeria, was one of the most significant.
5. Local indigenous languages of the region around Freetown: Mende, Temne, Vai, etc.

From the above we can see first, that Standard English was not significantly involved in the formation of Krio, except in the very earliest stages before the Freetown colony was founded. The model (or 'target language') for learners of Krio has always been a *creole*. Secondly, large numbers of freed slaves were coming into the colony for many years, bringing new African languages with them. It is possible that a *pidgin* form of Krio developed which was used for communication among the newcomers, or between the newcomers and the existing community; also, since a pidgin form of English was widely spoken along the coast, some of the newcomers may have been familiar with it already. Finally, the pidgin Krio may itself have creolised through being learnt by the children of the newcomers; and this cycle may have repeated itself several times as new generations of freed slaves arrived in the colony. Thus modern Krio is likely to be the product of the following stages:

1. The intial pidginisation of English on the African coast.
2. The creolisation of that Pidgin English, either in Africa (around the coastal trading centres) or in the Caribbean (on the plantations).
3. Contact between several types of Creole English (North American, Jamaican, West African) around the time of the establishment of the Freetown settlement.
4. Repidginisation of this creole as its speakers came into contact with freed slaves newly brought from other parts of Africa, some of whom spoke only African languages, and some of whom may have known a type of pidgin English similar to Krio.

5. **Recreolisation** of the pidgin Krio, as it became the first language of the generation born in the Freetown colony.
6. Continuing influence from African languages, both local and distant.
7. Influence from Standard English as Freetown came under British colonial administration and Standard English became the language of schools and government.

Krio is a good example of how pidginisation and creolisation take place in multilingual settings, often of great complexity. If multilingualism continues to be a feature of the community, and the other conditions are right for it to happen, the cycle of pidginisation and creolisation may take place again. While it is clear that African languages (especially Yoruba) and Standard English have had an influence on the lexicon of modern Krio, a comparison with West African Pidgin English (Chapter 4), Sranan (this chapter) and Jamaican Creole (Chapter 7) show that it has strong links with both the pidgin tradition of West Africa and the creoles of the Caribbean.

Although it is mainly a spoken language, Krio has from time to time been used as a literary medium. Shakespeare's *Julius Caesar* was translated into Krio by Thomas Decker (n.d.; orthography is that of the source):

> ... *Way Caesar been leck me, are cry for am; way good been meet am, are gladdy for day; way e been tranga are respect am; but, way e want-want are kill am.*

Note: *are* = 'I', phonetically [aː].

As Caesar loved me, I weep for him; as he was fortunate, I rejoice at it; as he was valiant, I honour him; but as he was ambitious, I slew him.
(Act III, scene 2)

Other literary works have occasionally appeared in Krio. In the 1990s Krio has been introduced into primary education, but this is still experimental.

5.2 Krio Text

The following text is by Arthur de Graft-Rosenior, a journalist with an interest in education and development issues. It appeared in *African Farmer*, December 1991, pp. 50–51. The majority of articles in this issue of *African Farmer* were in English only. This article was unique in being published in two versions, one in English and one in Krio. The translation below each line of the Krio version is a 'literal' one which relates each Krio word to its English source (words in *italics* are not of English origin). The free translation below is by the author, and is the one which appeared in *African Farmer*.

Note on orthography: The orthography here is phonemic, and is the orthography used by the author, with the following exception. Krio distinguishes between high-mid and low-mid front and back vowels, thus *skel* /skel/ 'scale' has a closer vowel than /sɛl/ 'sell' and /fo/ 'four' is distinct from /fɔ/ 'for'. The author has indicated this distinction by using capital letters for the more open vowels, so that the headline as printed reads: *Isatu Koroma: Mi Savis di Mek KOsatament DEn TOn Bak Kam Mit Mi Ol Tem.* Since this is somewhat difficult to read I have adapted the text in line with another convention which is sometimes used to represent Krio vowels. In this version of the text, *the more open vowels are indicated by a following h.* Thus *skel*, 'scale'; *sehl*, 'sell'; *fo*, 'four'; *foh*, 'for'. The above quote from Decker's translation of Julius Caesar in this orthography would be as follows:

> ... *We Caesar bin lehk mi, a kray foh am; we gud bin mit am, a gladi foh de; we i bin tranga a respekt am; boht, we i want-want a kil am.*

Isatu Koroma: Mi Savis di Mek Kohsatament Dehn
Isatu Koroma: me service *di* make customer them

Tohn Bak Kam Mit Mi Ol Tem
turn back come meet me all time

Smol-skel fama dehn na Afrika (noh lehk uman dehm), kin ohlwez mehnsho
small-scale farmer them in Africa (no like woman them), can always mention

dehn behteh wan bay ohw dehn ebul foh fid, drehs, fehn ples foh slip,
them better one by how them able for feed, dress, find place for sleep,

ehn ehdyuket dehn pikin dehm.
and educate them child them.

Bay da we de nohmoh, Isatu Koroma we de na SaLon behteh insehf foh tru.
By that way *de* no more, Isatu Koroma w(ho) *de na* Sierra Leone better himself for true.

Wit 1.8 hehkta (4.5 eka) Land na Lehsta vilej,
With 1.8 hectares (4.5 acres) land *na* Leicester village,

we de 5 kilomita from Fritohn, di neshon in kapital,
w(hich) *de* 5 kilometre from Freetown, the nation him capital,

Ms. Koroma na wan pan boku* uman dehm we di plant vehjitebul ehn spays
Ms Koroma *na* one 'pon *many* woman them w(ho) *di* plant vegetable and spice

foh sehl na Fritohn makit dehm.
to sell *na* Freetown market them.

In man, we na lebra, wit in fo big pikin, na dehm kin ehp am foh avehst
Him man, w(ho) *na* labourer, with him four big child, *na* them can help him for harvest

ehn sehl di vehjitebul we du foh fid di famul ehn sehn di pikin dehn go skul.
and sell the vegetable w(hich) do for feed the family and send the child them go school.

In man di wok Le 600 ($3.50) foh mohnt.
Him man *di* work Le 600 ($3.50) for month.

Ms Koroma in yon gadin di gi am Le 1,800 foh wik.
Ms Koroma her own garden *di* give him Le 1,800 (US$11) for week.

* Note: *boku*, 'many' from French *beaucoup*.

Isatu Koroma: Service Keeps Customers Coming Back

Small-scale farmers in Africa, especially women, often measure success by their ability to feed, clothe, house and educate their children. By this standard, Isatu Koroma of Sierra Leone is truly successful.

With 1.8 hectares (4.5 acres) of land in Leicester village, 5 kilometres from Freetown, the nation's capital, Ms Koroma is one of many women who grow vegetables and spices to sell at markets in the capital. With the help of her husband, a day labourer, and their four oldest children, she harvests and sells enough vegetables to feed the family and send the children to school. Her husband earns Le 600 (600 Leones, US$3.50) a month. Ms Koroma's garden brings in Le 1,800 (US$11) a week.

5.3 Exercise

1. Go through the text in 2.4.2 and note the following:

   (a) Two distinct functions of *na*.
   (b) Two distinct functions of *di*.
   (c) The function of *de*.
   (d) The function of *foh*.

2. How are plurals indicated in Krio?

3. How is possession indicated in Krio?

Compare your findings with the grammatical notes on West African Pidgin English (Chapter 4) and Sranan (this chapter). What similarities or differences do you notice?

6   CASE STUDY 5: AFRIKAANS – A CREOLE OR A 'CREOLOID'?

Lexifier: **Dutch**
Languages in contact: **Dutch, creolised Portuguese, Malay, Khoi (Hottentot), possibly German, French and Xhosa**
Relative numbers: **not established, but the Dutch were a significant proportion**
Outcome: **partial creolisation (disputed)**

6.1   Introduction

The Dutch East India Company established a station at the Cape of Good Hope in 1652, as a mid-way stop for its ships trading with the Far East. Cape Town, which grew around this settlement, was populated by the Dutch, other European settlers including Germans and French Huguenots, the indigenous Khoi-speaking inhabitants of the area (sometimes known as Hottentots) and slaves from the East Indies, usually characterised as 'Malays'.

Today, a majority of South Africa's ethnic Europeans call themselves Afrikaners and speak a language called Afrikaans, at one time known as Cape Dutch. Afrikaans also has a large number of native speakers among the racially mixed ethnic groups ('Coloureds' and 'Malays'). Nonstandard varieties are spoken by both white and mixed-race groups, and a pidginised variety known as Fly Taal is spoken by Africans in some urban areas (see Chapter 1).

In the nineteenth century Britain became the dominant imperial power in Southern Africa, giving rise to discontent among the descendants of the Dutch settlers, many of whom migrated inland. Towards the end of the nineteenth century, and again early in the twentieth century, Afrikaans became associated with Afrikaner nationalist (specifically, anti-British) cultural movements. At the establishment of the Union of South Africa in 1910, the Dutch language was given equal official status with English. However, the Afrikaans cultural movement pressed for Afrikaans rather than Dutch to be official. This was recognised by law in 1925. Today, Afrikaans has a thriving literature with numerous daily papers and other periodicals and large numbers of books. It has its own monolingual radio and television channels.

Lexically Afrikaans shows only a few significant differences from Dutch, though some very common words are affected (e.g. Afrikaans *baie*, 'very', Dutch *zeer*; Afrikaans *min*, 'few', Dutch *weinig*). Gramatically, however, Afrikaans shows considerable simplification when compared with Dutch. Verbal paradigms are reduced and regularised, noun cases (which were still present in seventeenth-century Dutch, though being lost) are absent, and grammatical gender in nouns (still present in Dutch) is missing.

Debate has raged among interested parties for about a century over whether Afrikaans can be called a creole. The grammatical differences between Dutch and Afrikaans are of an order which has not occurred in any other overseas 'offshoot' of a European language, though there have been several over a similar timespan (French of France and Canada; English in Britain and North America; Portuguese in Portugal and Brazil). The simplification shown by Afrikaans in its grammar is the sort which typifies creoles; however, Afrikaans grammar is complex in other ways which make it similar to Dutch but unlike other creoles. For example, Afrikaans word order, like that of Dutch and German, is different in main clauses (SVO) and subordinate clauses (SOV). Compared with the differences between, say, Mauritian Creole and Standard French, the differences between Afrikaans and Dutch do not seem nearly so great. There is a degree of mutual intelligibility between the two languages, particularly the written languages. For this reason, even those creolists who believe that Afrikaans has been through a process of creolisation would regard Afrikaans, at least in its standard form, as *partially* rather than fully creolised.

A 'feel' for the extent of differences between Standard Afrikaans and Standard Dutch is given by the following sentence:

Dutch:
Ik	**zei**	**hem**	**dat**	**ik**	**het**	**glas**	**gebroken**	**hebbe.**
I	say-PAST	him	that	I	the	glass	PAST-break-en	have

Afrikaans:
Ek	**het**	**vir**	**hom**	**gesê**	**dat**	**ek**	**die**	**glas**	**gebreek**	**het.**
I	have	for	him	PAST-say	that	I	the	glass	PAST-break	have

'I told him that I broke/have broken the glass.'

The possibility of Afrikaans having creole origins was embarrassing for the White political movement which had promoted it as the vehicle of (Afrikaner) nationalism. The majority of Afrikaner academics could not accept the possibility that Afrikaans had its origin in a contact language used by slaves and servants, insisting instead that Afrikaans derived from Dutch dialects through 'spontaneous', i.e. normal, if slightly accelerated, processes of language change. One Afrikaans academic who promoted the idea of Afrikaans as a creole, Marius Valkhoff (1966), was severely criticised by South African academics in the opposite camp. Until recently, the 'Afrikaans-as-creole' theory had wide acceptance *outside* South Africa but was given little credence within the country. The debate is still unresolved, though not simply for political reasons. The problem is that Afrikaans, though it has some creole-like features and arose in social conditions which *could* have given rise to a creole, is not a *clear* case of creolisation. Afrikaans has therefore sometimes been labelled a '**creoloid**', meaning that it has creole-like features but is not a full creole. Much research still needs to be done to improve our understanding of the processes that take place during language contact. As Paul T. Roberge writes in the conclusion of his paper on the formation of Afrikaans, 'in the history of Afrikaans it was not always Dutch or substratum grammar, but three linguistic traditions – European, African (Khoikhoi) and Asian – that have met and hybridized with one another to produce a new whole that is truly more than the sum of its parts' (1993, p. 87).

6.2　Afrikaans Text

This text is taken from the Readers' Letters column of the community newspaper *Grassroots* (January 1984), which was published during a period of intense political struggle in South Africa in the 1980s. The majority of the paper is in English, but a few of the contributions are in Afrikaans. This reader's address and name (as well as her complaint) indicate that she is of mixed race ('Coloured') though her Afrikaans is more or less Standard, apart from lexical borrowings from English (e.g. *slippers* for Standard Afrikaans *pantoffels*) and the nonstandard spelling/pronunciation of the demonstrative *daai* (= *daardie*).

DIS	**'N**	**SKANDE**	**DAT**	**ONS**	**SO**	**MOET**	**LEWE!**
it-is	a	shame	that	we	so	must	live

LIEWE	**GRASSROOTS**
dear	Grassroots

ALMAL	**het**	**die**	**vakansie**	**geniet,**	**lekker**	**onstspan,**	**lekker**	**geëet,**
everyone	has	the	vacation	enjoy	nicely	relax		nicely	PAST-eat

maar	**wat**	**van**	**ons**	**'pensioners'?**	**Oor**	**die**	**Nuwe**	**Jaar**
but	what	of	us	pensioners	over	the	new	year

het	**ek**	**niks**	**gehad**	**nie,**	**niks**	**geld,**
have	I	nothing	PAST-had	NEG,	nothing	money

niks	**lekkergoed**	**nie.**
nothing	nice-thing	NEG

Ek	kry	eenennegentig	rand	elke	maand.
I	get	one-and-ninety	rands	every	month

Hoe	kan	ek	regkom?	...
how	can	I	right-come	

Krismis	was	daar	niks	in	die	huis	nie.
Christmas	was	there	nothing	in	the	house	NEG

Ek	kon	nie	eens
I	can-PAST	NEG	even

'n	overall	of	'n	paar	slippers	gekoop	het	nie.
an	overall	or	a	pair	slippers	PAST-buy	have	NEG

Dis	'n	skande	dat	ons	so	moet	lewe.
it-is	a	shame	that	we	so	must	live

Kyk	hoe	baie	kry	die	wit	mense.
look	how	much	get	the	white	people

En	hulle	het	nie	eens	die	geld	nodig	nie.
and	they	have	NEG	even	the	money	need	NEG

Hulle	kan	hulle	'servants'	met	daai	geld	betaal.
They	can	they	servants	with	that	money	pay

Ek	kan	nie	eens	iets	vir	my	kleinkinders
I	can	NEG	even	something	for	my	grandchildren

gekoop	het	nie.
PAST-buy	have	NEG

Dis	regtig	'n	skande...
it-is	truly	a	shame

IT'S A DISGRACE THE WAY WE HAVE TO LIVE LIKE THIS!

DEAR GRASSROOTS
EVERYONE enjoyed the holidays, relaxed well, ate well, but what of us poor pensioners? Over the New Year I had nothing, no money, nothing nice.

I get 91 rands every month. How can I manage?

At Christmas there was nothing in the house. I couldn't even have bought an overall or a pair of slippers. It's a disgrace that we have to live like this.

Look how much the white people get. And they don't even need the money. They can pay their servants with that money.

I couldn't even buy something for my grandchildren.

It's really a disgrace . . .

6.3   Grammatical Notes

In these notes the grammar of Standard Afrikaans will be compared with that of Standard Dutch (ABN, *Algemeen Beschaafd Nederlands*). Non-standard varieties of Afrikaans show considerably more differences.

6.3.1   *Pronouns*
The Afrikaans personal pronoun system preserves all the contrasts of person, number, and gender which exist in Dutch. However, some of the pronoun forms are different (*hulle*, 'they' instead of Dutch *zij*, 'they', from *hun lui* 'their people', formed on analogy with Dutch *jullie, jouw lui* = 'your people'). Particularly striking is the second person plural subject pronoun *ons*, which has the form of the object pronoun in Dutch. Thus Dutch makes the distinction *wij/ons* ('we/us') while Afrikaans has only *ons* for both. This is reminiscent of many creoles where the object forms of the lexifier pronoun become the only pronoun form in the creole, e.g. Sranan *mi* and *den*.

6.3.2   *Gender*
All Dutch nouns have either 'common' gender or 'neuter', which is not indicated on the noun itself but can be seen in the form taken by the definite article: *de man*; *de vrouw*, 'the woman'; but *het glas,* 'the glass'; *het huis*, 'the house'; *het geld*, 'the money'. Afrikaans lacks gender in nouns altogether: *die glas*; *die huis*; *die geld*; *die mense*, 'the people'.

6.3.3   *Determiners*
In addition to the invariant definite article *die* and indefinite article *'n* [ə], a reduced form of *een*, 'one', Afrikaans has demonstratives *hierdie, daardie* (*daai*), formed from a compound of *hier*, 'here', and *daar*, 'there', + *die*. Compare Dutch *deze/dit*, 'this', and *die/dat*, 'that'.

6.3.4   *Verb forms*
Afrikaans verbs, with a very small set of exceptions (the verbs for 'be', 'have', and some modals) are invariant in form except in the past tense, having no inflections for person or number. Dutch verbs, by contrast, have obligatory inflections, e.g. *ik kom, hij komt, wij komen* ('I come, he comes, we come', etc.).

While Dutch has both a simple past tense formed by inflecting the verb stem, e.g. *ik zag* 'I saw', and a compound tense formed by the verb *hebben*, 'to have', + past participle, Afrikaans has only one past tense, modelled on the second of these, with the form of *het* + past participle, e.g. *ek het geskop*, 'I kicked', where the past participle is formed by affixing *ge-* to the verb stem. Such participle formation is very regular in Afrikaans, less so in Dutch; e.g. Afrikaans *gebreek,* 'broke', *gekoop,* 'bought'; compare *ek breek,* 'I break', *ek koop,* 'I buy'; Dutch *gebroken* (compare *ik breek*), *gekocht* (compare *ik koop*).

6.3.5 *Word order*

Dutch (like German) has subject-verb-object word order in main clauses, but is verb-final in dependent clauses. Use of an auxiliary verb or modal even in a main clause causes the main verb to appear at the end of the sentence. In spite of the complexity of Dutch in this respect, Afrikaans word order behaves identically to Dutch.

Compare:

No auxiliary:	***almal geniet die vakansie***, 'everyone is enjoying the vacation'
With auxiliary:	***almal het die vakansie geniet***, 'everyone enjoyed the vacation'

Main clause:	***ons moet so lewe***, 'we must live like this'
Embedded clause:	***dis 'n skande dat ons so moet lewe***, 'it's a disgrace that we must live like this'

This is one area of Afrikaans grammar which is *not* simplified with respect to Dutch, and is arguably more complex than in many other languages.

6.3.6 *Possessives*

Afrikaans possession is shown by the invariant particle *se* thus: *Jan se skoene*, 'Jan's shoes'. Although the Dutch equivalent would follow the same order, it involves a morpheme suffixed to the possessor: *Jans schoenen*. The Afrikaans construction has a similar pattern to that of Creole Portuguese *sua* and Malay *punya* (see den Besten, 1978) and the same construction is also found in the Caribbean creole Papiamentu using *su*.

6.3.7 *Reduplication*

Reduplication has a number of functions in Afrikaans which are not present at all in Dutch. For example, a verb reduplicated may be used adverbially: *die kinders het sing-sing aangekom*, 'the children arrived singing'.

6.3.8 Negation

Probably no aspect of Afrikaans has received more attention from linguists than the double negative *nie . . . nie*, e.g. *hulle het **nie** eens die geld nodig **nie***, 'they don't even need the money' (literally, *they have **nie** even the money need **nie***). 'Europeanists' have tried to relate it to the French double negative *ne . . . pas* since French settlers were a significant element in the Cape population in the second quarter-century of European settlement. However, the French construction only superficially resembles the Afrikaans one: French *ne* precedes the verb (or auxiliary verb, if there is one) while in Afrikaans the first *nie* always follows it. Compare the French translation of the above sentence: *ils **n**'ont même **pas** besoin de l'argent*, 'they don't even need the money' (literally, *they **ne** have even **pas** need of the money*). Other writers have suggested Flemish dialects as the source, while those in favour of the creole-origin theory have ascribed it to influence from a Khoi language (den Besten, 1986). The truth remains elusive as the textual record of the development of Afrikaans is sparse; but almost certainly language contact between Dutch and non-European languages is responsible.

7 CONCLUSION

In this chapter we have looked at examples of five different creoles, each of which has a different history and a different set of factors which have contributed to making it what it is. Clearly, different historical circumstances, social conditions and input languages have resulted in different outcomes; yet certain similarities are apparent. Simplification of inflections in comparison with the lexifier language is apparent in every case. A regularisation of the system of tense and aspect marking is also seen in each of these cases, so that tense, modality and aspect are marked immediately before the verb by a separate particle. This is true even in the case of Afrikaans, which, although it shows less radical simplification than other creoles, has nevertheless reduced the Dutch system of tense marking so that it falls in line with the other languages studied in this chapter. Can these *shared structural features* be accounted for in terms of the process of creole formation? In the next chapter we will look at theories about the origins of creoles with a view to answering these questions.

KEY POINTS: Creoles

CREOLES
- are the result of contact involving two or more languages;
- develop out of a prior pidgin;
- may develop gradually from a stable pidgin or abruptly from a rudimentary pidgin;
- have native speakers of their own but may also be spoken in pidgin form by some speakers;
- are grammatically simpler than their lexifier languages;
- usually share structural features such as preverbal tense, modality and aspect marking.

6 Creole Origins

1 DIFFERENCES AND SIMILARITIES BETWEEN PIGINS AND CREOLES

1.1 Pidgins, Creoles, and Language Acquisition

In the previous chapter we looked at some of the specific characteristics of individual creoles. In this chapter we will ask some more general questions about how creoles come into existence and about the relationship between creoles and pidgins.

Pidgins and creoles both have their origins in language contact. Both share structural features such as grammatical simplicity and small vocabularies when compared with their lexifiers. Nevertheless, there are important differences between them from the point of view of language acquisition. Pidgins, at least before they become established languages in a whole community, are always acquired as second languages and usually after the age of adolescence. One of the key assumptions of modern linguistic theory is that the structure of human language must be such that it is possible for all children of normal intelligence to acquire it within a fairly short space of time (roughly, between ages 1 and 5) (see, for example, Chomsky, 1986, chapter 3). This is seen as imposing fairly strict constraints on the possible structures of human language, a linguistic 'blueprint' which applies universally. There can be no exceptions because a language which violated the constraints would be 'unacquirable'. Any language which can be *normally transmitted* to children (in Thomason and Kaufman's sense) must comply with the 'blueprint'. (In practice, of course, linguists do not agree on exactly what the constraints are. The principle is not invalidated, however, by the discovery of normally transmitted languages which violate proposed constraints.)

Of course, pidgins are in many ways just like other languages; they have a vocabulary, a sound system and grammatical rules, albeit simple ones. In discussing theories of pidgin origins, we saw that the typical features of pidgins apparently help to make them learnable – for adult second language learners. We also saw that adults learning a second language probably use a different set of strategies from those used by children acquiring a first language. We saw in Chapter 2 that it was useful to make a distinction between *language acquisition* – whereby a child acquires a language natively – and *language learning*, the process of gaining competence in a second or subsequent language. This distinction is the basis for a potentially very important difference between pidgins and creoles. Creoles may originate through abnormal transmission, but they are acquired by children and therefore must comply with the 'blueprint'. However, pidgins are the result of second language learning; although they have to be 'learnable' in the sense that adults can *learn* them, *they do not have to be* 'acquirable' *by children*. This means that there is at least a theoretical possibility that pidgins do not have to comply with the 'blueprint' for human language.

The exact consequences of this theoretical possibility are not immediately obvious. It is easy to imagine 'made up' languages which are too difficult to learn (as in Václav Havel's play *The Memorandum*, where the vocabulary is so complex and specific that it is almost impossible to memorise). However, pidgins, with their manifest simplicity and small vocabularies, seem poor candidates for this kind of complexity. Rather than think in terms of pidgins being too complex for children to learn, we should consider whether there are other ways in which pidgins might 'contravene' the blueprint. The best way to do this would seem to be to compare pidgins – contact languages *without* native speakers – with creoles – contact languages *with* native speakers.

This is not as easy as it might sound, however. For one thing, we have seen that pidgins develop through a series of 'fuzzily defined' stages, from jargon through to expanded pidgin. While jargons are rather unlike 'normal' languages, expanded pidgins look and function very much like languages with native speakers. Which pidgin stage should we use as a basis for comparison?

A different kind of question arises with creoles. Although we now have information about a very wide range of pidgins, most of the creoles which have been well described have quite similar origins. The creoles of the Atlantic Ocean area – the Caribbean, the coastal parts of North and Central America, and West Africa – all have connections with each other through European colonisation and the slavery system. This link also applies to the creoles of the Indian Ocean (Mauritius, the Seychelles, Réunion). In the Pacific zone, although the slavery connection is absent, the European connection is still there, as the monogeneticists have reminded us. All these creoles involve European lexifiers with indigenous substrates – African substrates in the case of the Atlantic and Indian Ocean creoles. One of the theories of pidgin and creole origins, the 'common core' theory, suggests that these creoles should be quite similar. If these creoles turn out to be similar to each other, but interestingly different from pidgins spoken elsewhere, can we be sure that this is not simply due to the similar 'mix' of languages which has produced most of the creoles that are available for study at the moment?

1.2   Some Suitable Cases for Comparison

There are, fortunately, a few cases where both the pidgin stage and the creole stage of 'the same' language are reasonably well documented. From Papua New Guinea, we have Tok Pisin, which is still a pidgin for most of its speakers, but has a growing number of first-language speakers. In Hawaii, Derek Bickerton and others have made extensive observations both of Hawaiian Pidgin English and of Hawaiian Creole English.

1.2.1 Tok Pisin

In Tok Pisin, if comparisons are made between the current (expanded) pidgin stage and the creole stage, we find that the structural differences are fairly subtle. Suzanne Romaine writes (1988, p. 155):

> It is apparent that the structural differences between an expanded pidgin and an incipient creole will be minimal. The same applies to functional differences, which emphasize the problem in using the criterion of native speakers as the defining feature of creoles to distinguish them from pidgins.

Nevertheless, there are some changes which have been observed. Both Sankoff (e.g. 1977) and Mühlhäusler believe that phonological differences between 'pidgin' Tok Pisin and 'creole' Tok Pisin are significant. Mühlhäusler writes (1986, p. 210):

> my own observations on Tok Pisin creolization suggest that the pronunciation of children can indeed be very different from that of second-language adults. Recordings made of children playing were virtually unintelligible to their parents, primarily, it would seem, because of their more 'advanced' phonology.

'Advanced' phonology here means phonetic realisations which involve reduction and possibly deletion of some of the elements of the underlying phonological form. We have already seen how the adverb *baimbai*, 'by-and-by, soon', has been grammaticalised to a future marker, at the same time losing much of its phonetic 'contents' to become [bai] or just [bə]. *Speed of delivery* seems to be one of the key differences between the pidgin and creole varieties of Tok Pisin: put simply, children can and do speak their native language faster than adults speaking a second language. With the advent of rapid speech styles in young creole speakers comes phonological reduction, especially of function (as opposed to content) words. Some examples given by Romaine (1988, p. 139), from an 11-year-old creole speaker, include:

/disla/ from /dispela/	'this'	
/blem/ from /bilong en/	'of him'	
/lo/ from /long/	'at, to, in'	

Another change, discussed by Gillian Sankoff (1977), Suzanne Romaine (1993) and Jean Aitchison (1996, pp. 17–29) affects both the syntax and the phonology. The predicate marker *i-* is being lost. This feature of the syntax, which seems to have developed from English *he* through grammaticalisation, only became a stable feature of New Guinea Pidgin grammar around 1930. In earlier texts and for older speakers it is patchily present. However, its use is now declining, strikingly so in the case of the youngest speakers. (In the text from the newspaper *Wantok* in Chapter 1, for example, the verb *gat*, 'have', in the sentence *ol meri long kantri tude i gat bikpela wari long en*, is prefixed by the predicate marker, while the same verb in the headline *Ol meri gat bikpela wari yet* lacks it.)

The explanation suggested by Sankoff is that having lost independent meaning and without a necessary syntactic function, it has been reduced in its phonetic form, effectively to nothing. Aitchison concludes after reviewing the evidence that '*i* is gradually on the decline. A plethora of interacting factors are all slowly eroding its use. But the process of atrophy is not a straightforward one. Considerable variation occurs, which has not yet been tidied up into a fully categorical system.'

It is worth pointing out that these differences between the pidgin and creole varieties of Tok Pisin are not necessarily confined to creole Tok Pisin speakers. They indicate trends which were present in the expanding pidgin as well.

1.2.2 *Hawaiian Pidgin and Creole Englishes*

Much more substantial differences are reported by Bickerton (1981) between Hawaiian Pidgin English (HPE) and Hawaiian Creole English (HCE). Hawaiian Pidgin English had its origins in the sugar plantations developed in Hawaii in the 1870s after it was colonised by the United States. Large numbers of migrant labourers came there to work from the whole Pacific region, as well as from Portugal and Puerto Rico. The exact date of the emergence of HPE is not known; Bickerton believes it developed after the development of an earlier Hawaiian-based pidgin, but there is evidence of an English-based pidgin or jargon from the 1880s. Bickerton in the 1970s was able to find and record HPE speakers who had arrived as early as 1907, though few speakers remain alive. HCE on the other hand is widely spoken in Hawaii today and is a topic of some interest and debate among the local population, for whom it symbolises (like many creoles) both solidarity – 'Hawaiian-ness' in the face of massive migration from the mainland USA – and social inferiority, as it is viewed as 'Broken English'.

Bickerton notes (1981, p. 14) that:

Among HPE speakers who arrived prior to 1920 the following features are largely or completely missing: consistent marking of tense, aspect and modality; relative clauses; movement rules, embedded complements, in particular infinitival constructions; articles, especially indefinite.

We have seen that pidgins in an early stage of development typically lack just these features; HPE therefore does not seem unusual. However, HCE *does* have all of these. For example, the tense, modality and aspect marking system is not only consistent, according to Bickerton, but quite well-developed, with 'an auxiliary which marks tense, *bin* ..., and auxiliary which marks modality, *go* (sometimes *gon*); and an auxiliary which marks aspects, *stei*' (1981, p. 26). Similarly, while articles appear 'sporadically and unpredictably' in HPE (p. 22), HCE speakers use the definite article *da* for 'all and only specific-reference NPs [Noun Phrases] that can be assumed known to the listener', and the indefinite article *wan* for all and only specific-reference NPs that can be assumed unknown to the listener' (p. 23).

In other words, the tense, modality and aspect system and the article system of HCE are systematic and rule-governed. The form which a speaker will use is predictable if the context is given. By contrast, speakers of HPE are inconsistent and unpredictable in the way they mark these categories.

The contrast between HPE and HCE is essentially that between an unstable, undeveloped pidgin and a 'normal' (i.e. non-pidgin, non-creole) language which happens to have a relatively simple grammar. In spite of the structural instability and poverty of Hawaiian *Pidgin* English, Hawaiian *Creole* English shares many similarities with stable and expanded pidgins, and with other creoles. This is one of the cornerstones of Bickerton's *Language Bioprogram Hypothesis* about the origins of creoles, which we shall examine shortly.

1.2.3 Hawaiian Creole English text
The following short story is one of several that can be found on the World Wide Web at http://www.lava.net/~pueo/pidgin.html and is reproduced by kind permission of the author. The orthography is that of the original.

Deaf Ear
by Neal Oribio

My Ungko ... he tink my Antee steh going deaf. My Antee ... she no like go doctor, but.

One time ... my Ungko wen go look da doctor. My Ungko wen tell da doctor ... 'Hoy, doctor. I tink Mada steh going deaf. She no like come doctor, but. What can do, eh?'

Da doctor wen tell my Ungko ... 'We will need to determine the seriousness of her hearing loss.'

'How can, but?' My Ungko wen tell da doctor again. 'Mada no like come look you.'

Da doctor wen scratch his chin. 'Perhaps we can try something without her noticing.'

'Shoots!' My Ungko wen ansah. 'What you like try?'

So da doctor wen explain... 'You might try asking a question... from across the room... when she is not looking at you... use your normal volume for speaking... if she does not respond... on your next visit... tell me how close you were when she responded.'

'Kay-den'... my Ungko wen tell da doctor... 'I going try 'em.' Enden my Ungko wen go home.

My Antee... she steh wash da dishes. My Ungko... he steh behind... by da door sai. So, my Ungko wen aks my Antee... 'Hoy, Mada... where get my reading glasses?'

My Antee... she still steh wash dishes, but. So, my Ungko... he wen go take chree steps. Enden he go aks again... 'Hoy, Mada... where get my reading glasses?'

Still yet... my Antee still steh wash da dishes. My Ungko... he wen go take chree mo steps. Enden he go aks one mo time... 'Hoy, Mada... where get my reading glasses?'

My Antee wen go turn aroun'... she get all piss-off kind look ontop her face... she go tell my Ungko... 'Hoy, Fada... I told you two time already... steh by da television... you steh deaf-ear, or what?'

Pau...

Ungko: uncle
steh: 1.   aspect marker, e.g. *steh going deaf*, 'is going deaf'
        2.   be in a place, e.g. *steh by da television*
wen: past tense marker
aks: ask
get (in *where get my reading glasses*): existential marker; *to be*
pau: finish

1.3   Similarities between Creoles

As mentioned previously, most creolists are agreed that there are striking resemblances between creole languages, even those that have unrelated lexifiers, unrelated substrate languages, and no geographical connections. Of course, there is much less agreement on exactly *what* the resemblances are. A number of 'checklists' of creole features are in existence. For example, Bickerton (1981, chapter 2) provides a list of twelve features which he believes are shared by all 'true creoles' but which are not necessarily associated with pidgins (for discussion of this, see below). These features may, of course, also occur in non-creole languages; but a language which has *most* or *all* of these features is likely to be a creole.

1.   *Movement rules* which cause focussed constituents to occur in sentence-initial position.

2. *Articles* similar to the HCE system described above: a definite article for presupposed-specific NP; an indefinite article for asserted-specific NP; and zero for nonspecific NP (Bickerton, 1981, p. 56).

3. *Tense-modality-aspect (TMA) systems* which use exactly three pre-verbal particles (see below).

4. **Realised and unrealised complements** of verbs which are distinct and are indicated by different means.

5. *Relativisation and subject-copying*: most creoles have relative pro-nouns, at least when the head noun is also subject of the relative clause.

6. *Negation*: non-definite subjects and constituents of VPs (Verb Phrases) must be negated as well as the verb itself, leading to 'double negatives' as in the Guyanese **non** *dag* **na** *bait* **non** *kyat*, 'no dog bit any cat' or 'no dog didn't bite no cat' (Bickerton, 1981, p. 66).

7. *Existential and possessive* are expressed in the same way, i.e. 'there is' is usually expressed in the same way as 'has' or 'has got'.

8. *Copula*: 'practically all creoles show some similarities in this area', for example locative complements are usually introduced by a special verb which is used just for this purpose (as in Sranan, see Chapter 5). There are several variations on this, however.

9. *Adjectives as verbs*: in many creoles, the adjective has been analysed as a subcategory of stative verbs (i.e. verbs which describe a *state* rather than an action). This means that adjectives take verbal TMA markers and do not require a copula.

10. *Questions*: the word order in yes/no (polar) questions, according to Bickerton, is identical to that in statements (this does not apply to 'wh-questions', which use words like *what?*, *who?* etc.).

11. *Question words* are always bimorphemic, as we saw in Chapter 2, Section 6.2, for pidgins.

12. *Passive equivalents*: creole languages usually have no morphologi-cally marked passive voice, but use a pattern where an objectless active verb may be interpreted as a passive, e.g. Jamaican Creole /di tri plaan/ 'the tree plant', i.e. 'the tree was planted'.

Most, possibly all, of these features can be found in non-creole languages. For example, English has 1, 2 and 5, and nonstandard varieties of English have 6 as well; French has 7, e.g. *il y a*, 'there is', *il a*, 'he has'. Chinese and many other languages have 9, and many languages have 10. We can therefore be sure that most of these features are not *confined* to creoles. What would be striking would be to find all twelve of the features together in one language. According to Bickerton, this is characteristic of creoles.

If every creole could be shown to have all these features, the twelve features would indeed be an impressive set of 'blueprints' for creole grammar. Unfortunately, even by Bickerton's own admission, several of the 'twelve features' have exceptions or apply doubtfully in some cases. This is not only not surprising, it is inevitable, as all languages change, and creoles, which usually remain in contact with other languages, are more likely than the average language to change rapidly. Therefore, even if exceptions to 'the twelve' are relatively easy to find, we would need to check historical evidence to see whether they have always been exceptions.

Several other 'checklists' have been drawn up, for example Markey's (1982, p. 200): this partly overlaps with Bickerton's and adds SVO word order, the absence of grammatical gender, lack of case (i.e. subject/object distinctions in nouns and pronouns) and a few other features. Taylor (1971, p. 294) offers another 'list of twelve', though these are described only as 'common to at least two lexically differently based groupings' (p. 293). Items on the list include 'the third person plural pronoun serves as nominal pluralizer' (i.e. plurals have the form NOUN + 'they'), 'the word for *give* also functions as dative preposition "to" or "for"', and several which concern individual lexical items, such as '*na* is employed as a general locative'. These apply specifically to the Atlantic creoles (Caribbean and West Africa) only, though the point that there is a *general* locative preposition might be valid further afield.

Muysken and Veenstra (1994, p. 124) provide another list, this time of features 'which have been claimed to be fairly general across creoles'. The main newcomer to this list is the use of *serial verbs*, which will be discussed in detail below.

All this shows that there is, in fact, broad agreement that creole languages show similarities to each other which are not explainable by reference to their lexifier languages, *and* that there is a fair amount of agreement about what these similarities are. But there is *no* agreement over the reason or reasons for these similarities. Once again, the theories which were discussed as explanations for pidgin genesis (in Chapter 3, Section 3) are brought into play: the *monogenetic* theory (which originally was intended to account for creole as much as pidgin origins); the 'common core' hypothesis; the *foreigner talk* theory; and theories laying emphasis on substrate influence and universals. We discussed most of these in depth as potential explanations for the characteristics of pidgins, in Chapter 3. In so far as some pidgins, like Tok

Pisin, appear to give rise to creoles through nativisation of the pidgin, the arguments for and against these theories hold for such creoles as well. There is still something to explain, however, as some creoles appear to originate without a pidgin stage. Furthermore, even when there is a pidgin precursor to the creole, it may be radically different, as Hawaiian Pidgin English is from Hawaiian Creole English.

Mufwene (1986) points out that there are two approaches to explaining creole genesis which are fundamental, namely, universalist approaches and substrate approaches. All other theories or proposals concerning the origins of creoles have to make reference to those two: for example, the foreigner talk theory will only account for similarities of structure in terms of universal patterns of simplification, while the 'common core' hypothesis must refer to features of the substrate as well as of the lexifier languages. We will therefore concentrate in the rest of this chapter on discussing those two approaches.

1.4   Exercise

Choose any three pidgins or creoles from those that have been described in detail earlier, or for which you have enough grammatical information, and look at them with respect to the first three features on Bickerton's list above. To what extent do they seem to conform to Bickerton's requirements? What problems are there?

2   UNIVERSALIST APPROACHES TO CREOLE GENESIS

2.1   The Bioprogram Hypothesis

Derek Bickerton's **Language Bioprogram Hypothesis** (LBH) (Bickerton, 1981) is the only theory of contact language origins which deals exclusively with *creole* genesis. In particular, it deals with creoles which come into being in situations where the only lingua franca is 'a highly variable, extremely rudimentary language state such as has been sometimes described as a "jargon" or "pre-pidgin continuum" rather than a developed pidgin language' (p. 5). In such a situation, a child acquiring a first language is in a very different situation from most children. A child learning, say, Japanese has a 'ready-made, custom-validated, referentially adequate' language to learn, and moreover has adult carers and siblings who *already* know the language and can assist the process. The child growing up surrounded by jargon speakers, by contrast, is immersed in something 'quite unfit to serve as anyone's primary tongue; which, by reason of its variability, does not present even the little it offers in a form that would permit anyone to learn it;

and which the parent, with the best will in the world, cannot teach, since that parent knows no more of the language than the child' (p. 5). Since the child *must* acquire a native language, the only option is for him or her to take the 'chaotic', variable input presented by the pidgin and use it to develop a new language, using an innate 'blueprint' – the *language bioprogram*. Thus, unlike children in a 'normal' language-learning situation, these children do not learn, by induction from talk offered to them by adults, the linguistic rules of the older generation. Instead, they acquire a set of rules which did not previously exist, using lexical items from the adults' pidgin, but guided by innate principles given in the bioprogram.

The diagram in Figure 6.1 illustrates how language acquisiton would take place, in case (A) in a normally transmitted language, and in case (B) where the 'language bioprogram' comes into operation.

Hawaiian Creole is Bickerton's 'classic case' of a creole which is unlike the pidgin that preceded it. How, he asks, has the creole acquired the structures which it has, when it can be shown that Hawaiian Pidgin English had virtually none of them? Only some innate mechanism could have allowed Hawaiian-born children, hearing such irregular and chaotic input, to come up with a set of regular rules. Furthermore, according to Bickerton, virtually the *same* set of rules – the 'twelve features' – are found in other creoles which have arisen under similar circumstances, i.e. without a stable prior pidgin. Again, some innate mechanism is implied.

Bickerton is explicit about what he means by *creole*: to be called a creole, a language must meet two conditions (p. 4):

1. It must have arisen out of a prior pidgin which had existed for not more than a generation,

2. ...among a population where at most 20 per cent were speakers of the 'dominant language' (i.e. lexifier) and where the remaining 80 per cent were linguistically diverse.

(A) 'Normal' language situation – language N

(B) 'Creole genesis' situation – Pidgin P, Creole C

Figure 6.1

This definition includes some of the Atlantic and Indian Ocean creoles as well as Hawaiian Creole English, but excludes Tok Pisin and its relative Bislama, as well as West African Pidgin English, on the grounds of too long a pidgin stage. Bickerton has since altered his position on condition (2), taking into account the fact that the proportion of speakers of the various contributing languages may vary considerably over time, for example, due to importation of slaves in 'waves' rather than evenly over time (see Bickerton, 1984). In such cases, the extent to which the creole displays the structures prescribed by the bioprogram will depend on the extent to which the model offered by the lexifier (the 'dominant language') is diluted by new arrivals. If the community is relatively stable, a pidgin may develop which has some of the structure of the dominant language: as this pidgin is less 'inadequate' as input to the creole, the creole-acquiring child will have less need to resort to the bioprogram, and the resultant creole will resemble the pidgin, and the lexifier, more.

The bioprogram itself, according to Bickerton (1981, chapter 3), 'programs' four major semantic distinctions, each of which has structural consequences. These are:

1. Specific–nonspecific. *Consequence*: the article system.   (Feature 2)
2. State–process. *Consequence*: differential marking of statives and non-statives in creoles.   (Affects TMA system, Feature 3)
3. Punctual–nonpunctual. *Consequence*: universal marking of nonpunctual verbs in creoles.   (Affects TMA system, Feature 3)
4. Causative–noncausative. *Consequence*: the existence of 'passive equivalents'.   (Feature 12)

2.2   Commentary on the Language Bioprogram Hypothesis

The LBH has been important in motivating research in the field of creole studies and has attracted great interest, partly because of its more general relevance to theories of language acquisition. At the same time, it has been widely criticised. The grounds for the criticism will be dealt with in turn.

2.2.1   There are too few test cases for the LBH to be evaluated
Bickerton's definition of *creole* excludes many languages one might want to call creoles, including some that share most of the 'twelve features'. In many cases, there is just not enough historical evidence to make it clear whether Bickerton's definition is met or not.

2.2.2   Some creoles by Bickerton's definition do not display the
         expected features
Mühlhäusler (1986, pp. 222–4) discusses such a creole, *Unserdeutsch*, which arose among the indigenous New Guinean students at a boarding school run

by Germans and 'appears to be a case of an insufficient jargon turning into a creole within one generation'. Mühlhäusler compares Unserdeutsch and Tok Pisin with Bickerton's twelve-feature list and finds that Unserdeutsch displays at most four of the expected features, while Tok Pisin has eight. This suggests that Tok Pisin is a better candidate for creolehood than Unserdeutsch, though only the latter meets Bickerton's criteria.

2.2.3   Bickerton's claims about the universality of tense, modality and aspect marking in creoles are not borne out by evidence from other creoles

Bickerton is specific about the structure of TMA marking in creoles, which is one of the main features of creoles which the bioprogram claims to account for. He writes (1981, p. 58): 'A majority of creoles, like HCE, express tense, modality and aspect by means of three preverbal free morphemes, placed (if they co-occur) in that order.' The three particles have specific functions: the *tense particle* signals 'anteriority' ('very roughly, past-before-past for action verbs, and past for stative verbs' – a state of 'before-ness', in other words); the *modality particle* signals 'irrealis' (futures, conditionals and other 'unrealised' states); and the *aspect particle* signals 'nonpunctual' ('progressive–durative plus habitual–iterative' – roughly speaking, repeated or ongoing states).

Such a strong claim is of course vulnerable to being disconfirmed by a counter-example, and many have been found. In his introduction to a volume devoted entirely to studies of pidgin and creole TMA systems, John Victor Singler (1990, p. xii) notes that of the seven languages represented, only two – Haitian Creole and Eighteenth-Century Nigerian Pidgin – conform to Bickerton's formula for anterior tense marking. Some do not mark anteriority at all. Singler goes on to point out that 'a crucial feature of Bickerton's system is the neat compartmentalisation of tense, mood and aspect'; however, these three attributes of a verb (or the activity it denotes) are difficult to separate, and it is their *interaction* which has 'given rise to the pidgin and creole TMA systems furthest from Bickerton's stereotype'.

2.2.4   The LBH as formulated by Bickerton does not take into account the social and historical realities of creole formation

There are two aspects to this objection. On the one hand, Bickerton's scenario assumes that the creole-acquiring children have no alternative language to learn. According to Bickerton, this is because 'none of the available vernaculars would permit access to more than a tiny proportion of the community' and 'the cultures and communities with which those vernaculars were associated were now receding rapidly into the past' (1981, p. 5). However, it is likely that any child growing up in such a situation will learn the native language(s) of his or her carers as well as the pidgin/creole. In other words, *bilingualism* rather than monolingualism in the creole is likely to be the norm in such a community. This changes things somewhat, because we now need to know about the *interactive* effects of acquiring both a 'normal' language and a pidgin/creole at about the same time. If the child is not sure what a language 'should be like', he or she may turn to the parental language, rather than the bioprogram, for guidance. This also suggests a mechanism by which substrate influences could come to have an effect on the creole, through speakers being bilingual in both a substrate language and the emerging creole. On this topic, Thomason and Kaufman write (1988, p. 164):

> In our opinion, [Bickerton] has not provided convincing evidence for his strong claims about the communicative setting. It is far simpler, and more consistent with the evidence from directly observable multilingual communities, to assume that different generations constitute one speech community, not two, and that both adults and children contribute to the development of an early-creolising creole.

Secondly, researchers such as Singler (1986) have objected that historically, creoles did not come into being in the type of society which Bickerton posits. Children were not plentiful on the slave plantations – for several reasons, including a lack of women and high rates of sterility, abortion and infant mortality, all explainable by appalling conditions which are well-attested. In practice, these were childless societies for a long period. Therefore, the nativisation of the pidgin to a creole is likely to have taken a much longer time than Bickerton suggests.

2.2.5 Non-creole languages do not adhere to the bioprogram 'blueprint', and creole languages change with time to deviate from it

This objection relates to the wider implications of the LBH. Since the language bioprogram is an innate part of every child, a child learning *any* language is 'guided' by the bioprogram. Bickerton produces evidence from studies of acquisition of 'normal' languages like English and Turkish which, he claims, show that where a language has structures that conflict with the bioprogram 'blueprint', these are harder to learn (i.e. they are the subject of more errors, and are acquired later). The question is, how did these conflicting structures get to be there in the first place? Why would languages develop structures that are 'unnecessarily' difficult for children to learn, when the bioprogram prescribes the adequate minimum? As Mufwene (1986, p. 151) puts it: 'if all languages can be assumed to have started from the same bioprogram, what accounts for linguistic diversity?' Furthermore, some creoles seem to have developed structures different from those which the bioprogram would predict. What impetus would there be for languages to change in a direction away from the bioprogram?

A similar objection runs along the following lines: there must be universal principles underlying every child's acquisition of grammar, not only because the number of possible structures is quite limited, but also because the input is *always* inadequate (or 'degenerate' as Chomsky describes it, 1965, p. 31). It is not just children acquiring a creole who are faced with constructing a language from variable and incomplete data, it is *everyone*. Therefore, creoles should not be a special case, and the *real* bioprogram is nothing more than the set of principles which constrain *all* language learning. Creoles are therefore not special in this respect.

While the incompleteness of the data which children have to work with is doubtless universal, the above argument does not take into account the possibility that in the case where the child is exposed to an unstable pidgin, the data is not merely *incomplete* but also *inconsistent* and *unsystematic*. The child in such a situation will therefore be unable to find positive evidence for structures (since there are none). By contrast, a child learning a 'normal' language will be able to find evidence for structures which exist in the language, even if the data itself is not 'organised'.

For a detailed discussion and critique of Bickerton's position from the viewpoint of child language acquisition, see Romaine (1988, pp. 275–95).

2.2.6 *Substrate language influences can explain much of what the bioprogram is intended to account for*

This objection is potentially the most serious for Bickerton as it offers not merely a refutation of his hypothesis but an alternative explanation of the same data. Bickerton has dubbed those linguists who prefer substrate explanations 'substratomaniacs', which has raised the temperature of the debate without necessarily improving its quality. We shall discuss substrate approaches in more detail in Section 3 below.

2.3 The LBH: Conclusion

Singler (1990, p. ix) notes that 'creolists have in general rejected the LBH, at least in its strongest form, as the principal means of accounting for the shared properties of creoles'. Some of the main objections have been discussed above. The balance of evidence suggests that even if something like the bioprogram is operating in creole acquisition, it does not work in quite the way that Bickerton suggests. It is possible, of course, that the LBH *itself* is valid, even though Bickerton's 'twelve features' may be the wrong ones to characterise creoles. At the very least, a theory is needed which is more robust, in other words one which can account for similarities among creoles more generally (without so many exclusions) and can explain the differences which do exist. Such a theory will also have to take into account the fact of bi- or multilingualism within pidgin/creole speaking communities, and the differing historical circumstances in which they come into being. It will also need to connect with more general theories about language acquisition and the innateness of linguistic knowledge, for example those of Chomsky (e.g. 1986).

2.4   Other Universalist Approaches

Although Bickerton's bioprogram hypothesis is the most widely debated universalist approach to creole genesis, it is not the only one. However, at the time of writing it is the only one which addresses itself exclusively to creole genesis. Other universalist approaches treat pidginisation as a similar or at least related process to creolisation, on the assumption that creolisation involves the nativisation of an existing pidgin, even though it may be a very rudimentary one. These other approaches were discussed in detail in Chapter 3.

3   SUBSTRATE APPROACHES

3.1   Context of the Debate

An emphasis on the contribution of substrate languages has been favoured especially by researchers working on the creoles of the Caribbean region. These show interesting resemblances not only to each other but also to various languages of West Africa. Since the cultural heritage of the creole speakers of African descent is largely African – a fact which is beyond dispute and which is probably better understood now than a century ago – logic suggests that at a deep level, their linguistic heritage should be as well. An early dramatic statement of this was made by Suzanne Sylvain in her 1936 study of Haitian Creole. After a detailed discussion of both French and African aspects of the language, she concluded (p. 178) 'we are in the presence of French which has been cast in the mould of African syntax or, since languages are generally classified according to their syntactic ancestry, an Ewe [West African] language with French vocabulary'.

Interestingly, we learn through a personal communication from Robert A. Hall, Jr, cited by Holm (1988, p. 38), that Sylvain had been required to write this by her mentor and that it did not truly reflect her own opinion – or the rest of her book, which was much more even-handed. Even at this early stage in creole studies, the role of the substrate was a touchy issue.

Much more recently, on the basis of a detailed syntactic analysis, Claire Lefebvre and her associates have put forward the hypothesis that Haitian Creole is a relexified form of Gbe, a West African language of the Kwa group (Lefebvre, 1986).

In order to understand and evaluate the debate about the influence of African substrate languages on the Caribbean creoles, it is necessary to look at the social and political context of the debate. For a long period the very existence of the creole languages concerned was denied, the colonial elite and expatriates alike preferring to see them simply as inferior versions of the lexifier language. A partial change in attitudes, the advent of political independence for many of the countries concerned, and new interest in the African cultural heritage of their populations has stimulated interest in the African *linguistic* contribution. This has not quite had the effect of raising creole languages to respectability on a par with European languages (it is difficult to generalise about this since attitudes vary from place to place) but it has chimed with the interests of radical 'back-to-Africa' movements such as Rastafarianism as well as a more general popular desire to establish independence from Europe – symbolised in this case by European languages. None of this is to say that the interest in 'proving' the African influence on creole languages is just politically motivated or unscientific; this would be grossly unfair to the many serious scholars doing high quality comparative work in this field. It does mean, however, that research which emphasises the African heritage of the creoles in question connects with a popular interest in language and cultural history, which research with an alternative focus – emphasising the role of universals, say – does not. As a result, the complexity of the issues is sometimes lost in the rhetoric of claims about the importance of substrate influence.

3.2 Substratist Methodology

Substratist claims usually take the form of identifying particular syntactic, morphological or lexical features of a creole language which resemble structures of an African language that can be shown to have been present in the slave population at the time of formation of that creole language. Evidence is thus of two kinds:

1. Evidence that the creole structure resembles that of a particular African (usually West African) language.
2. Evidence that the West African language identified as a possible source was in fact present in the mix of languages which contributed to the pidgin/creole.

Direct evidence of the second type is relatively easy to produce. Most of the substrate languages have left some lexical traces in the form of words for African cultural practices. The personal names of African slaves are a matter of historical record. A search through dictionaries will often establish the origins of particular words or personal names. Corroborative evidence comes from historical documents such as lists of slaves embarked and disembarked at particular points by slaving ships. These enable us to guess the languages spoken by the slaves who were shipped to the various colonies – though not with much accuracy, since the ports where the slaves were embarked were usually not where the slaves originally came from, and numerous languages may have been spoken locally. This fact is offset somewhat by the fact that many of the languages of West Africa share many of their structures; though they are *lexically* dissimilar, their *grammars* have a lot in common.

A good example of the kind of methodology just described is that of Frederic G. Cassidy in his book *Jamaica Talk*. Cassidy cites a Jamaican official document of 1789 as a source of figures for the number of slaves landed from various parts of the West African coast over two separate periods. He obtained lists of slaves' tribes in eighteenth-century reports and accounts of the Jamaican colony. He concludes (1961, p. 17):

> The information afforded by these names is incomplete, yet it points much the same way: we may safely conclude that at the time when the basis of Jamaican folk speech was laid, the largest number of slaves came from the area of the Gold Coast [now Ghana] and Nigeria, and were therefore speakers of the Niger–Congo or West Sudanese languages.

Evidence of the first kind is more problematic. It is easy to compare structures superficially and find likenesses. For some researchers in this field, this has been convincing enough evidence that the African structure *is* the source of the creole structure. Their methodology has attracted criticism from scholars such as Bickerton (1981, p. 48):

> substratomaniacs, if I may give them their convenient and traditional name, seem to be satisfied with selecting particular structures in one or more creole languages and showing that superficially similar structures can be found in one or more West African languages.

A more rigorous method would require that it be shown that the structural similarity was not simply coincidental. The problem here is that all languages show *some* similarities – as they must, if universal principles constrain language acquisition. Intuitively, we may have a sense of which similarities are 'striking' and which are 'unsurprising' similarities. Only 'striking' similarities are of use in trying to establish substrate influence. 'Unsurprising' similarities are no more than we would expect by chance, given the nature of human language.

Unsurprising similarities are probably uncontroversial for the most part. For example, if two languages share the requirement that all syllables have the structure CV(N) (consonant, vowel, optional nasal consonant), this would probably be an unsurprising similarity. Many unrelated languages share this structure, suggesting that it is more 'natural' or less 'marked' than others. On the other hand, if two apparently unrelated languages both allow consonant clusters such as /zmrz/, this might be taken as a *striking* similarity, since clusters like this are rare among the world's languages.

In trying to explicate the notion of 'unsurprising' and 'striking' similarity, we have had to use terms like 'natural', 'rare' and 'marked'. *Markedness* is a relatively well-developed concept in phonology and may provide a way of measuring how 'striking' phonological similarities between creoles and their substrates are. However, markedness in syntax and morphology is much less clear and well-theorised, and it is here that the main controversies about substrate influence lie. To make a convincing argument about substrate influence, it is necessary to show that structure shared by the creole and substrate language is a *marked* one, so that the likelihood of the similarity being due to chance is small. But how marked is marked? How improbable or 'striking' must the similarity be in order to count? And how do we measure markedness effectively for this purpose? These are problems which the substratists have been slow to address, making themselves vulnerable to criticism from 'universalists'. For example, Dalphinis (1985, p. 10) gives 'suffixation of the definite article and pronouns' as in the Haitian creole *liv-la*, 'the book', as an example of one of 'eleven language features ... common to Creoles and African languages' (p. 8). Yet there are numerous non-African languages with suffixed definite articles (for example, Norwegian and Bulgarian) so that this similarity might well have arisen by chance. Similarly, his 'non-differentiation of the third singular' (i.e. lack of gender distinction in third person pronouns) is common in the world's languages, although it is unusual in European languages. Of course, these are genuine *similarities* between creole languages and (some) African languages; the problem comes in attributing a cause-and-effect relationship to them. Some additional evidence is needed in order to claim that the African structures are the *source* of the creole ones.

3.3   The Substance of Substratist Claims

The kinds of resemblances between creoles which were discussed above in 1.3 are also the focus of substratists' interest. Since most of the Caribbean creoles can be assumed to share part of their substrate – although the exact details may be hard to determine – features that are common to the creoles, or to subgroups of them, should also be common to the substrate, if the substratists' hypothesis is correct. Indeed, Singler (1986, p. 144) points out that 'many of Bickerton's creole properties are common to Kwa languages and indeed are often West African areal features'.

We will here look briefly at some of the creole structures which are most frequently mentioned as deriving from an African substrate.

3.3.1 *Lexical calques*

These are 'literal translations' of idioms and were mentioned in Chapter 2 and in Chapter 4, Section 6.2 (where examples are given). Even where the pattern of the creole idiom exactly matches that of the African one, there is room for doubt about the source. Mufwene (1986, p. 147) questions Alleyne's (1980) analysis of creole compounds like *ay waata* (Jamaican), *wata woyo* (Saramaccan) – both literally 'eye water' with the meaning 'tears' – and *mout waata* (Jamaican), *wata buka*, 'mouth water' (Saramaccan), i.e. 'saliva'. Alleyne relates these to African influence, but Mufwene points out that English words such as *eye lid* and *eye lash* could have very well served as models to the Jamaican creole compounds too. One could also argue that such 'semantically transparent' compounds would be favoured by universal principles of simplicity and transparency and so could be expected to occur in many languages. They would then fall into the category of 'unsurprising similarities'. This objection might not apply to other more culture-based compounds such as Sranan *bun-ede*, 'good head' ('good luck') and *atibron* 'heart burn' ('anger'), which seem to reflect cultural beliefs about the bodily source of emotions and personal qualities.

3.3.2 *Predicate adjectives as verbs*

This is Bickerton's 'Feature No. 9'. In many creoles, the adjective has been analysed as a type of stative verb, with the result that no copula is used with the adjective in the predicate. I have proposed such an analysis (Sebba, 1986) for Sranan **predicate adjectives** (those which are 'predicated of' a subject, e.g. *they are smart*; **attributive adjectives**, which modify a noun directly, e.g. *smart cookies*, seem to require a different analysis) though this has been disputed by Seuren (1986). Other creoles of the Caribbean region, including Jamaican, Guyanese, and other English-lexicon creoles; Haitian, Dominican and other French-lexicon creoles, seem to require a similar analysis, though the Portuguese/Spanish-lexicon creole Papiamentu does not. Taylor (1951) gives some examples:

Sranan: a   liba   disi   bradi
               the river this broad
               'this river is broad'

Jamaican: **di man kriezi**
               'the man is crazy'

Dominican: **mun   sot**
               people stupid
               'people are stupid'

In many West African languages, the predicate adjective seems to behave like a verb. Dalphinis (1985) gives an example from Ewe (spoken in Ghana):

Ewe: è   **bija**
            it   red
            'it is red'

Similar examples could be found in Akan, Yoruba and many other West African languages which are known to have had speakers among the slave populations of the Caribbean.

Again, the similarity is not in dispute but its significance is subject to question. Many languages outside the Caribbean and West Africa have the same feature, for example Chinese and Japanese. No-one suggests that these are part of the substrate of the Caribbean creoles. This is not to say that the African structure is *not* the source of the creole one, but unequivocal evidence is lacking.

3.3.3   Cleft and predicate cleft
Many languages have a focussing construction like the English **cleft**, as exemplified by (b) and (c) below:

(a)   We are discussing creoles.
(b)   It is creoles we are discussing.
(c)   It is we who are discussing creoles.

To an English speaker, (a), (b) and (c) mean the same thing in truth-conditional terms (i.e. they are either all true or all false under a particular set of circumstances) but they each have a different focus. While (a) is the most neutral, (b) might be an answer to '*Are you discussing pidgins?*' while (c) might be an answer to '*Is the group by the window discussing creoles?*'

Most Atlantic creoles have a similar construction, e.g. Sranan:

Sranan: **Na   wi   e   taki   abra   kriorotongo**
              is   we   ASP   talk   about   creole-language
              'It is we who are discussing creoles'

The Sranan construction is different from the English in that it uses the equative copula *na* (sometimes called a *highlighter* in this context) without a subject corresponding to the English 'dummy *it*' and does not require any relative pronoun or complementiser to introduce the rest of the sentence. A less common construction, not found in English but found in the Atlantic creoles and West African languages, is **predicate cleft**. Notice that in Standard English we cannot say something like '*It is discussing creoles we are*' in order to bring the verb into focussed position. But many of the

Atlantic creoles have a construction which allows just this, e.g. the four below (data from Bynoe-Andriolo and Yillah, 1975):

Sranan:

Na	**feti**	**wi**	**mus**	**feti**	**te**	**wi**	**kon**	**fri**
is	fight	we	must	fight	until	we	come	free

'We have to *fight* for our freedom!'

Krio: **Na wok i de wok**

Haitian Creole: **Se travay li ap travay**

Papiamentu:

Ta	**traha**	**e**	**ta**	**traha**
is	work	he	ASP	work

'He's really working!'

These predicate cleft constructions are similar to the 'ordinary' cleft, but involve 'copying' the verb into focussed position, with the result that the verb occurs twice. The first occurrence of the verb is always 'bare', lacking tense and aspect markers. Adjectives can undergo predicate cleft exactly like verbs.

Similar constructions are to be found in West African languages, e.g. (data from Bynoe-Andriolo and Yillah, 1975):

Temne: kìbulɔ kɔmɔ bulɔ (yaŋ)
Yoruba: iṣẹ l'o nṣẹ.
            'it is work he works', i.e. 'he's really working'

Predicate cleft is not a common construction in the world's languages. It looks like a good candidate for a 'marked' syntactic structure. It is therefore interesting and potentially significant that it occurs in many of the Atlantic creoles *and* in West African languages of the Kwa group, which are known to form a major part of their substrate.

3.3.4 *Serial verbs*
Serial verbs (also called verb catenation or verb chaining) will be discussed in more detail in the case study of Sranan in Section 5. In this section we will just note that series of verbs occurring together in the same sentence are a feature both of most Atlantic creoles and of West African languages – in particular, the Kwa sub-family of the Niger–Congo language family. Two specific similarities have interested substratists:

(1)   The use of the verb meaning 'say' as a complementiser (e.g. *he believes say*...meaning 'he believes that...'), which is found in Sranan Tongo, Krio, Gullah, US Black English, Negerhollands and Berbice Creole Dutch

(Holm, 1989, p. 185) as well as in Akan (Twi/Ashanti/Fanti), spoken in Ghana, and in many other African languages, including the Bantu subfamily. For example:

Sranan:

    A taygi mi *taki* **a nyan bori kba**
    he tell me say the food boil already
    'S/he told me that the food was already cooked'

Ewe (Niger–Congo family, Kwa group) (example from Lord, 1976):
    me nyá *bé* **édzo**
    I know 'say' he-left
    'I know that he left'

Compare the following Sranan sentence, where *taki* is used as the main verb:

    a *taki* **furu ogri sani**
    he say many ugly thing
    'S/he said a lot of bad things'

Scholars are not agreed on the significance of the fact that 'say = that' is apparently confined to the English- and Dutch-lexicon Atlantic creoles and is not found in Papiamentu or the French-lexicon creoles (see Holm, 1989, for discussion).

(2) The use of the verb meaning 'give' to mean 'for' (e.g. *they bought this give me* for 'they bought this for me'). This is found in Sranan, Saramaccan, São Tomé Portuguese Creole, Gullah, Haitian, and Negerhollands as well as other English-lexicon and French-lexicon creoles of the Atlantic region. It is also found in West African languages of the Kwa group, e.g. Akan, Gã and Yoruba.

Sranan:

    A tyari a nyan gi mi
    he carry the food give me
    'S/he brought food to/for me'

Yoruba:

    nwón tà á fún mi
    they sell it give me
    'They sold it to me'

Compare the Sranan sentence below, which shows *gi* used as a main verb:

    Kofi ben gi mi wan bun bruku
    Kofi PAST give me one good trousers
    'Kofi gave me a nice pair of trousers'

These two types of serial verb use are not confined to West Africa and the Caribbean (Chinese has similar verbal structures, for example: see Sebba, 1987), but they are not common elsewhere, and thus seem to qualify as 'highly marked' constructions. Certainly the correspondences between the West African and Caribbean uses of these constructions are very close. They would seem to be good candidates for constructions which come directly from substrate sources.

3.3.5 *Phonological features*

Substrate influence on the phonology of creoles is relatively uncontroversial, as transfer of native-language sound patterning to a pidgin, and from there to the developing creole, would have been effectively unavoidable. Creole lexicons typically show the phonological effects of their first speakers' pronunciation of European words: simplification of consonant clusters, e.g. Sranan *tranga*, *tori* from English *strong*, *story*; epenthetic vowels (added to create open syllables), e.g. Jamaican *ratta*, 'rat'; and unrounding of front rounded vowels (common in French but not in the languages of West Africa), e.g. Haitian Creole *yo* /yo/ from French *yeux* /jœ/ 'eyes' (see also Chapter 8 for a discussion of the orthographic problems this causes). For a detailed discussion of the phonology of creoles, see Holm (1989, vol. 1, chapter 4).

Probably the most striking result of substrate influence on the Caribbean creoles is the role of tone in these languages. Most African languages have phonemic tone (see the discussion of Fanakalo, Chapter 2), although, as noted there (Section 5.3), some African pidgins do not. Several Caribbean creoles, however, make use of tone for lexical and/or syntactic purposes: for example, Papiamentu (Portuguese/Spanish lexifier) and Saramaccan (English-lexifier with a high proportion of Portuguese lexis). For more information on the topic of tone see Devonish (1989).

4   CREOLE GENESIS: A SUMMING-UP

4.1   Substrate versus Universals

There is no doubt that some substratists have been too casual in claiming substrate origins for creole features. It is important that they should not weaken their case through over-zealousness. There are two areas in particular on which substratists need to concentrate. First, it is necessary to have some metric, or measurement, by which to decide on the significance of a feature, F, which is common to a substrate language S and a creole C. If there is a reasonable likelihood of F being found in any two languages which do not necessarily share any part of their history, it is not a good candidate as a feature resulting from substrate influence. Developments in language typology may help with the development of measures to assess these 'reasonable likelihoods'.

Secondly, substratists must give an account of exactly how the substrate features come to be present in the creole. According to Bickerton (1986, p. 314), 'Substratists...have to describe *exactly* and *explicitly* how, in creolization, syntactic structures got from substratum languages into creole languages' (emphasis in original). While this goal may not be possible in every case, it is at least one which needs to be worked towards. Here, theories of bilingualism and multilingualism may be helpful in revealing the kinds of language-learning processes that may go on. We also need to back this up, in many cases, with a better understanding of the historical situation surrounding the formation of the creole. Another factor – again connected with language typology – is the question of how similar the substrate languages are to each other. Singler has argued (1988, 1992) that *homogeneity* – i.e. typological similarity – of the substrate languages is an important factor and can account, for example, for the substrate impact on Tok Pisin. Where substrate languages are more diverse, universals may have a greater role to play.

On the question of universals, Mufwene (1986) brings some interesting data to bear. *Kituba* and *Lingala*, two Bantu-lexicon pidgins of Zaire, have both undergone restructuring in comparison with their lexifiers, and both in a similar (and by now familiar) way. In place of a highly agglutinative morphological system where single words, built up by means of affixes, translate a complete sentence of English, we find a much less agglutinative system, for example (Mufwene, 1986, pp. 134–5):

Kikongo (ethnic language):	**n-diá**	'I am eating'
	n-dì-ìdì	'I ate'
Kituba (pidgin):	**móno kéle diâ**	'I am eating'
	móno dià-áka	'I ate'

Mufwene points out that the pidgin system resembles that of the Kwa languages of West Africa, although this resemblance is clearly not due to substrate influence, as the Kwa languages are not spoken anywhere near to Zaire. Rather, they seem to result from the kinds of universal processes which have had much the same effect in the transition from Zulu to Fanakalo (Chapter 2). However, the structural resemblances of the Atlantic creoles to the Kwa languages are often cited as evidence of Kwa substrate influence on the creoles in question. The Kituba data shows that universals may produce the same effect – a 'Kwa-like' structure – although Kwa languages were not involved at all.

To quote the title of Mufwene's paper (1986): 'The Universalist and Substrate Hypotheses Complement One Another'. They are not, in other words, mutually exclusive. It is hardly possible that universals do not play some role in the formation of creoles. On the other hand, the influence of typologically similar substrate languages seems to have continued for many generations in places like Surinam, and it would be strange if a creole developing in a context of widespread bilingualism did not show the influence of substrate language structures.

4.2 Abruptness versus Gradualism

We have already seen in this and the previous chapter that the period of time over which creolisation takes place is a major issue among creolists. According to Bickerton (1981), a 'true' creole arises only out of a prior pidgin which has existed for not more than a generation (see above), though later Bickerton (1988, p. 268) relaxes this somewhat, to 'one or two generations'. Taking the more restrictive of these conditions, we can say that in Bickerton's view true creoles are characterised by being formed through a process of *abrupt* creolisation, in Thomason and Kaufman's terms. In contrast to this, Jacques Arends (1993) puts forward a case, based on a detailed historical study of Sranan, that creolisation is a *gradual* process.

The history of Surinam shows that for many generations newly arrived or 'salt-water' slaves outnumbered those born on the plantations because the death rate among slaves was so high. During this period Sranan must have had more the character of a pidgin than of a creole, being spoken mainly as a second language. Furthermore, children were a rarity rather than the norm on the plantations for at least the first century of the colony's existence. 'Creolisation' in the sense of nativisation of the language by children could therefore not have taken place except very slowly as the proportion of locally-born slaves slowly increased. As successive generations of slaves, native speakers of African languages, arrived in Surinam, they had to learn the local language – the developing pidgin Sranan. The substrate influences identified in modern Sranan are the result of features transferred from their native languages, and have thus developed over a long period.

Thus for Arends creolisation is a process with the following characteristics (1993, p. 376):

1. It is a gradual rather than a catastrophic process, extending over several generations.
2. It is a continuous rather than a discrete process, i.e. there is no clear break between pidginisation and creolisation.
3. It is a process carried out by adults rather than by children.
4. It is a process of second rather than first language acquisition.
5. It is a differential rather than a uniform process.

4.3   Pidgin X = Creole X?

Let us now return briefly to a question we opened up at the start of this chapter. Is a creole necessarily *different* from its predecessor pidgin, and if so, how? Arends concludes (above) that there is *no* clear break between pidginisation and creolisation. Bickerton would argue that such a difference must exist, if the appropriate conditions are met. Arends bases his arguments on a study of written records of Sranan. Bickerton bases his claims largely on data recorded from Hawaiian informants, speakers of Hawaiian Pidgin English, who were still alive in the 1970s. Fortunately, we can also turn to Papua New Guinea for data from Tok Pisin, which is in the process of creolisation at the moment. In summarising the findings concerning the predicate marker *i-* (discussed above in 1.2.1), Jean Aitchison concludes:

> The overall conclusion is that *i-* is gradually on the decline. A plethora of interacting factors are all slowly eroding its use. But the process of atrophy is not a straightforward one. Considerable variation occurs, which has not yet been tidied up into a fully categorical system. The situation found here suggests that young creoles are sometimes glamorized in the literature, and presented as instantaneous, neat systems. In practice, the neatening-up process might not be complete for generations (cf. Arends [above]) – in line with the finding that first-language speakers can often tolerate more variability than second-language speakers. Such changes are probably not being carried out by babies, but by stable groups of speakers, interacting among themselves.   (Aitchison, 1996, p. 29)

What all this certainly shows is the importance of having clear data, whether in the form of historical records or actual spoken data, in trying to reach any conclusions about the relationships between pidgins and creoles. Since the circumstances of formation of each creole are different, we should be prepared to accept that there may be different outcomes. What is important is that theorising should be based on sound data and careful empirical studies.

4.4   Exercise

Compare the tense and aspect systems of the following languages: Tok Pisin (Chapter 2, 2.1.2); Fanakalo (Chapter 2, 9.3.2); Mauritian Creole (Chapter 5, 3.3.2); Sranan (Chapter 5, 4.5.3). Do the similarities and differences you notice support a substratist hypothesis or a universalist one?

5 CASE STUDY: SUBSTRATE AND DEVELOPMENT IN SRANAN

In this case study, we will look at two aspects of Sranan Tongo, the creole described in detail in the previous chapter. In 5.1 we examine *serial verb structures*, a relatively unusual syntactic feature found in a number of creoles. In 5.2 we will look at the *derivational processses* at work in the Sranan lexicon. In considering serial verbs, we will see that there are numerous similarities between Sranan and some African languages, which suggest a possible substrate explanation. In looking at lexical processes of derivation, we will see that Sranan possesses a range of strategies for enlarging the referential capacity of the lexicon, for which a substrate explanation is unnecessary.

5.1 Serial Verbs

While probably in most languages just one main verb per clause is the norm, some languages permit chains or series of finite verbs to be present in the same clause. Such structures are usually called *serial verb structures*. (See Sebba, 1987, for a detailed cross-linguistic study of serial verbs; Lefebvre, 1991, for more recent research developments.) Example (1) from Sranan gives an idea of what such structures are like. They clearly do not correspond to any structures found in English or other European languages.

(1) **Rudy ben**   *tyari* **den**   **buku** *kon*   **na**   **ini a**   **oso**
     Rudy PAST carry the-PL book come LOC in the house
     'Rudy had brought the books into the house'

In (1), *tyari* and *kon* are both finite verbs; in other words neither is an auxiliary or modal verb, and neither is dependent on the other in the way that *come* is dependent on *want* in a sentence like *I wanted to come into the house*. The tense marker *ben* occurs only once, before the first verb, but determines the tense of both verbs, because both actions have to be interpreted as simultaneous.

   Sentence (2) is from Akan (the name of a group of closely related Ghanaian languages which includes Ashanti, Fanti and Twi) from the Kwa language group of Niger–Congo.

(2) *ɔde*   **pɔŋ**   **no**   *baae*
     3PERS-take-PAST table the come-PAST
     'S/he brought the table'

The structure of (2) is almost exactly the same as (1), with the difference that in Akan, both verbs are marked for tense; however, the tense must be the same for both verbs (one of the tense markers is thus redundant).

The fact that serial verbs are an 'areal feature', confined to very specific geographical regions and language groups, suggests that they are sufficiently highly marked for the correspondence between (1) and (2) to be a 'striking similarity' which suggests substrate influence. The similarities become stronger when we look at the range of different types of serial verbs which are found in Sranan and in the Kwa language group.

5.1.1   Directional serial verbs: 'go/come'
Sentences (1) and (2) are illustrations of this type, which indicate direction away from or towards a reference point.

5.1.2   Other motion verb complements: 'fall down', 'come out', etc.
A number of other verbs can function as complements of motion verbs: (3) and (4) are examples.

(3) **Sranan:** **Kofi** *fringi* **a** **tiki** *fadon*
               Kofi throw the stick fall-down
               'Kofi threw down the stick'

(4) **Yoruba:** **Olu** *ti* **ọmọ** **náà** *ṣubu*
               Olu push child the fall
               'Olu pushed the child down'

5.1.3   Instrumental serial verbs: 'take'
These indicate the means or instrument whereby something is done, and have the form *take* X *do* Y, e.g. (5) and (6):

(5) **Sranan:** **Mary** *teki* **a** **aksi** *fala* **a** **bon**
               Mary take the axe fell the tree
               'Mary felled the tree with an axe'

(6) **Yoruba:** **Mo** *fi* **ada** *ge* **igi**
               I take machete cut tree
               'I cut the tree with a machete'

5.1.4   Goal-indicating verbs: 'hit', 'pierce', 'fall down', etc.
Like *go* and *come*, these are usually complements of motion verbs. The first verb may be transitive or intransitive. If it is transitive, the *object* of the first verb is *subject* of the second verb, e.g.

(7) **Sranan:** **Mi** *fringi* **a** **ston** *naki* **Amba**
               I throw the stone hit Amba
               'I threw a stone at Amba (and hit her)'

(8) **Akan:**   me*tow*   **bo**   **no**   me*bɔɔ*   **Amma**
                  I-throw-PAST stone   the   I-pierce-PAST Amma
                  'I threw the stone at Amma (and hit her)'

Note that the English translation requires some clarification because in the Sranan and Akan sentences both verbs represent *completed* actions: hence the stone actually struck its victim rather than just going in the victim's direction.

5.1.5 *Lexical idioms*

Often two verbs operating in tandem have an idiomatic meaning, i.e. one that is not transparent from the meanings of the separate verbs. This suggests that the combination should have the status of a single discontinuous lexical item. For example:

Akan: *gye* 'accept' + *di* 'eat' = 'believe'

Anyi-Baule: *kã* 'touch' + *klé* 'show' = 'say, tell'

Yoruba: *la* 'cut open' + *ye* 'understand' = 'explain'

Lexical idiom serial verbs seem to be found in all the West African languages which have serial structures, but they are less easy to find in creoles. The Sranan examples that exist are certainly more transparent than their African counterparts:

Sranan: *bro* 'breathe, blow' + *kiri* 'kill' = 'blow out (candle)'

5.1.6 *Grammatical function I: Dative/benefactive: 'give'*

This type of construction was mentioned above in 3.3.4, where examples were given. The verb 'give', as second in the series, fulfils a role comparable to the English preposition *to* or *for*.

The 'give' serial construction, like the 'say' construction below, appears to have been subject to grammaticalisation in some languages, including Sranan. In such cases, the serial 'give' becomes re-analysed as a preposition, with the result that it has some or all of the normal prepositional properties and loses its verbal properties. For discussion, see Jansen et al. (1978) and Sebba (1987).

5.1.7 *Grammatical function II: Complementiser: 'say'*

This type of construction was also mentioned above in 3.3.4. The verb normally meaning 'say', following a verb like 'think', 'believe' or 'know', functions as a complementiser, equivalent to English *that*.

The 'say' serial construction in African languages has been the subject of some discussion, as the verb 'say' seems to have undergone re-analysis as a complementiser and lost its verbal properties in some languages. This may also be true of *taki* in Sranan, but it is difficult to find ways of distinguishing between *taki* as a verb and *taki* as a complementiser. For discussion see Lord (1973) and Sebba (1984).

5.1.8 *Grammatical function III: Comparative constructions*

A verb meaning 'pass' or 'surpass' may be used to form comparatives. In Sranan, either the verb *pasa* or the verb *moro*, 'surpass' (which can also function as an adverb meaning 'more'), may be used:

(9) **Sranan:**   **Anansi koni** *pasa* **tigri**
                   Anansi cunning pass tiger
                   'Anansi is more cunning than tiger'

(10) **Yoruba**:   **Omo náà gbon ju**   **asarun**
                   child the clever surpass tsetse-fly
                   'The child is cleverer than the tsetse fly'

We have now seen that serial verbs exist both in West African languages such as Akan, Yoruba and Anyi-Baule – all of which are known to have had speakers who were taken as slaves to the Caribbean – and in Sranan Tongo. Furthermore, for each different type of serial verb which can be found among the West African languages, Sranan has a more or less exactly corresponding construction. This is true even of the three constructions ('give', 'say' and 'surpass') which seem to have undergone grammaticalisation to varying degrees. Serial verb constructions are not widespread in the world's languages, but seem to be confined to a few geographical areas: they seem to be a good example of a marked syntactic construction.

However, the evidence for substrate influence is not unequivocal. Serial-like constructions have also been found in other creoles and creolising languages which have no African substratum. Bickerton (1981, p. 131) reports traces of serial-like constructions among the oldest Hawaiian Creole speakers, in particular the use of directional *come* and *go* after a main verb. Bickerton ridicules the suggestion that this is due to Chinese influence, but in fact it cannot be ruled out, as Chinese has exactly this kind of construction, and was one of the substrate languages in Hawaii. Harder to explain by reference to the substrate are instances of serialisation in Tok Pisin, reported by Sankoff (1984). Sankoff reports a range of 'verb chaining' structures some of which closely resemble the directional serial verbs of

Sranan, e.g. *em i salim mi kam*, 'he sent me come = he sent me (here)'. There is no apparent substrate source for these.

Bickerton (1981) rejects substrate explanations and regards serial verbs as a consequence of the fact that rudimentary creoles lack categories which mark grammatical relations, such as prepositions and morphological case-markers. According to him, 'verb serialisation is the only solution to the problem of marking cases in languages which have only N and V as major categories' – which he argues is the case with creoles, until such time as they develop other categories. Other languages, he says – like the West African serialising languages – have developed them as a response to the need for case-marking as existing prepositions have decayed.

This argument is not convincing if we bear in mind that most creole languages (as well as pidgins) do in fact have prepositions – though only a few of them. The fact that the category exists suggests that serial verbs are not simply a response to a need that prepositions can fulfil. It is also apparent from the range of functions which serial verbs in languages like Sranan perform, that case-marking is not the main purpose of serial verbs (though of course it may be their *original* purpose; once the construction is there, any language would probably tend to maximise the use of it). It also seems, on the basis of the available data, that serial verbs in Tok Pisin are not primarily used as case-markers (there are several well-documented prepositions which can do this; see Chapter 2).

Once again, we have to rely on some notion of markedness to tell us whether the serial verbs of Sranan are 'direct descendants' of the serial verbs of West Africa. The range of different functions seems to be the most significant factor in this. Both Hawaiian Creole English and Tok Pisin have serial verbs documented, but with a restricted range of functions (and low frequency in HCE). By contrast, Sranan serial verbs are frequent and widespread, and exactly mimic a range of uses found in West Africa.

5.2   Derivation in the Sranan Lexicon

If there seems to be some compelling evidence for substrate influence in a language like Sranan, does the substrate have to account for *all* the structural characteristics of the language? Could some of the language's structures be developed independently, without being based on the substrate? In order to begin to answer this question, in this section we will look at the expansion of the Sranan lexicon by studying the processes by which nouns are derived. Sranan, in common with many pidgins and creoles, has quite limited morphology. Also in keeping with other contact languages, the size of the Sranan lexicon is not great even now and the 'basic' lexicon at the time of the creole's formation was undoubtedly smaller. There is a need for productive morphological processes to increase the referential range. Sranan has two morphological processes which it uses to do this, *reduplication* and *compounding*, while *multifunctionality* is also important.

5.2.1 Reduplication

Some of the oldest words in Sranan seem to be the names of animals, which have been formed by reduplicating the word from the lexifier language. We find **konkoni**, 'rabbit' (from obsolete English *coney*), and **puspusi**, 'cat' (English 'pussy'), as well as **moysmoysi**, 'mouse', from Dutch *muis*.

Another set of reduplicated words – presumably old, because of their meanings – refer to body parts: **gorogoro**, 'throat', **fokofoko**, 'lungs'. The origins of these words are not known with certainty.

The above examples show that reduplicated forms exist in Sranan, but they do not show that reduplication is productive. In fact, reduplication *is* productive and has several different functions.

We find that many words for *instruments* are derived from verbs by reduplication. For example: **ariari**, 'rake', from **ari** (verb: 'to rake'); **kankan**, 'comb', from **kan** (verb: 'to comb'); **nanay**, 'needle', from **nay** (verb: 'to sew') (from Dutch *naaien*).

Reduplication can also be used to create nouns from adjectives, for example **moymoy**, 'finery', from Dutch *mooi*, 'beautiful'.

Reduplication of verbs may also produce a verb with an altered meaning, for example **wakawaka**, 'wander about', from **waka**, 'walk'; **takitaki**, 'chatter', from **taki**, 'talk'; **tantan**, 'stay intermittently', from **tan**, 'stay' (English *stand*).

Reduplication can also be used to derive adjectives from nouns, e.g. **tiftifi**, 'cogged, indented', from **tifi**, 'tooth' (English *teeth*). Here **tiftifi** means 'toothed' in a figurative sense: it cannot be used to describe, say, an animal which has teeth. There are other examples of reduplicated adjectives (derived from adjectives in this case) with figurative meanings: **bakabaka**, 'underhand', from **baka**, 'back, behind', and **brokobroko** as in **brokobroko tongo**, 'broken language', from **broko**, 'broken'. A similar kind of figurative meaning seems to attach to some reduplicated adverbs, e.g. **afuafu**, 'moderately', from **afu**, 'half', and **wanwan**, 'one at a time', from **wan**, 'one'.

Reduplication of adjectives can also produce an intensive meaning, e.g. **bisibisi**, 'very busy', from **bisi**, 'busy'; **libilibi**, 'lively', from **libi**, 'living, alive'.

5.2.2 Compounding

Compound nouns are common in Sranan. We find *noun + noun* compounds such as **Sranan + man**, 'Surinamese person', *adjective + noun* compounds like **bigi + futu**, 'big foot' = 'elephantiasis' (a disease which causes the leg to swell), and *verb + noun* compounds like **sidon + preysi**, 'sit-down place' = 'seat'. The nouns *ten*, 'time', *preysi*, 'place', *man*, 'person/man', *uma*, 'woman', and *sani*, 'thing', combine freely with most nouns, verbs and adjectives to produce a compound noun with transparent meaning.

5.2.3 Multifunctionality

Many Sranan nouns are derived from verbs without any change in form, e.g. *bro* (verb: 'blow, breathe'; noun: 'breath'). In other cases, reduplication may be involved (see above). *Abstract* nouns can be derived from any unreduplicated adjective which denotes a quality, e.g. *ogri* (adjective: 'ugly, bad'; verb: 'badness, evil'), *fri* (adjective: 'free'; verb: 'freedom'). This process is completely productive, with the result that English and Dutch names for such abstract qualities are systematically absent from the lexicon of Sranan (Sebba, 1981, p. 109). *Freyheti*, 'freedom', from Dutch *vrijheid*, is listed in Wullschlägel's dictionary (1856) as a word of Missionary origin. It seems to have dropped out of use altogether. Since Sranan *fri*, derived by a regular process, has the same meaning, borrowings like *freyheti* are redundant.

5.2.4 Productivity and constraints

The observation that a borrowing from Dutch is redundant as Sranan has its own word-creation processes is an important reminder that creole languages have their own resources and are not dependent for all their linguistic needs on the lexifier or substrate languages. The Sranan lexicon has a complexity of its own. Part of this is the operation of constraints which prevent the formation of homophonous words by reduplication. For example, the noun *freyfrey*, 'fly', is one of the reduplicated animal names mentioned in 5.2.1. It might be expected that the verb *frey* 'to fly', would be reduplicated on the pattern of *nanay*, 'needle', to mean 'an instrument for flying', i.e. 'wing'. In fact, this does not happen; the word for 'wing' is the unreduplicated form *frey*. The reduplicated animal name *freyfrey* seems to 'block' the formation of any potential homophone. Possibly the same principle is at work in producing two non-homophonous derived nouns from the verb *tay*, 'tie': *taytay*, 'bundle', and *tetey*, 'string, rope, muscle' (i.e. 'instrument used for tying').

5.3 Commentary

We have seen in this section two aspects of the grammar of Sranan: on the one hand, the syntactic phenomenon of verb serialisation, and on the other, the lexical processes of reduplication, compounding and multifunctionality. While in the case of serialisation, there seems to be a strong argument for seeing African substrate influence as responsible for establishing the patterns, in the case of the lexicon we can see that Sranan has its own resources for deriving new lexical items on the basis of words originally from

English and Dutch. Even if these lexical processes could be shown to be patterned on existing ones found in West African languages – which so far has *not* been shown – the processes themselves are Sranan ones.

Thus while substrate influence may account for some aspects of the grammar of a creole language, it is necessary to keep this in perspective. As a pidgin or creole develops, it creates its own resources for further development. This has been documented for Tok Pisin by Mühlhäusler (see Chapter 4), and is partly demonstrated above for Sranan. What this suggests is that while pidgins and creoles must be seen as the products of multilingual contact situations – because that they certainly are – they also have to be seen, at least once they have stabilised, as autonomous systems with their own pathways of development. It is probable that substrate influence is most significant when it confirms a tendency already present in the pidgin or creole grammar, or coincides with universal principles which are already pointing the language in the same direction.

5.4   Exercise

1. Which, if any, of the derivational processes described in 5.2 do you think are responsible for each of the following Sranan words? Where a Sranan source word is given, how does the derived form relate to it in terms of meaning and grammar?

dreyten	'dry season' from *drey* 'dry' + *ten* 'time'
babari	'noise, tumult' from *bari* 'shout' (English *bawl*)
singi	'song' or 'sing' (English *sing*)
tyatyari	'thing for carrying things on the head' from *tyari* 'carry' (English *carry*)
fufuruman	'thief' from *fufuru* 'steal' + *man* 'man'
draydray	'hesitate' from *dray* 'turn' (Dutch *draaien*)
wiwiri	'grass, hair' from English *weed*
krinkrin	'completely' from *krin* 'clean' (English *clean*)
monkimonki	'monkey'
langa	'length' or 'long' (probably from Dutch *lang*, 'long')
fonfon	from Sranan *fon* 'to punish' (origin unknown)
bruyabruya	'very untidy, pell-mell' from *bruya* 'confused' (origin unknown)

2. The Sranan words for 'life' and 'belief' are **libi** and **bribi** respectively.

    (a) By which of the derivational processes can these be related to the Sranan verbs *libi*, 'live', and *bribi*, 'believe'?

    (b) How can we be sure that the nouns *libi* and *bribi* are not derived directly from the English nouns *life* and *belief*?

KEY POINTS: Creole Origins

Creoles tend to share certain features (see Section 1.3 for list). How can we account for this?

- Universalist approaches: universal processes have the most important effect on the structure of the creole.

Bickerton's *Language Bioprogram Hypothesis*: the child acquiring language in a pidgin-speaking environment 'creates' a creole on the basis of an innate blueprint.

- Substrate approaches: the substrate provides many of the most important syntactic, morphological, phonological and lexical structures of the creole.

Abrupt vs *Gradual* creolisation:

- *The Language Bioprogram Hypothesis*: a creole has to be formed rapidly, within one generation. There is little or no substrate influence as language is not transmitted normally from adults to children.

- *The Gradualist Hypothesis*: Creolisation takes place among adults, over several generations. Substrate influences may appear gradually over a long period as new waves of substrate language speakers arrive.

7 Continuing Contact: Life after Creolisation

1 A MULTILINGUAL COMMUNITY

Creole languages are never born into the stillness of a monolingual community, but always – necessarily – amid the hubbub of a multilingual one. As we have seen, language contact can take several forms, and when the conditions of contact are present for a creole to appear, we can be sure that several other phenomena of language contact – pidginisation, foreigner talk, borrowing, code switching – are there as well. What is more, this situation is likely to last for a long time. In theory a creole could emerge as the sole language of a community within a generation or two, and there would be an end of language contact: but in practice, there does not seem to be a single case of this in recent history. Language contact is a pervasive phenomenon, and contacts which are intense enough to give rise to a new language altogether, tend to endure.

In the Caribbean, for example, the intensive language contact of slavery times led to the emergence of creolised forms of English, French, Spanish/ Portuguese and Dutch under conditions of contact in which slaves speaking a large number of different and mutually unintelligible African languages (and often deliberately put together with other slaves with whom they had no common language, to make it harder for them to conspire to escape) acquired reduced forms of the European languages in question. The slave-owners and colonisers did not go away at this point, but continued to practice slavery in the same region – though not always in the same territory – for several centuries. European languages thus continued to remain in contact with African languages, while both remained in contact with the new language – the creole. In some places, indigenous languages of the Americas were still spoken as well. Soon after the abolition of slavery, in several territories in the Caribbean and Indian Ocean (Surinam, Guyana, Trinidad and Mauritius, for example), indentured labourers were imported from the Indian subcontinent or East Asia, adding further to the linguistic complexity.

What all this means is that, while the emergence of a creole can in one sense be seen as the end point of a process which starts with language contact and ends with language birth, it can also be viewed as the beginning of a new process, in which the creole is a newcomer in an existing cocktail of languages in contact. In the previous chapter we saw that there is evidence of an enduring influence of African languages on Caribbean creoles. In this chapter we shall be concentrating on the relationship between the creoles and their lexifier languages, first taking the English-lexicon Jamaican Creole as a case study.

2 CASE STUDY: JAMAICAN CREOLE

2.1 Historical Background

Prior to 1509, the Caribbean island of Jamaica was inhabited by the Arawak people. Spanish settlement started in that year, and continued unprofitably until in 1655 a British force expelled the Spanish. By this time there were no Arawaks left in Jamaica. From 1656 onwards planters began to settle in Jamaica from other English colonies, and slaves were imported from Africa and from elsewhere in the Caribbean. The European population of Jamaica included Scots, Irish, Welsh and French, but the English were in the majority from this time.

The large sugar plantations of Jamaica required slave labour, and for most of the next two centuries slaves continued to be brought to Jamaica from Africa. All seem to have come initially from West Africa, and most would have spoken Kwa or Bantu languages. About 1000 of the earliest slaves in Jamaica came from Surinam with their owners in 1771 after the expulsion of the British by the Dutch, so that about 10 per cent of the slaves in Jamaica at that 'linguistically critical' time were Surinamese (Holm, 1989, p. 470).

A feature of the 17th and 18th centuries in Jamaica was *marronage* – slaves escaped into the mountains, where they set up villages beyond European control. The descendants of these escaped slaves or *Maroons* continue to live in quite isolated, linguistically conservative, communities.

Slavery was abolished in 1833. Some of the emancipated slaves subsequently moved to remote mountainous areas to farm, preserving older forms of the language (Le Page and De Camp, 1960). Jamaica continued to be ruled as a British colony until Independence in 1948. Today, most Jamaicans are Creole speakers, but the prestige language is Standard English and many who actually speak the Creole will claim to be speakers of English. Three centuries of contact between Standard English and the English-lexicon creole have created a situation where few speakers speak the 'broadest' creole, or 'basilect' as their main variety. Most Jamaicans speak a variety intermediate between the basilect and Standard English. Local variations also occur, as well as varieties of creole distinctive to particular groups, such as Rastafarians (see Pollard, 1994).

2.2 Jamaican Creole Text

The cartoon which follows is a small extract from *Kowaiti Bay*, a comic book published by the Diabetes Association of Jamaica. The characters are all neighbours in a poor part of Kingston. At the start of the extract, Kan Kan brings news to her friends that Tata Bishop, who practises *obeah* (magic healing) on his neighbours with little success, has been knocked down by a car.

Yes, a car knocked down Tata!

My father!

And we were just talking about him a little while ago!

So where is he now?!

Looks like a doctor knocked him down so ... He took him into his car and carried him to the hospital!

... if you back monkey he'll fight tiger ...

What's that you say, Miss Black?

Ohh my father, me and him had an argument about that *obeah* [magic] thing there, and I told him to go talk to the doctor and nurse at the clinic and see if they will teach him some of the right things to do to help ...

the poor people down in Kowaiti Bay when they're sick ... Kan Kan, do you know which hospital he's gone to?

It's the big one 'cause the doctor came from that hospital!

Figure 7.1 Extract from a cartoon strip from *Kowaiti Bay* (Jamaica)

Tata...tata...how are you
doing?

Ohh my dear Lord...Tata how did you
let this happen to you?

I never let it happen, ask Kan Kan,
she saw everything...

Now, who's to look after me?

Figure 7.1   (*continued*)

...Ohh, that will solve itself in time, don't worry your head here, thoughts,...worries aren't good for your poor head!

...the day I got hit it was the doctor I was going to see!

Ohh, so that's how that doctor man was there!

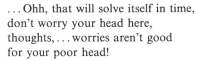

...which doctor was where?

The one whose car hit Tata!

Whose car hit who?

...then you didn't know that it was a doctor's car that hit you?

Figure 7.1 (*continued*)

Note on orthography. The orthography used here is based on Standard English spelling with some modifications to draw attention to the Jamaican pronunciation. The modifications are not always consistent. Apostrophes are sometimes used to represent consonants which are pronounced by Jamaican speakers using Standard English, but that are omitted by the speakers here, who are using Creole. For example, the spelling ***docta'*** seems to be intended to indicate that this word is pronounced without a final /r/, i.e. the spelling represents the pronunciation /dakta/. On the other hand, the motivation for spellings like *yu* and *lik* is not clear, as these words are pronounced much the same whether in Jamaican Standard English or in Creole. There is also a *phonemic* orthography developed for Jamaican Creole by Frederic Cassidy and used by Cassidy and Le Page for the *Dictionary of Jamaican English* (1967/1980). At the moment this is mainly used by linguists for linguistic descriptions of Jamaican and related languages. In the grammatical notes below, Jamaican words will be represented in the Cassidy phonemic orthography, which may make them look different from the same words in the cartoon. For comparison, the speech from the first two panels of the cartoon are given below in the Cassidy orthography:

> Yes, kyar lik doun **Tata**!
> Mi faada!
> An wi jos a taak bout im a likl wail!

> So we him de **nou**?!
> Luk laik a dakta man lik im doun so...
> Im tek im intu im kyar an kyari im gaan tu di **haspital**!

2.3 Grammatical Notes

2.3.1 *The pronoun system*
Where Standard English has separate forms for subject, object and possessive pronouns, Jamaican Creole (JC) has just one form for all three: sometimes this form is derived from the subject and sometimes from the object form in British English.

	singular	plural
1	mi/a	wi
2	yu	unu
3	im	dem

These are the forms found in the broadest creole, i.e. that least influenced by Standard English. Many speakers do differentiate gender in the third person singular, thus: *im/shi/it*.

2.3.2 Plurals

In JC the norm is *no* marking; ***dem*** may be added after a noun (especially one referring to people) to show plural, e.g. *di gyal-**dem***, 'the girls'.

2.3.3 Tense and aspect

JC has aspect markers ***a*** (progressive) and ***go/wi*** (future), which can combine with the anterior tense marker ***ben*** to give combinations like:

mi a waak	'I am walking'
mi ben waak	'I walked'
mi ben a waak	'I was walking'
mi ben go waak	'I was about to walk'

The form of the anterior tense marker is variable: it can take the form *bin*, *en*, or (in more English-influenced varieties) ***did*** or ***di***, as in the text: *mi an 'im di hav' agument*. Whichever form it takes, it is an invariant particle and cannot be regarded as an auxiliary verb.

A verb without any preverbal marker often has past meaning, e.g. *car lik down Tata*, and many other examples from the text.

Future tense is marked by ***wi***, e.g. *if yu back monkey im wi fight tiger*.

2.3.4 The copula

Locative complement: ***de***

> *Kingston de a Jamaica*, 'Kingston is in Jamaica'
> From the text: *wey him deh now?!* 'Where is he now?'

Equative: ***a***

mi a di tiicha, 'I am the teacher'

Adjectival complement: **copula absent**
dem sik, 'they are sick'
di man taal, 'The man is tall'

2.3.5 Possession

(a) X ***fi*** Y: *di pikni fi Mary* ('Mary's children')

(b) Y X: *Mary pikni*
    (from the text) *mi father*; *a docta' car* ('a doctor's car')

Note: ***fi*** is also a verbal marker corresponding to English *to*, e.g. (from the text) *mi tell im fi gu talk to di docta' and nurse at di clinic si if dem wi teach im some a di right tings fi do fi help . . .*

2.3.6   Serial verbs

Some of the structures mentioned in Chapter 6 as possible substrate structures are present in Jamaican Creole and illustrated in the text, for example:

Use of the verb meaning 'say' as a complementiser (Section 3.3.4): *yu neva know **seh** is a docta' car lik yu?!* (You never knew 'say' it was a doctor's car that hit you?)

Directional serial verbs: ***go/come*** (Section 5.1.1): *'Im tek 'im into im car an carry 'im **gone** to di hospital!*

2.4   Exercise

1.   Compare the pronoun system of Jamaican Creole with that of Sranan (Chapter 5). Make a note of any similarities you find.

2.   Compare the tense and aspect system of Jamaican Creole with that of Sranan. Make a note of any similarities you find.

3.   Compare the copula system of Jamaican Creole with that of West African Pidgin English (Chapter 4). Make a note of any similarities you find.

4.   Compare the uses of Jamaican Creole *fi* with your notes on *foh* in Krio (Chapter 5). Note any similarities and differences.

5.   Make a list of all the plurals in the Jamaican Creole text (use the meaning rather than the marking to decide if a word is being used in the plural). How accurate is the description of the plural in 2.3.2? What is unaccounted for?

3   THE POST-CREOLE CONTINUUM

3.1   The 'Ladder of Lects'

One of the problems facing a linguist aiming to describe the language of Jamaicans is its *variability*. As mentioned above, there are relatively few Jamaicans who speak only the broadest form of Jamaican Creole. Equally, there are relatively few who speak Standard English, although this is the language of official functions and the media. The majority speak 'something in between'. To take a simple example, the broadest creole translation of Standard English *I am eating* would be *mi a nyam*. These sentences differ from each other lexically (*eat* vs *nyam*), morphologically (*I* vs *mi*) and syntactically (Auxiliary verb *am* with aspect suffix *-ing* vs TMA particle *a*). It is very hard, in fact, to see how these could be considered to be different renditions of the same sentence *in the same language*. However, if we examine all the possible ways that Jamaicans might express this concept, we would find at least these additional possibilities: /mi a iːt, mi iːtɪn, a iːtɪn, a ɪz iːtɪn/ (*me a eat, me eatin', I eatin', I is eatin'*).

De Camp (1971) was the first to describe the Jamaican situation as a dialect continuum linking the broadest creole (which he calls 'bush talk') with the local version of Standard English. Here is his description (1971, p. 350):

> ...no one can deny the extreme variability of Jamaican English....[I]n Jamaica there is no sharp cleavage between creole and standard. Rather there is a linguistic continuum, a continuous spectrum of speech varieties ranging from the 'bush talk' or 'broken language'...to the educated standard....Many Jamaicans persist in the myth that there are only two varieties: the patois and the standard. But one speaker's attempt at the patois may be closer to the standard end of the spectrum than is another speaker's attempt at the standard....Each Jamaican speaker commands a span of this continuum, the breadth of the span depending on the breadth of his social contacts.

We can conveniently visualise the continuum as a ladder. At one end (see Figure 7.2), we find a form of Jamaican Creole which is markedly different from Standard English in a whole range of ways': This variety is now called, in 'continuum' terminology, the **basilect** – the 'lect' (variety) at the base of the continuum. This is therefore the 'bottom rung' of the ladder,

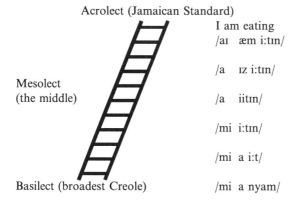

Acrolect (Jamaican Standard)

I am eating
/aɪ æm iːtɪn/

/a ɪz iːtɪn/

Mesolect
(the middle)

/a iitɪn/

/mi iːtɪn/

/mi a iːt/

Basilect (broadest Creole)   /mi a nyam/

Figure 7.2 The Jamaican Post-Creole continuum

reasonably accurately reflecting the fact that the basilectal Jamaican Creole is likely to be used by those who are economically worst off, and have least access to education. Basilectal Jamaican Creole, like any 'pure' language, is necessarily something of a theoretical construct. Since every speaker is likely to 'command a span of this continuum', as De Camp puts it, it is unlikely that any speaker will use the basilectal form of the creole all the time. Nonetheless, Jamaicans probably have an intuitive feel for what the basilectal forms are, even if they do not use them.

At the top of the 'lect ladder' we find the **acrolect**, or 'peak' (Latin *acer*), which is actually just the local Jamaican variety of Standard English. The acrolect is at most marginally different from British Standard English in grammar and morphology, and apart from the use of local lexical items for things Jamaican, it is lexically almost the same as well. In terms of its phonology, it is somewhat different, and has much in common with the Jamaican basilect. It could reasonably be called 'Standard English with a Jamaican accent'. Unsurprisingly, the acrolect is usually the preserve of the educated Jamaican elite – professionals and the economically well-off. Standard English is the language of prestige and is offered as a model in education and the media, but generally it is only the wealthier Jamaicans who grow up speaking it.

All the varieties between the acrolect and the basilect are given the name *mesolect* – the 'middle'. It is here, of course, that the majority of speakers are – the 'in-betweens'. The mesolect represents a continuous range of lects, each shading into the next, each more or less Creole-like and more or less Standard-like depending on its 'rung' of the 'ladder' (see Figure 7.2).

3.2 Social History and the Continuum

Let us compare the linguistic situations in Jamaica and Surinam. They are surely comparable. Both countries were settled by the English at almost the same time, are located in the same part of the world and practised similar types of plantation farming using slaves from West Africa. In each an English-lexicon creole developed. In fact, if we compare the grammar of basilectal Jamaican Creole – in so far as we can separate it out – with that of Sranan, we find some significant similarities. The pronoun systems, TMA marking, possession marking and use of the copula are all very similar – a fact which cannot be explained by reference to the lexifier, English, which is different from both in these respects.

Here, however, the resemblance between these two creole-speaking communities ends. In Surinam, there is no 'continuum' (although there are varieties of Sranan which have been lexically influenced by Dutch, and some speakers code-switch between Sranan and Dutch). All varieties of Sranan are extremely unlike English, and there is virtually no mutual intelligibility. In Jamaica, on the other hand, there is a situation which can be modelled by a continuum, and Jamaican Creole as spoken by most Jamaicans is sufficiently like English for them to regard it as a form of English – usually regarded as 'broken' or 'bad'.

The reason, of course, is that while Jamaican has remained in contact with its lexifier, Sranan has not. English has not existed as a model for Sranan speakers for the last three centuries. In Jamaica, by contrast, English (not necessarily in a Standard form, but at least more or less as spoken by British native speakers) has continued to be present and to be held up as a model of correctness.

This fact in itself is not enough to explain the existence of a continuum. In Haiti, the official language has been French ever since the establishment of the French colony there, and it coexists with the French-lexicon Haitian Creole. But there is nothing like the Jamaican continuum in Haiti; the situation is much more like one of diglossia (see Chapter 1), with a small elite bilingual in French and Haitian Creole, and a large majority of the population monolingual in the Creole. (See Chapter 8 for a case study of Haitian Creole.) The Haitian case seems to be analogous to the Jamaican one, but the absence of a continuum or something like it requires explanation.

De Camp (e.g. 1971) thinks of the Jamaican situation as a **post-creole continuum** reflecting a change in social conditions after the emancipation of the slaves. In this scenario, the liberalisation of social relationships and increased (though still limited) access to education in the post-emancipation period enabled the continuum to emerge, as pressure to assimilate to Standard English affected different social groups to different extents. On this view, it represents the next stage in the pidgin/creole life cycle, as the creole slowly 'reunites' itself with its lexifier. As pointed out by John Rickford (1987, p. 32), this means that all the mesolectal varieties have actually developed more recently than the acrolect or basilect, 'representing a filling in of the linguistic space between creole and standard language that parallels the filling in of the social space between the highest and lowest castes of colonial society after Emancipation'.

An alternative view is presented by Alleyne (1980, p. 184), who cites the differential access to the slave owners (and their language) enjoyed by different types of slaves even in the earliest days of the colony. 'Field slaves', those who actually spent their working lives cultivating and cutting sugar cane, had virtually no contact with the European masters; however, their (African) overseers had some direct contact. The domestic slaves, meanwhile, worked in the houses of the slave owners and were spoken to directly by them. This hierarchy (in terms of both status, and access to native speakers of the lexifier language) gave rise, according to Alleyne, to 'a certain cultural and behavioural differentiation in the slave population' which produced a range of language varieties closer to or further away from the English of native speakers. On this view, the continuum has its origins in the plantation society, and is not recent.

3.3   Implicational Patterns in a Continuum

We saw above that between the 'basilectal' creole *mi a nyam* and the 'acrolectal' *I am eating*, there were a range of other forms which might be heard in Jamaica, for example, /mi a iːt, mi iːtɪn, a iːtɪn, a ɪz iːtɪn/. But what of *I am nyaming, mi am a nyam, I a eat*? These forms do not seem to occur (except possibly the last, among Rastafarians, who have a preference for using *I* rather than *mi* in most contexts). Why should this be? Intuitively, some lexical forms are inappropriate in certain contexts. The connotations of *nyam* are such that it would not be expected to figure in the kind of conversation where Standard English forms like *I am ...ing* would be used. However, this does not explain the non-occurrence of forms like *I a eat* and *mi am a nyam*. If the different forms which do occur are simply the result of random mixing of two 'extreme' varieties – the acrolect and the basilect – then we are left without an explanation.

In fact, it has been argued by De Camp, C.-J. N. Bailey (1973), Bickerton and others that what we find in a creole continuum is an *implicational hierarchy*. What this means is that the occurrence of a particular form in the speech of a speaker, means that the same speaker will necessarily use certain other forms as well. For example, a speaker who uses *mi* for the first person singular pronoun will use the *a* progressive aspect marker with the bare stem of the verb, e.g. /mi a iːt/, while a speaker who uses *be* V + *ing* to form a present progressive tense will use the form *I* rather than /mi/ for the first person singular.

De Camp (1971, p. 355ff) gives an example involving seven speakers and six linguistic features, each of them with a Standard English variant and a broad creole variant, in Jamaica. The features in question are the following:

(1)

	Standard variant	Creole variant
A:	child	pikni
B:	eat	nyam
C:	/θɪk/ contrasts with /tik/	/tɪk/ for both
D:	/ðen/ contrasts with /den/	/den/ for both
E:	granny	nana
F:	didn't	no ben

Features A, B and E are lexical; C and D are phonological; while F is syntactic/morphological. Arbitrarily, let us say a speaker has the value + if s/he uses the Standard variant and – for the creole variant, thus +A –B etc. De Camp's seven speakers each use a different combination of these seven features, namely:

(2)

1.	+A	+B	+C	–D	+E	+F
2.	–A	+B	–C	–D	+E	+F
3.	–A	+B	–C	–D	–E	–F
4.	–A	–B	–C	–D	–E	–F
5.	+A	+B	+C	+D	+E	+F
6.	+A	+B	–C	–D	+E	+F
7.	–A	+B	–C	–D	+E	–F

From this it appears that Speaker 4 uses only the creole forms, while Speaker 5 uses only the Standard ones. The remainder might be called 'mesolectal' speakers. However, the distribution of the features they use is not random. This becomes obvious if we first rearrange the table to rank speakers in terms of the number of 'plus' features they have:

(3)

5.	+A	+B	+C	+D	+E	+F
1.	+A	+B	+C	–D	+E	+F
6.	+A	+B	–C	–D	+E	+F
2.	–A	+B	–C	–D	+E	+F
7.	–A	+B	–C	–D	+E	+F
3.	–A	+B	–C	–D	–E	–F
4.	–A	–B	–C	–D	–E	–F

The most 'Standard' speaker is now at the top and the most 'creole' one at the bottom. If we now rearrange the table a little more we can see the *implicational* nature of the variation we are considering:

(4)

5.	+B	+E	+F	+A	+C	+D
1.	+B	+E	+F	+A	+C	–D
6.	+B	+E	+F	+A	–C	–D
2.	+B	+E	+F	–A	–C	–D
7.	+B	+E	–F	–A	–C	–D
3.	+B	–E	–F	–A	–C	–D
4.	–B	–E	–F	–A	–C	–D

We can now see that a speaker who is '+E' is also necessarily '+B', while a speaker who is '+A' is necessarily '+B', '+E' and '+F' – in other words, a speaker who uses the word *child* rather than /pikni/ will also use *granny*, *didn't* and *eat*. However, such a speaker may or may not have a contrast between *thick* and *tick*. At the same time, if a speaker uses the form *no ben* (–F) rather than *didn't* (+F) then that speaker will also use /pikni/ for 'child', and lack the contrast between *thick* and *tick* as well as the contrast between *thin* and *then*. This will be much clearer if we re-draw our table as a more conventional 'implicational scale' table:

(5)

	B	E	F	A	C	D
5.	+	+	+	+	+	+
1.	+	+	+	+	+	−
6.	+	+	+	+	−	−
2.	+	+	+	−	−	−
7.	+	+	−	−	−	−
3.	+	−	−	−	−	−
4.	−	−	−	−	−	−

What this suggests is that there is a true 'continuum' of different combinations of features – it is not the 'all or nothing' represented by Speakers 4 and 5 – but that these are also hierarchically ordered, so that if a speaker has a particular feature he or she will also necessarily have certain others. This does not have to be the case. If there were just random mixing of the Standard and creole variants, we would expect a different picture, perhaps something like this:

(6)

	B	E	F	A	C	D
5.	+	+	+	+	+	+
1.	+	+	−	+	+	−
6.	−	+	+	−	+	−
2.	−	+	−	+	−	+
7.	+	−	+	−	+	−
3.	+	+	−	−	−	+
4.	−	−	−	−	−	−

Table (6) is not *scalable*, in other words it is impossible to arrange it to show an implicational hierarchy like the one in table (5). On the other hand, if what we had were completely discrete varieties – 'Standard English' and 'Creole' – which speakers *never* mixed, we would expect a table like (7):

(7)

	B	E	F	A	C	D
5.	+	+	+	+	+	+
1.	+	+	+	+	+	+
6.	+	+	+	+	+	+
2.	−	−	−	−	−	−
7.	−	−	−	−	−	−
3.	−	−	−	−	−	−
4.	−	−	−	−	−	−

De Camp's table reflects the linguistic behaviour of just seven of his speakers. We could object that the fact that seven individuals display a scalable implicational hierarchy in their speech does not tell us much, as there may be hundreds of other Jamaicans who mix randomly, producing a table like (6). Therefore, it is first of all necessary to be able to apply scaling techniques to a fair-sized random sample of speakers if any claims are to be made about the behaviour of the community as a whole. Secondly, there needs to be an *index of scalability* which indicates how scalable the data actually is. A table like (5), where all the pluses lie above the diagonal and all the minuses below it (or vice versa) is considered 'perfect' or 100% scalable. In practice, according to Guttman (1944), who first developed the technique of implicational scaling, scales need only be 85% perfect to approximate perfect scaling. What this means is that in a table like (5), (a 6 × 7 matrix with 42 cells) up to 6 pluses and minuses could be in the 'wrong' places (minuses above the diagonal or pluses below it) and it would still suggest strongly that an implicational hierarchy was involved. More deviations than that, however, would suggest either that there was no implicational hierarchy, or that something was wrong from a methodological point of view (e.g. the variables had been badly defined, or the speakers' behaviour had been noted incorrectly).

3.4 The Continuum as History

Bickerton (1973, 1975) develops a view of the continuum which sees it as a mirror of the linguistic history of a community. On this view, each speaker has *polylectal* competence, i.e. command of a number of separate *lects* or self-contained grammars (cf. the quote from De Camp in 3.1). These lects differ from each other minimally, by the presence or absence of a single rule, and constitute the 'ladder' of grammars which link the two 'end' lects – the basilect and the acrolect.

Bickerton's continuum research relates mainly to Guyana, a country adjacent to Surinam in mainland South America where the linguistic situation is quite comparable to that in Jamaica. It was settled by the English at much the same time, cultivated by slave labour, and while a broad Guyanese Creole (often called *Creolese*) can be identified, the official language and language of the elite is Standard English. Between these two exists a continuum, much like that in Jamaica. For Bickerton, the Guyanese continuum represents a process of *decreolisation*, as the original Guyanese Creole has gradually assimilated to English. As Bickerton puts it (1975, p. 16):

> it would seem reasonable to suppose that the extreme creole varieties in modern Guyana represent survivals from a relatively early stage in creole development, and that, if Guyana had not come under pressure from standard English, all Guyanese speech, rather than a relatively small proportion of it, would closely approximate contemporary Sranan. Equally, had this pressure from English been more strongly and evenly applied, all Guyanese speech might have evolved into a variety of English differing from the standard no more, say, than Black English differs from White English in New York.

The continuum thus results, in this scenario, from the fact that the rural Guyanese (especially those of East Indian origin) had virtually no contact with Standard English; the educated urban elite (of African extraction) had a high level of access to it; while 'the remainder of the population, strung out between these extremes, advanced, at an uneven pace and not without sidesteps and hesitations, in the direction of the superordinate language' (p. 17). While originally subscribing to De Camp's view that the continuum was of recent (i.e. post-Emancipation) origin (see 3.2 above), Bickerton now accepts Alleyne's view that the basis of the continuum was there from the start, inherent in the types of social relationships which came with the slavery system. This does not alter the historical interpretation of the continuum significantly, however, because (as pointed out by Rickford, 1987, p. 33) the numerical predominance of the field slaves – those with the least exposure to Standard English – would have meant that decreolisation for most people in Guyana began only after Emancipation.

It follows, says Bickerton, that a *synchronic* study of the Guyanese continuum amounts to a *diachronic* view of the development of Guyanese language systems. The 'step-by-step, lect-by-lect' progression through the mesolect mirrors the stages of approximation to Standard English achieved by the 'top rank' of speakers at each stage. Hence what we have is a dynamic 'creole system' which displays past changes while itself changing. *Decreolisation* is the process whereby speakers progressively alter the grammar of the basilect so that the output comes to resemble the output of the acrolectal grammar.

To take one example, the basilectal anterior tense marker *bin* is replaced in mesolectal varieties in Guyana by *did*. Bickerton notes that 'one very characteristic strategy of the decreolisation process is the replacement of morphemes of non-standard appearance by others which, on the surface, look like – or at least, look more like – morphemes of standard English'

(1975, p. 69). Bickerton adds that often the replacement is superficial; the grammar does not change, just the morpheme representing the basilectal grammatical category. This is what happens in the case of *did*, which is not the past tense of *do* for mesolectal Guyanese speakers, but simply an invariant morpheme (like *bin*) marking anteriority. However, it *sounds* more like Standard English, so that replacing *bin* with *did* in an utterance like *mi bin sen it*, 'I sent it', can be seen as a step in the direction of Standard – both subconsciously by the speaker, and from an analytical point of view, by the linguist.

3.5 The Continuum Questioned

There are a number of important theoretical issues underlying the continuum hypothesis (see Rickford, 1987, chapter 1, for a more detailed discussion). These, and the methodology of the continuum's advocates, have been critiqued and called into question by other researchers. In this section we will look at some of these critiques.

3.5.1 Methodology: scalability
The scalability of data is crucial to the continuum hypothesis as only if there is genuinely an implicational hierarchy can there be said to be a 'creole system' consisting of a 'continuum of lects', each minimally differing from the next, which links the two extremes.

Bickerton has been criticised for his use of scaling, in particular by Romaine (1982, 1988). One criticism concerns whether empty cells (i.e. those for which there is no data) have to be counted in as part of the total. For example, is table (8) scalable or not? It has 42 cells, but only 30 are filled. Of these 30, 2 are deviant (one plus below the diagonal, one minus above), so we could claim that it is $28/30 = 93\%$ scalable. But how do we know that the unfilled cells would be filled with pluses and minuses in the 'right' places? If we treat unfilled cells as potentially deviant, we get a much worse figure: $28/42$ or 67% scalable, not enough to show a convincing implicational hierarchy.

(8)

	K	L	M	N	O	P
1.		+	+		+	+
2.	+	+		+	+	−
3.	+	+	+	+	−	
4.		+	+	+	−	−
5.	−	+	−	−	−	−
6.		−		−	−	−
7.						+

As Romaine points out, if speakers who produce very little data are moved up or down, improved scalability may result – for example, by moving Speaker 7 to the top, we could eliminate one deviant cell. Yet we would not have a very good reason for doing this – or indeed, for placing Speaker 7 anywhere else.

This is not an argument to dismiss Bickerton's work out of hand, but it indicates that careful attention must be given to statistical methods and sample sizes before making claims about scalability. According to Le Page (1984, p. 6), shortly before his death De Camp stated that he regretted that implicational scaling had been taken up so avidly by other linguists, and that he had himself been able to scale only 30 per cent of his Jamaican data.

3.5.2   Unidimensionality

The classic continuum model assumes that there is only one *dimension* of variation, i.e. that all variation can be arranged on a single line linking creole with Standard. This has been contested by researchers such as Washabaugh, and Le Page and Tabouret-Keller. De Camp himself raised the possibility that some variation might lie outside the single Creole–Standard dimension – for example, geographical variation, but felt that this was not significant. Other variables, such as age and gender, he felt could be accounted for within the unidimensional continuum since, for example, the speech of the young tended to be closer to Standard English than that of older people.

Washabaugh (1977) showed that in Providence Island, part of the territory of Colombia where a creole similar to Jamaican Creole is spoken, there was a 'basilect vs acrolect' (locally called *broad talk* vs *speakin*) dimension of variation, but also a stylistic 'careful' vs. 'casual' (*sweet talk* vs *bad/brawlin talk*) dimension. Rickford, responding to this, suggests that throughout the West Indies the operative distinction may be 'sweet talk' vs 'broad talk': 'it is most unlikely that the careful/casual contrast does not involve some elements of the acrolectal/basilectal opposition' (1987, p. 25). This reflects a view widely held by variation theorists, that 'variation on the style dimension within the speech of a single speaker derives from and echoes the variation which exists between speakers on the "social" dimension' (Bell, 1984, p. 151; he calls this the 'style axiom').

Le Page's critique is more wide-ranging. Le Page and Tabouret-Keller's research (see 1985, chapter 4) was carried out mainly in two locations – Belize and St Lucia – where multilingualism and language contact is the norm. In Belize, the main components of the linguistic situation are Standard English, English-lexicon Creole, Spanish and Maya; in St. Lucia, Standard English, English-lexicon Creole and French-lexicon Creole (*Kweyol*). Le Page and Tabouret-Keller stress that one dimension of variation cannot account for the linguistic complexity of these societies, and stress the need for a *multidimensional* model. For Le Page and Tabouret-Keller, speakers' choices of particular variants, or particular languages through which to express themselves, are 'acts of identity' by means of which speakers associate themselves with groups that they identify around them. In so doing, they locate themselves within multidimensional linguistic space. For example, Le Page and Tabouret-Keller's Belizean informants located themselves along dimensions which might be labelled 'Spanish', 'Carib', 'Creole' and 'English/book learning'.

The diagram in Figure 7.3 is Rickford's (1987, p. 27) interpretation of how three of Le Page's informants (the Belize schoolgirls MP and GM, and the 'old lady' OL) could be positioned in multidimensional space.

Calling Bickerton's (1975) model 'simplistic' in the way he links variability with language change (in terms of decreolisation), Le Page and Tabouret-Keller write (1985, pp. 198–9):

> Such a model necessarily implies a linear sequence of varieties within 'a language', with the implication that all innovation starts from the same source and travels in the same direction; and that innovation in phonology is paralleled by a similar sequence of innovation in different parts of the grammar and lexicon. None of these suppositions can be sustained.... Although it is clear from our Belize and St. Lucian examples that language changes are taking place, it is also clear that not all change is in the same direction, towards the same target.... At any moment in time each of us can select from a variety of possible models, each socially marked; change only takes place when the social rules of the possible models change, and the behaviour of the community is re-focussed as a result.

Although Le Page and Tabouret-Keller reject the *unidimensional* continuum model, they are by no means in favour of a model which views language varieties as discrete, clearly bounded entities. Rather, they are in sympathy

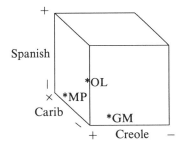

Figure 7.3   Locations of three Belizean speakers in multidimensional space

with the general notion of a continuous linguistic space in which speakers place themselves by their linguistic behaviour, but reject the notion of a single, unidirectional progression from Creole to Standard.

3.5.3 Nondiscreteness

However, other researchers have questioned the claim of *nondiscreteness* or continuity of the linguistic system in Guyana and Jamaica; in other words, they have denied the very existence of a continuum. Among these researchers are a number who are themselves members of the language communities in question, for example Lawton (1980), a Jamaican, who favours a model of two discrete language systems with code switching between the two. Gibson (1982), a Guyanese, also favours a two-language system. In her view, the acrolect – Standard English – is different from all other varieties, which together may be taken as varieties of Creole and share an underlying grammar. Beryl Loftman Bailey, a Jamaican, similarly 'preferred to operate with two distinctly divergent poles, and to regard all performances which occur within the continuum as belonging to one or the other of these poles' (1971, p. 341). In her pioneering 1966 study of Jamaican Creole syntax, Bailey attempted to describe the structures of 'the form of language which is syntactically, phonologically, and lexically farthest removed from the Jamaican standard', but she notes that this is an 'idealised construct' (1971, p. 342).

For each of these native speakers who rejects the notion of a continuum, however, there is at least one who does not. For Guyana, Rickford (1987, and many other works) strongly favours a continuum explanation. While accepting that there are communities in Jamaica and Guyana which are linguistically as complex as Belize and St Lucia, he feels that the uni-dimensional continuum is still the descriptive goal to be worked toward. Among Jamaicans, Frederic Cassidy (1961) and Dennis Craig (1980) favour the continuum view.

While an approach that treats 'Standard' and 'Creole' as separate lan-guage systems is incompatible with a unidimensional continuum analysis, it can be accommodated within a multidimensional approach like that of Le Page and Tabouret-Keller. Since in this approach, a 'language' is never a discrete entity, but a speaker's construct, it is possible to have 'Standard', 'Creole', and other languages or language varieties which speakers identify in their environment as dimensions of the linguistic space. Speakers will then place themselves in this multidimensional space (in different positions on different occasions). Code switching between varieties may be seen as one kind of 'act of identity' by which speakers position themselves at a given moment; choice of a particular morpheme or a particular lexical item may be another. Despite its rejection by some theorists, the multidimensional model (which could, of course, be reduced to a unidimensional model in some very simple situations – if any are that simple!) may offer a way of modelling linguistically complex communities, of which 'continuum' situations might form a subset.

3.5.4 Making the ends meet

A fundamental theoretical problem with the continuum concept is raised by Le Page. How can we be sure that the linguistic units of the basilect match with those of the acrolect? As Le Page and McEntegart put it (1982, p. 109),

> To what extent does one end of a diglossic system share the same tense/ aspect/mood system or even the same basic divisions of predication (stative/active, inceptive/completive/progressive etc.) as the other? To what extent is the phonology of a broad spoken vernacular based on the same distinctive feature system and the same morpheme-stock as the speech of educated literates in the same society?

Le Page and McEntegart's point is that 'variation' has to be between *tokens of the same type* (p. 110, their emphasis), i.e. one must compare like with like. For example, how could we quantify 'variation' between a basilectal system which had a distinction between completive and noncompletive aspect, and an acrolectal system which made distinctions only in terms of tense? The two 'ends' of the supposed continuum would not match up with each other. In practice, as we saw, speakers tend to introduce morphemes which approximate the acrolectal form (like *did* as an anterior tense marker in the Guyanese system). For speakers 'emerging' from the basilect, it is clear that this morpheme has acrolect-like form, but it functions as part of the basilectal TMA system. However, it is not clear how speakers close to the acrolect make the transition from the Creole TMA system to the Standard one. They already have forms like *did* which resemble acrolectal forms, but their system still is fundamentally different. There must, it seems, be a sudden transition – and hence a break in the continuum – at the point where speakers begin to use the TMA system of Standard English rather than that of Creole. This suggests that there are just two underlying systems – Creole and Standard English – with most of the variation taking place within the Creole system.

3.5.5 The relevance of social factors

The relevance to the continuum of *social* factors is the subject of disagreement among researchers. Bickerton regards a social account of variation as irrelevant to the continuum hypothesis (i.e. the continuum can be described independently of social factors); other proponents of the continuum have, however, taken social factors into account (e.g. Rickford). Le Page (1980) points out that the motivation of the speaker for moving across the continuum is not explained – implying that such an explanation is an essential part of an account of these phenomena. In Le Page's own model, 'the individual creates for himself the patterns of his linguistic behaviour so as to resemble those of the group or groups with which from time to time he wishes to be identified, or so as to be unlike those from whom he wishes to be distinguished' subject to certain constraints on the individual's ability to identify the groups and make the necessary behavioural adjustments (Le Page and Tabouret-Keller, 1985, p. 181). This model thus attempts to account for both *where* and *why* an individual positions him/herself in multidimensional linguistic space. At the same time, the notion of *diffuse* linguistic norms (discussed in Chapter 1, Section 3.4) helps to account for the large amount of variation. While this greater scope of explanation may make Le Page and Tabouret-Keller's model preferable, it should be pointed out that this does not actually offer counter-evidence to the continuum hypothesis, which does not attempt to account for the social aspects of continuum phenomena.

3.6   The Continuum: Conclusion

All researchers seem to agree that there is something in the linguistic situation of Jamaica, Guyana and similar creole-speaking territories which needs to be explained by means of a model. In some ways the continuum model states the obvious: that the higher the social and economic status of the speaker, the closer is his/her speech to Standard English. That 'obvious' fact has turned out to be difficult to prove, however, as questions have been raised about the reliability and scalability of the data, the validity of the assumptions of unidimensionality and discreteness, and the relationship of the continuum to the historical development of the creole. Ultimately, the choice between a unidimensional model, a multidimensional model, and any other model which may be proposed will not be made simply on the basis of data collected in one or other territory, but on the basis of the *explanatory* power of the model, as it applies to that and to other situations.

Perhaps one weakness of the continuum model is that it is so specialised, giving an account of one very specific type of situation ('decreolisation') but not adaptable more generally to situations of language contact. In fact, some linguistic situations not involving creoles have also been described using the continuum metaphor: for example, the series of stages between Gaelic-influenced English and Standard English used by Catholic speakers in the north of Ireland (O'Donnell and Todd, 1980; see also Harris, 1984, on the 'decreolisation' of Hiberno-English). This situation is similar to that of a creole and standard language in contact, in that it involves speakers assimilating, under social pressure, to a prestige standard which is not their native language. However, it is likely that a multidimensional model could account equally well for such a situation, taking into account both the linguistic and social factors in the context.

In Section 4, we will look at *recreolisation*, a phenomenon which presents another challenge to the notion of a 'post-creole continuum'.

3.7 Exercise

Go through the Jamaican Creole text in 2.2 again. Make a note of which parts are more like Standard English and which are more creole-like. Suggest reasons for any systematic variation you find. Discuss whether a 'continuum' approach, a 'code switching' approach or some other approach seems best for describing your small sample of Jamaican data.

4 RECREOLISATION

If Jamaica and Guyana represent linguistic contexts characterised by *decreolisation* – a movement away from Creole towards the Standard – there are nevertheless other contexts which may be characterised by *recreolisation* – a movement by speakers towards the more 'creole' end of the linguistic spectrum. In Bickerton's (1975) continuum model (see above), the continued presence, and prestige, of Standard English in Guyana provided the linguistic pressure to cause speakers to modify their grammars, stage by stage, in the direction of the acrolect. In Britain today – where Standard English is both more widespread and more accessible than in the Caribbean – some speakers are modelling their language on *basilectal* creole.

To understand this phenomenon – which is not explainable without reference to the social context, let us first take a striking example. The following is a transcription of a conversation between two boys, 'Mike' and 'Edgar', aged about 15, in a London school.

Transcription conventions: Underlining indicates an utterance identifiable as Creole on phonological or grammatical grounds. Parts which are unclear are in round brackets ( ). A glottal stop is indicated by %. Numbers in round brackets indicate pauses measured in seconds, e.g. (0.8) = a pause of eight-tenths of a second. Braces ([) indicate overlapping speech.

M:	a me no know if me a go down dere you know
	(0.2) this week (man) (me no know)
	⎡I dunno if I'm going to that man
E:	⎣seen ⟨*seen* = agreement marker⟩
(0.2)	
M:	(it's) on Wednesday you know wha'I mean
E:	seener
M:	(like room with me)
(1.8)	
E:	cho (0.8) (s) who de 'eights down dere
M:	me no know (0.8) bwo:y (1.2) (Jesus in on it)
(2.0)	

```
E:    cha:::
M:    ⟨clears throat⟩ is Roger 'ere
E:    ye::ah (.) them (did bim bow chest 'im) me di-
      me did check 'im dis morning you know wha' I
      mean ⎡dem 'bout him
M:         ⎣m::
M:    wha' happen to B
(1.0)
E:    me no know (1.0) 'im just come back today same
      time as you bu% me no see 'im
(0.6)
M:    uh 'im ge%s (.) ge% suspended
E:    yeh man
M:    Jesus Christ
(2.4)
E:    me no see 'im (1.0) me see Pe%er an dem (lo%)
      bu% me no see dem
      (0.2) me no see – me no see B ⟨sucks teeth⟩
      (anyway I see de other ( ) widout de ?faakiyaa ha
      you know      /zai ni ai ai/)
M:    is it
E:    yeah ⎡gyel dem di other guy: dem usual gel
M:         ⎣wha% gyel
E:    walk de park
M:    uh huh huh dem punkoot yes me know them huh huh
      me know dem ⟨punkoot = 'girl'⟩
```

Both M and E appear to be using a mixture of local London English (marked by some local features of pronunciation, especially glottal stops for /t/) and something similar to Jamaican Creole. Utterances like *me no know if me a go down dere* (by Mike) and *me no know, 'im just come back today* (by Edgar) have to be placed squarely at the Creole end of the spectrum.

This in itself might not be too surprising, since Caribbeans who grow up in London could be expected to know London English as well as the Creole of their parents. However, these are precisely the most surprising things about this conversation. The speaker 'Mike' is not Caribbean at all, has never left England, and has no connections with Jamaica, other than through friends. 'Edgar' is actually black and of Caribbean parentage. However, reports from several researchers confirm that irrespective of which part or parts of the Caribbean young Black British speakers come from, the creole which they use is a form of *Jamaican* Creole. For many, this means that they speak a different creole from their parents.

Elsewhere in Britain we find the same phenomenon. Fiona Wright (1984) describes the language behaviour of young black people in Birmingham as involving a target maximally distinct from the Standard. She terms this 'recreolisation' and identifies it as a process of *focussing* in the sense used by Le Page, discussed in Chapter 1, Section 3.4 – in other words, a process of 'zooming in' on a set of norms which speakers have identified (Le Page's 'focussing' metaphor is drawn from photography, though he does not use the term 'zooming in'). According to Wright, the Birmingham speakers are 'focussing on phonological and morphological patterns, lexicon and syntactic structures which are distinct from Standard English' (Wright, 1984, p. 37).

A third case of recreolisation is described by Shirley Tate (see Tate, 1984; Sebba and Tate, 1986), who studied a group of young Dominicans in Bradford, West Yorkshire. In most British cities Jamaicans outnumber other Caribbeans, but in Bradford, Dominicans form the largest Caribbean group. Dominica is one of the Eastern Caribbean islands where a French-lexicon creole is used, which is spoken by the first generation of immigrants. Tate (who is herself Jamaican-born) found that the group she studied used Jamaican Creole with a level of competence comparable to born Jamaicans – in spite of having no ancestral connection with Jamaica.

These examples of Caribbeans by descent in three British cities show clearly that there is not a uniform, simple progression from Creole to Standard. It is probably quite true that the parents of these second-generation migrants have 'decreolised' their language to some extent, though living and working among speakers of British English (not, in general, *Standard* English). This process has been partly documented, for phonology, by John Wells (1973), but it results in a haphazard and only partly successful assimilation to British norms. But their children show a different kind of linguistic behaviour: on the one hand, they have – almost without exception – a native-like command of the local British vernacular: London English in London, Birmingham English in Birmingham, etc. On the other hand, they have a more-or-less good command of Jamaican Creole – in a broad or basilectal form. This is in *addition* to any knowledge of a creole language (such as the French-lexicon Dominican Creole, or the English-lexicon Grenadan creole) which they may learn from parents and carers. For these young Black British, their linguistic behaviour consists mainly of *code switching* between the first two language varieties mentioned.

In the next section we will look at a detailed case study of Black British language use.

5   CASE STUDY: LONDON JAMAICAN

5.1   Historical Background

Migration of people of African descent to Britain is not a phenomenon of this century alone, but the majority of Afro-Caribbeans now in Britain were either born here or came from the Caribbean in the 1950s and 1960s. From the late 1960s onward, immigration laws were tightened to make entry more difficult; as a result, most younger Caribbeans now living in Britain were born here and may or may not have first-hand knowledge of the Caribbean.

The first generation of migrants came with distinctive language varieties associated with their birthplace: Jamaica, Guyana, Trinidad, St Vincent, Grenada, etc. The creoles spoken in these places are all lexified by English but are somewhat different from each other. The first generation of migrants were mostly not from the poorest in their societies, but were relatively highly educated and skilled: their usual language was therefore likely to be some way along the spectrum towards Standard English, even if they also had competence in basilectal creole. Evidence is that the first generation kept their separate cultural identities as Jamaicans, Guyanese, etc. in spite of being lumped together, in the eyes of the native British, as 'West Indians'. To some extent they kept their linguistic identities as well, although they have assimilated towards local British norms over time (see above).

However, shared exeriences of race and class – taking the brunt of the racial attitudes of the indigenous British, while finding themselves at the bottom of the British socioeconomic heap irrespective of their social class in the Caribbean – seem to have had a profound effect on the second and subsequent generations of Caribbeans, many of whom now prefer to be identified as 'Black British' rather than 'Jamaican', 'Trinidadian' or 'Guyanese' (for a detailed account of this, see Gilroy, 1987). The fact that the Caribbean social structure has not been reproduced in Britain – the majority of Caribbeans in Britain being working class – means that there is no convincing evidence of a 'post-creole continuum' among British-born Caribbeans.

Linguistically, the behaviour of Black British speakers is characterised by the use of at least two, possibly more, language varieties: minimally the local British English and a type of Jamaican Creole (often called *Patois*), as well as, usually, Standard English; also, possibly, other Caribbean creoles, and other languages spoken in the multicultural environment.

The choice available to most speakers is exemplified by a three-way phonological choice in the pronunciation of the Standard English (RP) word *thing*:

London English
   (Cockney)   *fing* /fɪŋ/

                                        thing /θɪŋ/ RP

                    ting /tɪŋ/
           Jamaican Creole/Patois

On any given occasion, a speaker may – and *must* – locate him or herself in this 'multidimensional space' by making a choice of one of the three variants above (or of another, chosen from an altogether different language such as Dominican French Creole). There are, of course, other phonological differences between these three language varieties, but often there is only a two-way contrast, with London English (LE) patterning like Standard English/RP. Some more phonological examples are:

	Creole	LE	RP
word-final /l/ as in *well*	[l]	[ʊ]	[ɫ]
/ð/ as in *with*	[d]	[v]	[ð]
/au/ as in *how*	[ou]	[æ:]	[aʊ]
/ʌ/ as in *love*	[ɒ]	[ʌ]	[ʌ]

5.2 London Jamaican Text

This conversation took place between two British-born girls of Jamaican parentage, aged about 15, in a school in South-East London in 1982. The girls were left alone in a room with a tape recorder and asked to have a conversation in 'Jamaican'. To the extent that the situation was not a very natural one, the conversation must be seen as a kind of performance – especially as they were specifically asked to use a particular language variety. Nevertheless the language forms which they produce are typical of many other conversations recorded with other participants in the same and other parts of London. (For more such conversations and commentary, see Sebba, 1993.)

Transcription conventions: Underlining indicates an utterance identifiable as Creole on phonological or grammatical grounds. Parts which are unclear are in round brackets ( ). A glottal stop is indicated by %. Numbers in round brackets indicate pauses measured in seconds.

J: ⟨whisper⟩ you start

C: all right, we went to this party on Sa%urday night you know Jane and I (.) and I tell you boy de par%y was well rude, you know, well rude
(1.0)

J: whe you a seh? ⟨*seh* = 'say'⟩

C: mi seh dis party well rude!
(0.6)

J: that good, was it?

C: yeah! me tell you seh dere some boy down de boy, (0.4) I seh (0.4) z – 'e was (my) (ting) for the night

J: was it? <u>did 'im give you what you a look for?</u>

C: <u>no sir, no sir, not mean it in dat way I just mean de phone number an' t'ing</u>
(1.0)

J: <u>im did phone you?</u>

C: <u>no man me phone 'im, you know wha' I mean?</u> <u>me na really like give out de phone number an' t'ing</u>

J: is it? so how comes <u>you just tell me about it now?</u>

C: 'cause like <u>seh (0.5) feel like tell you</u> y'know

J: $\begin{bmatrix} \underline{\text{me spar}} \;\langle spar = \text{'friend'}\rangle \\ \text{I see} \end{bmatrix}$

J: I see so did you enjoy yourselves

C: <u>seen man</u> (.) <u>de scene up dere 'ard</u> y'know (.) <u>place call nations</u> (.) I tell you <u>you go dere and you riot all night</u>

5.3 Commentary

In the above conversation, both speakers use Jamaican Creole phonology and intonation – but not consistently. Some formulaic utterances could equally be called 'Creole' or 'English', for example, *you know what I mean* and *you know*. Some utterances are 'pure' English, for example, *we went to this party on Sa%urday night you know Jane and I* and *so did you enjoy yourselves?* We therefore have to recognise that code switching between London English and Creole is a factor even in a supposedly 'Creole' or 'Patois' conversation like this one. This conclusion is amply supported by many other recordings (see Sebba, 1993) which show systematic switching between Creole and British English; in fact, this conversation is unusual in that *so much* Creole is used. It is common to find the use of Creole limited to a few utterances in the course of quite a long conversation.

The form of the 'Creole' used here is itself very interesting. Although there are some utterances which could be called 'basilectal', others include forms which are closer to Standard – and the speakers sometimes use both. For example, *de par%y was well rude* uses the Standard English past copula *was*, and could equally well be Standard English with a Creole pronunciation (though the glottal stop in *par%y* is a specifically London feature, not present in Jamaica!); by contrast, *dis party well rude* is identifiably Creole, not only by virtue of pronunciation, but also because the copula is absent before the adjective *rude*.

Of particular interest are J.'s questions *im did phone you?* and *did 'im give you what you a look for?* Both are obviously intended to be Creole, as shown by the form of the subject pronoun (*him*) and the phonology. The first of these, *im did phone you?* would certainly pass for Creole in Jamaica, as it uses the same word order as the corresponding statement. The tense marker *did*, which corresponds to other Jamaican forms like *bin* and *en*, has to be treated within Jamaican Creole grammar as an invariant particle, not the past tense of an auxiliary verb *do* as in English. However, *did 'im give you what you a look for?* seems to be modelled on the English *did he give you*... with subject–auxiliary inversion moving *did* to first position. This is not possible in 'real' Jamaican creole for the reason just mentioned. We either have to propose that J. has 'made up' a rule of subject–tense marker inversion, or that she has modelled her Creole on English, treating *did* as an auxiliary, and applying the *English* rule of subject–auxiliary inversion.

In fact (as I argue in Sebba, 1993, pp. 54–5), some speakers seem to treat Creole as a sort of special register of London English, and derive Creole forms from London English forms by means of adaptation rules. Thus we get *London* Jamaican forms (but not *Jamaican* Jamaican forms) like /bava buːt/ 'bovver boots' (Jamaican /bada/ from 'bother'), [fruː] for 'through' (Jamaican [truː]), and [lʊər] for 'law' (Jamaican [laː]). In each case, the London Jamaican form seems to be an adaptation of the London English pronunciation, in accordance with a set of conversion rules which tell the speaker, for example, to pronounce [ɒ] as [a] (London English [lɒt], Jamaican Creole [lat]). These rules must be determined by speakers inductively, by generalising from correspondences they recognise. Mis-adaptations arise when one London form has two Jamaican equivalents; thus in London, *poor* rhymes with *law* for many speakers, but in Jamaica, they never do: [pʊər] preserves the historic /r/ and high back vowel, while [laː] is r-less and has a much more open vowel. By mis-adapting *law* on analogy with *poor*, a speaker may derive [lʊər] – a form which Jamaicans would probably not recognise at all. Similarly, as shown in the diagram in 5.1, London /f/ corresponds to Jamaican /t/ in 'thing', but it *also* corresponds to Jamaican /f/; hence the forms *frough* /fruː/ and *breaf* /bref/ which occur within Creole utterances in my London data where Jamaican Creole would have /truː/ and /bret/.

5.4 Sociolinguistic Aspects of London Jamaican

If recreolisation is a fact, the question remains: why? The answer, in sociolinguistic terms, must be: because speakers are *attracted* to the creole forms, or rather, to the image they convey. Since creole has little overt prestige, we have to assume that it has *covert* prestige, an attractiveness for young British Caribbeans which derives from its associations with solidarity, Black Britishness, and being a *non-legitimated* language variety.

Patois stands as a symbol of *solidarity* in as much as it is different from the language of most white people, and often unintelligible to them. However, as we saw in Section 4, there are white people who use London Jamaican. These are nearly always individuals who have a network of black friends – but even for them, the question of whether and when they may use creole without giving offence is a delicate one. This is documented in detail by Roger Hewitt (1982, 1986). At the same time, Patois is a symbol of *Black Britishness* – partly because it is different from 'White British' speech, but also because it is different from the Creole speech of the Caribbean. For many young speakers, its association with popular cultural movements like Reggae music and Rastafarianism is a source of pride, and it is because these cultural movements are originally Jamaican, as well as because the Jamaicans are numerically dominant in most Black British communities, that Jamaican Creole has become the model.

Finally, Patois has the value of being a *non-legitimated* variety. Precisely because the use of Creole is not sanctioned by schools, and is often frowned on by parents, it offers a form of oppositional behaviour (a more or less harmless one, although children who use Creole to respond to a teacher may get a very negative reaction). In this respect London Jamaican has some resemblance to Fly Taal (see Chapter 1) used by urban black youth in South Africa. Fly Taal could also, perhaps, be seen as a kind of 'recreolisation' as it represents a form of Afrikaans which is self-consciously maximally deviant from the Standard.

The symbolic power of Creole may be revealed by an anecdote. When I was making some recordings in an East London school a boy of about 12, who had a reputation for making up rhymes and 'toasting' (reciting to music), left me a message on the tape recorder when I was out of the room. I had previously used a little bit of Creole to demonstrate the sort of language I was interested in. This was the message he left on the tape, in the form of a song:

> *De man t'ink him is a black yout' yah*
> *But if him go round to Leyton Youf*
> *Im gonna get him raas kick!*

> 'The man thinks he's a black youth here,
> But if he goes round to Leyton Youth [a mainly black youth club]
> He's going to get his arse kicked!'

This I took to be a clear indication of a 'hands off our language' attitude, though expressed in a friendly sort of way. Not all Creole speakers have this attitude; but in view of the symbolism which attaches to Creole, non-group members (white people especially) must tread carefully or risk causing offence and alienating themselves. Note, incidentally, the alternation between *yout'* /juːt/ ('a youth') and *youf* /juːf/ 'youth' as in the name of the club.

One final point needs to be made with respect to London Jamaican. It is mainly a phenomenon of adolescence and early adulthood. Thus the under-twelves seem to use Creole much less than teenagers, although there are some fluent younger speakers. This fact is in keeping with the observation that some speakers 'make up' Creole by adapting English, using a set of rules which sometimes give wrong output (see 5.3). For these speakers, Creole is a 'second dialect', a language variety which they acquire after London English, their native language variety. The cultural attraction of Creole, and particularly its value as a non-legitimated variety, are things which assume greater importance after puberty. This also helps to explain how 'recreolisation' has involved focussing on Jamaican Creole rather than individuals' 'mother tongue creoles': it is often not learnt in the family home, but at school and from the peer group, at a relatively late age.

6 CONTINUA AND CODE SWITCHING: CONCLUSIONS

Whether or not the 'unidimensional continuum' model is appropriate for some parts of the Caribbean, we can see that any model which takes a simple progression from Creole to Standard as its basis is not adequate. The social value which attaches to different varieties of language – *and the way those varieties are identified and labelled by speakers themselves* – is a crucial factor in explaining phenomena like 'recreolisation' and the linguistic behaviour of speakers in Belize and St Lucia. What young Black British speakers label 'Creole' or 'Patois' would not always pass for Creole in Jamaica. Nevertheless, their target is Jamaican Creole, in so far as they are able to identify and imitate it. At the same time, they are native speakers of the local British English, and are able to switch confidently (and sometimes, meaningfully) between the two. We also find, as speakers try to 'create' Creole by adapting their English by means of inductively determined rules, that various 'deviant' forms (or 'mistakes') arise as a result.

All of this suggests that in a community with diffuse linguistic norms – which probably the majority of pidgin and creole-speaking communities are – linguistic behaviour is too complex to be modelled by a unidimensional continuum. The linguistic choices which speakers make are subject to influences from a number of different language varieties, each with different values and exerting different amounts of pressure, depending on the power relations in the society. Standard languages, especially Standard English, exert a strong attraction; but values such as solidarity and rejection of authority may equally strongly push speakers away from the Standard towards a creole or pidgin.

7   EXERCISE

Some questions to discuss:

What linguistic (or other symbolic) ways of signalling different group allegiances do we have?

What type of motivations could account for the 'White Creole Speaker'?

When we speak, what conscious choices do we make about how we speak, and at what linguistic levels are these choices (e.g. pronunciation, grammar, vocabulary)? What unconscious choices do we make?

KEY POINTS: Beyond creolisation

The post-creole continuum: may exist where a creole remains in contact with its lexifier.

- *basilect* (base) – the broadest form of creole;
- *acrolect* (top) – may exist where the lexifier remains in contact with the creole: the standard form of the lexifier;
- *mesolect* – any 'lect' (variety) which lies between basilect and acrolect.

An individual speaker may command a range of lects.

Implicational hierarchy (hypothesis): Standard (acrolectal) forms are acquired in a particular order so that speakers who use certain forms can be predicted to use certain others. This reflects the historical process of *decreolisation*.

Features of some post-creole communities:

- *Decreolisation* – a movement away from Creole (*basilect*) towards the Standard (*acrolect*). Implicational hierarchy results from the fact that decreolisation always follows the same pattern.
- *Recreolisation* – a tendency by speakers to focus on the more 'creole' end of the linguistic spectrum.

Code switching: may take place between 'creole' and 'standard'.

8   Pidgins and Creoles: Issues for Development

1   DEVELOPING LANGUAGES

Just as countries today may be described as 'developing countries' – meaning that they are expanding economically and educationally, usually (whether appropriately or not) on a Western model, so it makes sense to describe many languages of the world as 'developing languages' – meaning that they have yet to realise their full potential as linguistic resources. Most expanded pidgins, and many creoles, would fall into this category.

By calling these languages 'developing' I want to emphasise that in spite of negative popular attitudes in many parts of the world – and often from their own speakers – they nevertheless have the potential to fulfil the same functions as any of the 'developed' languages, if only they are given the respect and resources that this demands. This is, of course, the opposite of the traditional viewpoint that pidgins and creoles are worthless 'lingos', not even deserving to be called languages at all.

In much of this chapter, the key considerations will be ideological – issues of belief, power and political will – as well as linguistic. The attitudes about language of those who hold power in a society are very significant, not only in determining the relative status of languages, but often in maintaining the existing power relations so that things cannot change. In many countries where the overwhelming majority of the population speak a creole language, nevertheless all the functions of the State are carried out in some other language. This necessarily limits the ability of the majority to participate in decisions which affect their own lives. Hubert Devonish, a strong advocate of the use of Creole for official purposes in the Caribbean, has written (1986b, p. 37):

> ... the practice of democracy cannot be restricted to three minutes in a polling box every five years. Democracy as it is presently practiced in these countries blocks, on grounds of language, the access of the mass of Creole speakers to information concerning political issues and decisions which affect their lives. ... The evidence suggests that the political elite in these countries are not entirely unaware of the linguistic problems which exist in their communication with the public. It seems likely that they are aware of the communication gap and manipulate it to their own advantage.

It is reasonable, therefore, when we find pidgins and creoles stigmatised even in places where they are the majority language, or unable to rise in status even when government policies acknowledge their importance, that we should ask 'exactly who is benefiting from this state of affairs?' as well as 'who would benefit from changing it?'

In this chapter we shall look at four important areas of language development: pidgins and creoles as standard languages; pidgins and creoles as written languages; pidgins and creoles in education; and pidgins and creoles as official languages.

2   PIDGINS AND CREOLES AS STANDARD LANGUAGES

In Chapter 1, we saw how historically the growth of empires with the need for a common administrative language, coupled with the mass medium of printing, promoted the creation of 'standard' print-languages which gave economic and political power to their speakers, while disempowering others who spoke 'dialects'. Given the power and influence of standard languages in the world, it is clearly an important issue whether pidgin and creole languages can be standardised in the same way as other languages have been.

There are four substantial problems which historically have stood in the way of pidgin and creole languages becoming standard languages: *status, difference, variability and development*. We look at each of these in turn.

2.1   The Problem of Status

Pidgins and creoles nearly always have low status, even when they are majority languages. Typically, there is a situation of *diglossia* in communities where pidgins and creoles are spoken. In a diglossic situation, one language (the 'high' language) will take on the 'important' functions (those which are overtly valued in the society) such as administration, education and 'high' culture (including literary writing). The 'low' language – in this case, the pidgin or creole – will be used for other functions associated with everyday life and communication within the family. One part of the community – the elite – may reject the pidgin/creole even for these functions, preferring to use the 'high' language for all purposes. The whole society is likely to regard the pidgin or creole as the language of the lower social classes and appropriate only for less valued functions. It is likely to be seen as unsuitable for any 'serious' purpose (including literary writing).

Obviously, the issue of status is closely linked with the question of who holds power in a particular society where a pidgin or creole is spoken. It is those who have power within a society who are able, by and large, to define what is 'standard' and what is 'inferior'. During colonial times, the colonial masters – expatriates and the locally born elite – were able to define the standard language of the colonising country as the norm, with local languages, including pidgins and creoles, as inferior or substandard. Independence has swept away the expatriate elites in many countries since about 1960 – but the status of pidgins and creoles in many places is unchanged. Even where there have been positive changes in status for developing languages, often there has been little practical improvement. This may be due to power being held by an elite who can comfortably use the official Standard or lexifier language. They may have a vested interest in keeping the majority uninformed and controlling their access to national institutions.

2.2   The Problem of Distance

Distance (the term is used here in the sense of Heinz Kloss, 1967, who uses the German term *Abstand*) here refers to the perception (or lack of it) of two languages as separate entities, with 'space' between them, as shown by substantial differences in vocabulary and grammar. Dutch and German, for example, though closely related, have enough differences (are 'distant' enough from each other) to be recognised as separate languages. Just the opposite – extensive overlapping, especially in vocabulary – is typical of creole languages which are still in contact with their lexifiers (Jamaican Creole, say, rather than Sranan Tongo). We saw in Chapter 1 that it is not possible to distinguish between 'language' and 'dialect' other than on the basis of social attitudes or beliefs. Because there is little perceived 'distance' between the two, the creole will be thought of as a dialect of the lexifier; but because of its association with the poorer socioeconomic classes and those who lack power in the society, it invariably is regarded as an *inferior* ('debased', 'corrupt', 'broken' etc.) version of the lexifier language. Since as much as 90 per cent of vocabulary may be common to the creole and the lexifier, it is easy for the creole's detractors to claim that it is not really a separate language at all – just a bad form of the lexifier.

Where the creole and the lexifier have parted company and are so dissimilar that it would be absurd to treat them as one language, as in Surinam, the creole may still be seen as lower in status but at least will be accepted as a *separate* language with its own norms of correctness.

2.3   The Problem of Variability

Bound up with the distance issue is another problem which is particularly serious for languages in a 'post-pidgin' or 'post-creole' continuum. The classical model of standardisation assumes a stage of dialect selection, in which one dialect is chosen to be the basis for the standard language. In most cases where this has happened historically (excluding recent cases of standardisation which have involved the intervention of linguists and state agencies, as in some developing countries), the 'special' dialect happens to be the one spoken at the centre of power and authority. The 'Queen's English' is no misnomer; the same could be said for the 'Queen's Castilian' presented to Isabella by Nebrija in 1492 (see Chapter 1).

Creoles and pidgins present two difficulties in the light of this. First, they are typically absent from the centres of power, which is just where the standard or lexifier language is most used. Secondly, the amount of variability inherent in a situation where the pidgin/creole and its lexifier are in contact makes it difficult to pick an appropriate variety (or 'lect') for standardisation. In many respects, the basilect – the variety with *least* in common with the Standard – is the ideal one to pick, as it has norms clearly differentiated from the lexifier. Choosing this variety seems to be the solution to the problem of *distance*. Yet this only creates a new range of problems: how do we identify the 'true basilect'? And given that in most 'continuum' situations, the majority of the population are *not* basilectal speakers, how do we justify choosing the language of a minority as the basis for a standard?

Issues of this kind have presented problems for standardisation in Haiti (see Case Study, Section 3.5 below), where there have been debates over whether the front rounded vowels of French (the vowels of French *tu* /ty/ and *peur* /pœr/) are part of Haitian Creole or not. In the most basilectal Haitian Creole, French words containing these vowels have lost either the rounding (becoming front unrounded /i e /) or the frontness (becoming back rounded /u o/) in keeping with a system in which front vowels are unrounded, while back are rounded (Hall, 1966, p. 28). However, many Haitians who also know some French use the front rounded vowels in words where they would occur in French. In fact, the front rounded vowels function as social prestige markers: they symbolise upward mobility and higher social status (Schieffelin and Doucet, 1994). Now should the Haitian Creole writing system allow for these sounds to be written, or are they (like the nasal vowel used by some English speakers in the word *restaurant*) marginal and not in need of representation? Haitian linguists, politicians and educators have had to make this decision (see below).

Creoles with complex continua such as Guyanese and Jamaican present even more problems, affecting phonology, grammar and lexicon. How can a *focussed* standard be defined in a *diffuse* linguistic situation? Who will decide what is 'real Creole' and what is not? One response is to say that the concept of a standard as a *single* variety, a 'chosen one', is unnecessary. There may be a *range* of acceptable standard varieties, just as some variation is acceptable in Standard English (*dreamt* vs *dreamed*; *I shall* vs *I will*; *two cacti* vs *two cactuses*; etc.). Even so, this is likely to increase the complexity of the undertaking rather than simplify it. Devonish (1986a, p. 115) makes a specific proposal along these lines:

(i) develop a description of the range of intermediate varieties of Creole along the continuum, all of which would be considered as acceptable forms of Creole, and (ii) identify certain forms which are the most common... which could be recommended for use by journalists, broadcasters and others who find themselves in important positions as disseminators of information in Creole.

Devonish stresses, however, that this is not intended as a way of creating a 'standard variety' of Creole, but is 'intended purely as a medium for identifying the most efficient variety of Creole for communicating with as wide a cross-section of the population as is possible'.

2.4 The Problem of Development

In order to be used successfully for 'high' functions such as administration, education and culture (i.e. for uses we typically associate with writing), a language has to develop stylistic registers which speakers feel are appropriate to these purposes. 'Writing as you speak' is commonly felt to be wrong and there is probably no language where the written and spoken registers are identical. However, these written and formal registers have to be developed where they do not already exist. All languages have the potential to develop in terms of style, register and vocabulary, but this kind of development presents special difficulties for pidgins and creoles.

Historically, it has been unusual for a language to develop rapidly from being an unwritten, unstandardised language into a written language in which all the 'high' functions of language can be carried out. Usually, there is an *existing* standard language in the community which is used for most or all functions, which is slowly phased out as a newly-standardised (or standardising) language becomes the norm in more and more domains of life.

Creole languages have a special problem in this regard. As pointed out by Joseph (1987), historically nearly all languages have been standardised on the basis of an existing model – the relevant model always being the established 'high' language of the community, which the newly standardised language starts to replace. There are many examples of this in history. The literary standard of Latin was modelled on the Ancient Greek literary language, which for the Romans was the language of the 'classics'. Much later, the modern European standard literary languages, including English, were shaped with reference to Latin, the language of education and administration of medieval Europe. One consequence – massive borrowing of Latin words into the new standard languages – still gives English its character today, and makes a good deal of technical terminology in English identical with that of, say, French, Swedish or Dutch.

The special problem which stands in the way of creoles developing as standard literary languages is a consequence of this. As they develop, the obvious model for them to follow – perhaps the only one which they *can* follow – is the 'high' language already used in the community. This is often the lexifier. So the creole must model itself on the lexifier in order to develop. But in order to be recognised as a separate language, the creole must put *distance* between itself and the lexifier; otherwise it will still be perceived as a 'substandard dialect' of the lexifier. The creole is thus caught in a trap, between developing on the model of the lexifier on the one hand, and distancing itself from the lexifier on the other. (For a discussion of this in more detail, see Joseph, 1987; also Sebba, 1994.)

It may be argued that the pidgin or creole does not have to model itself on the lexifier. It may choose another model, or it may draw on its own resources. This has happened in the past – for example, in the case of Ancient Greek, according to Joseph (1987) – but is rare. It is most likely to happen if writers using the pidgin or creole themselves gain enough authority and status to define a standard language on their own terms – some Shakespeares, Dantes or Luthers are needed! This is possible, but rare in history – and it can only happen if writers actually *use* the pidgin or creole for 'high' functions such as literature. This itself can be problematic, as we shall see in Section 3.

The problems of status, distance, variability and development are closely interrelated. A creole cannot develop without establishing a distance from its lexifier. But establishing distance in the face of low status and a belief that the creole is just a 'debased' form of the lexifier is not easy. Choosing a 'distant' standard from a point on a continuum is not straightforward. Development will help the language's status, but perhaps only at the expense of making it no more than a dialect of the lexifier. To say that these problems cannot be solved is much too pessimistic. In some cases, all that is needed may be the will and the resources to solve them. This brings us back to the question of who benefits by leaving things as they stand.

3   PIDGINS AND CREOLES AS WRITTEN LANGUAGES

3.1   Literacy in Pidgins and Creoles

Although there is clearly a link between standardisation and writing, it is quite possible for a language to be written down without standardisation having taken place. English was a written language for many centuries before a standard emerged. The arrival of printing (and more recently, technologies such as desk-top publishing, which have made printing relatively cheap and accessible in most parts of the world) tends to act as a catalyst, speeding up standardisation. Nevertheless we can consider separately from standardisation the question of pidgins and creoles as *written* languages.

Since, for linguists, much of the interest in pidgin and creole languages lies in their linguistic structure or in the social and historical conditions which brought them into being, most of the recent research into pidgins and creoles has concentrated on the *spoken* language. Less interest has been focussed on written pidgins and creoles, and on issues concerned with literacy in these languages.

In discussing pidgin and creole literacy (in the sense of reading and writing), we should also be clear that the absence of writing in a society does not mean the absence of 'literature'. Many of the creoles now in existence, as well as the extended pidgins like Kamtok (Cameroonian Pidgin) and Tok Pisin have bodies of *oral* literature such as traditional tales, riddles and songs. Some of this oral literature has been recorded, typically by anthropologists in the twentieth century: the Sranan traditional story in Chapter 5 ('Why Dog Goes About Naked') is an example. The anthropologists who noted it down, Melville and Frances Herskovits, altogether collected 146 tales, 106 riddles and 174 proverbs in their book (1936). Likewise, there are rich collections of creole-language folklore from, for example, Jamaica, Haiti, Louisiana, the Cape Verde Islands and Mauritius.

Some pidgins have essentially no indigenous written literature – in other words, if they are written down at all, they are written down by curious visitors, colonial administrators or plantation managers, usually for their own purposes. Much of our knowledge about pidgins in the eighteenth and nineteenth centuries or earlier comes from such sources; however, such writing does not constitute an indigenous literature. Neither do the mass of dictionaries, grammars and textbooks – of greatly varying completeness and quality – produced over the centuries by missionaries, scholars, linguists and amateurs. Bible translations exist in many pidgins; sometimes these are the work of indigenous writers, and sometimes not (it is not always easy to find out).

Creoles, as the only available languages for many of their speakers, often are written down informally from a relatively early stage. Though most of their speakers will have been unable to read or write, nevertheless some will have learnt to do so, perhaps from missionaries. Religious texts are often the earliest type of printed literature in a creole.

Among early known writings in pidgins and creoles, personal diaries are quite important. The late eighteenth century diary of an Efik trader from Calabar, Antera Duke, was mentioned in Chapter 4. As might be expected if Antera Duke had been taught to read and write Standard English but actually spoke an early form of West African pidgin, this diary contains a mixture of apparently pidgin forms mixed with Standard English ones. In the late nineteenth century a Surinamese preacher, Johannes King, who had learnt to read and write Sranan when he was in his thirties, wrote detailed diaries about his experiences wandering in the interior of Surinam. These have now been published (De Ziel, 1973).

Extract from the Diaries of Johannes King

Note on transcription: in this text, the orthography mainly follows Dutch conventions. Thus **oe** = [u] (toe = [tu], English *two*); **j** = [j] (joe = [ju], English *you*); **é** = [ei] (dé = [dei], English *day*).

[5 August 1892]

En te débroko fosi, na satra sabaten, wi go doro dape na kriki de. Ma di wi no ben doro na na kriki mofo ete, a ben libi toe oekoe langa ete, wi si wan kampoe agen nanga dri man soema en dri oema, nanga fo pikin. Wi haksi den hoepe na kriki de, disi den kari Gran-kriki. En den sori wi; den taki: a de krosibé dia, toe hoekoe langa nomo wi sa waka, joe doro dape. Ma te oen doro dape oen no moese kari na kriki nen na hen mofo. En efi oen kari hen nen na hen mofo, na kriki sa meki trobi nanga oen. We di na man taki so, nomo wi alamala lafoe, bikasi no wan foe wi piki hen no wan wortoe moro. En di wi doro na na kriki mofo, wi kari na kriki nen: Gran-kriki, na hen mofo, foe espresi, meki den féfi heiden soema, di ben go nanga wi, moese si fa didibri de kori den heiden soema foe soso.

(*Translation by Mark Sebba*)

And when day first broke on Saturday, we went through to where the creek is. But when we had not yet reached the creek's mouth, it still lay two hoekoe *distant, we saw another camp, with three men and three women, and four children. We asked them where the creek was, which they called 'Great Creek'. And they showed us; they said: it is close by here, only walk two* hoekoe *and you'll get there. But when you get there you must not call the creek by its name in its mouth. And if you call its name in its mouth, the creek will make trouble for you. Well, when the man spoke so, we all started to laugh, because none of us answered him a single word. And when we reached the creek's mouth, we called the creek's name: Great Creek, in its mouth, to express how the five heathen people, who had come with us, should see how the devil deceives heathen folk for nothing.*

Historical factors such as the liberation of the slaves, the introduction of schooling on a broader (though usually not universal) basis and the advent of modern, relatively cheap, printing methods have had their effect on literacy among pidgin and creole speakers. However, the result is not always an increase in the amount of written pidgin or creole. This is because *primary* literacy (the first language a person learns to read and write, as opposed to speak) is often not in the creole, but in the lexifier or another standard language. Although literacy rates (in the sense of the numbers of people able to read and write) may increase, if literacy is not in the pidgin or creole, but in some other language, the amount of writing *in the pidgin or creole* will not necessarily increase – and may actually decline, as the standard language outweighs it in prestige.

While governments – particularly colonial governments – have usually done very little to promote writing in pidgin or creole languages, *language movements* started by writers and publishers themselves have sometimes played an important role in establishing a creole language as an independent entity and enhancing its status – and have sometimes been central to nationalist movements. The Afrikaans Language Movements in the nineteenth century and early twentieth century are one such: they successfully established Afrikaans as an independent literary language with its own norms separate from Dutch, eventually leading to a constitutional change by which Afrikaans replaced Dutch as an official language in South Africa in 1925. The Language Movements were closely linked to Afrikaner Nationalism, culminating in the establishment of an Afrikaner Nationalist government in 1948. (It should be said that only Afrikaans speakers of European descent were involved in these movements; ironically in view of the fact that they were promoting a creole, they were exclusively white and many believed in the superiority of the Europeans as a race.)

Another partially successful language movement was that of Surinam. In the 1940s Koenders, a teacher, began a campaign for the recognition of Sranan as a language on an equal footing with others. This campaign was carried on partly through a monthly publication, *Foetoe-boi* ('foot-boy', i.e. 'servant'), which carried articles in Dutch and Sranan. In the 1950s Surinamese students studying in the Netherlands formed a cultural movement called *Wi Eegie Sanie* ('Our own things') with language as a main focus. Out of the *Wi Eegie Sanie* movement a political party (the PNR) developed, led by Eddy Bruma, a leading Sranan poet. As one of the pro-independence parties in Surinam, the PNR came to power as part of the coalition government which led Surinam into independence in 1975. While the cultural effects of *Wi Eegie Sanie* have been profound, it has to be said that Dutch remains the official language of Surinam and that the position of Sranan has changed little since 1975. (Information from Devonish, 1986a.)

The development of pidgins and creoles as written languages presents an interesting mix of social, political and practical problems. Probably the most immediate of these, and very important, is the question of *orthography* – a spelling system for the language. Since a lot has been written on this topic and several aspects are controversial, we will look at it in some detail.

3.2 Orthographic Principles

There are basically two approaches to orthographic (spelling) systems for pidgin and creole languages: *phonemic* and *etymological*. The *phonemic* approach involves treating the pidgin or creole as a language in its own right, without historical connections to any other, and producing a spelling system which has one, and only one, symbol per phoneme of that language. Thus the outcome of the phonemic approach will be a 'tailor-made' orthography which represents the sounds actually used in the language. The **etymological orthography** treats the pidgin or creole as a dialect of the lexifier, and uses the conventional spelling of the lexifier for words which identifiably originate from the lexifier. Other words are spelt using the conventions of the lexifier, with modifications if necessary.

Two methods of spelling Jamaican Creole provide a good illustration of the differences between these approaches. The only phonemic spelling system so far proposed for Jamaican Creole was devised by Frederic Cassidy (1961) and used by Cassidy and Le Page for the *Dictionary of Jamaican English* (1967/1980). Since its first publication, it has been widely used by scholars writing *about* Creole in the Caribbean, but has never been used by writers writing *in* Creole. An example was given in Chapter 7, Section 2.2. Here is another example of a transcription of a spoken text, Version A using the Cassidy orthography, Version B using an etymological style of transcription.

A:
> So afta mi dadi lef im, Mama liiv
> an gaan hosl outsaid no,
> far shi laik si i moni kom iin,
> yu nuo, shi no laik fi nuo se
> wel den di man a liv afa im uon.

B:
> So afta mi daddy lef im, Mama leave
> an gaan hustle ohtside noh,
> for shi like see di money come een,
> you know, shi no like fi know say,
> well den, di man a live offa im own.

(From L. Emilie Adams, 1991: *Understanding Jamaican Patois*. Adams has adapted the Cassidy orthography in Version A; I have standardised it back again for the sake of having a straightforward comparison. MS)

If you have learned to read and write Standard English (whether or not you are a speaker of Jamaican Creole yourself) you will probably find the

B version easier to read at first. Words like *hustle* and *know* are spelt the same way as in Standard English (in spite of being pronounced in a distinctively Caribbean way) and are instantly recognisable. In Version A, although the sounds of the words, as pronounced in Jamaica, are faithfully represented, the connections are harder to make.

But notice that we have been looking at this from the point of view of someone whose *primary* literacy (i.e. first language for reading and writing) is in Standard English. The etymological approach would not have any advantage for a reader who did not *already* know how to read Standard English. It would, in fact, have substantial drawbacks: the spelling of Standard English notoriously lags centuries behind pronunciation, and besides was designed for English, not Creole. Many Creole words do not have conventional spellings in Standard English, because they exist in Creole only.

Although linguists are apparently unanimous in preferring the phonemic orthography of Version A, writers themselves, as mentioned above, have largely ignored it. Most writers using Jamaican Creole (or its offshoots, such as British Creole) and other Caribbean creoles continue to use etymological orthographies: in other words, traditional English spellings, with modifications. The result of this is a large amount of variation in spelling, with no standardisation at all. Each writer is free to make up his or her own spelling for particular words in an effort to make them 'sound' more Creole. A small survey of published texts using the etymological approach yielded a long list of variants, of which the following (adapted from Sebba, 1994) is an example (the Cassidy spelling is also given for reference):

Standard sp.	Used by writers	Cassidy
mouth	*mout', mout*	mout
thing	*t'ing, ting*	ting
nothing	*nutten, not'n', notin'*	notin
no	*nuh, noh, nu*	no
hold	*hole, hol'*	huol
say	*seh, sey*	se
do	*dhu, duh*	du
can't	*cyan, cyaan, kaan, kean*	kyaan
(be)cause	*caw, cau', caa*	kaa
boy	*bwoy, bway*	bwai
of	*af, ah*	af

While writers, when asked, usually say that their aim is to represent the sound of Creole, it is clear that there are a variety of ideas about the right way to do this. In some ways, Jamaican Creole is in a similar position now to that of English itself about 500 years ago. There is no generally agreed (i.e. conventional) way to spell the written language. It remains to be seen whether, as happened in the case of Standard English, pressure from editors and printers forces Creole writers to adhere to certain 'standards' which will gradually acquire the force of 'convention'.

3.3   Which is Best: Phonemic or Etymological?

The hand-lettered hospital sign from the Solomon Islands in Figure 8.1 shows a mixture of mainly conventional English spellings (e.g. *time*, which in a phonemic spelling would be *taim*) and a few phonemic ones (*plis*, *pikinini*). Here Solomon Islands Pijin (very similar to Tok Pisin) is forced into a strait-jacket of Standard English spelling.

For Tok Pisin, which has had its own phonemic orthography (in several versions) for decades, orthography is no longer a problem. The language is so different from English (and so few speakers are able to read and write English

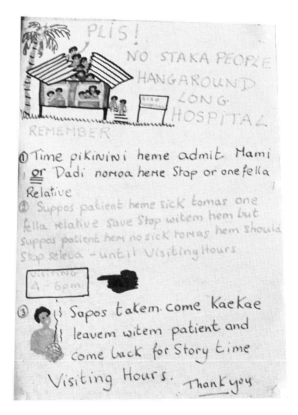

Figure 8.1   A hospital sign in the Solomon Islands – the English spellings suggest that it may be the work of a European (*photograph courtesy of Chris Calvert*)

competently) that only phonemic spelling is widely used nowadays. But for writers wanting to write in pidgin and creole languages where there is no officially approved orthography, spelling is a practical problem which each writer solves as best she or he can. We have already seen various examples of this: a written version of a spoken text from Nigeria (Chapter 4), two texts in Krio (Chapter 5) and some Jamaican Creole (Chapter 7). Meanwhile, linguists debate the issue of what kind of orthography is best – if any.

Todd (1990, p. 80) rejects teaching people to write using pidgins and creoles, and is against introducing 'individual orthographies' for them altogether:

> If they use the standard English orthography they save money on printing but make the pidgin or creole appear at best dialectal, at worst inferior. And if they use a tailor-made orthography they teach a set of spelling conventions which will inevitably clash with those of standard English. . . . the majority of what [pidgin and creole speakers] read and write will, of necessity, be in Standard English, whether it be an examination paper, a novel, an official notice or a letter of application for employment.

This argument assumes that the standard (or lexifier) language will inevitably have official status, while the pidgin or creole does not, wherever pidgins and creoles are spoken. This is true in most cases (Papua New Guinea being an important exception) but does not *have* to be true. Irrespective of the actual status of the pidgin or creole, most linguists writing on this issue stress the advantages of a pidgin or creole having its own, phonemic writing system. For example, Hellinger, writing about the Creole of Belize, Central America, a close relative of Jamaican Creole, lists the advantages of a 'genuinely creole orthography':

> [it] will strengthen the structural and psychological identity of the creole; it may in fact initiate or support a recreolization process; it will provide a source for higher prestige and may therefore facilitate native speakers' identification with the creole language and culture. (Hellinger, 1986, p. 67)

Introducing an official creole orthography based on *English* conventions, she says, would have severe negative consequences: it would strengthen 'the widespread conception of the creole as an inferior variety of English'; it would obscure real differences between Creole and Standard English, and hasten the decline of Creole as an entity separate from English (i.e. promote rapid decreolisation).

Cassidy himself, the 'inventor' of the phonemic orthography for Jamaican Creole, makes a point about the need for the creole to maintain *distance* from the lexifier:

> The more the creole differs phonemically from the lexicalizing language, the more it must differ in its orthography. It should be taught and learned as a system of its own.   (Cassidy, 1993, p. 136)

He is against the use of 'personal spellings' by writers:

> But hit-or-miss, personal spellings prevail. This is unfortunate because it portrays the creole language as erratic, unsystematic, and ignorant – which further makes writers feel no obligation to get it right.   (ibid.)

Meanwhile, for Nigerian Pidgin (NP) (now becoming a creole in some places), Elugbe and Omamor (1991, p. 120) advance very similar arguments to those of Hellinger, in favour of a 'tailor-made' orthography:

> The problem of a conflict between an NP orthography and that of English will arise only if the orthography designed for NP is a cosmetic alteration of Standard English orthography. It is thus necessary that an orthography for NP should be a modern orthography, based on the principle that NP is a Nigerian language in need of a writing system based on a clear understanding of phonology.

Against this we need to remember that writing is used for different purposes, by different writers and for different audiences. Standard languages have enormous economic and social power – English most of all. As Peter Roberts (1988, p. 134) says, 'West Indian authors face a situation in which the standard form of English is stable, full of conventions, powerful and dominant in all literature written in English.' It is not surprising that most *literary* writers of English-lexicon creole choose to make their work look more, rather than less, like Standard English by using its normal spelling conventions, with modifications.

Ultimately, it will be state policies which determine the type of orthography used for most pidgins and creoles. Where a pidgin or creole is given some official status, a phonemic (or at least 'tailored') spelling system usually receives official support at the same time. Elsewhere, it is often left to writers to work out their own system, usually an etymological one.

It is also possible to envisage hybrid systems. These may be a practical solution to the particular problem of variability and code switching, especially in Caribbean creoles. Lise Winer, in a detailed discussion of different types of orthography which might be used for Trinidadian Creole (another Caribbean Creole with many similarities to Jamaican, and likewise part of a 'dialect continuum') suggests that 'the variation typical of such "continuum" situations is salient to its speakers and should be representable' (Winer, 1990, p. 263). In some contexts, she says, a 'Modified English' approach (using conventional English spellings, appropriately adapted) may be best. In others, a phonemic system may be appropriate.

3.4 Official Orthographies: Phonology meets Ideology

The last word has not been said on orthographies for pidgin and creole languages. Perhaps surprisingly, in an area where practical concerns and sensitivity to the needs of speakers and writers might seem the only important considerations, we find that spelling is among the most hotly argued and problematic issues for some developing creoles. The phonemic/etymological divide is not just to do with practicalities, but to do with ideologies: with cultural allegiances to the lexifier (or the colonising power it represents) or to the creole (and a developing or consolidating sense of nationalism). This becomes very apparent in the case of Haitian, which we shall now discuss as a case study.

3.5 Case Study: Haitian Creole

Haitian Creole (*Kreyòl* in some orthographies) is one of several French-lexicon creoles of the Caribbean. All have their origins in the system of slavery and plantation labour, and all have some similarities, although there are also differences between them.

Haiti achieved its independence from France in 1804, a rare example of a slave colony where the slaves liberated themselves and set up their own government. This is not to say, however, that there were no class divisions. The divide between the well-off elite on the one hand and the urban working class and rural poor is sharper in Haiti than in many other places. This divide shows itself linguistically in the fact that while 5 to 10 per cent of the population – the elite – speak the local variety of Standard French, alongside the Creole, at least 90 per cent of the population are monolingual in Creole. At the same time, in 1984 only 20 per cent of the population were estimated to be able to read and write in any language (Holm, 1989, p. 385).

The fact that, apart from a small elite, Haiti is a monolingual Creole-speaking country, added to the low rate of literacy, means that promoting literacy in Creole is an urgent necessity. *How* creole is to be written is therefore a matter of great national importance.

There have been several different orthographies in use in Haiti up to the present. The earliest attempts to write Haitian Creole used the 'etymological' approach, treating Haitian as a dialect of French and using Standard French orthography with modifications. For example, Georges Sylvain (1929/1971) produced a free translation of LaFontaine's fables in Haitian Creole using a Gallicising (French etymological) orthography. (This example is quoted from Hall, 1953, p. 218.)

> Rivé bò la-riviè,
> Li ouè nan d'leau-là, qui té clè,
> Gnou lott chien, laidd, vòlè, gros gé,
> Avec moceau mangé
> Pi gros, pi goût, passé pa li.

('Arriving at the river's edge, he saw in the water, which was clear, another dog, ugly, thieving, dirty, with a bit of food bigger, tastier, than his.')

In the 1940s an Irish Protestant missionary, Ormonde McConnell, proposed a phonemic orthography, which was revised on the advice of an American literacy expert, Frank Laubach. The same verse in the resulting McConnell–Laubach orthography would be written thus:

> Rivé bò lariviè,
> Li wè nâ-dlo-la, ki té-klè,
> Gnou lòt chê, lèd, vòlè, gro-jé,
> Avèk moso mâjé
> Pi gro, pi gou, pasé pa li.

A further revision of this system was proposed by Pressoir, who replaced the circumflex accent (indicating a nasalised vowel) with *n*, and replaced other characters with alternatives which brought the Haitian orthography closer to that of French.

> Rivé bò lariviè,
> Li **ouè nan** dlo-la, ki té klè,
> Gnou lòt **chin**, lèd, vòlè, gro jé,
> Avèk mòso **manjé**
> Pi gro, pi gou, pasé pa-li.
>   (Valdman, 1978:117)

In 1979, Kreyòl was introduced by law into Haitian schools, along with yet another orthography. This official orthography was designed by Haitian linguists in collaboration with French linguists. In the official orthography our verse would now read:

> Rive bò lariviè,
> Li **wè nan** dlo-la, ki te klè,
> Youn lòt **chen**, lèd, vòlè, gro je,
> Avèk mòso **manje**
> Pi gro, pi gou, pasé pa-li.

It is easy to see that there are a number of practical issues which may influence one in favour of one or another of these orthographies. For example, the McConnell–Laubach orthography might be regarded as having too many diacritics (accents and symbols written above characters), particularly the circumflex (^). These are said to slow down writing and typing. However, as Schieffelin and Doucet (1994, p. 176) explain, the real arguments concerning which orthography to adopt are much more to do with beliefs and principles.

> …arguments about orthography reflect competing concerns about representations of Haitianness at the national and international level, that is, how speakers wish to define themselves to each other, as well as to represent themselves as a nation.

There are basically two camps: the *pro-phonemicists* say that the Creole must be written in a coherent, systematic, logical way. They are concerned that the orthography should be easy to learn for monolingual Creole speakers, so it is important that it should represent the actual sounds of their speech. The main supporters of this view are to be found in the Ministry of Education, the Catholic Church and literacy agencies. Some linguists also share these views.

On the other side are the *pro-etymologists* who believe that the Creole must stay as close as possible to the French orthographic system. They believe that this will facilitate learning of Standard French – which they believe should be the ultimate goal of the education system – and reflect the French origins of the Creole. In this camp we find mainly literati, members of the intelligentsia, teachers, and the middle classes – members of the elite who want to distance themselves from Creole.

There is also an 'intermediate position', which states that the orthography should be phonemic, but should use the conventions of French orthography to represent sounds which are common to both languages.

As Schieffelin and Doucet point out, the *look* of Kreyòl when it is written down has become a major bone of contention. The letters *w*, *k* and *y* are seen by the pro-etymologists as 'Anglo-Saxon' imports. McConnell and Laubach, who used these letters on the basis that they were part of the International Phonetic Alphabet, were viewed by some as agents of American imperialism, preparing the way for English (with its 'Anglo-Saxon' consonants) to replace French in Haiti. The pro-etymologists would argue for 'French' letters and combinations such as *ou* and *c* or *qu* to represent the sounds given by *w* and *k* in the McConnell–Laubach system and the 1979 official orthography.

As mentioned above, there is also a more linguistic issue: whether or not the orthography should have a way of representing the front rounded vowels which some Haitians use. The official orthography does not represent them, because they are regarded as 'marginal' to the Creole (although, of course, they are a 'central' part of French). The pro-etymologists, naturally, are not happy with this.

We see here just how potent the symbolism of orthography is, and how these discussions reveal some of the underlying ambiguities which Creole speakers feel toward their language. Pro-etymologists want to see Haitian Creole as 'part of' French, in the same way that Haiti will be 'part of' the French-speaking community of states (*la francophonie*). They want this even if the cost is the creation of unnecessary educational difficulties for the majority of the population. Pro-phonemicists, meanwhile, can be seen as wanting linguistic 'independence' for Haitian, even if this means separation from *la francophonie*. At a deep level, the debate about *w* and *k* is a debate about 'who we, Haitians, are'.

3.6   Exercise

Look again at the following texts: the speech of 'Peter' in Chapter 1, Section 1; the phonemic version of it in Chapter 1, Section 6.2; the quotation from Decker's version of Julius Caesar in Chapter 5, Section 5.1 and its phonemic version in 5.2; the Jamaican Creole text in Chapter 7, Section 2.2 and its phonemic version in the 'note on orthography' below. What advantages and disadvantages can you see in using (a) etymological spelling systems, and (b) phonemic spelling systems? Which do you think would be more appropriate for each language, and why?

4   PIDGINS AND CREOLES IN EDUCATION

4.1   Mother Tongue in Education

One of the most important functions a language can have in a society is as a medium of education. Languages which have this function automatically gain status from it. In addition, the fact that large numbers of people will become literate in the language mean that it is more likely to be used in the high-status, 'powerful' domains such as administration and the media.

In many parts of the world, the only officially sanctioned language(s) of education, except perhaps at the most elementary stages, are European Standard languages. Education systems based on English, French or Portuguese are part of the colonial inheritance of many otherwise multi-lingual countries. However, there is agreement among educational linguists that the greatest benefits from the point of view of learning and cognitive development come through education in a person's *native* language. Thus, for example, a document produced by a committee of experts for UNESCO in 1951 declared (UNESCO, 1951, p. 691):

> On educational grounds we recommend that the use of the mother tongue be extended to as late a stage in education as possible. In particular, pupils should begin their schooling through the medium of the mother tongue, because they understand it best and because to begin their school life in the mother tongue will make the break between home and school as small as possible.

This could be taken as a cogent argument for encouraging the educational use of *creole* languages where they are spoken. These are, after all, native languages for their speakers ('mother tongues' in the terminology of the UNESCO document) and are often not mutually intelligible with the European lexifier. In fact, this has happened – to a limited extent – in some places. Creole languages now have an officially sanctioned place in education in several countries: *Haitian Creole* in Haiti, *Krio* in Sierra Leone, *Crioulo* in the Cape Verde Islands, *Papiamentu* in the Netherlands Antilles. In the Seychelles, an island republic in the Indian Ocean where the creole spoken is similar to that of Mauritius (Chapter 5), the first four years of education are in the creole, locally known as *Seselwa* ('Seychellois').

4.2 Pidgins in Education

Pidgins, however, are different. They are no-one's native language or mother tongue. Do they, then, have a possible role in education? Not all writers on this topic are agreed that they have; however, the arguments in favour seem compelling, if we remember the role that pidgins have in many parts of the world as lingua francas. The UNESCO experts' view (1951, p. 697) was that there were regions where

> a pidgin tongue is freely used over a wide area as a lingua franca between peoples in habitual social contact, and the children become familiar with it from an early age. When this is the case, it can be used as a medium in the schools. There are, however, two main objections to this: (a) when the pidgin contains elements based upon a European language, it is feared that the use of the pidgin in schools will make it harder for pupils to learn the European language correctly; (b) the people are often opposed to it because of its association with economic and social subordination.

The crucial point is that in spite of not being a native language for its speakers, a pidgin is nevertheless an *indigenous* language, and a lingua franca with which children may become familiar before starting school. This is certainly the situation in parts of New Guinea and West Africa. It is thus a practical solution to the problem of multilingual schools and limited resources – and a solution, furthermore, that does not disadvantage or disempower anyone. The anthropologist Margaret Mead, in a paper given at a conference on the future of Tok Pisin in New Guinea (*Tok Pisin i go we? –* Where is Tok Pisin going?), gave the following view:

> All the educational findings that show that it is important that children learn to read in their mother tongue – arguments that are very cogent – are irrelevant to the Papua New Guinea situation. It would be impossible to train a teacher corps whose different members could teach in one or more of the 500 to 700 languages. . . . [I]t will be necessary to have some common language for the country that is not the mother tongue of any indigenous Papua New Guinean group, for no Papua New Guinean group is large enough to claim any sort of priority. The choice clearly lies between Pidgin and English. But the problem is how are teachers who do not know the particular local language of any Papua New Guinean group to teach English without an intermediate language. Pidgin is that intermediate language.   (Mead, 1975, p. 52)

It is not necessary to think of pidgin-medium education as a 'second best' alternative to mother-tongue education, in a situation like that described above. While learning through the medium of a pidgin may cause initial difficulties for some children, the big advantages are in terms of resources – which can be concentrated on just one language – and in putting everyone on an equal footing, as pidgin is not the property of any one ethnic group. While educational policy in Papua New Guinea remains officially based around Standard English, one cannot help having the suspicion that Tok Pisin is probably used quite widely in the classroom. In Nigeria, according to Elugbe and Omamor (1991, p. 134), teachers in Benin and other places use pidgin with pupils when communication – which is 'officially' in Standard English – breaks down. Elugbe and Omamor (1991) along with Todd (1990) believe that this is sound educational practice. Elugbe and Omamor further advocate the use of Nigerian Pidgin as the official language of classrooms where a majority of pupils are native or near-native speakers.

Todd, however, is in favour of a strictly limited role for pidgins in education.

> A limited use of pidgins and creoles in oral instruction is justified, on pedagogic grounds, in early stages of education. Socially too it is acceptable since it is likely that future linguistic contact for the majority of pupils in any area will be regional rather than international. At first sight, the use of pidgins and creoles in the teaching of reading and writing might also seem to be reasonable. This is not, however, the case. There is little doubt that individual orthographies could be worked out for each pidgin and creole, but which part of the spectrum should be isolated as the norm? And whose pronunciation should be selected as the model? It could

be argued that [texts in the pidgin or creole might] facilitate the acquisition of the reading and writing skills in the pidgin or creole, skills which might then be transferred to reading and writing in standard English. This is possibly true. Pidgin and creole texts might indeed contribute to this acquisition, but at what cost? Even waiving financial considerations, the psychological cost would veto such a project.

(Todd, 1990, p. 80)

This is, of course, one of the objections referred to by the authors of the UNESCO document, and it is an objection which many of the local elite, who have access to English or other standard languages by virtue of their position in society, would agree with. To insist that literacy should only be through the medium of the European standard language, however, is in effect to exclude a large proportion of children – whether in Papua New Guinea or in Nigeria – from literacy altogether. Most of the problems listed by Todd – lack of norms for pronunciation, lack of an orthography, etc. – are purely practical problems which can be solved, given adequate resources. The more serious problem is an 'ideological barrier' which denies that pidgins (or creoles) are valid languages at all, and regards only Standard European languages as worth learning. Todd writes (Todd, 1990, p. 81):

many speakers of pidgins and creoles, even while adulating the languages, worry that they might be educationally limiting. They prefer their children to be taught to read and write the internationally-sanctioned variety of English, using the conventions of Standard English spelling.

Against this view, Elugbe and Omamor point out that defining 'literacy' to mean 'literacy in Standard English' is to deny the potential of indigenous languages generally (1991, p. 137):

It is doubtful if anyone, linguist or otherwise, who wishes to be taken seriously, will advocate a situation in which more than two decades after independence from colonial rule in Nigeria, the indigenous languages are barred from the classrooms because meaningful literacy should suppo- sedly boil down to literacy in a standard European language as Todd implies.

They argue (1991, p. 120) that

the so-called limitations of pidgin in education do not exist in fact. Although it may appear that the lexicon of a pidgin is limited, its capacity for extension should not be underestimated.... In developing Nigerian languages to enable them to cope with the demands of modern education, we have designed orthographies, prepared teaching materials, and compiled metalanguages for technical aspects. All these can and should be done for pidgin.

What is apparent from this debate is that any pidgin which is to be used educationally must be provided with resources to develop. This at the moment is generally not happening. The view that educational use of a pidgin will be limiting and, in the long run, delay and damage national development is a very persistent one among the educators and legislators of pidgin-speaking countries – not surprisingly, for these are the very people who have been educated through the medium of European Standard languages and so reached their present positions.

4.3   Creole on the Curriculum?

Much the same kind of debate concerns the use of creole as an educational medium in the Caribbean. Where English-lexicon creoles are seen simply as inferior, bad, or broken versions of English, there is little sympathy for making them languages of education:

> If the language of the barrack yard and the market place is to be the accepted mode of expression in the school-room, in the office and in life generally, all books would be useless, there would be nothing for our children to learn and we could well close the schools and universities, save the high wages of these experts and set them free to go and plant peas and gather nutmegs where they could give full play to this dialect stuff.

> (Letter to the *Trinidad Guardian*, quoted in Edwards, 1979)

This is not to say that no progress has been made. Devonish (1986a) discusses changes in education policy in countries such as Jamaica, Trinidad and Tobago, and Guyana, which mean that Creole is at least recognised as the home language of many children entering school. Although the goal of school is still to teach the child literacy in Standard English, new materials have had to be developed to help children make the transition from the 'home language' (Creole) to the 'school language' (Standard). Devonish points out that with the expansion of education in the post-independence Caribbean, the assumption of a corps of teachers proficient in Standard English has become unworkable; in fact most teachers now come from Creole-speaking backgrounds and have much in common, linguistically, with their pupils. Official policy has recognised this to some extent, but there is no possibility for the foreseeable future of accepting English-lexicon Creole as a *medium* of education.

In the non-Commonwealth Caribbean, the story is somewhat different. In Haiti, as mentioned above, an official Haitian Creole orthography was adopted for use in schools in 1979. Along with this came potentially far-reaching reforms. Creole was to be the medium of education as well as a school subject for the first four years of primary schooling. During this period, French would be taught as a foreign language, with literacy in French introduced gradually, and later than for Creole. After the first four years, vocational education in Creole and French, or more advanced education mainly in French, would be available.

This plan met with considerable resistance, principally from the French-speaking elite (see Devonish, 1986a, pp. 64–5). This resistance seems to have ensured the maintenance of the status quo to a large extent. According to Appel and Verhoeven (1994), 90 per cent of Haitian teachers are still not familiar with the official orthography.

In Aruba, Bonaire and Curaçao, the Netherlands Antilles, the creole Papiamentu was introduced as a subject in all grades of primary school in 1983 for one hour a day. However, the language of instruction for all subjects remains Dutch. In 1993 a new plan for primary education was issued; this proposes to make Papiamentu the medium of instruction throughout the primary school, with Dutch treated as a foreign language (Appel and Verhoeven, 1994, p. 73). Opposition, as usual, comes from those who believe that Papiamentu is too much of a 'minor language' and cannot fulfil the required educational functions. Appel and Verhoeven note that it remains to be seen whether lack of human and financial resources will obstruct this reform.

In Britain, there has occasionally been discussion of the role of Creole in the classroom. At one time in the 1970s, when a significant proportion of Caribbeans in British schools were actually Caribbean-born, there were proposals that Creole had a role to play. Jim Wight, one of the authors of a set of materials intended to help Creole-speaking children acquire British English, considered that a positive value should be placed on Creole as a way of enhancing the self-image of Creole-speaking pupils, and 'older children can be encouraged sometimes to explore their own dialect and write in the style and manner of their culture' (Wight, 1971, p. 5). At the same time, some Caribbean parents actually wanted Creole to become a school subject. The majority, however, among both educators and parents, seemed to take a much more traditional stance. The familiar beliefs – that Creole was an inferior form of English, that use of the Creole would damage children's chances at school or prevent them from getting jobs, and that there were too many practical barriers to teaching Creole – prevailed to prevent any large-scale classroom use of Creole. However, a certain amount of Creole writing was allowed and encouraged in some schools (see Sebba, 1993, Chapter 9 for more discussion).

At present, although there are numerous users of Creole in British schools, and a certain amount of Creole writing continues to be done, there is no case to be made for Creole as a 'mother tongue'. Virtually all Creole users now at school in Britain are actually first-language speakers of British English. For these, Creole may be a second dialect or another native language (see Sebba, 1993); in any case, they are not in need of 'mother tongue' instruction merely to overcome a language barrier. Some people, however, might like the opportunity to study a creole as a subject. There is some provision for studying Creole as part of 'language awareness'; however, the prospect of any more than this becoming possible, given the current priorities for education funding in England, is very remote.

5 PIDGINS AND CREOLES AS OFFICIAL LANGUAGES

In this section, by 'official language' I mean a language which is used for administrative purposes by national or local government, and which is acknowledged by the laws of a particular country as having that role. Many languages which in practice have these functions are not 'official' languages – for example, English at the time of writing is not the official language of the United States of America (there is no 'official' language). Nevertheless, official documents, court cases, educational institutions and other functions of government are usually expected to use English. There are also cases where the status of 'official' language is largely symbolic. Irish is an official language in the Republic of Ireland but is spoken natively only by a small – and not politically powerful – minority. Nevertheless, the association of Irish with nationalist and cultural goals – plus of course the fact that *historically* it was the language of most Irish people – has ensured it official status which is constitutionally guaranteed.

In looking at the use of pidgins as official languages, we could therefore consider three possibilities. A pidgin or creole might be:

1. an official language in 'word and deed', i.e. one which both has official status (e.g. in the constitution) and is actually used for administrative purposes;

2. an official language in practice – for example, with an acknowledged role in administration or education – but without this being specified in law;

3. an official language mainly for *symbolic* purposes, without being used much in practice.

In fact, as we have already seen, most pidgins and creoles, whatever their importance as communicative systems for their speakers and even for administrative purposes, have low status and are therefore unlikely to be, or to become, official languages. In fact, as far as I know, no pidgin or creole has ever been the *sole* official language of a country. The closest any language has come to this is probably Afrikaans, which for about 70 years shared that status with English in South Africa. Afrikaans was, however, very unusual in that it was not considered to be a creole language, and its speakers were a politically powerful group.

Elsewhere, it is only in the South Pacific that pidgins have had a measure of success in becoming official languages. In Papua New Guinea, Tok Pisin is an official language alongside English. In practice, there is use of both languages in official contexts (for example, in parliament). In Vanuatu, Bislama – which is similar to Tok Pisin – has official status, alongside French and English. Bislama is a major means of inter-group communication in Vanuatu, which has 105 indigenous languages, and in the 1970s its use spread to many domains of life (Holm, 1989, pp. 536–7). Because of the unusual way in which the colonial administration of the former New Hebrides Condominium was shared between the British and the French ('so inefficient and cumbersome that it was popularly known as the Pandemonium' – Molisa et al., 1982), both French and English became official languages of Vanuatu at independence in 1980, and are still the languages of education. In this situation Bislama has a special advantage, as a language neutral between English and French. This may be part of the reason for its relative success as an official language. It is now the main spoken language of government (Holm, 1989, p. 536).

Elsewhere in the world, there are few real possibilities for pidgin or creole languages to become official languages at this time. Even where the pidgin or creole is acknowledged in official policy to have some role in education or literacy, this is nearly always the limit of the language's recognition.

One argument against the adoption of a creole language as an official language comes up time and again. This is the argument that a country benefits by having a *national* language which is also an *international* language. There is no doubt truth in the argument that, say, people with a native command of English have an advantage in a world where English is such an important means of communication. Native speakers of English in Britain, the United States and elsewhere do not have to learn English in order to go on to higher education, engage in international trade, or use the Internet. This advantage is obvious, but can be overstated. There are people all around the world who have successfully learned a second language for such purposes. At issue in the creole-speaking countries like Guyana, Jamaica, Trinidad and Grenada is the question of whether advantages accrue to them just by virtue of their *calling* themselves English-speaking, when for the majority of the population, English is in effect a foreign language. Devonish writes (1986a, p. 114):

for the large mass of the primarily Creole-speaking populations, the prevailing situation has no such advantage. In fact, the prevailing situation has two huge disadvantages for Creole speakers. It excludes them from access to both the official language of internal communication and the language of external communication. These functions are both performed by English.

Devonish points out that, in practice, 'recognition' of a creole often means that a kind of *diglossia* is promoted. In Grenada during the revolutionary period of the early 1980s, for example, official rhetoric held that both English and Creole complemented each other as each had its own important functions. Devonish shows that in practice this meant maintaining the status quo by preserving English in all the 'high' functions – 'the official, public–formal and sole written language variety in the country', while Creole remained the preserve of everyday informal communication for most people. 'These two language varieties complemented each other in the same way as do the rich man in his castle and the poor man at his gate, each with his estate clearly ordered' (Devonish, 1986a, p. 138).

What this shows is that where an official policy of 'bilingualism' is promoted, it is important that the creole have *genuinely* equal status with the European language. While it is unlikely that both will be equally used in all domains – this would be a very unusual situation – it must not be the case that all the 'high' functions are fulfilled by a European language and all the 'low' functions by a creole. This simply reproduces the low status of the creole while providing a convenient camouflage through a policy of 'equality'.

6 CONCLUSIONS

It is not possible to make any general predictions about the future status and functions of pidgins and creoles. Historical factors will determine what happens in each separate situation. What we can say with reasonable certainty is that there will be no positive changes in the status quo unless there is a political will to make those changes. Along with that will must come resources to enable linguists, teachers and writers to develop appropriately the full resources of the language.

Where this does not happen, the outlook is not entirely bleak. Pidgins and creoles continue to be used day-to-day in many functions, in many parts of the world. There is a great deal of writing in some pidgins and creoles – particularly in creoles such as Sranan, Papiamentu and Jamaican Creole (or its offshoot, British Creole). For example, there are a number of daily newspapers published in Papiamentu (see Figure 8.2) as well as occasional novels and volumes of poetry. The existence of this writing, and its quality, may help to raise the status of the languages in question and this in turn may change public attitudes towards the use of creoles in some functions from which they are now excluded. This is necessarily a gradual process, however, and one which could easily be halted by external factors.

èxtra

DIARASON 24 DI MEI 1978

GRAN ESPECTATIVA PA CONGRESO DI HANDICAPTNAN

WILLEMSTAD.—
Diadomingo awor lo tin inaugurashon di e 5 Congreso di Mentalmente Retarda di Caribe, den Hotel Hilton Curacao. Ayera 'den un rueda di prensa esaki, a keda comproba ku, Totalica tuma e encargo aki riba dje, pa organisa e Congreso aki na Corsou. Totalica ta miembro di C.A.M.R. (Caribbean Association on Mental Retardation), kendenan ta organisa sorto di congresonan aki cada 2 anja. E idea pa trece e congreso aki na Corsou ta pa krea mas cordinashon entre e famianan na cas y con trata e muchanan handicapt mas positivo. E trabounan pa yega na e congreso aki, tin un durashon di un anja, pa'sina por coordina esaki bo den otro. Ta lamentable cu e congreso aki ta ser presencia cu mas extranjeronan como personajenan local.. E congreso aki lo bai trata "handicaptnan sivico y situashonan familiar". E panelistanan pa e anochinan aki lo ta Dr. M. Thorburn di Jamaica y Dr. Allan Rocker di Canada, direktor Canadian Association on Mental Retardation, kendenan ta miembronan di differente comishonnan internashonal.

E organisashon di Corsou ta worde forma pa e comishon di: Zr. Josepha Wouter, direktor di conferencia; Ana Kelle, Bertha Minguel y Ellen Isenia, kendenan ta encarga cu e trabounan di secretaria: Frank Elenburg, Jan van hal, henk van het Wout kendenan ta encarga cu financien; Frido Romer, Jet Grootens, Hertha develaar, kendenan ta encarga cu registrashon, transporte y acomodashon ; Myrna Lecks, Drs. Nelson Coffie, Drs. L. van der Veen, kendenan tin e pa atende programmashon y pa actividadnan social Maritza Eustatius, Cornell Beaujon, Monica Kapel, Lucia Whiteman; cu relashonnan publico y coordinador, Anita De Costa Gomes, miembro di directiva di Totalica T. Linzey. E fondo cu e comishon aki tin actualmente ta 72.000 florin, pa duna colaborashon na e congreso aki. Subsidionan di tantu Gobierno Central como Insular a bini. Tambe nos por bisa di Kon. Juliana Fonds di Hulanda, C.C.C. (ris di Sticusa), aknon di hendemenan di sticker y cen di inscripshon. Totolica tin e intershon di yega na nan segundo proyecto cual e prome ta e "Pasadia". For di principio di anja 1976, e peteshon pa pone e congreso aki na nos isla a ser pidi, caminda señora Anita De Costa Gomez, kende a bai Sto. Domingo pa e congreso di 76 y hopi interes a ser pone den Cosrou, pa yega na e congreso aki. Tin 20 paisnan cu lo participa na e congreso aki, cualnan ta Venezuela, Costa Rica, Canada, Antigua, Bahamas, Barbados, Bermuda, Cuba, Haiti, Jamaica, Hulanda, Panama, Puerto Rico, Rep. Dominicana, Tortola, Surnam. St. Lucia, St. Vincent, Trininidad, Turks y Islanan Caicano y Antiyanan Nerlandes. Manera nos a splica ariba caba e congreso aki lo worde inuagura diadomingo awor y esaki lo worde efectua pa e prome Ministro di Antiyas señor Boy Rozendaal. E donashonan cu a bini for di e siguiente jatancinan ta, 20.000 florin di Gobierno insular, 10.000 di Gobierno Central, di C.C.C. 7250 florin y di Kon. Juliana Fonds 10.000. Na Hulanda nan no gusta di duna sorto di dunashonnan aki, pero ya cu e comishon aki tabata den un combersashon personal·cu e service club aki, nan a yega na e idea di colabora tog cu Corsou. Lamentable ta e majoria di nos hendenan no a participa na e congreso aki, cual ta uno cu lo bai duna Corsou un bon propagandashon pa nos Comishon mentalmente retarda. Mas o me-

Sigi lesa riba pagina 12

CUIDO DENTAL TA UN URGENCIA

DIADOMINGO AWOR TELETON

WILLEMSTAD— Ayera prensa a reuni cu e fundashon nobo pa kwido di djente, kendenan lo bai na cuminsa cu un tarea importante na beneficio di nos comunidad. Den e rueda aki a bini sali na cla cu un Fundashon nobo a ser lanta pa yega na un mihor sistema pa kwido di djente. E fundashon aki lo bai carga e nomber di "Fundashon Servicio Emergencia Dental" di Wit- Gele Kruis. Esaki ta especial pa hendenan cu no tin moda o cen pa ranca djente, cu ta molestiando nan. Diadomingo awor lo tin un teleton pa yegana e suma cu ta den nesesidad. Si nos wak abienaarnan ta hanja sierto "vergoeding" pa cuido di dokter, esaki ta locual cu obrero nan no ta hanjabdo actualmente.

Ta ser calcula cu tin 50 pa 80 mil habitante di nos isla cu tin e nesesidad aki, pa mea nan djente, cu ta molestiando nan. Pa yega na e fondonan aki, varios instancianan a sermaera, cualnan ta "servico clubnan", kendenan lo bai duna nan colaborashon pa e fundashon aki. Plannan pa yega na un clinica nobo, caminda e edificio di Wit-Gele-kruis na Santa Maria ta urgente y plannan pa yega na un clinica dental na Mgr. Verriet Instituut a ser liquida pa via cu e clinica nobo no ta mas cu 200 km for di e central di e servicio di Wit- Gele kruis. Lo bai tin 8 dentista pa duna servicio completamente gratis. Durante di e funshonamentu di e clinica aki nan lo bai cobra solamemente 2 florin, pero tur esakinan ta gastunan pa material, cual ta ser huza pa rancamentu di e djente.. Tambe Gobierno tin entenshon di liquida e 'liestal camaan" cu tin actualmente, pa busca 5 dental car nobo, pa buta na lugar di esakinan. Pero e servicio di dental na akol ta mustra hopi otro for di esus cu e comishon di Servicio di Emergencia Dental di Wit-Gele Kruis. Ainda e comishon aki no tin idaanan fiho pa duna servicio durante di week-end, pero esaki por bai ser studia den transcurso di e dianan cu ta mercando. E comishon aki ta consisti di; Johannes van Kouwen,kende ta presidente, Ronald Orteia, secretario, Geertruida Gerlings- Wytema, kende tin encargo di financien, Eric de Brabander, miembro di comishon di dentistanan lokal, Leslie Celestina, tambe miembro di e comishon ya menahora, Fred van Dalen, miembro di comishon di dentistanan. Itala Schob- Franka,miembro y Guillermo Thomas, kende tambe ta fungi como miembro. Nos ta spera cu e pueblo den su totalidad lo sabi di contribui na e "Teleton" aki, pa hanja fondo pa duna servicio dental, na bendenan cu no tin e moda di ranca djente. Y nos tambe lo duna e apoyo necesario na e fundashon aki, ya cu akinan tambe un parti di nos comunidad lo por worde proteha..

SPLICASHON DI A.H.T.S.

WILLEMSTAD.- Na augustus 1972 Antilliaanse Hogere Technishe school a habri su portanan pa tantu estudiantenan di Corsow como di e otro islanan di Antiyas.

Apertura tabata tin como consecuencia cu mester a hanja acomodashon pa alohá estudiantenan di e otro islanan , locual a conduci na institushonnan di Campus AHTS.

Durante di e programa di SAD, School Advies Dienst, lo duna aplicashon di e funcashon di AHTS, via di TeleCuracao pa mis or di atardi awe.

Figure 8.2 A daily newspaper in Papiamentu, the Spanish-lexicon creole of Aruba, Bonaire and Curaçao

7   EXERCISE

1. Discuss the arguments for and against having primary and/or secondary education through the medium of a specific pidgin or creole (for example, Tok Pisin or Sranan). Make sure you are clear about *who* would benefit or be disadvantaged in each case.

2. Imagine that you have been given the job of implementing a government decision to introduce primary school teaching through the medium of a pidgin, where previously the lexifier language (say English) had been used. What kinds of training and resources would you need? What specific difficulties might you encounter? (Consider it from your own perspective and those of the pupils, the teaching staff and the parents.)

3. Should pidgins/creoles be made official languages? Discuss this question with reference to a few specific cases.

KEY POINTS: Literacy, Education and Standardisation

Problems for pidgin and creole languages becoming standard languages:

- status: usually low to start with;
- difference: pidgins/creoles are too similar to their lexifiers – can easily be dismissed as 'inferior dialects' of the lexifier;
- variability: no clear notion of which forms are 'correct' in the language;
- development.

Orthographic (spelling) principles

- *phonemic*: represents sounds of language and de-emphasises connection with the lexifier;
- *etymological*: stresses connection with the lexifier.

Pidgins and creoles in education

- using mother tongue in education usually benefits learners;
- some pidgins/creoles are now used in primary education;
- practical difficulties (e.g. lack of a standard form, lack of texts) often prevent pidgins/creoles from being used in classroom.

Pigins and creoles as official languages

- some pidgins (e.g. Bislama, Tok Pisin) used for official purposes;
- no creoles (except Afrikaans) have official status but some are developing a role in administration.

9 Conclusions

1 INTRODUCTION

In this final chapter I want to deal with some of the remaining issues concerning pidgins, creoles and contact languages which have not been discussed in earlier chapters. Some of these questions are new ones in the study of contact languages (for example, the question of whether sign languages are creoles), while others are old questions ('Why study pidgins and creoles?') but have found new answers in the recent history of the field.

2 SOME CONTROVERSIES AND QUERIES: MIXED LANGUAGES, SIGN LANGUAGES, AND AFRICAN–AMERICAN VERNACULAR ENGLISH

2.1 Mixed Languages

Mixed languages have only recently become a focus of interest for linguists. While it seems likely that in the future they will become a separate field of study, at the moment they occupy a niche within the general area of creole language studies. However, creolists would be the first to agree that mixed languages – which often have great morphological complexity – sit uneasily alongside the 'classical' creoles, which are characterised by relative grammatical and morphological *simplicity*. The attempt by Bakker and Mous (1994, p. 5) to define a 'mixed language' shows why they are of interest to creole scholars:

> A very rough approximation is that a mixed language has its lexicon and grammar from different sources. On the basis of the lexicon one would classify such languages as belonging to one language family and on the basis of the morphology, syntax and general grammatical characteristics one would classify them as belonging to another language family.

'Grammar from one source and lexicon from another' is a formula often used to characterise pidgins and creoles, as for example the description by Sylvain (1936, p. 178) of Haitian Creole as 'an Ewe [West African] language with French vocabulary' (see Chapter 6). However, the inadequacy of such descriptions as applied to pidgins and creoles soon becomes apparent when we compare their grammatical structures with those of the input languages.

264

We invariably find a large amount of simplification in pidgins and creoles, as demonstrated in Chapter 2 and elsewhere in this book.

Mixed languages by contrast retain the grammatical complexity of their 'grammatical host' language, but replace all or part of the vocabulary with items from another, unrelated language, through a process which has been termed *relexification*. In Chapter 3 we saw that some scholars have suggested that a process of relexification was involved in the formation of some pidgins and creoles, accounting for grammatical similarity in spite of differences in lexicon. I gave the example of an Ecuadorian mixed language, Media Lengua (Muysken 1981, 1994), as evidence that relexification was more than a theoretical notion, and had apparently taken place in at least one case.

2.1.1   The case of Mbugu

In fact, as early as 1971, Goodman had reported, at an important conference on Pidgin and Creole studies, 'the strange case of Mbugu'. Mbugu or Ma'a (Goodman, 1971; Mous, 1994) is spoken by the Mbugu people who live in the Usambara mountains of Tanzania. Mbugu exists in two varieties. The first, 'normal' or 'high' Mbugu, is similar to Pare, another local language, which is from the Bantu group. The second, which its speakers call the 'real' or 'inner' Mbugu, has essentially the same grammar as the other variety, but a large proportion of lexical items of non-Bantu origin. These have been identified as coming from the Cushitic language family (a group of languages mainly found in the Horn of Africa, which includes languages such as Somali). In fact, according to Mous (1994, p. 175), the 'normal' and 'inner' Mbugu languages are actually registers of the same language, and most speakers will use both in an ordinary conversation.

Like Media Lengua, inner Mbugu shows the results of mixing the vocabulary of one language (or language group) with the grammar of another. But how exactly did this come about? The Mbugu are in some respects culturally different from their Bantu-speaking neighbours – in particular, they are cattle-keepers, which suggests a Cushitic culture. Normal Mbugu is clearly a Bantu language and would be unremarkable but for the existence of inner Mbugu. Inner Mbugu thus has the appearance of a Bantu language whose vocabulary has largely been replaced by Cushitic lexical items – in other words, relexified. However, in the absence of any historical evidence of this, we cannot be sure, and Mous mentions a number of alternative theories of the origin of inner Mbugu (1994, pp. 197–8). Thomason and Kaufman, for example, argue (1988) that Ma'a is the result of a Cushitic language undergoing massive borrowing from a Bantu language, on the grounds that much of the most *basic* vocabulary of Ma'a is Cushitic. If Ma'a were originally Bantu, we might expect that the most fundamental vocabulary would be Bantu. Mous does not accept this argument. His conclusion (1994, p. 199) is that

It is crucial that proficiency in Inner Mbugu (Ma'a) implies proficiency in Normal Mbugu. ... Inner Mbugu is a lexical register that was created by speakers of Normal Mbugu. They did this consciously and on purpose, to set themselves apart from their Bantu neighbours.

Strange as the case of Mbugu may be, it is not at all unique. Bakker and Mous (1994) published the edited proceedings of a conference which discussed no less than fifteen cases or possible cases of 'language intertwining'. I shall give just two more examples here.

2.1.2   Michif

Michif (Bakker, 1994b) is spoken by some (not all) of the ethnic group called Métis, descendants of French-speaking fur-traders and their Amerindian wives. The Métis now speak a variety of languages and are dispersed over a wide area of Canada and the northern United States. The number of speakers of Michif is small and ageing, as children no longer acquire the language. Michif is best described as a mixed language resulting from a 'blend' of French with the Amerindian language Cree. However, while Ma'a shows a reasonably neat 'split' between grammar (Bantu) and lexis (Cushitic), Michif is less straightforward:

Michif is a language with French nouns, numerals, articles and adjectives, Cree verbs, demonstratives, postpositions, question words and personal pronouns, and further possessives, prepositions and negative elements from both languages. Not only is there a fairly neat distribution of the two languages across these grammatical categories, both languages lost little or nothing of their complexities.   (Bakker, 1994b, p. 16)

2.1.3   Mednyj Aleut

Mednyj Aleut or *Copper Island Aleut* (Golovko, 1994) is spoken by a very small number of speakers who (before their removal in the 1960s to another island) lived on Copper Island (Russian *Mednyj*), one of the Commander Islands group which lies east of the peninsula of Kamchatka in the Bering Sea in the extreme far east of the Russian Federation. In Mednyj Aleut the majority of the vocabulary is of Aleut origin. Aleut is a Native American language related to Inuit ('Eskimo') and with a polysynthetic type of morphology. The verb stems, however, carry Russian tense, number and person markers: also of Russian origin are 'the subjunctive marker, negator, subjective pronouns, the infinitive, conjunctions and clause markers' (Golovko, 1994, p. 114). Russian is an Indo-European language which is also morphologically complex.

The following is an example of a sentence from Mednyj Aleut (Golovko, 1994, p. 115). Russian elements are in italics, the rest is Aleut:

jesli	*by*	*oni*	ukaala-ag'aa-*l-i*	huzu-um	*by*
if	SUBJ	they	here-move-PAST-PL	all-REFL	SUBJ

txichi	qala-chaa-*l*
REFL-PL	be glad-CAUS-PAST

'If they came, everybody would be glad'

Compare the Russian equivalent (elements shared with Mednyj Aleut are in bold):

jesli	**by**	**oni**	prijexa-**l-i**	**vse**	**by**	obradova-**l-i-s'**
if	**SUBJ**	**they**	come-**PAST-PL**	**all**	**SUBJ**	be glad-**PAST-PL-REFL**

There are a number of hypotheses about the origins of Mednyj Aleut, but the exact manner of its coming into existence remains unknown. It is certainly the product of the Russian colonisation of the Aleutian Islands during the nineteenth century, which led to the emergence of an ethnically mixed population, the descendants of Russian fur-traders and the native Aleutians (who, however, were resettled on Mednyj Island from elsewhere in the island chain). The 'creoles', defined as a separate ethnic group by the Russian–American Company which exploited the islands, were between Russians and Aleuts in the social hierarchy. The existence of the 'creoles' seems to have been a key factor in the development of Mednyj Aleut. (See Golovko, 1994 for more details.)

According to Golovko (1994, p. 117), Mednyj Aleut

was 'constructed' by adults. Still the question remains: which adults were responsible for [its] emergence? Were they the Aleut wives of Russian husbands, or the Russian husbands themselves... or bilingual creoles who strived to identify themselves as a separate ethnic group. The last possibility is the most likely one.

It is obvious that Copper Island Aleut was 'invented' by bilingual speakers of Aleut and Russian, for whom Aleut was the mother tongue and Russian a second language.

While mixed languages are clearly different from creole languages in that they retain the morphological complexity of their input languages, their origins in language contact and (apparently) ethnic mixing suggest that creolists have something to learn from them. Bakker (1994b, p. 24; see also 1992) argues that two types of circumstances give rise to 'language intertwining'. The first is that a settled, formerly nomadic group, require a secret language for communication about business in the presence of strangers. Such a language will have the lexicon of the original language and the grammatical system of the host country. Though not given by Bakker as an example, Mbugu/Ma'a seems to fit this scenario, as the ethnic Mbugu are slightly different in culture and appearance from their Bantu-speaking neighbours. Bantu provides the grammatical structure of inner Mbugu while the vocabulary is Cushitic.

A second possibility is described as follows by Bakker (1994b, p. 24):

> a group of men speaking language A invades the territory of language B. They massively marry local women. Their descendants, if they will stick together and form a new ethnic group, develop a new language with the grammatical system of the language of the mothers and the lexicon of the language of the fathers.

Bakker cites Michif as an example of this scenario: Canadian French-speaking men intermarrying with Cree-speaking women. Mednyj Aleut represents a very similar case, and likewise connected with the fur trade. The linguistic outcomes, though different, show significant similarities.

So what can creole studies learn from looking at mixed languages? A first lesson is that the outcome of language contact always depends on the social circumstances which surround that contact. Even where a new language results, it is not always appropriate to label that language a pidgin or creole in the sense which has been developed in this book. The terms 'pidgin' and 'creole' have to be restricted to languages which show simplification when compared with the input languages.

Secondly, we should be aware that the key factors in the two scenarios described by Bakker as leading to language intertwining may also play a role in pidgin/creole genesis. The need for a 'secret language' – which we might reinterpret as the need for a language which *marks* its speakers as a separate group, even when the language is not strictly 'secret' – may lead to the adoption of a pidgin or creole by a community who originally were speakers of another language. In Section 3 we will see an example of this from Brazil.

Perhaps more significantly, the *gender* of speakers may be a significant element in determining the form of the language which results from language contact. Little attention has been given so far by creolists to this issue. It has usually been assumed that the roles of men and women in pidgin and creole formation have been similar, or that any differences were not significant. The study of language intertwining, however, suggests that if there were consistent differences between the languages of the men and women involved in a case of creole genesis – for example, if most of the women spoke the same language or related languages while the men did not – we would expect that to affect the outcome. An interesting case to compare in this regard is that of Pitkern (Pitcairnese), described in Chapter 5. We know that in the

Pitkern case, the majority of the male founders of the settlement were speakers of some variety of English, while the women were speakers of Tubaian or Tahitian. In this case, the outcome was not Tahitian with English lexicon, as would be expected in a clear case of language intertwining. Rather, the resultant language looks like a creolised English with some Tahitian grammatical features and lexis. Why these differences in outcome in different cases? In spite of the difficulties of doing historical research into this, the gender of the 'founding speakers' may be a promising line of inquiry in creole studies.

2.2 Sign Language

There are some interesting parallels between the history of the field of *Sign Languages* (or *Signed Languages*) and the field of pidgin and creole studies. In both cases, the languages in question were misunderstood and looked down on by those who did not speak them, and to some extent by linguists – who in general simply ignored them. The few linguists who took them seriously put their careers at risk by doing so. Much more recently, however, both creole studies and sign language studies have become important fields of study and the objects of substantial amounts of research.

Sign languages are the native and normal mode of communication used by Deaf people. (By convention, 'Deaf' with a capital D is used to indicate those people who identify themselves as belonging to a culture distinct from that of hearing people; 'deaf' with a small D is used of anyone who is audiologically deaf.) Recent research has shown beyond doubt that sign languages meet all the criteria for being considered true human languages: in other words, they are not simply haphazard sets of gestures or impoverished communicative systems, as was believed at one time. Like spoken languages, they can be used to convey an infinite set of messages and can encode ideas of great complexity. When used by native signers, they have all the creativity and subtlety of spoken languages. Their main, and obvious difference from spoken languages is that they make no use of sound (though they do make use of lip movements). As with spoken languages, signed languages differ from community to community: thus while most hearing people in Britain and America have a common spoken language (English), American Sign Language and British Sign Language are not mutually intelligible.

The connections between creole studies and sign language studies are not limited to similarities of history. A case has been made for treating sign languages as creoles. To see why this should be, we have to look at how sign languages are acquired by their users. While the transmission of spoken languages from generation to generation is straightforward in most cases – creolising languages being the exception, discussed in detail earlier – the transmission of sign languages is generally more complex. This is because the great majority of deaf children are born into families where both parents are hearing. Estimates suggest that only 5 per cent of deaf children are born to parents who are both deaf, while another 5 per cent have one deaf and one hearing parent (Brennan, 1992, p. 3). These facts, together with differing arrangements for educating deaf children in different places and different educational systems, mean that Deaf people come to acquire sign language through a number of different routes.

Deaf children born to deaf parents who use sign language are those most likely to acquire sign language in a manner which corresponds to 'normal transmission' of spoken language. (This term is discussed in Chapter 5.) They will be surrounded by sign language from birth and can truly be termed 'native signers'. Since hearing parents generally do not know sign language, deaf children born into hearing families are unlikely to learn sign language at the age when hearing children begin to learn spoken language, and may come to it much later or not at all. Some may acquire it when they start to attend a school for Deaf children, while others may not come into contact with it at school but later, through socialisation with Deaf signers. At the same time, in most countries if not all, the Deaf child will be surrounded by the main spoken language used in his or her community, and will be expected to learn how to communicate through lip-reading, speech or writing in that language. Thus in Britain and the USA, Deaf people are expected to reach a standard comparable with that of hearing people in their use of written English and as far as possible in spoken English as well. Deaf people accommodate these expectations of hearing people to varying degrees – and by no means all Deaf people would accept that deafness is a form of 'disability' which can be 'alleviated' by becoming 'educated' in hearing people's language.

Nevertheless most Deaf people will have some knowledge of the language of hearing people, and are thus bilingual, although not in the conventional sense of knowing two *spoken* languages. Under these conditions of unequal power, spoken language exerts an influence on sign language. British Sign Language (BSL), for example, often incorporates the initial letter of the fingerspelt form of an English word into the sign for the same word: the 'C' handshape for communicate, the 'N' handshape for 'national'. (Finger-spelling is a way of using handshapes (the manual alphabet) to represent the letters of the written form of a spoken language such as English; it is not itself a 'sign language'). Some sign language words are represented just by their initial letter from the manual alphabet, sometimes repeated (Y for 'year', DD for 'daughter'), while other words have no sign (at least, none so far) and have to be 'borrowed' from English in a fingerspelt form.

All of this shows that sign languages (at least British and American sign languages) involve a fairly high degree of contact with spoken languages. It is quite reasonable to examine them for signs of the kinds of phenomena associated with contact languages like pidgins and creoles. Some linguists have in fact argued that 'sign languages may usefully be grouped with pidgins and creoles' (Edwards and Ladd, 1984, p. 75). Viv Edwards and Paddy Ladd compared the structure of BSL with the list of twelve most frequently occurring creole features given by Bickerton (1981), and found that BSL followed Bickerton's 'creole' pattern in eight cases, and deviated from it in four, some of which could by explained by the difference in modality (i.e. the use of gesture and facial expression rather than speech). On the basis of these structural similarities and developmental similarities, they argue that BSL should be considered to be a creole. Margaret Deuchar (1987) examined five specific characteristics of creoles discussed by Bickerton (1981), and found them all in British Sign Language as well as some others. They are:

1. *Aspect marking is closest to the verb, then modality, then time.* In fact, Deuchar argues, aspect marking is simultaneous with the verb; for example, the sign TALK can be inflected for 'durative aspect' (i.e. indicative that it continued for some time) by fast repetition of the movement. (By convention, words in capitals indicate the sign with the corresponding gloss.) Modality is expressed by separate lexical items which come immediately before or after the verb; WILL ASK for 'I will ask', AGREE WILL YOUNG for 'the young will agree'. Tense marking is furthest from the verb, but in sign languages there is really *time* rather than tense marking, and this is carried out by temporal adverbials like BEFORE, NOW, TOMORROW, which may be 'at some distance from the verb', rather than tense markers (Deuchar, 1987, p. 85).

2. *Existential and possessive share the same lexical item.* In many creoles the *existential* 'there is' and the *possessive* 'I/you etc. have' are both indicated by the same word. The same is true in American, British and French sign languages; for example, in BSL the sign for both 'have' and 'there is' is an open hand closing into a fist in front of the signer (ibid.).

3. *There is no copula.* This is a widespread feature of pidgins although not so widely shared by creoles. BSL, ASL (American) and FSL (French) all seem to lack copulas, for example, HE NO-GOOD, 'He is no good', in BSL.

4. *Adjectives behave as verbs.* This point is related to the last and has been observed in a number of creoles, for example Sranan and Jamaican Creole. It is also found in sign languages, which can, for example, add negative and durative inflections to signs whose English translations are adjectives.

5. *There is no passive construction.* According to Deuchar this is true at least in British, American, Danish, French, Russian and Swedish sign languages.

Deuchar goes on to argue that sign languages are 'new emerging languages of the same kind as creoles' (p. 86) on the grounds that they share not only these structural similarities, but developmental similarities as well. Her argument is based on the notion that 'limited input' from adults to children accounts both for the similarities among creole languages (this is Bickerton's argument) and for the structural features of sign languages.

> Just as a creole first develops as a child's first language, on the basis of rather limited input from a pidgin, sign languages are generally learned by children on the basis of rather limited sign language input. This is because the majority of deaf children's parents are hearing and do not sign to them, or sign in a very limited way.... [C]hildren sign among themselves, but... it seems that they in fact 'invent' a sign language system which is only influenced by very limited input from the adult sign language.
> (Ibid., p. 86)

We saw in Chapter 6 that Bickerton's Language Bioprogram Hypothesis has remained controversial and is by no means accepted by all creolists. Rejection of the LBH is based both on theoretical grounds and on actual counter-examples. Some of the strongest criticism has come from creolists who hold that substrate influence can account for shared similarities among creoles. Clearly, however, influence from a substrate (in the sense of a non-creole language which is native to many or all members of the pidgin/creole community) cannot be a factor in sign language acquisition. Spoken languages are initially inaccessible to deaf children, even though they may become accessible later, through lip reading or writing. In this respect, sign languages provide a better test of the LBH than do spoken creoles.

The nature of sign language transmission must be a crucial factor in evaluating the claims made for the Language Bioprogram Hypothesis. In Chapter 5, 'creole' was defined as *a language with native speakers which results from language contact without normal transmission.* If deaf children indeed 'reinvent' sign language in each generation with restricted input from adult signers, and on each occasion conform to the 'language blueprint' of the LBH, this would provide striking evidence for the Language Bioprogram.

However, other explanations might also be available, for example: even if sign language does not exactly conform to the model of 'normal transmission', it is not learnt by each generation in complete isolation from previous generations. If that were so, we would expect major differences, in addition to any structural similarities, between the sign languages of different generations. But this is not what we find; rather, we find smallish differences, on a par with those in other, 'normally transmitted' spoken languages. It is more realistic to think of a sign language tradition which is passed down, via adult signers and older deaf children. This tradition may be less direct and more broken than in the case of spoken languages, and so may lie somewhere between 'normal' and 'abnormal' transmission. Nevertheless, it is not on a par with the almost instantaneous creation of a new language system on the basis of fragmentary output, which is the scenario required by Bickerton's LBH.

Secondly, since acquisition of sign language generally takes place later than that of spoken language – except for children of parents who are signers – its simpler structure may be the result of this later learning. Since we know that for spoken languages native-like acquisition becomes more difficult with increasing age even for children, we may assume that the same is true for the acquisition of sign languages. This suggests that the structure of sign language may reflect a somewhat reduced ability to acquire complex structures.

Thirdly, we need to take into account the models of sign language which are offered to learners. Except in the case of deaf children of deaf parents who are signers, the child acquiring sign language is likely to learn it from a variety of people – deaf peers, deaf adults, and hearing adults – who will themselves be more, or less, 'native-like' in their signing ability. Only a minority of these will have learnt to sign in early childhood and thus be truly 'native signers'. These conditions are somewhat like those of *tertiary hybridisation* (Chapter 3), where a language is modelled for learners by non-native speakers, leading to the acquisition of a simplified variety. In this case, the creole-like features of sign languages would be attributable to language contact, but not to creolisation in the sense of the Language Bioprogram.

Fourthly, we should admit that sign language studies are still at an early stage, and that, given the difference of mode (speech vs sign), it is very difficult to make direct comparisons. It is still possible that the 'creole-like' features of sign language may turn out to be a consequence of some other factor, as yet undiscovered, which characterises languages in the signed mode.

It is interesting to note that in sign language studies, concepts developed in the study of language contact have been significant. In the United States, the term 'Pidgin Sign English' has been used to refer to language varieties which lie on the continuum between American Sign Language and manually represented English, reflecting the fact that such varieties appeared to result from contact between ASL and English, and to be simplified with respect to both. Rejecting the idea that this continuum of varieties is a pidgin in the sense in which we have used it in this book, Cokely (1984) instead argues that it derives from a combination of *learners' grammars* (speakers of English with a partial knowledge of ASL, and users of ASL with a partial knowledge of English) and simplified registers – what we have called *foreigner talk* (Chapter 3). Users of each language make judgements about the fluency of speakers of the other language with whom they interact, and these judgements lead them to produce more or less simplified registers of their own language for the benefit of their interlocutors. Thus deaf ASL users simplify their signing for hearing people who are not so fluent in sign language, while English speakers simplify their (signed version of) English to make it more accessible to users of ASL. In this situation, it is likely that neither group will progress to full fluency in the 'native' version of the target language, but will at best achieve fluency in the simplified version modelled by the target-language users. Thus the resultant continuum of 'inter-languages' is not a pidgin, although as Cokely points out (p. 26), the *processes* of pidginisation may be involved. This discussion in fact echoes much of what we noted in Chapter 3 in connection with *Gastarbeiterdeutsch*, in which both learners' grammars and foreigner talk seem to be involved.

Ceil Lucas and Clayton Valli also conclude that it is misleading to think of an ASL 'pidgin' brought about through 'contact signing' between Deaf and hearing people. They say (1992, p. 92): 'the data reveal that the morphological and syntactic system of contact signing cannot simply be characterized as 'reduced English' or as a pidgin. Sociolinguistically, it does not fit the criteria for defining pidgins, either,' as the social context 'does not match the situations in which pidgins have been said to arise. It is a maintained bilingualism, one outcome of which is contact signing' (p. 93).

To conclude this section, it is clear that sign language studies and contact language studies have some common areas of interest, and furthermore, that each can benefit from insights from the other field. Without going so far as to say that 'sign languages are creoles' we can certainly say that creolists and sign language researchers should keep in close touch with one another.

2.3   African-American Vernacular English

In this section we will look at the question of whether *African-American Vernacular English* (also known as *Black English Vernacular* or BEV, and *American Black English*), widely spoken by people of African descent in the United States, is or is not a creole language. This is a complex and much-discussed issue, in which social and political factors have also played their part. Therefore, I will give only a summary of the issues in this book. There are a number of volumes devoted entirely to this subject. (See, for example, Edwards and Winford, 1991; Ewers, 1996.)

2.3.1   Contact languages in North America
The North American continent has been home to a variety of different contact languages. *Chinook Jargon*, *Mobilian Jargon*, and *Delaware Jargon* (Chapter 1) were based on indigenous Amerindian languages but were used solely for inter-group communication and do not appear to have creolised.

However, at least two well-documented creole languages are spoken today in the United States. *Lousiana Creole* is a French-lexicon creole which is spoken in the state of Louisiana on the Gulf of Mexico, and has some features in common with the French-lexicon creoles of the Caribbean region such as those of Haiti, St Lucia, Martinique, Guadeloupe and French Guiana (Cayenne). All of these trace their origins to the plantation slave labour system and contact between French and languages of West Africa. (See, for example, Lefebvre et al., 1982.) The Sea Islands, off the coast of the south-eastern state of South Carolina, are home to an English-lexicon creole, *Gullah*, which is sometimes treated as a dialect of English but is clearly a creole and which shares many features with the English-lexicon creoles of the Caribbean area. In particular, it has elements of phonology and syntax (for example, preverbal tense/aspect markers) which make it resemble creoles like Jamaican and Guyanese. Furthermore, research by Lorenzo Dow Turner (1949) revealed numerous African 'survivals' in Gullah, showing beyond doubt that its origin lay in language contact between English and the languages of plantation slaves. Gullah is still spoken by perhaps a quarter of a million people (Holm, 1989, p. 491) in low-lying areas along the coast of the south-eastern United States and the offshore islands. Understandably, it is under considerable pressure to assimilate towards English, and has undergone extensive decreolisation. Gullah was used by Dubose Heyward (1885–1940) in his novel *Porgy*, which was made into the folk opera *Porgy and Bess* by George Gershwin.

2.3.2 Creoles and the plantation system

Given that there is indisputable evidence for at least two creoles with plantation origins in specific regions of the United States, one might wonder whether the plantation system, the source of many creole languages in the Americas, had given rise to other English-lexicon creoles. All the states of the American South had operated plantation agriculture and practised slavery prior to the Civil War of 1861–5: should a creole not have developed as a result? But while creoles were the linguistic outcome of the plantation labour system in many places, there are a few clear instances where it was not so. In Brazil the majority of the population, whether or not descendants of African slaves, speak a variety of Portuguese which lacks the features associated with Creole Portuguese elsewhere (but see Section 3 below). In Cuba, although a nonstandard variety of Spanish emerged among African slaves (*Habla Bozal*), it is not certain that this was a creole (see Holm, 1989, pp. 306–9), and today most Cubans speak Spanish, not a Spanish-lexicon creole – in spite of the Caribbean being full of creole-speaking islands. Therefore, the existence of plantations and African slave labour does not guarantee that a creole will emerge. It seems that there are other necessary conditions for creolisation which have to be met – for example, the ratio of whites to slaves must be sufficiently small, social conditions must be such that the slaves have virtually no access to the Europeans' language, and no one language must predominate among the slaves. But even when these conditions are met, we cannot be certain that a creole will be the result.

2.3.3   An African-American creole?

We now come to the main issue of this section: is African-American Vernacular English (AAVE), the language variety of a large proportion of African-Americans, a creole or a dialect of English? This is a question which is still undecided at the time of writing, as both views have their proponents and opponents. The difficulty results from the fact that while clearly AAVE shows substantial differences from English dialects spoken in the United States, it is not self-evidently the product of creolisation in the same way as most of the creoles discussed in this book. The non-linguistic evidence for creolisation is circumstantial – the existence of plantations and African slaves of mixed linguistic origin. As we saw above, this does not guarantee that a creole will develop. On the other hand, the linguistic evidence for a creole is not as strong as elsewhere. If AAVE has its origins in a creole, it has certainly decreolised and assimilated to American English to a large extent. The same could be said, say, of Jamaican Creole: but in Jamaica, the 'broad', basilectal creole is still spoken, and the range of varieties between the basilect and Standard English is there for all to observe. Thus critics of the creole-origin theory for AAVE point to the lack of a clearly creole 'basilect', or a continuum which indicates beyond doubt that a basilect must have existed, even if it has died out.

Proponents of the view that AAVE is a dialect of English have tended to take the view that AAVE derives from a conservative variety of English which was brought to North America by the English colonists. In most of the colonies (later states) where slaves were part of the labour system, the ratio of whites to blacks was too high to permit the formation of a creole: rather, the slaves learnt more or less the same English as their masters. The Gullah-speaking region was an exception to this. According to this view, AAVE is a dialect of English which has preserved features now extinct in the language of white Americans, as a result of the relative social isolation of the African-American population, compounded by such factors as poverty and illiteracy.

On the other hand, proponents of the view that AAVE is a creole point to linguistic features of AAVE, including its rhythm and intonation patterns, which give it a different 'feel' from the English of white Americans. (See, for example, the work of Geneva Smitherman, 1977, expecially chapters 4 and 5, on tone rhythm, intonation and discourse styles.) They point to connections, both linguistic and social, between Gullah and AAVE and their speakers (see, for example, Dillard, 1972). They assert the unlikelihood of AAVE developing from English without creolisation in a situation which was known to have given rise to creoles elsewhere, and where one creole – Gullah – was known to exist. While AAVE may be more similar to Standard English than we might expect of a creole, in at least two cases – Barbados and Réunion (mentioned in Chapter 5, Section 3.1) – a higher ratio of whites to slaves has apparently led to a creole that is closer to the standard language than other creoles which developed from a similar mix of languages.

A major focus of the debate over AAVE has been a single category of the grammar – the copula. One of the striking differences between (white) American English and AAVE is the use of the verb *to be*. As we saw in Chapter 5, Section 4.5.4 (for Sranan Tongo) and Chapter 7, Section 2.3.4 (for Jamaican Creole), the copula is one site of difference between Standard English and English-lexicon creoles. In AAVE, we find four possible realisations of the copula where Standard English and most of its dialects have only two (Labov, 1982, p. 179):

(1a)   He is tired out
(1b)   He's tired out
(1c)   He tired out
(1d)   He be tired out

Form (1d) is different from the others in that it represents a category which AAVE does not share with Standard English, representing 'habitual' or 'repeated' action. Some examples given by Dillard make the difference clear (Dillard, 1972, p. 45):

(2a)   He be waitin' for me every night when I come home
(2b)   He waitin' for me right now

In AAVE, these sentences would be incongruous if *be* were omitted in (2a) or inserted in (2b). This seems to be a clear enough indication that the *aspect* system of AAVE is different from that of Standard English, so that in that respect, at least, their grammars are dissimilar.

In AAVE as in Standard English the sentences (1a) and (1b) would be treated as possible alternatives with identical meaning. However in AAVE, (1c) occurs as well, and is a third alternative form. We have seen that in Caribbean creoles such as Sranan and Jamaican, forms like (1c) are the norm rather than the exception. From the perspective of the debate as to whether AAVE is a creole or an English dialect, there are two possible interpretations of this data:

(3a)   AAVE is like the Caribbean creoles in lacking a copula in sentences such as (1c). Through a process of decreolisation, the more standard forms (1a) and (1b) have been introduced into the language as alternative forms.

(3b)   AAVE is like English dialects in that the copula is subject to a
        (phonological) process of contraction, e.g. *he is → he's*. However, in
        AAVE, this process can go a step further and delete the copula
        altogether, under conditions where other dialects would simply
        contract it.

In an extensive study of the AAVE copula, Labov and his co-researchers
reached the conclusion that, where other dialects of English can *contract*,
AAVE can contract or *delete* the copula, but where other dialects can
neither delete nor contract, AAVE cannot delete or contract (Labov, 1969,
1972, 1982).

Thus in this respect, AAVE appears to behave like a dialect of English.
Labov's conclusion was that AAVE

> is best seen as a distinct subsystem within the larger grammar of English.
> Certain parts of the tense and aspect system are clearly separate
> subsystems in the sense that they are not shared or recognised by other
> dialects. . . . but the gears and axles of English grammatical machinery are
> available to speakers of all dialects, whether or not they use them in
> everyday speech.   (Labov, 1972, pp. 63–4)

Labov's conclusion, stated above, appears to favour the hypothesis that
AAVE is a dialect of English. However, this was not the end of the story.
Baugh (1980, reprinted in Edwards and Winford 1991) was able to
demonstrate that the same syntactic environments which favoured deletion
of the copula in AAVE were *also* those that favoured its absence in Gullah
and in Jamaican Creole. Here now was evidence that creole grammar was
influencing the linguistic behaviour of speakers of AAVE. Baugh's data also
suggested that AAVE, having started out with a creole grammatical system,
could be seen as having decreolised to a greater extent than Gullah or
Jamaican.

The combination of studies like Labov's and Baugh's enabled a synthesis
of views to take place among linguists studying AAVE. In 1978–9 an
important court case took place in Ann Arbor, Michigan, USA. The judge
was required to decide whether the language of black primary school
children was sufficiently different from English to be a barrier to their
learning through the medium of English. If so, then the school system would
be required to take account of that fact. The case was brought by parents
of children at a local school who were concerned that their children
consistently underachieved and were labelled educationally handicapped.
A number of linguists, including Labov, gave evidence as expert witnesses
on behalf of the complainants. The essence of their 'consensus' testimony
(Labov, 1982, p. 192) was that AAVE is a 'subsystem of English with a

distinct set of phonological and syntactic rules that are now in many ways aligned with the rules of other dialects', but also that 'it shows evidence of derivation from an earlier Creole that was closer to the present-day Creoles of the Caribbean'.

The lawyers for the School Board were unable to find expert witnesses to contradict this evidence. Consequently the judge ruled that the Ann Arbor School Board must make plans to enable teachers to identify speakers of Black English (AAVE) and to use that knowledge in teaching such children to read Standard English (Labov, 1982, p. 193).

In spite of the achievement of a consensus among linguists, to the effect that AAVE has historical connections with a creole while at the same time sharing most of its rules with English and thus being 'aligned' with other dialects, there are many unanswered questions. What exactly was the antecedent creole like? How exactly did the process of decreolisation work? And – a question which equally applies to other creoles – how can a language at the same time be a dialect of a standard language and have a distinctive, creole grammar?

The question of the AAVE copula has also refused to go away. Traute Ewers (1996), in a study based on a corpus of transcribed interviews with African-Americans collected in the 1930s (the HOODOO texts, which concern witchcraft and spirit practices), focussed entirely on the form and use of the copula. Her conclusion is that

> the use of *be*-forms in both corpora does not exhibit the kind of structural differences to be expected in the case of a creole origin and an ongoing case of decreolization. On the other hand, there are also a number of findings that cannot be traced back to English varieties or to the process of dialect levelling. (1996, p. 239)

Thus the question of the origins of AAVE remains open. This issue is certain to continue to attract scholarly interest for a long time to come.

3 WHOSE LANGUAGE?

Earlier chapters of this book have given ample evidence of how, in spite of their origins – often under circumstances of colonial domination, forced labour or slavery – pidgins and creoles nevertheless become accepted as useful, respected and even loved possessions of their communities. Such acceptance tends to develop over a period of time, and is dependent on what we might call the *linguistic ecology* of the community and its environment: what other languages are present, who speaks them, and what values attach to them, in both the cultural and the economic sense. In this section we look at two recent studies which show how a pidgin (in the first case) and a probable creole (in the second) have achieved a special status in particular communities where they are used.

We have already seen how Tok Pisin, formerly called New Guinea Pidgin, has become one of the national languages of Papua New Guinea, and has creolised in some parts of the country. Don Kulick, in his study of Gapun, a small, isolated village close to the northern coast of Papua New Guinea, shows how Tok Pisin has come to be integrated into the culture of the village with the consequence that the traditional language of the village is being lost:

> The villagers in Gapun speak a language they call Taiap Mɛr (Taiap Language). The language exists only in Gapun and is spoken actively by exactly eighty-nine people. Even by the standards of Papua New Guinea this is a small language. Since the late 1970s, however, the number of people who speak Taiap has been getting even smaller, despite the fact that the village population is the largest within memory. As of 1987, no village child under 10 actively used this village vernacular in verbal interactions. These children either speak or...are on their way to acquiring Tok Pisin. Many children under 8, expecially boys, appear not even to understand Taiap.   (Kulick, 1992, p. 7)

Why should there be such a massive shift away from Taiap to Tok Pisin? Kulick points out that the older villagers are unable to explain the loss of Taiap by the younger generation. None of them have actively encouraged it; all want their children to learn Taiap. They believe that Taiap has greater expressiveness, and stronger associations with their village and beliefs, than Tok Pisin. To explain the reasons for the shift, Kulick argues, requires an understanding of 'how the villagers view and express the self' (p. 19), which has changed in significant ways since the arrival of Europeans in Papua New Guinea. In the traditional culture of Gapun, two aspects of the self have enormous importance. Both are known by their Tok Pisin names: *hed* ('head') and *save* ('knowing'). *Hed* 'is the dimension of self which is individualistic, irascible, selfish, unbending, haughty, and proud', while '*save* is the sociable, cooperative side of a person. All people, but especially men, are expected to use their *save*, their "knowledge", to "suppress" (*daunim*) their antisocial *heds* and cooperate with their fellow villagers.'

How is this connected with language shift? Kulick (p. 20) elaborates:

> What was once a dual concept of personhood subsumed under one language has become a duality split along linguistic lines. *Hed* has become linked to the vernacular, which in turn has associations with women, the ancestors, and the past. *Save*, on the other hand, has come to be expressed through and by Tok Pisin, which in turn is strongly associated with men, the Catholic church, and modernity.

The distinctions between the old and the modern, Christianity and Paganism, education and lack of education, which have been introduced through contact with Europeans, have been given expression in Gapun culture by association with the concepts of *hed* and *save*, which are far older than the European contact. However, it is Taiap to which the negative values of *hed* and its associations of backwardness attach, while Tok Pisin is associated with *save*. 'The connections that came to be sedimented out in Gapun between Tok Pisin and *save* resulted in that language crystallizing into a valuable possession to be acquired and displayed' (p. 253). Thus,

> In using Tok Pisin, villagers are ... expressing an important and highly valued aspect of self; they are displaying their knowledge and social awareness, their *save*. But in doing this, they are also constituting a situation in which their vernacular is becoming less and less desirable and important. *In reproducing the self, Gapuners are changing the symbolic means through which the self can be reproduced.* ... [I]t is this dynamic which is ultimately responsible for – quite without conscious effort or approval on the part of anyone – language shift in Gapun.
>
> (p. 21; emphasis in original)

The extent to which Tok Pisin has become integrated with, and interpreted in terms of, local cultural beliefs in Gapun shows how strongly a pidgin, despite its origins in contact with outsiders, may become the cultural property of its indigenous users.

In a somewhat similar way, the Baré Indians of Amazonia have reinterpreted the Brazilian 'contact language' *Língua Geral* as the 'traditional language' of their community. Língua Geral, also known as Nheengatu, is actually a form of the indigenous language Tupi. Languages or dialects closely related to Tupi were once spoken over a wide area of Brazil. Língua Geral ('General Language') is thought to be a *koine* or 'lowest common denominator' of these related languages. It was developed by the early colonisers of Brazil – in particular, by Jesuits who established missions among the Indians – and soon became, as its name implies, the general language of a large part of the population. Even the majority of the European colonisers and mixed-race inhabitants of the interior were speakers of Língua Geral. Despite its indigenous origins, indigenous Brazilians who were not speakers of Tupi at first saw Língua Geral as a 'language of the Whites' (*língua dos brancos*) – a mark of the European culture which was imposing itself on the indigenous culture and language (Barros, Borges and Meira, 1994). From the mid-seventeenth century onwards, Língua Geral declined at the expense of Portuguese, which replaced it almost everywhere in Brazil. In the Amazon basin, meanwhile, Língua Geral had been taken up for use as a lingua franca by indigenous Indians whose languages did not belong to the Tupi family. Under these conditions Língua Geral appears to have undergone restructuring and possible pidginisation, though it is not clear that this definitely occurred (Holm, 1989, p. 605). Thus while Língua Geral is a 'contact language' (Portuguese *língua de contato*) in the sense that it originally arose through contacts between Europeans and indigenous people, it is probably a pidgin only in Amazonia, if at all.

What is interesting about the recent history of Língua Geral is that in spite of it originally being regarded as a 'Language of the Whites' among Amazonian Indians, some indigenous groups have reinterpreted its symbolism and adopted it as their own 'traditional' language.

The Baré (from the Arawak linguistic family) who have practically lost their original language...have adopted Língua Geral, with which they have long been acquainted, as their 'traditional language' vis-à-vis the white society, with a clear objective of ethnic differentiation and affirmation.... [T]he language has a fundamental role in marking a differentiation which simultaneously transforms them and keeps them Baré, or rather, a group distinct from the 'others'.

(Barros, Borges and Meira, 1994, p. 67)

For the Baré, Língua Geral has taken on the role of their 'traditional language' following the loss of the original Baré language. This means that the Baré people now acknowledge Língua Geral rather than Baré as the language of their traditional activities, although Portuguese will also be used for some purposes, including communication with Portuguese speakers from outside the community, who do not speak Língua Geral. (Portuguese is learnt throughout Brazil as either a first or second language.) While to other groups (at least in previous centuries) Língua Geral was a European imposition, although it originated in Brazil, for this group it has come to stand for *indigenous* Amazonian values.

In the case of both the Gapun villagers and the Baré people, we see a contact language being treated as *cultural capital* in a sense developed by the French sociologist Pierre Bourdieu (for example, in Bourdieu, 1991a, 1991b). For the speakers in question, the language is not valued merely as *functional* (i.e. in terms of its usefulness); it has come to have a symbolic value within the culture of the community concerned. In Gapun, the association between Tok Pisin and the positive values of *save* has led to a language shift at the expense of the traditional language Taiap. Among the Baré, the contact language has replaced their ancestral language as the medium of expression for their folk traditions. Here we can see the result not only of *language* contact, but of *cultural* contact as well; the creation of new and hybrid cultures (with language, of course, playing a key role) in times of rapid and widespread social change.

4   CONCLUSION: MARGINAL LANGUAGES?

John Reinecke, the Hawaii-based researcher who almost single-handedly put pidgin and creole studies on the agenda of linguistics in the first half of the twentieth century, entitled his Ph.D. thesis (completed in 1937) *Marginal Languages: A Sociological Survey of the Creole Languages and Trade Jargons*. For Reinecke, 'marginal' meant at the periphery of linguistic study, as well as at the periphery of society. 'Marginal' languages were often scarcely recognised as languages at all, being classified merely as broken or debased forms of 'proper' languages.

Fortunately, the attitude of linguists has undergone a major change since Reinecke was writing his Ph.D. Pidgins and creoles are now not only considered legitimate objects of study, they are regarded as sufficiently central to linguistics to warrant a mention, and sometimes a chapter or so, in most introductory general linguistics textbooks. But this positive attitude generally does not extend much beyond the narrow boundaries of academic linguistics. We have seen, especially in Chapter 8, that pidgin and creole-speaking communities are generally divided on the issue of to what extent their language should be promoted. While linguists and educators often take a positive stand with respect to the contact language, many governments do not. In this, they typically claim to have the support of the general population, who want to be thought of as speaking, or to have their children taught, a 'proper language'. Whether or not the majority of the population actually think like this, it is clear that the educated elite in many places have a vested interest in keeping the pidgin or creole in a subordinate position. Under such conditions, even when the pidgin or creole is publicly valued as part of the national culture, this is often conditional on the language 'knowing its place' and not presenting a threat to the established European official language. Thus we can say that even in countries where the majority of the population are pidgin or creole speakers, the languages in question are not particularly highly valued, widely studied, or well understood. Although this is not true everywhere, it is unfortunately true in many parts of the world.

Elsewhere, in spite of efforts by linguists to improve public understanding of pidgins and creoles, ignorance about them is still widespread, not least among those whose role is to inform the wider public. As part of a wider ranging project aimed at finding out how accurately linguistic matters were reported by non-specialist reference works such as atlases and encyclope-dias, I examined what several such publications had to say about pidgins and creoles. 'Depressingly little' was the answer in many cases, as pidgins in particular seem to be invisible to the compilers of many of these volumes. One reference atlas, for example, has an entry for Papua New Guinea which reads: 'Official language: English (but the people speak more than 700 languages)' (Kingfisher, 1993). There is no mention of Tok Pisin, which is also an official language, and the one which, as we have seen, enables communication to take place among speakers of those 700 languages (the figure may or may not be accurate).

Clumsy and misleading attempts to characterise creole languages are common – though less common than their existence being ignored altogether. The *Third World Guide* says of Haiti, for example: 'Most people speak creole, a local dialect combined with Spanish, English, French and African languages.' Several publications, in acknowledging that 'Creole' is one of the languages of certain countries, fail to make any distinction between Portuguese-lexicon, French-lexicon, and English-lexicon 'creole', potentially giving the impression that the same creole is spoken in, say, Haiti (French-lexicon) and the Cape Verde Islands (Portuguese-lexicon). The two books already mentioned, between them provide an impressive amount of misinformation about the languages of Surinam (see Chapter 5):

> Official language: Dutch. . . . Besides the official language, Surinamers speak a local dialect, Spanish, English, Hindi, Javanese and Chinese. (Kingfisher, 1993)

English and Spanish, though spoken, are very much foreign languages in Surinam (Hindi, Javanese and Chinese are important ethnic community languages there); but Sranan Tongo, a lingua franca for most Surinamese and probably the language with the largest number of native speakers in Surinam, has become a nameless 'local dialect'!

> Dutch and Spanish (official). Also spoken are English, Hindi, Javanese, and a creole dialect (called either Taki-Taki or Senango-Tongo [*sic*], depending on the region) based on African languages mixed with Dutch, Spanish and English.   (*Third World Guide 89/90*)

In addition to wrongly giving Spanish as one of the official languages of Surinam, the *Third World Guide* misspells Sranan Tongo and gives the outdated and potentially offensive name *Taki-Taki*. Disappointing, especially as the editors proclaim that it 'was about time that the Third World had its own reference book and we set out to make it'.

Thus Reinecke's term 'marginal' remains an apt metaphor, as outside of the discipline of linguistics, contact languages rarely receive the recognition they deserve. Furthermore, a 'margin' can only exist relative to something else: for example, the margin of the page on which these words are printed exists only by virtue of the fact that it is a part of the page which has not been printed on. If there were no blank space at all at the edges, there would of course be no margins; but it is also true that we would not speak of a margin if the *whole* page were blank. Extending this analogy to pidgins and creoles, it is still nearly always the 'languages of empire' which play the part of the printed text, pushing contact languages to the edge of the page. The analogy is quite appropriate when we consider that the position of *written* contact languages is particularly weak compared with that of the European standard languages like English, French, Spanish and Dutch. Even where spoken pidgins and creoles play a *central* part in the life of a community, their written forms, where they exist, are more likely to be on the margins. (There are a few exceptions to this, some of which have been discussed in Chapter 8.)

A newspaper published in the Netherlands, *De Surinaamse Krant* (Dutch for 'The Surinamese Paper') of September 1994, provides a nice illustration of the last point (see Figure 9.1). The newspaper clearly addresses itself to a readership who know both Dutch and Sranan, as Sranan is found in several places in the paper. (It is not safe to assume that all readers are native speakers of Sranan.) However, the text is overwhelmingly in Dutch. Individual words of Sranan Tongo are scattered throughout – for example, the name of the winning carnival troupe *Trafassi* ('Otherwise', from English *other* or *t'other* and *fashion*), which is on the front page – but there are only a small number of 'pockets' of Sranan where more than an isolated word can be found. On page 2, we find an advertisement for a *Surinaamse Culturele Winkel* (Dutch for 'Surinamese Cultural Shop') called *Kankantrie* (Sranan – a type of tree), which lists as available (Dutch *verkrijgbaar*) a long list of medicinal and cosmetic plants, giving their names in Sranan. On page 3, the headline *Puwema* (Sranan for 'poem') introduces a column about a Surinamese poet: but the text, including a short poem, is entirely in Dutch. On page 4, we find another poem, in eight verses each of four lines, about the current political and economic situation of Surinam. At first sight, the poem seems to be in Dutch; but on closer inspection, two words of Sranan occur in the third line, while there is a complete line of Sranan in the fifth verse (*Kondre man oen aartjie mie* – '(fellow) countrymen, listen (hark) to me'). Of the last two verses, the first is all in Sranan, and the second all in Dutch. Finally, in the Letters section on page 6, we find a letter from a correspondent who argues that Surinam is right to accept refugees from Haiti. The whole letter is in Dutch apart from the closing sentence: *Bon wintis e kon, deng tja a gowtoe djie alla sma.* 'When good spirits come, they bring gold for everyone.' Significantly, this is not a line of prose created by the letter's author, but a Sranan proverb.

There are books available, including novels, poetry and children's books, which are entirely, or almost entirely, written in Sranan. Yet it is striking how in the newspaper described above – a much more 'everyday' text than a book of poems or a novel – Sranan occupies a 'marginal' space. This is not to deny altogether its power for writers and readers – clearly the rallying cry of the poet, and the proverb quoted by the letter writer, gain in significance by being in Sranan rather than Dutch. Nevertheless the role of Sranan in this edition of *De Surinaamse Krant* could well be described as 'marginal'.

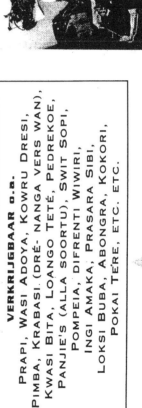

Figure 9.1 An advertisement from *De Surinaamse Krant* in Sranan and Dutch

It is chiefly there for its *symbolic* power, as the language which identifies Surinamese people *as* Surinamese. When it is used, it is often used *strategically* – as in the poet's call, *kondre man oen aartjie mie*: 'hear me, fellow countrymen!'.

From the example of *De Surinaamse Krant* we can see how Sranan occupies a position at the margins of the world of printed language, and yet has a symbolic power out of proportion to the amount of actual use. The same point could be made of London Jamaican (Chapter 7), Tok Pisin and Baré (this chapter), Fly Taal (Chapter 1) and many others. As we reach the end of this book, it provides an important reminder that the value of contact languages lies not only in their usefulness as means of communication, but also – and in some cases, mainly – in their power as symbols of group identity and shared values.

5 EXERCISE

At the end of Chapter 1 you were asked to 'have an argument with a friend, real or imaginary' in favour of or against using terms like 'baby talk' and 'broken' to describe Tok Pisin. In the light of everything you have learnt from this book, revise your discussion. Do you still hold the same viewpoint? What are the main ways in which you would change your line of argument?

EPILOGUE: WHY STUDY PIDGINS AND CREOLES?

At the end of this volume, it seems a good idea to ask: why go to the trouble of studying pidgin and creole languages? And if we do decide to study them, do they deserve to be studied as a special grouping, rather than each one being considered separately in its own right? My answer to the second question lies in the earlier chapters of this book. Pidgins and creoles have certain common characteristics which mean that it makes sense to study them as a group – not a homogeneous group, admittedly, because there is great diversity even among the small sample of pidgins and creoles described here, but a group whose common features may reveal something to us, both about those languages which are within the group and about those which are outside it. The first question, however, is less easy to answer. Why should we care enough about pidgins and creoles to want to study them?

In a discussion of this question, Peter Mühlhäusler (1992) offers a variety of answers, including the following:

- They can provide a model of unmonitored second language acquisition, i.e. a detailed study of pidgin evolution would enable us to watch the development of second language learning in a 'natural' state.

- They can give us a better understanding of the processes of linguistic accommodation which are active in intercultural communication. Pidgins provide us with 'real-life' examples of how speakers without a common language or even much in the way of shared culture can nevertheless achieve effective communication.

- A pidgin might be able to serve as a 'pivot language' for machine translation, i.e. translation by computer. For many years linguists and computer scientists have been trying to develop systems which will automatically translate one language into another. Such systems will be more versatile and efficient if, rather than simply being designed to translate from language A into language X, they can translate from A into a 'pivot' language P, and from P into X. The advantage becomes obvious if we want to translate between all the different languages of a grouping (for example, the European Union). If 10 languages are involved, we would have 100 different language pairs. If we could find a 'pivot' to translate each language to and from, we would have only 10 pairs (each language to and from the pivot language). Mühlhäusler suggests that a 'culturally neutral simple pivot language' is the ideal, and a pidgin might be well suited to this purpose; though he adds 'the potential of such a solution remains to be explored'.

In addition to these potential uses of pidgins and creoles, Mühlhäusler discusses what, to date, has probably been the main 'use' of pidgins and creoles for linguists since the resurgence of interest in this field in the last third of the twentieth century. This is their use as 'theory busters', i.e. as counter-examples to prevailing or generally accepted wisdom among linguists about the nature of language or the appropriate form of linguistic theory. In Chapter 1, I mentioned the nineteenth-century Austrian linguist Schuchardt, one of the first serious scholars of creole languages. For Schuchardt, creole languages were interesting for the way they provided challenges to the 'family tree' model of language relatedness.

Mühlhäusler believes that linguists like Schuchardt were 'right in maintaining that pidgins and creoles offered the best point of departure for rethinking the linguistic enterprise'. More recently, he argues, the study of pidgins and creoles has dealt a blow to the prevailing linguistic paradigm (structuralist and generative linguistics), which tends to treat languages as static objects, to be studied without reference to their history and development. Pidgins and creoles cannot be understood without reference to their history, and the work of De Camp, Bailey and others described in Chapter 7 has shown how the synchronic variation within creoles reflects historical changes in progress. This argues for a discipline of Linguistics which treats language change and development as central rather than peripheral, and language itself as dynamic and social rather than static and individual.

Mühlhäusler's next, and most important point, is that

> there is no *object* or thing that can be studied. All that one can perceive is people communicating with one another in real settings, using verbal signals together with many non-verbal devices.... [T]he observation of how people communicate by means of pidgins necessitates the acceptance of an integrationist's view of language (Harris, 1981), one that looks at the numerous interdependencies between communicative processes, setting and context.

In other words, the study of pidgins and creoles forces us to stop conceptualising language as a *thing*, an *object* which can be captured and put under the microscope and dissected using a set of tools developed by linguists. This conceptualisation of language as an object is usually referred to as the *reification* of language (Latin *res*, 'thing'; hence 'making language into a thing') and is an approach to the study of language used by many linguists (sometimes without realising it) and criticised by others, especially those whose main interest is in creole languages. (See, for example, Le Page, 1994). Instead of a neat, and tidily analysable object, we can instead see language as a *process*, or a set of *practices*, or a *space* in which social actions are carried out. Pidgins and creoles remind us, in other words, that without people interacting in a context, there can be no language. If this point seems obvious, it is worth noting that for much of the twentieth century, many linguists have subscribed to linguistic theories which treat social aspects of language, and communicative interactions, as marginal or irrelevant to the study of language. A focus on cognitive and structural aspects of language, however, is not incompatible with an interest in the social realities of language use. Indeed, the two are interdependent, a point made by Chomsky (1986, chapter 2).

In addition to these reasons for studying pidgins and creoles, there are others. We have seen in earlier chapters many of the aspects of pidgins and creoles which make them interesting to linguists. Grammatical and phonological complexity is reduced to a minimum in the simplest of pidgins, giving us a sort of 'base line' of what is absolutely necessary for communication where no common language exists. From this we may be able to learn something about the cognitive structure of language and how it is acquired (see, for example, Slobin, 1977). At the same time, development in pidgins and creoles is extremely rapid, so that a creole may develop over a short space of time (a decade or two), undergoing changes which would take a 'normally transmitted' language several centuries. This accelerated rate of development makes them useful 'laboratory animals' (a point made by Mühlhäusler in his paper mentioned above) for the study of languages generally, but also makes them interesting in their own right, both from the point of view of grammatical and lexical development, and from the point of view of how they function within society.

Lastly, pidgins and creoles are a group of mainly low-status languages which nevertheless serve extremely important communicative functions for their speakers. They provide many interesting and challenging problems for linguists and language planners who are looking for ways of enabling better lives for their speakers – for example through general educational programmes, rural development, or literacy programmes. Some of these have been discussed or described in Chapter 8 or elsewhere in this book. Although most of these problems are shared with other low-status and indigenous languages, pidgins and creoles do have some special problems – in particular the fact that they share so much of their lexis with high-status languages (their lexifiers). This is one reason why pidgins and creoles remain poorly understood, even by their own speakers. We could say, then, that one of the best reasons for studying pidgins and creoles is to enable us – and by 'us' I mean not just students of language but anyone who speaks a pidgin or creole language or lives in a country where a pidgin or creole is spoken – to come to a better understanding of this fascinating group of languages. Through such an understanding we can start to grasp the role that they play, or *could* play, in improving the lives of their speakers. If this book has contributed towards that aim, it has been well worth the effort of writing it.

KEY POINTS: mixed languages, sign languages, African-American vernacular

Mixed languages:

- are the result of contact between two languages, usually where one community assimilates another;
- are grammatically as complex as their source languages;
- are rare compared to pidgins and creoles.

Sign languages:

- are fully fledged languages;
- show some structural similarities to pidgins/creoles (e.g. lack of articles and copula);
- are often transmitted differently from spoken languages as deaf children of hearing parents usually learn to sign outside the home.

African-American Vernacular English:

- is historically connected with the Atlantic/Caribbean creoles, especially Gullah;
- has undergone extensive decreolisation;
- in some ways behaves like a dialect of English;
- in some ways behaves like a creole.

Glossary

Abrupt creolisation: where a creole comes into being, usually in less than one generation, before a stable pidgin has had time to emerge.

Acrolect: the language variety in a *post-creole continuum* which is closest to standard; the local variety of the *lexifier* language.

Adstrate: languages which have provided a grammatical or lexical 'stratum' or influence on a pidgin/creole. Used where clear *superstrate* and *substrate* languages are not identifiable.

Aspect: the grammatical encoding of the *completeness* or *incompleteness* of an action.

Attributive adjectives: adjectives which modify a noun directly. *See predicate adjectives*.

Basilect: the variety of creole that is 'deepest', 'broadest' or most different from the *lexifier* language.

Calque: a word or lexical expression which is made up of lexical items from the *lexifier* language but follows exactly the pattern or idiom of a *substrate* language.

Cleft and **predicate cleft**: constructions which focus an element of the sentence by moving it close to the beginning. **Predicate cleft** moves the verb to the front of the sentence but leaves a copy in the original position.

Code switching: alternation between languages by one bi- or multilingual speaker within the course of the same interaction, e.g. within the same sentence or within the same conversation.

Copula: the verb *to be* or its equivalent.

Creolisation: the process whereby a creole comes into existence.

Creoloid: a language which originated through language contact and which has creole-like features but is apparently not a full creole.

Decreolisation: the process whereby a creole becomes more like its *lexifier* as a result of social pressures.

Derivational morphology: morphology which marks word-class membership and may be used to derive a word of one class from a word belonging to another.

Diffusion: where a speech community has relaxed linguistic norms, so that a wide range of variation is possible, the community would be said to have *diffuse* linguistic norms. *See focussing*.

Diglossia: a linguistic situation where two languages are used within the same society but in rigidly differentiated circumstances, so that there are few or no circumstances where they could be used interchangeably.

Etymological (orthography): an orthography for a creole language which uses the spelling conventions of the *lexifier*, i.e. treats the creole as a dialect of the lexifier.

Extended (or **expanded**) **pidgin**: a pidgin which is not only grammatically and lexically stable but has extended its use into the everyday life of its speakers and is used in a wide range of activities.

Family tree model: a model of language change where a 'parent' language gives rise to two or more 'offspring' which developed from it through 'natural' processes of sound, meaning and grammatical change.

Focussing: the process whereby a community of speakers 'focus' on a set of linguistic norms. A language which has highly focussed norms is one where the range of acceptable variation is relatively narrow.

Foreigner talk: a special register of a language which is used for addressing non-native speakers of that language.

Gradualism: the hypothesis that creoles developed gradually, over decades or centuries, rather than abruptly in the space of a generation.

Grammaticalisation: the process whereby a mainly 'content' word (e.g. verb, adverb) becomes a mainly grammatical 'function word' (e.g. preposition, tense marker).

Inflectional morphology: morphology which marks grammatical relations such as tense, number or case.

Inflections: morphemes which mark grammatical categories such as plural, past tense, object, etc.

Input languages: all the languages significantly involved in the formation of a pidgin or creole.

Jargon: the most basic form of contact language, which lacks any stable or consistent norms of grammar and has a very restricted vocabulary drawn inconsistently from the languages involved.

Language acquisition: the process whereby a child acquires a language natively.

Language Bioprogram Hypothesis: the hypothesis that a 'biological blueprint' determines the form of language when children are exposed to a pidgin too fragmented to provide adequate input. See Chapter 6, Section 2.1.

Language convergence: a phenomenon where languages which coexist in the same community adjust their structures so that they become more similar to each other.

Language learning: the process of learning a second or subsequent *non-native* language.

Language mixing (also called *language intertwining*): a phenonemon whereby a new language comes into being with the grammar of one previously existing language, and the vocabulary of another.

Language of wider communication: a language which is used as a second language by a group in order to communicate outside their own speech community.

Lect: a language variety, compare *dialect, idiolect*.

Lexifier: the language which is the source of the majority of the lexicon (vocabulary) of a pidgin or creole.

Lingua franca: a *language of wider communication* which is widely used over a relatively large geographical area among a number of different groups.

Metaphorical extension: where basic items of vocabulary take on wider meanings through being used metaphorically.

Modality: the grammatical encoding of possibility, necessity, etc., typically expressed in English by use of 'modals' such as *can, must, may*, etc., in conjunction with the main verb, and in other languages by equivalents of these or by grammatical marking of the main verb.

Monogenesis: the theory that all present-day pidgins and creoles are descended directly or indirectly from an earlier Mediterranean pidgin.

Multifunctionality: where one word belongs to several word classes, e.g. functions as a noun, a verb and an adjective.

Nativisation: the process whereby a community takes on a new language as its native language, possibly adapting its phonology and grammar.

Normal transmission: the process by which languages are 'normally' passed from generation to generation, children learning the language from adults, older children and peers.

Orthography: a system of spelling a written language.

Pidginisation: the process whereby a language is reduced grammatically to become a pidgin.

Polygenesis: *polygenetic* theories hold that the different pidgins and creoles of the world may have originated independently of one another. Compare *monogenesis*.

Post-Creole continuum: a continuum of minimally different language varieties (*lects*) which is hypothesised to develop when a creole is in continuing contact with its lexifier language. *See also* **basilect**, **acrolect**.

Predicate adjectives: adjectives linked to their subject by a verb such as *be, appear, become*.

Realised and unrealised complements: a 'realised' complement of a verb is one where the action of the complement is understood to have taken place, e.g. in *she began to speak* we understand that she spoke, even if she did not finish. In an unrealised complement the action may not have taken place at all, e.g. *she promised to speak* does not tell us whether she actually spoke or not.

Recreolisation: movement of a *decreolised* creole *away* from the standard, i.e. to become more *basilectal*.

Reduplication: repetition of a morpheme or syllable, normally to fulfil grammatical function.

Relativisation: the process whereby a relative clause is formed. In some languages this involves *subject-copying*, i.e. using a pronoun to stand for the subject in the relative clause.

Relexification: the complete or nearly complete replacement of the vocabulary of a language by vocabulary from another language.

Restructured (English, French, etc.): varieties of a lexifier language which have undergone substantial *restructuring*.

Restructuring: changes in grammatical and/or lexical structure which are due to complete or partial pidginisation and/or creolisation of a language.

Stable pidgin: a pidgin which has reached the stage of having fairly stable and consistent grammatical and lexical norms of its own (different from those of its *lexifier*).

Stative: a verb which denotes a *state* (rather than an action). In some languages adjectives are stative verbs ('to be cold', 'to be red', etc.).

Substrate: the indigenous language(s) with which the *lexifier* came into contact during the formation of a pidgin or creole.

Superstrate: the *lexifier*, together with any other non-indigenous languages which came into contact with the *substrate* during the formation of a pidgin or creole.

Tense: the grammatical encoding of relations of *time* (past, present, future etc.).

Tertiary hybridisation: this is said to have occurred when a pidgin comes to be used for communication between speakers who are *not* speakers of the original target language, i.e. all its users are now second-language speakers.

Bibliography

Adams, L. Emilie (1991) *Understanding Jamaican Patois: An Introduction to Afro-Jamaican Grammar* (Kingston, Jamaica: Kingston Publishers).

Aitchison, J. (1996) 'Undergeneralisation and Overgeneralisation in Creole Acquisition', in: Wekker (1996), pp. 9–31.

Alleyne, M. (1980) *Comparative Afro-American* (Ann Arbor, Mich.: Karoma Press).

Anderson, B. (1983) *Imagined Communities: Reflections on the Origin and Spread of Nationalism* (London: Verso, revised and extended edition, 1991).

Appel, R. and Verhoeven, L. (1994) 'Decolonization, Language Planning and Education', in: Arends et al. (1994), pp. 65–74.

Arends, J. (1993) 'Towards a Gradualist Model of Creolization', in: Byrne and Holm, (1993), pp. 371–80.

Arends, J. and Bruyn, A. (1994) 'Gradualist and Developmental Hypotheses', in: Arends et al. (eds), pp. 111–20.

Arends, J., Muysken, P. and Smith, N. (eds) (1994) *Pidgins and Creoles: An Introduction* (Amsterdam: John Benjamins).

Bailey, B. L. (1966) *Jamaican Creole Syntax: A Transformational Approach* (Cambridge University Press).

Bailey, B. L. (1971) 'Jamaican Creole: Can Dialect Boundaries be Defined?' in: Hymes (1971), pp. 341–8.

Bailey, C.-J. N. (1973) *Variation and Linguistic Theory* (Washington, D.C.: Center for Applied Linguistics).

Baker, P. (1972) *Kreol: A Description of Mauritian Creole* (London: Hurst).

Baker, P. and Corne, C. (1982) *Isle de France Creole: Affinities and Origins* (Ann Arbor, Mich.: Karoma)

Bakker, P. (1992) *'A Language of our Own'. The Genesis of Michif, the Mixed Cree–French Language of the Canadian Métis*, Ph.D. dissertation, University of Amsterdam (to be published by Oxford University Press).

Bakker, P. (1994a) 'Pidgins', in: Arends et al. (1994), pp. 25–40.

Bakker, P. (1994b) 'Michif, the Cree–French Mixed Language of the Métis Buffalo Hunters in Canada', in: Bakker and Mous (1994), pp. 13–33.

Bakker, P. and Mous, M. (1994) *Mixed Languages* (Amsterdam: IFOTT).

Barbag-Stoll, A. (1983) 'Social and Linguistic History of Nigerian Pidgin English as Spoken by the Yoruba with Special Reference to the English Derived Lexicon' (Tübingen: Stauffenberg Verlag).

Barros, M. C. D., Borges, L. C. and Meira, M. (1994) 'A Língua Geral Como Identidade Construída', *Papia (Revista de Crioulos de Base Ibérica)*, 3(2), pp. 62–9.

Bauer, A. (1974) *Das melanesische und chinesische Pidginenglisch* (Regensburg: Verlag Hans Carl).

Baugh, J. (1980) 'A Reexamination of the Black English Copula', in: Labov (ed.), *Locating Language in Space and Time* (New York: Academic Press), reprinted in Edwards and Winford (1991), pp. 32–59.

Bell, A. (1984) 'Language Style as Audience Design', *Language in Society*, **13**, pp. 145–204.

Bhattacharjya, D. (1994) 'Nagamese: Pidgin, Creole or Creoloid?', *California Linguistic Notes*, **24**(2), pp. 34–50.

Bickerton, D. (1973) 'On the Nature of a Creole Continuum', *Language*, **49**, pp. 641–69.

Bickerton, D. (1975) *Dynamics of a Creole System* (Cambridge: Cambridge University Press).

Bickerton, D. (1981) *Roots of Language* (Ann Arbor, Mich.: Karoma Press).

Bickerton, D. (1984) 'The Language Bioprogram Hypothesis', *The Behavioural and Brain Sciences*, **7**, pp. 173–221.

Bickerton, D. (1986) 'The Sociohistorical Matrix of Creolization', *Journal of Pidgin and Creole Languages*, **7**(2), pp. 307–18.

Bickerton, D. (1988) 'Creole Languages and the Bioprogram', in F. J. Newmeyer (ed.), *Linguistics: The Cambridge Survey* (Cambridge: Cambridge University Press), pp. 268–84.

Bilby, K. M. (1983) 'How the "Older Heads" Talk: A Jamaican Maroon Spirit Possession Language and its Relationship to the Creoles of Surinam and Sierra Leone', *New West Indian Guide*, **57**(1–2), pp. 37–88.

Blackshire-Belay, C. (1993) 'Foreign Workers' German: Is it a Pidgin?' in: Byrne and Holm (1993), pp. 431–40.

Bloomfield, L. (1933) *Language* (New York: Henry Holt).

Bold, J. D. (1974) *Fanagalo Phrase Book Grammar and Dictionary* (Johannesburg: Hugh Keartland).

Bollée, A. (1980) 'Zum Projekt eines Dictionaire Etymologique du Créole', in: Bork et al. (eds), *Romanica Europaea et Americana* (Bonn: Bouvier Verlag), pp. 68–76.

Bourdieu, P. (1991a) 'The Production and Reproduction of Legitimate Language', in: Bourdieu (1991c), pp. 43–65.

Bourdieu, P. (1991b) 'Price Formation and the Anticipation of Profits', in: Bourdieu (1991c), pp. 66–102 .

Bourdieu, P. (1991c) *Language and Symbolic Power*, edited and introduced by John B. Thompson (Cambridge: Polity Press).

Brennan, M. (1992) 'The Visual World of BSL: An Introduction by Mary Brennan', in: D. Brien (ed.), *Dictionary of British Sign Language* (London: Faber and Faber).

Broch, I. and Jahr, E.H. (1981) *Russenorsk – et pidginspråk i Norge* (Oslo: Novus Forlag).

Broch, O. (1927) 'Russenorsk', *Archiv für Slavische Phonologie*, **49**, pp. 209–62.

Broch, O. (1930) 'Russenorsk tekstmateriale. Maal og Minne', *Norske Studier*, pp. 113–140.

Bynoe-Andriolo, E. Y. and Sorie Yillah, M. (1975) 'Predicate Clefting in Afro-European Creoles. Proceedings of the Sixth Conference on African Linguistics', Ohio State University Working Papers in Linguistics, **20**, pp. 234–9.

Byrne, F. (1987) *Grammatical Relations in a Radical Creole: Verb Complementation in Saramaccan* (Amsterdam: John Benjamins).

Byrne, F. and Holm, J. (eds) (1993) *Atlantic meets Pacific: A Global View of Pidginization and Creolization* (Amsterdam: John Benjamins).

Calloway, Rev. Canon (1868) *Nursery Tales, Traditions and Histories of the Zulus* (London: Trübner and Co.).

Cassidy, F. G. (1961) *Jamaica Talk* (London: Macmillan).

Cassidy, F. G. (1978) 'A Revised Phonemic Orthography for Anglophone Caribbean Creoles', paper presented at the Conference of the Society for Caribbean Linguistics, Cave Hill, Barbados.

Cassidy, F. G. (1993) 'A Short Note on Creole Orthography', *Journal of Pidgin and Creole Languages*, **8**(1), pp. 135–7.

Cassidy, F. G. and Le Page, R. B. (1967/1980) *Dictionary of Jamaican English* (Cambridge: Cambridge University Press).

Chaudenson, R. (1974) *Le lexique du parler créole de la Réunion* (Paris: Champion).

Chomsky, N. (1965) *Aspects of the Theory of Syntax* (Cambridge, Mass.: MIT Press).

Chomsky, N. (1986) *Knowledge of Language: Its Nature, Origin, and Use* (New York: Praeger).

Clark, R. (1979) 'In Search of Beach-la-Mar', *Te Reo*, **22**, pp. 3–64.

Cokely, D. (1984) 'Foreigner Talk and Learners' Grammar', *The Reflector*, vol. 8 (Winter 1984).

Cole, D. T. (1964) 'Fanagalo and the Bantu Languages in South Africa', in: Hymes, D. (ed.), *Language in Culture and Society: A Reader in Linguistics and Anthropology* (New York: Harper and Row), pp. 547–54.

Cook, V. (1993) *Linguistics and Second Language Acquisition* (London: Macmillan).

Craig, D. (1980) 'Models for Education Policy in Creole-speaking Communities', in: Valdman and Highfield (1980), pp. 245–66.

Dalphinis, M. (1985) *Caribbean and African Languages: Social History, Language, Literature and Education* (London: Karia Press).

De Bono, E. (1981) 'Disturbing Thoughts about Thinking', *Times Higher Education Supplement*, 8th May 1981, p. 10.

D'Costa, J. and Lalla, B. (eds) (1989) *Voices in Exile: Jamaican Texts of the 18th and 19th Centuries* (Tuscaloosa and London: University of Alabama Press).

De Camp, D. (1971) 'Towards a Generative Analysis of a Post-creole Speech Continuum', in: Hymes, D. (ed.), *Pidginization and Creolization of Languages*, Proceedings of a Conference held at the University of the West Indies, Mona, Jamaica, April 1968 (Cambridge: Cambridge University Press), pp. 349–70.

den Besten, H. (1978) 'Cases of Possible Syntactic Interference in the Development of Afrikaans', in: Muysken, P. (ed.), *Amsterdam Creole Studies II* (Amsterdam: Institute for General Linguistics of the University of Amsterdam).

den Besten, H. (1986) 'Double Negation and the Genesis of Afrikaans', in: Muysken and Smith (1986).

De Ziel, H. F. (ed.) (1973) *Johannes King: Life at Maripaston* (Netherlands: Verhandelingen van het Koninklijk Instituut voor Taal-, Land- en Volkenkunde).

Deuchar, M. (1987) 'Sign Languages as Creoles and Chomsky's Notion of Universal Grammar', in: Modgil, S. and Modgil, C., *Noam Chomsky: Consensus and Controversy* (Brighton: Falmer Press).

Devonish, H. (1989) *Talking in Tones* (London: Karia Press).

Devonish, H. (1986a) *Language and Liberation: Creole Language Politics in the Caribbean* (London: Karia Press).

Devonish, H. (1986b) 'The Decay of Neo-colonial Official Language Policies. The Case of the English-lexicon Creoles of the Commonwealth Caribbean', in: Görlach and Holm (1986).

Dillard, J. L. (1972) *Black English: Its History and Usage in the United States* (New York: Random House).

Edwards, V. K. (1979) *The West Indian Language Issue in British Schools: Challenges and Responses* (London: Routledge and Kegan Paul).

Edwards, V. K. and Ladd, P. (1984) 'The Linguistic Status of British Sign Language', in: Sebba and Todd (1984), pp. 83–94.

Edwards, W. and Winford, D. (eds) (1991) *Verb Phrase Patterns in Black English and Creole* (Detroit: Wayne State University Press).

Elugbe, B. O. and Omamor, A. P. (1991) *Nigerian Pidgin: Background and Prospects* (Ibadan: Heinemann Educational Books, Nigeria).

Enga Province Business Directory (1991) (Wabag, Papua New Guinea: Placer).

Ewers, Traute (1996) *The Origin of American Black English: Be-forms in the Hoodoo Texts* (Berlin/New York: Mouton de Gruyter).

Ferguson, C. (1971) 'Absence of Copula and the Notion of Simplicity: A Study of Normal Speech, Baby Talk, Foreigner Talk and Pidgins', in: Hymes (1971).

Flint, E. H. (1964) 'The Language of Norfolk Island', in: Ross and Moverley (1964), pp. 189–201.

Forde, D. (ed.) (1968) *Efik Traders of Old Calabar* (London: Oxford University Press).

Fox, J. A. (1973) 'Russenorsk: A Study in Language Adaptivity' (University of Chicago, mimeograph).

Fox, J. A. (1983) 'Simplified Input and Negotiation in Russenorsk', in: Anderson, R. (ed.), *Pidginization and Creolization as Language Acquisition* (Rowley, Mass.: Newbury House), pp. 94–108.

Gardner-Chloros, P. (1991) *Language Selection and Switching in Strasbourg* (Oxford: Oxford University Press).

Gibson, K. A. (1982) 'Tense and Aspect in Guyanese Creole: A Syntactic, Semantic and Pragmatic Analysis', D.Phil. dissertation, University of York.

Gilroy, P. (1987) *There Ain't No Black in the Union Jack* (London: Hutchinson).

Golovko, E. (1994) 'Mednyj Aleut or Copper Island Aleut: An Aleut–Russian Mixed Language', in: Bakker and Mous (1994), pp. 113–21.

Goodman, M. (1971) 'The Strange Case of Mbugu', in: Hymes (1971), pp. 243–354.

Görlach, M. and Holm, J. (eds) (1986) *Focus on the Caribbean* (Amsterdam: John Benjamins).

Gumperz, J. J. and Wilson, R. D. (1971) 'Convergence and Creolization: A Case from the Indo-Aryan-Dravidian Border', in Hall (1966).

Guthrie, Malcolm (1967–72): *Comparative Bantu: An Introduction to the Comparative Linguistics and Prehistory of the Bantu Languages*, in 4 volumes (London: Greggs).

Guttman, L. (1944) 'A Basis for Scaling Qualitative Data', *American Sociological Review*, 9, pp. 139–50.

Hall, R. A. (1943) *Melanesian Pidgin English: Grammar, Texts, Vocabulary* (Baltimore: Linguistic Society of America at Waverley Press).

Hall, R. A. (1953) *Haitian Creole: Grammar – Texts – Vocabulary*, Memoirs of the American Folklore Society, Volume 43 (Philadelphia: American Folklore Society).

Hall, R. A. (1961) 'How Pidgin English has Evolved', *New Scientist*, 9, pp. 413–15.

Hall, R. A. (1966) *Pidgin and Creole Languages* (Ithaca and London: Cornell University Press).

Hancock, I. F. (1969) 'A Provisional Comparison of the English-based Atlantic Creoles', *African Language Review*, **8**, pp. 7–32.

Harding, E. (1984) 'Foreigner Talk: A Conversational-analysis Approach', in: Sebba and Todd (1984), pp. 141–52.

Harris, R. (1981) *The Language Myth* (London: Duckworth).

Harris, J. (1984) 'Syntactic Variation and Dialect Divergence', *Journal of Linguistics*, **20**, pp. 303–27.

Heine, B. (1973) *Pidgin-Sprachen im Bantu-Bereich* (Berlin: Dietrich Reimer Verlag).

Heller, M. (ed.) (1988) *Codeswitching: Anthropological and Sociolinguistic Perspectives* (Berlin: Mouton de Gruyter).

Hellinger, M. (1986) 'On Writing English-related Creoles in the Caribbean', in: Görlach and Holm (1986).

Herskovits, M. J. and Herskovits, F. S. (1936, reprinted 1969): *Suriname Folk-Lore* (New York: Columbia University Press/AMS Press).

Hewitt, R. (1986) *White Talk, Black Talk* (Cambridge: Cambridge University Press).

Hewitt, R. (1982) 'White Adolescent Creole Users and the Politics of Friendship', *Journal of Multilingual and Multicultural Development*, **3**(3), pp. 217–32.

Highfield, A. and Valdman, A. (eds) (1981) *Historicity and Variation in Creole Studies* (Ann Arbor, Mich.: Karoma Press).

Hill, K. C. (ed.) (1979) *The Genesis of Language* (Ann Arbor, Mich.: Karoma).

Hinnenkamp, V. (1984) 'Eye-witnessing Pidginization? Structural and Sociolinguistic Aspects of German and Turkish Foreigner Talk', in: Sebba and Todd (1984), pp. 153–66.

Hinnenkamp, V. (1982) *Foreigner Talk und Tarzanisch* (Hamburg: Helmut Buske Verlag).

Hodgkinson, C. (1845) *Australia*, quoted in Sandefur (1979).

Holm, J. (1988) *Pidgins and Creoles*, vol. I: *Theory and Structure* (Cambridge: Cambridge University Press).

Holm, J. (1989) *Pidgins and Creoles*, vol. II: *Reference Survey* (Cambridge: Cambridge University Press).

Hosali, Priya (1992) 'Syntactic Peculiarities of Butler English', *South Asian Language Review*, **2**(2), pp. 58–74.

Hosali, Priya (1987) 'Morphological Features of Butler English', *Dibrugarh University Journal of English Studies*, **6**, pp. 51–67.

Hymes, D. (ed.) (1971) *Pidginization and Creolization of Languages* (Cambridge: Cambridge University Press).

Illich, Ivan (1981) 'Taught Mother Language and Vernacular Tongue', in: Pattanayak, D. P. (ed.), *Multilingualism and Mother-tongue Education* (Delhi: Oxford University Press).

Jansen, B., Koopman, H. and Muysken, P. (1978) 'Serial Verbs in the Creole Languages', *Amsterdam Creole Studies*, **2**, pp. 125–59.

Janson, T. (1984) 'A Language of Sophiatown, Alexandra and Soweto', in: Sebba and Todd (1984), pp. 167–80.

Joseph, J.E. (1987) *Eloquence and Power: The Rise of Language Standards and Standard Languages* (London: Frances Pinter).

Kallgård, A. (1991) *Fut Yoli Noo Bin Laane Aklen? A Pitcairn Island Word-List* (University of Göteborg, Sweden).

Katamba, F. X. (1993) *Morphology* (London: Macmillan).

Kingfisher Countries of the World: An A–Z Reference Atlas (1993) (London: Kingfisher Books).

Klein, W. and Dittmar, N. (1979) *Developing Grammars: The Acquisition of German by Foreign Workers* (Heidelberg: Springer).

Klein, W. and Perdue, C. (1993a) 'Utterance Structure', in: Perdue (1993), pp. 3–40.

Klein, W. and Perdue, C. (1993b) 'Concluding Remarks', in: Perdue (1993), pp. 253–72.

Kloss, H. (1967) ' "Abstand" Languages and "Ausbau" Languages', *Anthropological Linguistics*, **9**, pp. 29–41.

Knowles, G. (1977): *A Cultural History of the English Language* (London: Edward Arnold).

Koefoed, G. and Tarenskeen, J. (1996) 'The Making of a Language from a Lexical Point of View', in: Wekker (1996), pp. 119–38.

Kulick, D. (1992) *Language Shift and Cultural Reproduction. Socialization, Self and Syncretism in a Papua New Guinean Village* (Cambridge: Cambridge United Press).

Labov, W. (1969) 'Contraction, Deletion and Inherent Variability of the English Copula', *Language*, **45**, pp. 715–62.

Labov, W. (1972) 'Is Black English Vernacular a Separate System?' in *Language in the Inner City* (Philadelphia: University of Pennsylvania Press).

Labov, W. (1982) 'Objectivity and Commitment in Linguistic Science: The Case of the Black English Trial in Ann Arbor', *Language in Society*, **11**, pp. 165–202.

Lawton, D. (1980) 'Language Attitude, Discreteness and Code Shifting in Jamaican Creole', *English World Wide*, **1**(2), pp. 221–26.

Le Page, R. B. (1980) 'Projection, Focussing, Diffusion', *York Papers in Linguistics*, **9**.

Le Page, R. B. (1984) 'Introduction' to Sebba and Todd (1984), pp. 5–7.

Le Page, R. B. (1994) 'The Notion of "Linguistic System" Revisited', *International Journal of the Sociology of Language*, **109**, pp. 109–20.

Le Page, R. B. and De Camp, D. (1960) *Creole Studies I: Jamaican Creole* (London: Macmillan).

Le Page, R. B. and McEntegart, D. (1982) 'An Appraisal of the Statistical Techniques used in the Sociolinguistic Survey of Multilingual Communities', in: Romaine, S. (ed.), *Sociolinguistic Variation in Speech Communities* (London: Edward Arnold), pp.105–124.

Le Page, R. B. and Tabouret-Keller, A. (1985) *Acts of Identity* (Cambridge: Cambridge University Press).

Lefebvre, C. (1986) 'Relexification in Creole Genesis Revisited: The Case of Haitian Creole', in: Muysken and Smith (1986), pp. 279–300.

Lefebvre, C. (ed.) (1991) *Serial Verbs: Grammatical, Comparative and Cognitive Approaches* (Amsterdam: John Benjamins).

Lefebvre, C., Magloire-Holly, H. and Piou, N. (eds) (1982) *Syntaxe de l'haïtien* (Ann Arbor, Mich.: Karoma Press).

Lord, C. (1973) 'Serial Verbs in Transition', *Studies in African Lingusitics*, **4**(3), pp. 269–96.

Lord, C. (1976) 'Evidence for Syntactic Reanalysis: from Verb to Complementizer in Kwa', in Steever, S., Walker, C. and Mufwene, S. (eds), *Papers from the Parasession on Diachronic Syntax* (Chicago: Chicago Linguistics Society), pp. 179–92.

Lucas, C. and Valli, C. (1992) *Language Contact in the American Deaf Community* (London: Academic Press).

McArthur, T. (1993) 'Language Used as a Loaded Gun', *Education Guardian*, 20 April 1993, p. 3.

Mafeni, B. O. W. (1971) 'Nigerian Pidgin', in: Spencer, J. (ed.), *The English Language in West Africa* (London: Longman), pp. 95–112.

Markey, T. L. (1982) 'Afrikaans: Creole or Non-creole?', *Zeitschrift für Dialektologie und Linguistik*, **49**, pp. 169–207.

Mead, M. (1975) 'On the Crucial Importance of Neo-Melanesian, also called Pidgin English', in: *Tok Pisin i go we?*, Proceedings of a Conference held at the University of Papua New Guinea, 18–21 September 1973. Kivung Special Publication No. 1 (Linguistic Society of Papua New Guinea), pp. 51–3.

Mesthrie, R. (1989) 'The Origins of Fanakalo', *Journal of Pidgin and Creole Languages*, **4**(2), pp. 211–40.

Miller, M. R. (1980) 'Attestations of American Indian Pidgin English in Fiction and Nonfiction', in: Dillard, J. L. (ed.), *Perspectives on American English* (The Hague: Mouton).

Molisa, G., Vurobaravu, N. and Van Trease, H. (1982) 'Vanuatu: Overcoming Pandemonium', in: *Politics in Melanesia* (no author) (Suva: University of the South Pacific).

Mous, M. (1994) 'Ma'a or Mbugu', in: Bakker and Mous (1994), pp. 175–200.

Mufwene, S. (1986) 'The Universalist and Substrate Hypotheses Complement One Another', in: Muysken and Smith (1986), pp. 129–62.

Mühlhäusler, P. (1983) 'The Development of Word-formation in Tok Pisin', *Folia Linguistica*, **VII**, pp. 1–4.

Mühlhäusler, P. (1982) 'Tok Pisin in Papua New Guinea', in: Bailey, R. W. and Görlach, M. (eds), *English as a World Language* (Ann Arbor, Mich.: University of Michigan Press), pp. 439–66.

Mühlhäusler, P. (1986) *Pidgin and Creole Linguistics* (Oxford: Blackwell).

Mühlhäusler, P. (1992) 'What is the Use of Studying Pidgin and Creole Languages?', *Language Sciences*, **14**(3), pp. 309–16.

Muspratt, E. (1931) *My South Sea Island* (London: Travel Book Club).

Muysken, P. (1981) 'Halfway between Spanish and Quechua: The Case for Relexification', in: Highfield and Valdman (1981).

Muysken, P. (1994) 'Media Lengua', in: Bakker and Mous (1994), pp. 201–5.

Muysken, P. and Veenstra, T. (1994) 'Universalist Approaches', in: Arends et al. (1994), pp. 121–36.

Muysken, P. and Smith, N. (eds) (1986) *Substrata versus Universals in Creole Genesis* (Amsterdam: John Benjamins).

Nyembezi, S. (1957) *Learn Zulu* (Pietermaritzburg (South Africa): Shuter and Shooter).

O'Donnell, W. R. and Todd, L. (1980) *Variety in Contemporary English* (London: George Allen and Unwin).

Opanga, K. (1989) 'Humour by the Ringside', *Daily Nation* (Nairobi), 8 December, 1989.

Papen, R. A. (1978) 'The French-based Creoles of the Indian Ocean: An Analysis and Comparison', PhD dissertation, University of California at San Diego.

Perdue, C. (ed.) (1993) *Adult Language Acquisition: Cross-Linguistic Perspectives* (Cambridge University Press).

Perl, M. and S. Grosse (1994) 'Dos textos de "Catecismos para Negros" de Cuba y de Haiti-criollo o registro didactico?', *Papia*, 3(2), pp. 127–36.

Pollard, V. (1994) *Dread Talk* (Kingston, Jamaica: Canoe Press).

Pradelles de Latour, M.-L. (1984) 'Urban Pidgin in Douala', in: Sebba and Todd (1984), pp. 265–9.

Reinecke, J. E. (1937) *Marginal Languages: A Sociological Survey of the Creole Languages and Trade Jargons*, Yale University PhD dissertation (Ann Arbor, Mich.: University Microfilms International).

Rickford, John R. (1987) *Dimensions of a Creole Continuum: History, Texts and Linguistic Analysis of Guyanese Creole* (Stanford, Cal.: Stanford University Press).

Roberge, P. T. (1993) 'The Formation of Afrikaans', *Stellenbosch Papers in Linguistics*, 27 (monograph).

Roberts, P. (1988) *West Indians and their Language* (Cambridge: Cambridge University Press).

Romaine, S. (1982) *Socio-Historical Linguistics: Its Status and Methodology* (Cambridge: Cambridge University Press).

Romaine, S. (1988) *Pidgin and Creole Languages* (London: Longman).

Romaine, S. (1989) *Bilingualism* (Oxford: Blackwell).

Romaine, S. (1993) 'The Decline of Predicate Marking in Tok Pisin', in: Byrne and Holm (1995), pp. 251–60.

Romaine, S. (1994) 'Hau fo rait pijin: Writing in Hawai'i Creole English', *English Today*, 38(10:2), pp. 20–4.

Ross, A. S. C. and Moverley, A. W. (eds) (1964) *The Pitcairnese Language* (London: Andre Deutsch).

Royal and Historical Letters during the reign of Henry IV, vol. I (Rolls series).

Sandefur, J. R. (1979) *An Australian Creole in the Northern Territory: A Description of Ngukurr-Bamyili Dialects (Part 1)* (Darwin: Work Papers of Summer Institute of Linguistics, Australian Aborigines Branch, Series B, volume 3).

Sankoff, G. (1977) 'Variability and Explanation in Language and Culture: Cliticization in New Guinea Tok Pisin', in: Saville-Troike, M. (ed.), *Linguistics and Anthropology* (Washington, DC: Georgetown University Press), pp. 59–75.

Sankoff, G. (1984) 'A Sociolinguistic Perspective on Substrate: The Case of Tok Pisin Verb Chaining', paper presented at Sociolinguistics Symposium 5, Liverpool.

Sankoff, G. and P. Brown (1976) 'On the Origins of Syntax in Discourse: A Case Study of Tok Pisin Relatives', *Language*, 52, pp. 631–66.

Sankoff, G. and Laberge, S. (1974) 'On the Acquisition of Native Speakers by a Language', in: De Camp, D. and Hancock, I. (eds), *Pidgins and Creoles: Current Trends and Prospects* (Washington, DC: Georgetown University Press), pp. 73–84.

Schieffelin, B. B. and Doucet, R. C. (1994) 'The "Real" Haitian Creole: Ideology, Metalingusitics and Orthographic Choice', *American Ethnologist*, 21, pp. 176–200.

Schuchardt, H. (1891) 'Beitrage zur Kenntnisse des englischen Kreolisch III. Das Indo-Englische', *Englische Studien*, 15, pp. 286–305; reprinted as 'Indo-English' in: Gilbert, G. (ed.) (1980) *Pidgin and Creole Languages: Selected Essays by Hugo Schuchardt* (Cambridge: Cambridge University Press).

Schuchardt, H. (1979) *The Ethnography of Variation: Selected Writings on Pidgins and Creoles,* translated by T. L. Markey (Ann Arbor, Mich.: Karoma Press).

Schumann, J. (1978) *The Pidginization Process: A Model for Second Language Acquisition* (Rowley, MA: Newbury House).

Schuring, G. K. (1978) 'Tsotsi-Afrikaans', *Nuusbrief/Newsletter* (of the South African Association for Language Teaching) **12**(3), pp. 27–34.

Sebba, M. (1981) 'Derivational Regularities in a Creole Lexicon: The Case of Sranan', *Linguistics*, **19**, pp. 101–17.

Sebba, M. (1986) 'Adjectives and Copulas in Sranan Tongo', *Journal of Pidgin and Creole Languages*, **1**(1), pp. 109–22.

Sebba, M. (1987) *The Syntax of Serial Verbs* (Amsterdam: Benjamins).

Sebba, M. (1993) *London Jamaican: Language Systems in Interaction* (London: Longman).

Sebba, M. and Tate, S. (1986) 'You Know What I Mean? Agreement Marking in British Black English', *Journal of Pragmatics*, **10**.

Sebba, M. (1984) 'Serial Verb or Syntactic Calque? The Great Circuit of *Say*', paper presented at Annual Meeting of the Society for Caribbean Linguistics, Mona, Jamaica.

Sebba, M. (1994) 'Informal Orthographies: Phonology meets Ideology. Spelling and Code Switching in British Creole', Working Papers of the Centre for Language in Social Life, No. 62

Sebba, M. and Todd, L. (eds) (1984) 'Papers from the York Creole Conference, September 24–27 1983', *York Papers in Linguistics*, **11**.

Seuren, P. A. M. (1986) 'Adjectives as Adjectives in Sranan: A Reply to Sebba', *Journal of Pidgin and Creole Languages*, **1**(1), pp. 123–34.

Seuren, P. and Wekker, H. (1986) 'Semantic Transparency as a Factor in Creole Genesis', in: Muysken and Smith (1986), pp. 57–70.

Silverstein, M. (1972) 'Goodbye Columbus: Language and Speech Community in Indian-European Contact Situations'. Unpublished manuscript.

Singler, J. V. (ed.), (1990) *Pidgin and Creole Tense-Mood-Aspect Systems* (Amsterdam: John Benjamins).

Singler, J. V. (1986) 'Short Note', *Journal of Pidgin and Creole Languages*, **1**(1), pp. 141–5.

Singler, J. V. (1988) 'The Homogeneity of the Substrate as a Factor in Pidgin/Creole Genesis', *Language*, **64**, pp. 27–51.

Singler, J. V. (1992) 'Rejoinder: Nativization and Pidgin/Creole Genesis: A Reply to Bickerton', *Journal of Pidgin and Creole Languages*, **7**(2), pp. 319–33.

Slobin, D. (1977) 'Language Change in Childhood and in History', in: MacNamara, J. (ed.), *Language Learning and Thought* (New York: Holt, Rinehart and Winston), pp. 175–208.

Smith, N. (1987) *The Genesis of the Creole Languages of Surinam*, PhD, University of Amsterdam.

Smitherman, G. (1977) *Talkin' and Testifyin': The Language of Black America* (Detroit, Mich.: Wayne State University Press).

Sylvain, G. (1929) *Cric? Crac! Fables de la Fontaine. Racontées par un montagnard Haïtien et transcrites en vers creoles par Georges Sylvain* (Port-au-Prince: the Author, Port-au-prince) reprinted 1971 by Kraus Reprint, Neudeln/Liechtenstein).

Sylvain, S. (1936) *Le créole haïtien: morphologie et syntaxe* (Port-au-Prince and Wetteren: Imprimerie de Meester).

Tate, S. (1984) 'Jamaican Creole Approximation by Second-generation Dominicans? The Use of Agreement Tokens', MA thesis, University of York (England).

Taylor, D. (1951) 'Structural Outline of Caribbean Creole', *Word*, 7, pp. 43–59.

Taylor, D. (1971) 'Grammatical and Lexical Affinities of Creoles', in: Hymes, D. (1971), pp. 293–6.

Third World Guide 89/90 (Montevideo: Instituto del Tercer Mundo).

Thomason, S. G. and Kaufman, T. (1988) *Language Contact, Creolization and Genetic Linguistics* (Berkeley: University of California Press).

Thompson, R. W. (1961) 'A Note on Some Affinities between the Creole Dialects of the Old World and those of the New', in: Le Page, R. B. (ed.), *Creole Language Studies II* (London: Macmillan), pp. 107–113.

Todd, L. (1984) *Modern Englishes: Pidgins and Creoles* (London: Routledge and Kegan Paul).

Todd, L. (1990) Pidgins and Creoles, 2nd edn (London: Routledge, 1st edn published 1974).

Turner, L. D. (1949/1969) *Africanisms in the Gullah Dialect* (Ann Arbor, Mich.: University of Michigan Press).

UNESCO (1951) 'The Use of Vernacular Languages in Education: The Report of the UNESCO Meeting of Specialists, 1951', in: Fishman, J. A. (ed.), *Readings in the Sociology of Language* (The Hague: Mouton, 1970).

Valdman, A. (1978) *Le Créole: Structure, Statut et Origine* (Paris: Éditions Klincksieck).

Valdman, A. and Highfield, A. (1980) *Theoretical Orientations in Creole Studies* (New York: Academic Press).

Valkhoff, M. F. (1966) *Studies in Portuguese and Creole. With Special Reference to South Africa* (Johannesburg: Witwatersrand University Press).

Virahsawmy, Dev. (1982) *Li*, translated as *The Prisoner of Conscience* by Ramesh Ramdoyal (Moka, Mauritius: editions de l'Ocean Indien).

Wawn, W. (1893) *The South Sea Islanders in the Queensland Labour Trade: A Record of Voyages and Experiences in the West Pacific from 1875 to 1891* (London: Swan Sonnenschein).

Washabaugh, W. (1977) 'Constraining Variation in Decreolization', *Language*, **53**(2), pp. 329–52.

Wekker, H. (ed.) (1996) *Creole Languages and Language Acquisition* (Berlin/New York: Mouton de Gruyter).

Wells, J. C. (1973) *Jamaican Pronunciation in London* (Oxford: Blackwell).

Whinnom, K. (1971) 'Linguistic Hybridization and the 'Special Case' of Pidgins and Creoles', in: Hymes (1971), pp. 91–116.

Wight, J. (1971) 'Dialect in School', *Educational Review*, **24**(1), pp. 47–58.

Winer, L. (1990) 'Orthographic Standardization for Trinidad and Tobago: Linguistic and Sociopolitical Considerations in an English Creole Community', *Language Problems and Language Planning*, **14**, pp. 236–68.

Woolford, E. (1978) 'Topic and Clefting without Wh-movement', *Papers from the Eighth Meeting of the North-Eastern Linguistics Society* (NELS, VIII).

Woolford, E. (1979) 'The Developing Complementizer System of Tok Pisin: Syntactic Change in Progress', in: Hill, K. C. (1979), pp. 108–24.

Wright, F. J. (1984) 'A Sociolinguistic Study of Passivization Amongst Black Adolescents in Britain', unpublished PhD thesis, Department of Linguistics, University of Birmingham.

Wullschlägel, H. R. (1856): *Deutsch-Negerenglisches Wörterbuch* (1965 reprint, Amsterdam: S. Emmering).

Wurm, S. A. (1977) 'The Nature of New Guinea Pidgin', in: Wurm, S. A. (ed.), *New Guinea Area Languages and Language Study*, vol. 3: *Pacific Linguistics*, Series C, no. 40 (Canberra: Australian National University, Research School of Pacific Studies).

Wurm, S., Laycock, D. C., Mühlhäusler, P. and Dutton, T. (1979) *Handbook of New Guinea Pidgin* (Canberra: Pacific Linguistics).

Subject Index

abrupt creolisation *see* creolisation
acrolects, 211, 213, 214, 217, **220–3**
adjectives, 186
adverbials, 42
articles, definite and indefinite
  absence of, 38, 39, 40
  French in Mauritian Creole, **144–5**
  in Afrikaans, 164
  in creoles, 174
  in Hawaiian Creole English, 172
aspect *see* tense, modality and aspect

'baby-talk' *see* foreigner talk
basilect, 204, 211–14, 219, 220, 223, 230, 238
bilingualism, 179
  in language shift, 11
  communities, bilingual, 6
  in relexification, 75
borrowing of words, **117–19**

calques, 92, 119
  in creoles, 186
circumlocution, 85, **116–17**
cleft, 187–8
code switching, 6, 223
  between Sranan and Dutch, 212
  in bilingual communities, **12–13**
'common core' hypothesis, 77, 78, 175
complementiser, 114
consonants
  click, in Fanakalo, 108
  clusters, 110
contact languages, 2, 169
  expanding into creole, 135
content words, **111–13**
continuum, **212–25**
  social factors in, 223, 233
copula, 38, 39, 40
  deletion of, in Foreigner Talk, 85
  in AAVE, 277
  in creoles, 174, 187, 209
  in sign language, 271

  in Sranan, 154
  in WAPE, 132
  lack of, in Butler English, 125
creoles
  differences from pidgins, **169–71**
  similarities between, **173–6**
creolisation
  abrupt, 135, 136, 142, 147, 192
  creole genesis, **176–85**
  of Krio, **156–7**
  of pidgins, **15–16**
  of Tok Pisin, 170
  partial, **161–2**
creoloid, 162

decreolisation, 26, 218, 224
dialect, 7
  problems in defining, **2–3**
diffusion, 8–9, 224
diglossia, 11, 213, 223, 236

education
  pidgins and creoles in, **252–8**
embedding, **114–15**
extended pidgins
  beyond stable pidgin, **105–7**

family tree model, **9–10**, 34
  and normal transmission, 135, **168–9**
  challenge to, 34, 288
first-language transfer
  unimportant in pidginisation, 91
focussing, 8, 227
foreigner talk (FT), 77, 83, 84, 86
  and pidginisation, 91
  essential in communication, 86–90
  in creoles, 175
  similarity to pidgins, 85
  simplification in, 87–8, 90
gender, grammatical, 49–50, 268
  in Afrikaans, 164
  in creoles, 175
gender, of speakers, 128, **268–9**, 280

Name Index

Aitchison, J., 170, 193
Alleyne, M., 213
Anderson, Benedict, 8
Appel, R. and Verhoeven, L., 257
Arends, J., 192

Bailey, C.-J. N., 214, 220, 288
Baker, P., 144, 145
Bakker, P., 266, 267, 268
Bakker, P. and Mous, M., 74, 264
Bakker, P. and Muysken, P., 40, 48
Barros, M. C., Borges, C. D. and
    Meira, M., 281, 282
Bhattacharjya, D., 44, 117
Bickerton, D., 171–3, 176–82, 184, 186,
    191–3, 197, 198, 214, 217–19, 221,
    225, 271–3
Blackshire-Belay, C., 80, 81
Bold, J. D., 56, 58, 60, 61, 108
Bollée, A., 144
Broch, I. and Jahr, E. H., 63
Broch, O., 63, 84
Byrne, F., 149

Cassidy, F. G., 184, 208, 222, 247, 248
Cassidy, F. G. and Le Page, R. B., 244
Chaudenson, R., 141
Chomsky, N., 168, 181
Clark, R., 28, 76
Cokeley, D., 273
Cole, D. T., 61
Cook, V., 82, 96
Corne C., 141–2
Craig, D., 222

Dalphinis, M., 185
De Camp, D., 204, 211, 212, 213, 214,
    217, 218, 220, 288
den Besten, H., 166
Devonish, H., 235, 238, 239, 256, 257,
    259, 260
Dillard, J. L., 277

Edwards, V. K. and Ladd, P., 271, 274
Elugbe, B. O. and Omamor, A. P., 122,
    127,128, 129, 248, 254, 255
Ewers, Traute, 279

Ferguson, C., 84, 88, 89, 91
Fox, James A., 83, 105

Gibson, K. A., 222
Gilroy, P., 228
Golovko, E., 266–7
Goodman, M., 265
Gumperz, J. J. and Wilson, R. D., 13

Hall, Robert A., 28, 42, 66, 67, 76, 78,
    113, 118, 182, 238
Hancock, Ian F., 127
Heine, B., 113
Hellinger, M., 247
Hesseling, Dirk, 34
Hewitt, R., 232
Hinnenkamp, V., 31, 80, 85, 90, 91, 95
Holm, J., 18, 28, 29, 30, 32, 56, 63, 67,
    128, 137, 141, 146, 155, 182, 189,
    190, 249, 259, 282
Hosali, Priya, 124, 125, 126

Illich, Ivan, 7

Jansen, T., 32, 33
Joseph, J. E., 239, 240

Katamba, F. X., 44
Klein and Dittmar, N., 81, 82
Klein, W. and Perdue, C., 80, 81, 91, 92
Koefoed, G. and Tarenskeen, J., 148,
    237
Kulick, D., 280

Labov, W., 278–9
Lawton, D., 222
Lefebvre, C., 182, 275

311

Language Index